PEACEKEEPING IN AFRICA

Peacekeeping in Africa

Edited by
OLIVER FURLEY
ROY MAY

Ashgate
Aldershot • Brookfield USA • Singapore • Sydney

© O.W. Furley and R. May 1998

All rights reserved. No part of this publication may be reproduced, stored in a retrieval system, or transmitted in any form or by any means, electronic, mechanical, photocopying, recording or otherwise without the prior permission of the publisher.

Published by
Ashgate Publishing Ltd
Gower House
Croft Road
Aldershot
Hants GU11 3HR
England

Ashgate Publishing Company
Old Post Road
Brookfield
Vermont 05036
USA

British Library Cataloguing in Publication Data
Peacekeeping in Africa
    1. Conflict management - Africa 2.Reconciliation
    I.Furley, Oliver II.May, Roy
    303.6'9'096

Library of Congress Catalog Card Number: 98-71399

ISBN 1 85972 492 2

Printed and bound by Athenaeum Press, Ltd.,
Gateshead, Tyne & Wear.

Contents

List of contributors	vii
Acknowledgements	xi
List of abbreviations	xii
Map of Africa: political 1998	xvi

Part One: World Perspectives — 1

1 Introduction — 3
   Oliver Furley and Roy May

2 Peacekeeping in Africa: recent evolution and prospects — 13
   Margaret Carey

3 African perspectives: regional peacekeeping — 29
   Gerry Cleaver and Roy May

4 Peacekeeping in Africa, 1990-1996: the role of the United States, France and Britain — 49
   Mats Berdal

Part Two: Case Studies — 81

5 Zimbabwe's peace settlement: re-evaluating Lancaster House — 83
   Norma Kriger

6 Chad — 105
   Simon Massey and Roy May

7	Somalia *Peter Woodward*	143
8	Peacekeeping in Mozambique *Sam Barnes*	159
9	Angola: the search for peace and reconstruction *Barry Munslow*	179
10	Namibia *Donna Pankhurst*	207
11	Liberia: lessons for the future from the experience of ECOMOG *Gerry Cleaver*	223
12	Rwanda and Burundi: peacekeeping amidst massacres *Oliver Furley*	239

Part Three: Wider Issues — 263

13	NGOs and conflict resolution in Africa: facilitators or aggravators of peacekeeping? *Timothy Murithi*	265
14	The military, peacekeeping and Africa *Richard Connaughton*	287
15	Being peacekept *Christopher Clapham*	303

List of contributors

Sam Barnes worked in Mozambique for the UN from 1987 to 1994 in the co-ordination of humanitarian assistance during the war and the peacekeeping phase. She received a grant from the MacArthur Foundation for research and writing on the impact of humanitarian assistance in the stabilisation of Mozambique. She has worked for the United Nations as a consultant in post-conflict peace programming in Angola, Liberia, Tajikistan and Somalia. She is a contributor to edited works on Mozambique and has a forthcoming article on NGOs in peacekeeping operations in *Development in Practice*.

Mats Berdal is a Research Fellow and Research Co-ordinator at the Centre for International Studies at Oxford University. He is currently working on a book entitled *The UN and the Search for International Order after the Cold War*.

Margaret Carey is the Special Assistant of the Assistant Secretary-General for Peacekeeping at the United Nations.

Christopher Clapham is Professor of Politics and International Relations at Lancaster University. Author of *Africa and the International System: The Politics of State Survival* (Cambridge, 1996), he has recently edited a collective book, *African Guerrillas* (James Currey, 1998).

Gerry Cleaver is a lecturer in the School of International Studies and Law, Coventry University. He is also a member of the University's African Studies Centre where he is studying for his PhD on the practical problems associated with peacekeeping in Africa, a subject on which he has recently published articles. He teaches both African and Third World politics at undergraduate level as well as a course on African peacekeeping in the School's MA programme.

Richard Connaughton was formerly an officer in the British Army. His last appointment prior to early voluntary retirement in October 1992 was Colonel Defence Studies, during which time he established the Strategic and Combat Studies Institute (SCSI). After leaving the army, he founded the National and International Consultancy which specialises in undertaking politico-military studies. He is a regular contributor to a number of periodicals and journals and has written several pamphlets. His books include: *Military Intervention in the 1990s - A New Logic for War; Celebration of Victory; Shrouded Secrets* - Japan's war on mainland Australia 1942-1944; *The Nature of Future Conflict; The Battle for Manila;* and *Descent into Chaos* - the doomed expedition to Kinabalu. He is presently working on a book on General MacArthur and FDR and also a biography of General Nguyen Khanh. He undertook a Defence Fellowship at the University of Cambridge 1989/90 and was elected a Research Fellow of the Centre for Defence and International Security Studies, Lancaster University, in 1992.

Oliver Furley is an Honorary Research Fellow and formerly Head of the Department of Politics and History at Coventry University. Previously he taught for many years at Makerere University, Uganda, and also in the universities of St Andrews, Edinburgh, the West Indies and Duke University, North Carolina. He is co-author with Tom Watson of *The History of Education in East Africa*, NOK Publishers, USA, 1978, and of *Uganda's Retreat from Turmoil*, Centre for Security and Conflict Studies, 1987. He has contributed chapters and articles of East African history, politics and conflict studies. He is editor of *Conflict in Africa*, Tauris Academic Studies, 1995.

Norma Kriger is a Professor in the Department of Political Science, The Johns Hopkins University, Baltimore. She is currently supported by a grant for research and writing from the John D. and Catherine T. MacArthur Foundation. Her research fields are southern Africa, wars and revolutions. Her publications include *Zimbabwe's Guerrilla War: Peasant Voices*, Cambridge University Press, 1992; Baobab Press, 1996. She is currently completing a book entitled *Zimbabwe's Guerrilla Integration: Entitlement Politics*.

Simon Massey is a PhD student in the School of International Studies and Law at Coventry University where he completed his MA. His main research areas are the theoretical and moral bases for peacekeeping operations in sub-Saharan Africa and also the politics of Chad.

Roy May is the Director of the African Studies Centre, Coventry University. He is also Head of International and Political Studies. He teaches undergraduate and postgraduate courses in African politics, development, aid and Third World politics. His original interest in the area came from service with the Royal West African Frontier Force in Sierra Leone. He has published widely on Chad, the Franco-African relationship, the role of NGOs, militarism and peacekeeping in Africa.

Barry Munslow is Professor of Politics in the School of Politics and Communication Studies at the University of Liverpool. He has written extensively on Southern Africa and is a frequent visitor to Angola. He has just finished editing a book on *The Challenge of Sustainable Development in Mozambique*. He has also been active in the launch of an International Diploma in Humanitarian Assistance which prepares professionals involved in complex emergencies.

Timothy Murithi teaches at Keele University where he is completing his PhD in International Relations. His main areas of research are in peacemaking and democratisation in failed states. He is the Co-founder of the Forum on Africa and International Relations (FAIR), a working group of the British International Studies Association (BISA).

Donna Pankhurst is a Senior Lecturer in the Department of Peace Studies, University of Bradford and is an Africa specialist. She has published on land reform and democracy in Namibia; famine and the environment in Sudan; and survival strategies, gender and rural development in Zimbabwe. Her current research interests include the causes of conflict, methods of its settlement and resolution, and the analysis of democratic change in Africa. She is also working on wider issues of gender and conflict.

Peter Woodward teaches at the University of Reading, and was formerly at the University of Khartoum. His publications on north-east Africa include *Condominium and Sudanese Nationalism*, Rex Collings, 1979; *Sudan: The Unstable State*, Lynn Rienner, 1990; *Nasser*, Longman, 1992; and *Horn of Africa: State Politics and International Relations*, Tauris,

1996. He was Editor of *African Affairs*, the journal of the Royal African Society, from 1986 to 1997.

Acknowledgements

The editors wish to thank Professor Christopher Clapham for his advice and general overview of the book; Arthur Owens, Social Sciences librarian in the Lanchester Library, Coventry University, for his patience in answering innumerable research queries; Erica Milwain, Cartographic Unit, Coventry University, for producing the cover map, and Marcella Edwards, secretary of the Centre for African Studies, Coventry University, for her essential role in the production of the book.

List of abbreviations

ACRF	African Crisis Response Force
ACRI	African Crisis Response Initiative
ADFL	Alliance of Democratic Forces for the Liberation of Congo-Zaire
AFL	Armed Forces of Liberia
BMATT	British Military and Assistance Training Team
BSAP	British South Africa Police
CAR	Central African Republic
CARE	Co-operative for Assistance and Relief Everywhere
CCF	Cease-Fire Commission (Mozambique)
CFA	Central Franc Afrique
CIA	Central Intelligence Agency
CMF	Commonwealth Monitoring Force
COG	Commonwealth Observers' Group
CORE	Commission on Reintegration (Mozambique)
CSM	Conseil Supérieure Militaire (Chad)
CRNRP	Programme of Community Rehabilitation and National Reconciliation (Angola)
DHA	Department of Humanitarian Affairs (UN)
DTA	Democratic Turnhalle Alliance (Namibia)
ECOMOG	ECOWAS Monitoring Group
ECOWAS	Economic Community of West African States
EO	Executive Outcomes
FAA	Angolan Armed Forces
FADM	United Defence Force (Mozambique)
FAN	Forces armées du nord (Chad)
FAO	Food and Agriculture Organisation (UN)

FAP	Forces armées populaires (Chad)
FAPLA	Angolan People's Liberation Army
FAR	Forces Armées Rwandaises
FAT	Forces armées tchadiennes (Chad)
FRELIMO	Frente de libertaçao de Moçambique
FROLINAT	Front de libération nationale du Tchad
GDP	Gross Domestic Product
GNP	Gross National Product
GOA	Government of Angola
GPA	General Peace Agreement (Mozambique)
GUNT	Gouvernement d'union nationale de transition (Chad)
HAC	Humanitarian Assistance Committee (UN)
HIC	High Intensity Conflict
IAF	Inter-African Force
ICRC	International Committee of the Red Cross
IDP	Internally Displaced Person
IFOR	Implementation Force in Bosnia
IGNU	Interim Government of National Unity (Liberia)
JRDF	Joint Rapid Deployment Force
LIC	Low Intensity Conflict
MIC	Medium Intensity Conflict
MIOB	OAU International Observer Mission
MISAB	Inter-African Mission to monitor the implementation of the Bangui Agreements (CAR)
MPLA	Movimento Popular de Libertaçao de Angola
MRNDD	National Republic Movement for Democracy and Development (Rwanda)
MSF	Médecins sans Frontières
NATO	North Atlantic Treaty Organisation
NGO	Non-Governmental Organisation
NICON	Nigerian Contingent of IAF in Chad
NMOG	Neutral Military Observer Group
NPFL	National Patriotic Front of Liberia
OAU	Organisation of African Unity
ODA	Official Development Assistance
ONUC	United Nations Operation in Congo
ONUMOZ	United Nations Observer Mission in Mozambique
OXY	Occidental Petroleum Corporation
PES	Economic and Social Programme of 1994 (Angola)
PF	Patriotic Front (Zimbabwe)

PLAN	People's Liberation Army of Namibia
PRE	Programme of Economic Recuperation (Angola)
QRF	Quick Reaction Force
RENAMO	National Resistance Movement (Mozambique)
RGF	Rwandese Government Forces
RPF	Rwandan Patriotic Front
RSF	Rhodesian Security Forces
RSS	Reintegration Support Scheme
SADC	Southern African Development Community
SCF	Save the Children Fund
SDECE	Documentation and Counter-Espionage Service
SG	Secretary General
SNA	Somalia National Alliance
SNM	Somalia National Movement
SSDF	Somali Salvation Democratic Front
SWAPO	South West African People's Organisation
SWAPOL	South West African Police
SWATF	South West African Territorial Force
UANC	United African National Council (Zimbabwe)
UCAH	United Nations Humanitarian Assistance Co-ordination Unit
ULIMO	United Liberation Movement of Liberia for Democracy
UNAMIR	United Nations Assistance Mission for Rwanda
UNAVEM	United Nations Angola Verification Mission
UNCIVPOL	United Nations Civilian Police Contingent
UNDRO	United Nations Disaster Relief Co-ordinator's Office
UNFPA	United Nations Population Fund
UNHCR	United Nations High Commission for Refugees
UNICEF	United Nations Children's Fund
UNIDO	United Nations Industrial Development Organisation
UNITA	National Union for the Total Independence of Angola
UNITAF	United Task Force (Somalia)
UNOHAC	United Nations Office for the Co-ordination of Humanitarian Assistance (Mozambique)
UNOMIL	United Nations Observer Mission in Liberia
UNOSOM	United Nations Operation in Somalia
UNREO	United Nations Rwanda Emergency Office
UNSAS	United Nations Standby Arrangement System

UNSCERO	United Nations Special Co-ordinator for Emergency Relief Organisations
UNSGSR	United Nations Secretary General Special Representative
UNTAG	United Nations Transition Assistance Group
UNTSO	United Nations Truce Supervision Organisation
UPRONA	Union pour le progrés national (Burundi)
USEUCOM	United Nations European Command
USG	Under Secretary General
WCG	Western Contact Group
WEU	West European Union
WFP	World Food Programme
ZACON	Zairean Contingent of IAF in Chad
ZANLA	Zimbabwe African National Liberation Army
ZANU	Zimbabwe African National Union
ZAPU	Zimbabwe African People's Union
ZIPRA	Zimbabwe People's Revolutionary Army

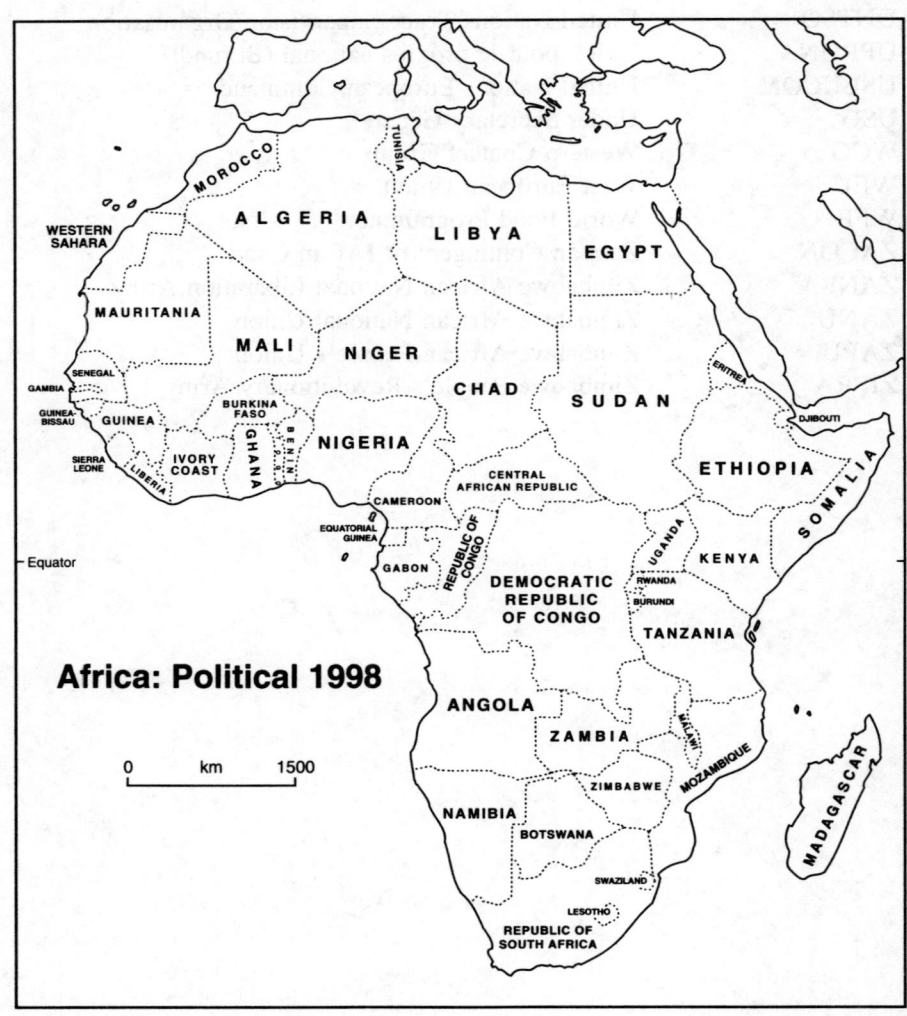

Part One
WORLD PERSPECTIVES

1 Introduction

Oliver Furley and Roy May

Peacekeeping operations have multiplied considerably in recent years, and as conflicts arise, the international community and regional organisations find themselves, willingly or not, drawn into ever more challenging and long-drawn out efforts to oversee and assist the implementation of peace agreements. Inevitably, books, articles and papers on the study of peacekeeping have proliferated, and international conferences on the subject are a frequent occurrence. Most of the books, however, cover world-wide peacekeeping as a whole, and tend to be theoretical in approach. There are few books concentrating specifically on Africa, and the aim in this book is to provide substantial background material, as well as covering the main peacekeeping operations of Africa.

The book will aim to cover all the important aspects of peacekeeping in Africa. Thus it will deal with the policies and actions of the international organisations concerned, such as the UN and the OAU, the participating African States, and the impact of sub-regional powers as well as the role of the big powers, USA, Britain and France, where their intervention in peacemaking and peacekeeping has led to blunders or sometimes intervention from motives of self-interest, as well as many examples of beneficial contributions to peacekeeping.

In the years that peacekeeping in Africa has been attempted, it has developed into an extraordinary range of functions. It is closely allied to 'peace-making', involving the political process of bringing the warring sides together, securing a cease-fire and establishing peace talks and helping to negotiate a peace accord. This is accompanied usually by UN civil and military missions to the country, collaborating with other international bodies such as the OAU or regional African organisations. Help is often required in setting up a transitional government as a factor of stability, where a fine balance has to be drawn between questions of sovereignty and foreign interference.

Peace-making then becomes peacekeeping, with a set of military requirements, monitoring the cease-fire, separating opposing military forces, demobilising soldiers or guerrilla fighters, and supervising the stockpiling and securing of arms. Peacekeeping forces may have the task of securing airports, road and rail links and the infrastructure generally. They may then help to establish a new integrated national army and police force, and provide training. On the civil front, peacekeeping may involve assisting the judiciary and especially help in safeguarding human rights and the protection of lives and property. The huge numbers of refugees and displaced persons which African conflicts have generated requires relief work of all kinds - emergency food supplies; the establishment of 'safe areas' and camps, sometimes with problems of demilitarisation within the camps; as well as the longer-term tasks of resettlement, rehabilitation and integration.

Finally peacekeeping has frequently led to efforts to secure a democratisation process, with elections as the final stage. This means peacekeepers are involved in the whole process of identifying and registering voters, observing the elections and verifying them as 'fair and free', and finally trying to persuade all sides to abide by the results. Lastly, in view of the frequently recurring failures at some of these hurdles, especially the last, above all the peacekeepers have to exercise infinite patience and try to maintain impartiality - difficult where in some cases peacekeeping blurs into 'peace enforcement'. This process has been labelled 'mission creep', as described in the chapter on Somalia.

It may be valuable at this stage to suggest some definitions that are used implicitly and explicitly within the work:

Peacekeeping

'The stationing of neutral, lightly armed troops as an interposition force following a cease-fire to separate combatants and promote an environment suitable for conflict resolution'.[1] A pre-requisite is the notion of consent based on a desire by the major warring parties for peace.

Peace enforcement

The intervention of troops from an external state or states into a situation of conflict with the purpose of imposing peace. There is the absence of consent from the warring factions and it may be synonymous with war fighting. It attempts to lead to the solution of the problem by superior firepower. 'Mission creep' is an unplanned move from *keeping* to *enforcement* and can be very dangerous for the troops involved. As General Rose has said, 'You cannot fight war from white-painted vehicles'[2]; the peacekeeping forces involved have been trained and equipped for a different type of mission.

Peacemaking

The political process that may accompany either peacekeeping or peace enforcement - an ongoing process.

Mandate

The official command or instruction by an authority. In the sense of peacekeeping, this can be taken to mean the precise terms and instructions which the peacekeeping force has to follow.

The problems for this are related to the capacity of the force to carry on its mandate, thus May and Massey show the difficulties of this in the case of the first OAU intervention in Chad in 1980. The mandate has to be realistic and clear (not capable of misinterpretation). Difficulties will arise when changes in external political alliances and internal political circumstances and military realities lead to a shift in the mandate. These problems are also highlighted by May and Massey who show that the purpose of the November 1981 mandate of the OAU was to reaffirm its support of the GUNT and request all member states of the OAU to support this government. They then show the nuanced shift in the February 1982 mandate of the OAU which asked the peacekeeping force to ensure the 'defence and security of the country' in effect withdrawing its previous recognition of the GUNT.

Humanitarian intervention

The provision of safe zones or camps for refugees, with shelter, food, medical supplies etc, can take place if the consent of the majority, if not all of the parties, has been obtained and perhaps some levels of force may be needed, for the protection of both the beneficiaries and the aid workers.

The middle section of the book consists of those African countries which present important examples of the successes and failures of all these tasks, from the disasters of Somalia to the comparative successes of Zimbabwe and Namibia. The last section will consult the wider issues, such as the role of both international and national NGOs which will be examined, as in many instances they have carried the main responsibility for effective peacekeeping at the grassroots level and in the organisation of relief work and rehabilitation. Finally, the future of peacekeeping will be discussed, with questions of regional peacekeeping and rapid reaction forces.

The end of the Cold War: 'Africa fatigue'

Several of the chapters refer to the watershed in international peacekeeping in Africa, when the Cold War ended in the late 1980s. Before then, the UN had enjoyed strong support by the big powers for intervention in Africa when it was thought necessary, and where it coincided with their strategic interests. Afterwards, strategic interest faded, and Africa ceased to be a stage where the East and West could play out their rivalries using surrogate African states in bids for dominance or influence. At the same time, and partly because of lack of controlling external influences, conflicts in Africa multiplied. Most of these have been intra-state conflicts, anarchical civil wars, in which the international community was loath to intervene. Several African countries earned the label 'failed states', and seemed beyond redemption.[3] This mood of disillusion re-enforced by the events in Liberia, Somalia and Sierra Leone which gave rise to 'Afro-pessimism' or Africa fatigue among the big powers, is exemplified by the widely quoted doomsday article of Robert Kaplan. Moreover, most of the recent conflicts have been ethnic or have had a strong ethnic element, and these are typically 'nasty, brutish and long', which made the peacekeepers' task uncertain when venturing into places that were not under the control of any recognisable authority.[4] A peacekeeping operation was supposed to follow a negotiated peace agreement, to which all parties in the conflict agreed, and after which they invited the UN or a regional body to come into the country and assist with the peace settlement. The chapter on the UN points to the difficulties the UN faces in summoning sufficient political will and commitment to peacekeeping operations in Africa by the main participating countries. Too often, they are slow in providing troops, logistic requirements and sufficient funds, and they are unwilling to face a long commitment in the field, where frequently peacekeeping has proved to be a far more lengthy process than previously planned. The result is that UN peacekeeping mandates have had to be extended, and participants have to be willing to support greater flexibility in their tasks, leading to the problems of 'mission creep'. Margaret Carey acknowledges that the UN itself has to reform some of its procedures, which have in the past occasioned fatal delays in launching peacekeeping operations. The whole process of securing a commitment in the UN to launch a peacekeeping operation, the drawing up of the mandate, persuading member states to commit funds, troops, supplies and logistics is in urgent need of reform, and points increasingly to the need for 'rapid reaction' or 'stand-by' forces, organised and based either centrally or regionally. This is an ongoing debate which is referred to many times in this book, and the assessment in the chapter by May and Cleaver points to the increasingly more frenzied efforts of the powers to develop an African crisis response initiative.

The grey area between peacekeeping and peace enforcement

The Zimbabwe chapter highlights one of the difficulties peacekeepers face when the peace settlement failed to address inter-party competition and was therefore not really a settlement. It merely 'created a new playing field for continuation of the deadly contest for military power'. In these circumstances, some of the roles of peacekeepers - demobilisation, disarming combatants, building a new national army etc, become almost impossible. Peter Woodward stresses this in the Somalia chapter, for with warlords leading rival clans, the UN force, UNITAF, was simply part of the political scene, to be manipulated by Somali players. Many of the chapters refer to this problem. In Angola, even though the peacekeeping operation appeared to complete the last stage with a 'fair and free' general election, one party, UNITA, refused to accept the result and resumed the civil war; showing that the peacekeeping process had been flawed in not securing the commitment of all sides to a settlement.[5] In Liberia, ECOMOG's peacekeeping force was faced with a near-impossible task of trying to preserve a whole series of peace settlements in a country ravaged by decentralised violence, with no recognisable war fronts, where opportunist leaders sprang up to fight in a 'privatised' war. In the end a major objective was achieved in the apparently successful election of a new President.

There is always a danger that a peacekeeping mission will find itself converted into a peace enforcement operation, which the UN did not vote for, which the contributing states did not support, and for which the available forces in the field were insufficient. Peace enforcement is a different kind of intervention, yet in Africa this type of 'mission creep' has been seen so often, as in Somalia, where UNITAF was required to try to *make* peace, not just maintain it. In Angola and Liberia, peacekeeping forces were required to reassert previous peace agreements, and this involved the use of force, ECOMOG having to increase its force greatly. Such actions, of course, tended inevitably to cancel out one of the main assets of peacekeeping missions - their neutrality. If they were perceived to be partial in the eyes of one side or another of the combatants, their authority was undermined and their forces were placed in danger of attack. In Somalia, as Woodward says, the meagre forces available ended up shut in their camps and the mission was ignominiously withdrawn.

These failures point to a so-called 'grey area' between peace enforcement and peacekeeping, where it is fatal to mix the two. The UN Charter (while not mentioning peacekeeping as such) made the necessary distinction, but Anthony Parsons writes 'Now, an unfortunate habit has developed of combining Chapter VI (mediation and peacekeeping with the consent of the parties) and Chapter VII (mandatory sanctions and the use of force). This practice led in Somalia to a confused mandate which combined seeking Somali co-operation and acquiescence with forthright coercive measures'.[6] Adam Roberts calls this the crisis in peacekeeping: the consent of parties in conflict to a UN operation is being downgraded as the distinction between peacekeeping and coercive action is blurred; 'There is a much more interventionist element in peacekeeping today and this is at the heart of the crisis'.[7] But if the peace is not kept, then peacekeepers find themselves in a different role of trying to enforce a restoration of the cease-fire or peace agreement. The dangers of this have been seen often enough in Africa: the 'vain aspiration to neutrality' as Christopher Clapham has put it, is usually impossible to maintain in such circumstances, and peacekeepers are accused of favouring one side, or changing to another, or freezing the military situation, to the disadvantage of one side.[8] Donna Pankhurst in her chapter on Namibia shows that UNTAG, trying to oversee a cease-fire which was broken, was caught out by the lack of clarity about what had been accepted in the first place. In Chad, as Roy May and Simon Massey point out, the cease-fire element was lacking consent when the OAU mounted its peacekeeping operation, and interestingly the OAU Charter was less able to cover forceful intervention than the UN Charter, as there was no equivalent of either Chapter VI or VII. What was lacking, and is still lacking in the OAU, is a full doctrinal framework for peacekeeping. For Chad, the OAU mandate for its peacekeeping force at first was to support the existing government, but when the opposition started gaining, they switched to a different mandate.

The wider tasks in peacekeeping

As conflicts in Africa continually vary widely in character, so do the tasks involved in peacekeeping. Adam Roberts lists new tasks which have arisen since 1988, and prominent among these is the humanitarian task of protecting the inhabitants in a threatened region, and refugees who have fled to new 'designated' areas or safety zones, or simply to camps where they have chosen to settle at random. Protecting designated areas can drag the UN into reprisal attacks by parties who oppose such intervention, he points out, as these activities often do not have the consent of all parties. Very often the protection of such zones and refugee camps involves safeguarding convoys of food and other supplies to them; Somalia provided the most prominent example of this, where lifelines had to be kept open by peacekeeping forces not sufficiently equipped or mandated to do it, and they even had to hire local armed groups to assist them. In consequent shoot-outs, the notion of UN impartiality of course suffered. The same was true in Rwanda where peacekeepers, first the French and then the UN force, could with some reason be accused of harbouring and assisting former members of the 'Interahamwe', the perpetrators of genocide. The protection of humanitarian aid became a major example of 'mission creep', and Olara Otunnu points out that this dangerous tendency to slide from peacekeeping to peace enforcement sometimes produced an imbalance between the preoccupation with humanitarian action and the need for a political process. Mozambique saw a combined strategy of humanitarian and political actions, but in and around Rwanda and to a lesser extent Burundi there was a major humanitarian effort but no comparable concerted efforts to find a political settlement to the conflict.[9] More recently, pressure by the OAU in imposing a boycott on Burundi until satisfactory democratic conditions are established, has redressed this imbalance somewhat, though with limited success.

The final chapter takes an unusual approach in examining the experiences, the aims and motives of the 'peace-kept' rather than the peacekeepers. Very often the recipients of a peacekeeping operation regard it as an unwelcome interference, or at best, as an opportunity to further the cause of this or that faction, utilising foreign funds or resources for their own purposes. Just as it was the colonisers in previous times who were frequently manipulated and 'utilised' in various ways, so it is today the 'peacekept' who have on occasion derived advantages from the peacekeepers.

Along with humanitarian aid, UN peacekeepers are instructed to ensure the safeguarding of human rights under the UN and OAU conventions.

Indeed, pressure from the major powers financing and supporting peacekeeping operations has led to the insistence that this is another vital role which peacekeepers should play. The large numbers of UN and OAU 'observers' for human rights issues, spread throughout conflict zones in Africa, bear testimony to this pressure. Further, in Rwanda especially and in the Democratic Republic of Congo, formerly Zaire (though there is no peacekeeping operation there) another task has been added, that of assisting the processes of bringing to trial the major violators of human rights. Thus in Rwanda, efforts are being made to do this, while the UN and OAU have set up the International Criminal Tribunal at Arusha, dealing with the main perpetrators of Rwandan genocide. It follows the establishment of the South African Truth and Reconciliation Commission which has the aim not only of bringing violators of human rights to justice but also of furthering the process of reconciliation among former conflicting communities. For the UN recognises that there can be no lasting peace without justice, or without comprehensive reconciliation among all sides. Thus justice and reconciliation take their place among the wider tasks of peacekeeping, with political settlement, economic reconstruction and social rehabilitation. This of course shades into the 'grey area' between peacekeeping and peace building. The mandates for peacekeepers normally have a termination date: the peacekeeping forces are not expected to take over these latter processes but to facilitate them, and once they have been set up securely, the military depart and hand over to civilian branches such as UNID, UNHCR, the World Bank and others, with UN observers, civilian police, trainers and advisers.[10]

A rapid reaction force?

Several chapters in this book refer to the need for a rapid reaction force. In Africa, the UN and the OAU have been both inadequate in conflict prevention and in speedy intervention to assist in ending a conflict by sending in a peacekeeping force. Richard Connaughton's chapter on 'The military, peacekeeping and Africa' reveals the inadequacies of some of these attempts. A solution to the latter weakness is sought either by a UN 'stand-by' force, or by regionally based forces. In 1994, Sir Brian Urquhart, a former UN assistant secretary-general for UN peacekeeping, urged a standing UN force of troops volunteered by leading countries, with an institutional mechanism to enable rapid mobilisation, and an assured budget. The OAU discussed such a force, and Kenya, Nigeria and Ghana were willing to comply. The chapter on regional peacekeeping deals at length with recent ideas for African rapid reaction forces which would operate on a regional basis. In West Africa, ECOMOG provided an example of a regional peacekeeping force in action, with positive success though demonstrating many pitfalls, as the chapter on Liberia shows. Regional stand-by forces may be the answer if there are agreed mechanisms for their rapid deployment, strong organisational support and adequate resources, including contributions from the major powers. The UN has also made new efforts, in setting up a 'High Readiness Brigade', under a Danish-Dutch-Canadian initiative, and Norway, Sweden, Poland and Austria have agreed to join.

The truth is, however, that instead of agreements being willingly drawn up for such interventions, the international community is still mulling over the lessons learnt from previous peacekeeping operations, and there is some hesitation in plotting a way forward. The chapter by Mats Berdal on the role of the United States, Britain and France shows this. The UN has set up a 'Lessons Learnt Unit' for peacekeeping, in a bid to build up an institutional memory so that hard experience can be turned to better account. Both Canada and Italy are going through agonising reappraisals of their roles as harrowing details of their troops' excesses in Somalia emerge. The French prime minister, M. Jospin, has announced a withdrawal from France's previous pro-active role in Africa (though the French presence there remains strong). Further, in the latest conflicts in Africa, the UN or the OAU have shown a marked reluctance to intervene. In the former Zaire, there has been an extreme humanitarian crisis as Kabila's rebel forces swept through the country and caused Rwandan refugees, numbering possibly one to two hundred thousand, to flee their makeshift camps and disappear into the bush. Disease, starvation and murderous attacks by soldiery took a huge toll. Anguished pleas for UN intervention were heard, but it was realised that a peacekeeping force would take at least six weeks of negotiations to get together. Instead, a 700-strong African force was proposed, to be financed by countries of the EU. The UN Security Council did not approve and turned to consider a UN force again, causing further delay. In the end, no peacekeeping force ever arrived.[11]

Again while a vicious civil war is waged in Congo, the UN has voted against sending a peacekeeping force. Instead the UN and OAU have sent a negotiator, Mahomed Sahnoun, and attempted cease-fires are not even holding. Perhaps the most discouraging factor in this is the shortage of UN peacekeeping funds. USA wants $100 million as compensation for its peacekeeping costs, and is also pressing for mandatory consultation with both Houses of Congress whenever a peacekeeping package is proposed.

Kofi Annan, the new secretary-general of the UN, knows that this reluctance of members is linked to the urgent need for reform of the UN, especially the Security Council. If he can achieve reforms, peacekeeping, which remains a vital function in many parts of the world, may be able to secure better support and become more effective in its complex tasks. This book aims to illustrate those tasks as seen in Africa and to analyse the issues at stake today.

Notes

1. Diehl, P. F. 'Operations other than war (OOTW): Missions Types and Dimensions', < http://www.ccsr.vivc.edu/People/gmk/Projects/UNCMCW/Documents/OOTW.html >, 20 September 1996.
2. Interview with Lt Col P. R. Wilkinson (author of the British Army's manual 'Wider Peacekeeping') at Coventry University on 23 February 1996.
3. Kaplan, R. D. (1994) 'The Coming Anarchy', *Atlantic Monthly*, February, especially pp. 44-60.
4. Cooper, R. and Berdal, M. (1993) 'Outside intervention in ethnic conflicts', *Survival*, Spring 1993, p. 140.
5. 'Peaceful settlements of disputes succeed only when all the parties, albeit each for a different reason, need a settlement simultaneously', Parsons, A. *From Cold War to Hot Peace. UN Intervention 1947-1994*, Michael Joseph: London, p. 136.
6. Parsons, A., op. cit., p. 206.
7. Roberts, A. (1994) 'The crisis in UN peacekeeping', *Survival*, 36, No. 3.
8. Clapham, C. (1995) 'Problems of peace enforcement: some lessons from the multi-national peacekeeping operations in Africa', in Cilliers, J. and Mills, G. *Peacekeeping in Africa II*, Institute of Defence Policy: South Africa, p. 145.
9. Olara Otunnu, 'Peacekeeping: from a crossroads to a future', in Cilliers, J. and Mills, G. (eds) op. cit., p. 55.
10. Barnett, M. (1995) 'The new UN politics of peace: from juridical sovereignty to empirical sovereignty', *Global Governance 1*, p. 93-94.
11. Michel Rocard, President of the European Parliamentary Committee on Development and Co-operation, 'Taking Two Steps Back in Africa', Le Monde and Guardian Weekly, 24.08.97.

2 Peacekeeping in Africa: recent evolution and prospects

*Margaret Carey**

The first peacekeeping operation, the United Nations Truce Supervision Organisation (UNTSO), was established in 1948. During the next four decades, however, Cold War rivalries within the Security Council limited the United Nations' ability to engage in peacekeeping as a means of ensuring international peace and security. From 1948 to 1988, only 15 peacekeeping operations were established. With the exception of the United Nations Operation in the Congo (ONUC) (now the Democratic Republic of Congo) in the early 1960s, these operations involved relatively straightforward mandates, usually limited to monitoring cease-fire agreements or the separation of forces between two States, through the deployment of unarmed or lightly armed military personnel. They were established at the invitation and with the consent of the States in conflict, on the understanding that the United Nations would act as an impartial broker and that the deployment of military personnel would not involve the use of force, except in self-defence.

I Post-Cold War developments

The end of the Cold War created opportunities for the Security Council to take action in the settlement of a number of conflicts once considered off-limits, and in the five years between 1989 and 1993, the Council established some 15 peacekeeping operations, including nine in Africa. Many of these operations were much more ambitious than the more

---

* Margaret Carey is the Special Assistant of the Assistant Secretary-General for Peacekeeping. The views expressed here, however, are personal and do not necessarily reflect those of the United Nations.

traditional operations described above and they challenged the old rules of peacekeeping.

A number of the new operations were established to assist states coming out of protracted civil conflict. Some of these conflicts had taken on a somewhat anarchic nature, involving a number of ill-defined irregular groups. They had ruined national economies, uprooted populations, and severely weakened government and civic institutions. In order to address these complex situations, most of the new operations were entrusted with ambitious mandates. Some involved the implementation of multi-faceted peace agreements, including national reconciliation, disarmament and demobilisation, creation of unified national armies and police forces, strengthening of civil administrations, delivery of humanitarian assistance, monitoring of human rights, and holding of elections. Others involved the protection of civilians and the delivery of humanitarian aid within states still engulfed in hostilities. These operations required the quick deployment of thousands of military and civilian personnel and the necessary logistic support, stretching the capacity of the United Nations Secretariat to respond effectively.

With the difficulties encountered in Somalia and the former Yugoslavia in 1993 and 1994, the international community began to reassess the viability of peacekeeping as a means of ensuring international peace and security. In fact, some went so far as to consider that peacekeeping was a thing of the past. But peacekeeping has achieved a number of successes around the globe, including Africa. In the light of the experiences of the past few years, the United Nations and regional organisations, as well as a number of Member States, are taking steps to improve their capacity for peacekeeping and adapt it to the requirements of the post-Cold War era. Africa deserves special focus in this regard. Many African states are politically willing to play a significant role in peacekeeping and have the personnel to do so. But many lack the resources to properly equip, train and maintain their troops on stand-by for quick deployment. At the same time, a number of African countries have, in recent years, witnessed internal conflicts, the resolution of which could be assisted with the support of the international community through peacekeeping. Before reviewing the lessons learned from United Nations' recent interventions in Africa and outlining prospects for the future, it would be worthwhile to review the basic principles of peacekeeping - consent, impartiality and the 'non-use' of force - as well as how United Nations peacekeeping operations are formulated and financed.

Consent

Peacekeeping operations are established by the Security Council, at the invitation and consent of the warring parties. The continued consent and co-operation of the parties is essential to the successful implementation of an operation's mandate. As peacekeeping has evolved in the post-Cold War era, the issue of consent and co-operation has become more complex and elusive. The main interlocutors in latter day peacekeeping operations are, in many cases, the leaders of ill-defined groups who often have little control over their fighters. Their consent and co-operation is required not only for the monitoring of a cease-fire, but for the implementation of a number of far-reaching objectives. It is not always forthcoming, adding difficulties to the implementation of Security Council mandates.

The use of force

The function of military personnel in peacekeeping is to help build confidence between the parties, by monitoring and assisting the implementation of the military provisions of an agreement, thus assuring each side that the other is not engaged in aggressive activity. In so doing, they help establish the ground upon which the parties can implement the political and military provisions of a negotiated settlement. The use of force is authorised only in self-defence. In some post-Cold War civil conflicts, where security is still very unstable and faction leaders may not have complete or even partial command of their forces, peacekeepers may be met with armed resistance. Where this is likely, the Security Council has authorised a wider definition of the use of force. In such cases, force may be used not only in self-defence but also in defence of a mission's mandate. The Security Council has also used the imposition of sanctions, as means of coercing parties to settle a conflict. Peace-enforcement can imply the offensive application of coercive measures, which, however, can have implications for the perception of an operation's neutrality and impartiality, thus adding another level of complexity to the implementation for Security Council mandates.

Impartiality

In assisting the parties to settle a conflict, the United Nations, on principle, acts as an impartial broker without, as stated in the United Nations Charter, 'prejudice to the rights, claims or positions of the parties concerned'. It is because the parties to a conflict trust that the United

Nations will act as a neutral broker, that they call on the Organisation to assist them in resolving the conflict. In complex, multi-dimensional, operations where the United Nations is called upon to assist in the implementation of a number of activities, maintaining the perception of impartiality can be difficult. When an operation's impartiality is called into question, its ability to carry out its tasks effectively is all the more difficult.

Resources for peacekeeping

Securing financial resources and manpower for peacekeeping is a difficult and complicated task which can influence an operation's ability to carry out its mandate effectively. When a peacekeeping operation is authorised, Member States are 'assessed' regarding the financial requirements necessary to cover its costs. Once the Security Council authorises the establishment of an operation, its budget is reviewed and approved by the General Assembly. However, the lag time between the Security Council's approval of the operation and the General Assembly's approval of the budget can affect the Organisation's ability to put peacekeepers on the ground in a timely manner. Resources for peacekeeping also involves securing the necessary troops, military personnel and logistic equipment from Member States. Achieving this is affected by the degree of interest Member States have in a particular operation. Each time an operation is established, the United Nations has to build the force from scratch, relying on the good will of Member States to provide troops, including their immediate equipment needs. Furthermore, some Member States willing to offer troops may not have the logistic equipment necessary to support them and the Secretariat finds itself trying to match troops provided by one state with logistics provided by another. It can take a number of months, therefore, to get the necessary troops and equipment to support them on the ground. While the budget of a peacekeeping operation is limited to the resources necessary to carry out its immediate tasks, there are usually a number of other activities critical to the overall success of the peace process that must be funded. Such activities include the demobilisation of forces, resettlement of refugees, strengthening of state institutions and security mechanisms, and the holding of free and fair elections. Some peacekeeping operations have limited resources for such activities, others have none. It is up to the international community to provide these resources on a voluntary basis and its willingness to do so will affect the implementation of the peace process and, consequently, the ability of a peacekeeping operation to carry out its mandate.

II Peacekeeping in Africa: four case studies

Since the end of the Cold War, six multi-dimensional peacekeeping operations have been established in Africa. All but one of these operations was established on the basis of a negotiated settlement and at the invitation of the parties. In considering the lessons learned from peacekeeping in Africa, this chapter will focus on four peacekeeping operations: the United Nations Observer Mission in Mozambique (ONUMOZ), the second United Nations Operation in Somalia (UNOSOM II), the United Nations Assistance Mission for Rwanda (UNAMIR) and the United Nations Observer Mission in Liberia (UNOMIL). Each of these operations has taught us certain lessons which have enhanced our understanding of the principles of peacekeeping. Drawing on these lessons, this chapter will provide some thoughts on the future of peacekeeping, particularly in Africa.

The United Nations Observer Mission in Mozambique (ONUMOZ)

The General Peace Agreement signed in Rome on 4 October 1992 by the Government of Mozambique and the Resistencia Nacional Mocambicana (RENAMO) covered a wide range of issues and was aimed at creating a 'lasting peace and effective democracy' in Mozambique, after 16 years of civil war. The parties requested the assistance of the United Nations and on 16 December 1992, the Security Council established the United Nations Observer Mission in Mozambique (ONUMOZ). The Mission was entrusted with a multiplicity of tasks, including to monitor and verify the implementation of the agreement, in particular to supervise the cease-fire, provide security for key transportation corridors; to monitor a comprehensive disarmament and demobilisation programme; to co-ordinate and monitor the provision of humanitarian assistance, and, ultimately, to verify national elections. In order to carry out these tasks, ONUMOZ was provided with some 350 military observers and 6,625 troops, assisted by an international civilian staff of 355 people. Later, a civilian police component of over 1,100 officers was added to the mission.

Despite the commitments made by all involved, the implementation of the General Agreement quickly ran into trouble. Within weeks of its signing, both sides had accused the other of violating the cease-fire.

Despite early planning, the United Nations encountered difficulties in securing troops from Member States and deploying them in a timely manner. This did not help to alleviate the deep mistrust between the parties. In addition, RENAMO's capacity to carry out its commitments, including participation in the various committees established to oversee the implementation of the agreement, was impeded by a lack of resources and an inadequate command and control structure. Another major difficulty in the implementation of the agreement, was the cantonment and disarmament of troops. Once the government agreed to proceed with the exercise, RENAMO continued to link its participation in the process to certain conditions. The two parties also took months to agree on the make-up of the Electoral Commission and there were significant delays in the formation of a national army. Given the delays, the timetable for the implementation of the agreement was extended from one to two years. Finally, on the first day of polling, the leader of RENAMO threatened to pull out of the elections.

In spite of the continuing mistrust and delays in the implementation of each stage of the peace process, the parties were ultimately able to muster the political will necessary to implement the agreement. Their ability to do so was, in a large part, due to the international community's active involvement in the peace process and its resolute support of ONUMOZ.

While ONUMOZ was established with the resources necessary to carry out its immediate tasks, it required the continued involvement of the international community in order to implement them. When the United Nations ran into difficulties in securing and deploying ONUMOZ troops, special efforts were made by several Member States to ensure they were deployed. The international community provided the financial resources necessary to carry out a number of tasks that were not funded under the ONUMOZ budget, but which were essential for the implementation of the agreement, including funds to enable RENAMO and other political parties to participate in the electoral process, the reintegration of displaced persons and demobilised soldiers into civil society and the formation of a unified army. The international community also showed the flexibility necessary to pursue the peace process, extending the mandate of ONUMOZ, despite delays in its implementation. More importantly, Member States provided their active and unified political support in encouraging the parties to implement the agreement. Such support was particularly critical when the leader of RENAMO threatened to pull out of the final stages of the electoral process. The ambassadors of various Member States in Maputo and the leaders of Mozambique's neighbouring states worked closely with the Secretary-General's Special Representatives in successfully convincing the parties to complete the peace process.

The United Nations Operation in Somalia (UNOSOM II)

The deployment in December 1992 of the Unified Task Force (UNITAF), led by the United States and comprising a total of 37,000 troops, enabled the international community to restore the flow of humanitarian assistance and put an end to the famine which was decimating the population of Somalia. However, when the Security Council established UNOSOM II, which took over from UNITAF on 1 May 1993, there were no functioning state institutions in the country and the factions continued to be heavily armed. Nevertheless, they had agreed to take a number of steps leading toward the establishment of a new central government and had reaffirmed an early agreement to cease fire, hand over their heavy weapons, and encamp and disarm their militias.

Given the high degree of insecurity, the Security Council authorised UNOSOM II to use enforcement powers in carrying out its mandate, which included the establishment of a secure environment throughout Somalia; disarming the factions; protecting United Nations and other international personnel; assisting the Somali people in rebuilding the country's economy and institutional structures and in achieving national political reconciliation. UNOSOM II was provided with an authorised strength of 20,000 troops, plus a military support unit of some 8,000 troops, and a civilian component of 2,800 staff. The United States maintained a Joint Task Force of some 17,000 troops in Somalia, which supported UNOSOM II in the field but were not part of the United Nations operations.

The establishment of UNOSOM was unprecedented in many ways: it was the first enforcement operation that was both organised and commanded by the United Nations. The tasks entrusted to it were wide-ranging and in some cases new for the Organisation, especially in regard to building government structures from the ground up and creating a national police force. Tension increased in Mogadishu in the months following the establishment of UNOSOM II, particularly between the Mission and the Somali National Alliance (SNA). A number of factors led to this situation, including attempts by UNOSOM II to forcibly disarm the factions, including the SNA. Against this tense background, on 5 June 1993, a UNOSOM II team engaged in the inspection of a weapons storage site was attacked and, by the end of the day, 24 UNOSOM II soldiers had been killed and 57 injured. UNOSOM II's investigation of the incident found evidence of an SNA conspiracy to commit premeditated acts of violence against the Mission. During the weeks that followed, UNOSOM II continued to take coercive measures in disarming the factions and, at the request of the Security Council took action to arrest and detain the SNA leader, General Aidid. On 5 October 1993, a US-led operation to arrest Aidid resulted in over 100 UNOSOM II and US deaths. This was a turning point for UNOSOM II.

After the 5 October incident, the US announced its intention to withdraw from Somalia. Due to a lack of sufficient manpower and logistic and financial resources, the Security Council decided in February 1994 that UNOSOM II would no longer use coercive measures, except in defence of its personnel, and would rely on the co-operation of the Somali people to carry out its mandate. This mandate marked the evolution of the Mission from a peace-enforcement to a peace-keeping operation. While in the first half of 1994, additional troop-contributing countries withdrew their contingents from Somalia, UNOSOM II continued to assist in the organisation of a number of local-level cease-fire agreements and reconciliation conferences, as well as the establishment of district and regional councils, an 8,500 police force and in strengthening the judicial system. Despite such achievements at the local level, however, the co-operation of the Somali factions necessary to achieve national reconciliation was not forthcoming. Agreements reached toward this end under the auspices of the United Nations unravelled and security continued to deteriorate, especially in Mogadishu, making it impossible for UNOSOM II staff to operate. In the end, the international community was unwilling to continue to finance such a large operation in the absence of significant progress toward national reconciliation and the Mission was withdrawn from Somalia in March 1995.

The United Nations Assistance Mission for Rwanda (UNAMIR)

The situation in Somalia was very much on the minds of the Member States as the Security Council deliberated on the establishment of UNAMIR and the operation was established on 5 October 1993 in an atmosphere of caution and fiscal austerity. It was provided with a modest mandate and modest manpower and resources. UNAMIR was established on the basis of a request from the Government of Rwanda and the Rwandese Patriotic Front (RPF) for assistance in the implementation of the Arusha Accords which had been concluded in August 1993. The principle function of UNAMIR was to create a climate of confidence necessary to enable the parties to implement the Accords, which included a cease-fire, establishment of a transitional government, integration of the armed forces, repatriation of refugees and the holding of elections, leading to the inauguration of a new government. UNAMIR's main tasks, however, were limited to the following: assist in ensuring the security of the capital city of Kigali; monitor the cease-fire; investigate non-compliance with any provision of the peace agreement; and provide security for the repatriation of Rwandese refugees and displaced persons. The implementation of a programme for disarmament and demobilisation, the creation of a unified army and gendarmerie, resettlement of displaced persons and the holding of elections would be carried out by the transitional government on the basis of voluntary contributions provided by the international community.

The Organisation of African Unity (OAU) had deployed a Neutral Military Observer Group (NMOG) of some 40 officers to Rwanda in July 1992 to monitor the cease-fire while political negotiations proceeded. Following the conclusion of the Arusha Accords, the OAU indicated that it did not have the resources necessary to oversee the implementation of the Accords and it was therefore agreed that NMOG observers would be incorporated into the proposed United Nations peacekeeping operation. UNAMIR was established with a total authorised strength of 2,545 lightly armed and equipped troops, as well as 126 international and 68 local staff. The Mission was to operate under the assumption that the co-operation of the parties would be forthcoming. In establishing UNAMIR, the Security Council urged Member States, the United Nations agencies and Non-Governmental Organisations (NGOs) to intensify their programmes of economic, financial and humanitarian assistance to Rwanda, including the process of democratisation. UNAMIR bore little resemblance to the multi-faceted peacekeeping operation approved just a year before to assist in the implementation of the peace agreement in Mozambique.

The United Nations soon ran into difficulties in securing the necessary troops and resources for UNAMIR, due in part to the commitments of potential troop-contributing countries in other United Nations peacekeeping operations, and the first contingent was not fully deployed until December 1993. Throughout the first months of UNAMIR's mandate, the parties continued to respect the cease-fire, but hesitated in providing the co-operation necessary to implement the political provisions of the Accords. While President Habyarimana was sworn in as President on 5 January 1994, in accordance with the Accords, the installation of the transitional government and the transitional national assembly was postponed as the parties were unable to agree on the members of these bodies. The impasse led to a deterioration in security, including politically motivated murders and assaults. By the end of March, the Secretary-General was compelled to note that in the event that sufficient progress was not achieved in the next two months, the Security Council should review the situation, including the role of the United Nations in Rwanda. The threat of a possible United Nations withdrawal was meant to pressure the parties to proceed with the implementation of the Accords. Unfortunately, this was not enough to encourage them to proceed.

President Habyarimana's death on 6 April 1994 led to a series of well documented events in Rwanda, which resulted in the massacre of over 500,000 people. UNAMIR's force level was too small and too lightly equipped to take offensive action in averting the crisis. The UNAMIR Force Commander noted at the time that a well-trained and equipped brigade could have deterred the violence before it grew to uncontrollable proportions. Yet, the international community was not willing to react quickly and provide UNAMIR sufficient troops, or to establish a multi-national operation such as UNITAF, necessary to stem the crisis and, perhaps, avert the genocide, which followed.

As the international community hesitated to become involved in settling the conflict, some UNAMIR contingents were unilaterally withdrawn by their governments from the operation. On 21 April, the Security Council decided to reduce UNAMIR's military strength to 270 troops who would assist in securing a cease-fire and in the resumption of humanitarian aid. It was not until 17 May 1994, at the urging of the Secretaries-General of the United Nations and OAU, and many African states, that the Security Council expanded UNAMIR to 5,500 troops and provided it with a more proactive mandate, i.e. to contribute to the security and protection of displaced persons, refugees and civilians at risk and to provide security and support for relief operations. While UNAMIR's rules of engagement did not include overt enforcement action, it was authorised to use force should certain elements try to prevent it from carrying out its mandate. Nevertheless, the necessary support for the expanded mission was not forthcoming. The countries willing to provide troops, which were mostly from Africa, required logistic support, but when logistic support was offered, the conditions were such that long and protracted negotiations were required to deploy it.

While the United Nations was trying to put together the expanded UNAMIR, France was organising a multi-national force, 'Operation Turquoise', which was authorised by the Security Council on 22 June to establish a 'humanitarian protected zone' in the south-west. The operation was established within a week and, by using deterrent force, saved thousands of lives, without having to take coercive action. Unfortunately, it was deployed too late, and had too restrictive an area of operations, to have had a more significant impact on stemming the massacres. On 18 July, the RPF declared a unilateral cease-fire and, the next day, installed a government of national unity in Kigali. UNAMIR, however, still had fewer than 500 troops on the ground. Its authorised strength was not fully deployed until September. With the war over, the new Government did not see the rationale for a large United Nations force, and resisted its deployment. Nevertheless, it consented to the presence of UNAMIR on the assumption that United Nations troops would bring with them resources for the rehabilitation of the country.

The people and infrastructures of Rwanda had been devastated by the civil war. While the Secretary-General launched an appeal for some $439 million for humanitarian and reconstruction assistance for the country, donors were slow to turn their pledges into concrete assistance, insisting that the new government undertake negotiations with the former Rwandese Government Forces (RGF) and broaden the participation of opposition groups in its administration. At the same time, millions of dollars worth of aid was provided to assist those who had taken refuge in camps in Zaire (now the Democratic Republic of Congo) and Tanzania. The government resented the disparity in aid flows and its resentment was taken out on UNAMIR as the visible representative of the international community in Rwanda. From that period until its withdrawal from Rwanda, UNAMIR experienced numerous difficulties in implementing its mandate. It did not have the tools necessary to foster the government's co-operation and it was especially difficult for the Government and people of Rwanda to understand why the Mission could not use the equipment and logistic resources at its disposal to assist it in rebuilding the country. While UNAMIR used its own resources to the extent possible to assist the Government, it was restricted by General Assembly and Security Council mandates from using the resources beyond the confines of its immediate Mission. In the absence of significant aid flows from the international community, the Government felt that UNAMIR as a peace-keeping mission did not respond to its priority needs. The Mission was finally withdrawn in March 1996.

The United Nations Observer Mission in Liberia (UNOMIL)

UNOMIL was the first United Nations peacekeeping operation established in conjunction with that of a regional or sub-regional organisation, in this case the Economic Community of West African States (ECOWAS). This posed particular difficulties and challenges for the United Nations. The tasks entrusted to UNOMIL were limited to observing and monitoring the implementation of the Cotonou Peace Agreement, signed by the warring parties in July 1993. The primary responsibility for the implementation of the agreement was assigned to the ECOWAS Monitoring Group (ECOMOG). The Cotonou Agreement provided for the formation of a transitional government headed by a Council of State; disarmament and demobilisation; and finally the election of a new government. UNOMIL was provided with 303 military observers, 60 military support personnel, 89 international and 139 local staff. While ECOMOG would require significant resources to carry out its tasks, the Member States of ECOMOG were not in a position to provide them. The resources required for ECOMOG would have to be provided on a voluntary basis. In his report on the establishment of UNOMIL, the Secretary-General noted that the Mission would not be able to fulfil its mandate unless ECOMOG received the support necessary to carry out its responsibilities. He established a trust fund through which Member States could voluntarily provide assistance for ECOMOG but despite the provision of some contributions (most notably by the government of the United States), the resources required for ECOMOG to carry out its mandate effectively were not, initially, forthcoming.

The Cotonou Agreement did not provide details as to how its provisions would be implemented. Throughout the latter part of 1993 and the first half of 1994, the parties engaged in protracted discussions over the manner in which they would proceed in implementing the agreement. As tension grew, the peace process broke down in September 1994, with the outbreak of fighting in some parts of the country. Throughout the following year, ECOWAS and UNOMIL made a number of attempts to re-start the peace process. These efforts culminated in the signing of the Abuja Agreement in August 1995. The people of Liberia, as well as the international community, were fairly optimistic that the factions would implement the Abuja Agreement. Instead of appointing representatives to the Council of State, the faction leaders themselves formed the Council, thus placing responsibility for the implementation of the agreement squarely on their own shoulders. However, when the faction leaders came to Monrovia to establish the Council, they brought with them a number of their fighters and weapons 'as security'. It soon become obvious that they did not have the necessary will to work together as an interim coalition government. The peace process was again delayed as the faction leaders procrastinated over how to proceed.

The Abuja Agreement collapsed in April 1996, with the outbreak of fighting in Monrovia, a city which until that time had been considered one of the only safe areas in Liberia. None of the factions won a military victory as a result of the fighting, but when they retreated from Monrovia, they left behind a humanitarian crisis and a devastated city. One development which emerged during this period, was the creation of a 'Mediation Team' composed of the Special Representative of the Secretary-General, the Special Representative of the Chairman of ECOWAS, the Field Commander of ECOMOG and the Ambassadors of Ghana, Guinea, Nigeria, Sierra Leone and the United States. Through a co-ordinated effort, the Mediation Team was able to encourage the factions to return to the negotiating table. In August 1996, the factions agreed to a new timetable for the implementation of the peace process. At the same time, ECOWAS took a number of decisions aimed at strengthening its oversight role in the peace process, including subjecting any faction found impeding the process to the imposition of sanctions. It was also decided that the process toward electing a new government would move ahead, with or without full disarmament, the implementation of which had been a major stumbling block in the past.

Following the tragic events of April 1996, the international community finally realised that unless ECOMOG was provided with the necessary resources to carry out its tasks, the peace process in Liberia would never succeed. Once it was provided with sufficient resources, ECOMOG was able to deploy its forces throughout Liberia and take steps to deter aggressive action from the factions. The factions were finally disarmed by the first part of 1997. The restoration of a climate of security, ensured by the widespread deployment of ECOMOG, was crucial to creating the confidence necessary to hold elections and for donors to provide assistance for humanitarian and reintegration programmes. On 19 July national elections were held in conditions of relative peace and security and a new government was installed on 2 August 1997.

III Lessons learned and prospects for the future

The United Nations operations described above reflected a new generation of peacekeeping, where the basic principles of peacekeeping - consent, the non-use of force, and impartiality - were significantly challenged. They had mandates which went way beyond the monitoring of a cease-fire or the separation of forces. They were deployed into messy, insecure situations where consent and co-operation were complex and elusive issues and where one was not always sure who the protagonists were. The lessons learned from these operations demonstrated that certain conditions must be in place in order for them to succeed. These conditions include the following: *Foremost*, the warring parties must be ready to put aside the military quest for power and pursue the settlement of the conflict through peaceful means. *Second*, a clear political strategy is necessary to address the underlying causes of the conflict and prescribe steps toward national reconciliation. *Third*, an operation's mandate must clearly set out the tasks entrusted to it. *Fourth,* the international community must be ready to provide both its political and financial support to the operation; it must match the tasks of a mandate with the provision of the manpower, logistic and financial resources necessary to carry them out and these resources must be deployed quickly. These conditions are applicable to peacekeeping world-wide. In Africa, they were in place for the most part in Mozambique and, later, to a certain extent in Liberia. But they did not exist in Rwanda and Somalia.

In recent months, a number of possible United Nations peacekeeping operations have been planned for the former Zaire (now the Democratic Republic of Congo), Burundi, Sierra Leone and the Republic of Congo (formerly Congo Brazzaville). These operations were never established by the Security Council because the basic conditions for success were not in hand. Yet, while the Security Council has shown a reluctance to establish peacekeeping operations, including in Africa, where the conditions for success have been elusive, African states have continued to act collectively in addressing crises on the continent. The OAU continues to take a lead role in negotiating political settlements to crises throughout the continent. ECOWAS is playing a lead role in assisting the parties in Sierra Leone to resolve the conflict in that country. An Inter-African Mission to Monitor the Implementation of the Bangui Agreements (MISAB) is presently deployed in the Central African Republic, with the assistance of the Government of France.

With African countries and organisations taking a growing interest in addressing conflicts on the continent, the co-ordination of such efforts with those of the United Nations will become increasingly important. In this connection, the United Nations and the OAU have taken steps to strengthen co-ordination both at the political and technical levels. The two organisations fielded a joint Envoy to address the recent crises faced by countries in central Africa. This experience was particularly valuable in ensuring the co-ordination of response at the political level. The United Nations is presently working hand in hand with ECOWAS in developing plans for a response to the crisis in Sierra Leone. Such joint efforts are likely to continue in the future. But as the lessons of peacekeeping in Africa have shown, their success will require the active participation of the international community as a whole, especially in terms of financial and logistic support for African peacekeepers and to support programmes essential to peacekeeping, such as demobilisation, reintegration, human rights, electoral assistance, institution building, etc.

African states are also taking an increasing interest in ensuring their preparedness for peacekeeping world-wide, including in Africa. Currently, 17 African countries are contributing almost 2,700 troops, military observers and civilian police observers to United Nations operations throughout the world. In co-ordination with the OAU and the United Nations, a number of African states have launched programmes for training peacekeepers. The OAU, as well as sub-regional organisations such as the Southern African Development Community (SADC), are taking steps to develop a collective African capacity for crisis management. The United Nations, for its part, is pursuing efforts, including with African states, in regard to the development of Stand-by Arrangements, Rapidly Deployable Mission Headquarters, training and streamlining procedures for quick deployment of personnel and equipment. All these efforts are aimed at preparing the international community to be able to respond to crises quickly and effectively.

A number of donor states, particularly France, the United Kingdom, the United States and the Nordic countries are assisting African countries in this regard. But effective response to crises requires not only well trained troops. The requirement of logistic and equipment support necessary to deploy those troops, and for them to carry out their tasks, is still to be satisfactorily addressed.

IV Conclusion

While the international community, including African states, has clearly learned from the lessons of the past, the most essential lesson - that the maintenance of international peace and security is a collective effort - can not be forgotten. For peacekeeping to be an effective tool in the resolution of conflicts, the international community will have to continue to strengthen its capacity to respond through co-ordinated efforts both politically and in terms of concrete support for peacekeeping. In this connection, peacekeeping operations in Africa, whether led by the United Nations or a group of African states, will remain a collaborative effort, demanding the involvement of the international community as a whole.

3 African perspectives: regional peacekeeping

Gerry Cleaver and Roy May

Introduction

Recent events in Central Africa have strengthened the contemporary debate over the need for a capacity amongst the states of sub-Saharan Africa to conduct military operations designed either to maintain or establish peace, in order to assist in the relief of humanitarian crises. The emphasis on the requirement for an essentially African capability in this field has developed as a consequence of a series of events that have followed the end of the Cold War.

At that time, in the prevailing atmosphere of relief and optimism there was a general perception that the United Nations, freed from the entanglements of superpower rivalry, would be able to adopt a more proactive role as the guardian of the world's peace. The success of the UN in such a role was of course dependent on the support it received from the USA and initially this appeared to be forthcoming, especially following the successful convergence of US and UN policies in the eviction of the Iraqis from Kuwait in 1991.

However problems arose for this 'New World Order'[1] when attempts were made to translate a policy for dealing with aggressive tyrants into one applicable to the humanitarian and political crises of Africa. The debacle in Somalia convinced US policy-makers that they needed to radically review their level of commitment to UN peacekeeping operations. The resulting policy changes, encapsulated in Presidential Decision Directive 25 in May 1994, led to a virtual embargo on the use of US ground forces and severe budgetary cutbacks. The US also used its position of leverage within the UN to impose constraints on future UN operations.[2] The new policy orientation meant that in order to receive US support, future UN peacekeeping operations would have to be, amongst other things, of a predetermined duration, be in response to a genuine threat to international peace and be properly budgeted for. The impracticality of these preconditions to action are obvious and US's insistence on them, effectively hamstrung the UN in its peacekeeping operations. The tragic consequences of this were most immediately apparent in Rwanda.

In the case of Rwanda, the precipitate withdrawal of the Belgian contingent of UNAMIR, after securing the safety of Westerners, the apparent disinterest of the US, the questionable role of France and the failure of the UN to reinforce its ongoing mission and alter its mandate to deal with genocide, all combined to support a growing belief within Africa that Africa's problems could only be effectively addressed by Africans themselves. It was argued that the assumption of responsibility by Africans for peacekeeping in Africa would have the advantage of granting them not only ownership of the problems but also of the solutions. The exclusion of outside powers and the 'Africanisation' of peacekeeping forces might help avert future instances where it could be inferred from the actions of those forces that black African lives were of less value than white European ones. It is also important to emphasise that the impetus behind the moves to establish African peacekeeping structures and forces comes as much from a largely disinterested international community seeking to disengage from a marginalised continent as from Africans themselves, who now recognise that if they don't take action, there is little likelihood that anyone else will.

The evolution of the debate on African peacekeeping

In examining the debate on African peacekeeping, two major themes emerge. Firstly there is a general consensus amongst all the interested parties on the desirability of indigenous African peacekeeping structures and secondly that the establishment and maintenance of such structures will be fraught with problems both political and practical. In the latter category the issues of finance and logistics appear to predominate. A number of states and international organisations, including the USA, Britain and France, have all, in varying degrees, expressed support for, and a willingness to assist the establishment of, African peacekeeping forces and institutions. The French position was made clear by the then Prime Minister, M. Balladur, during a tour of Africa in July and August 1994 when France launched its own, albeit UN endorsed, intervention into Rwanda, *Operation Turquoise*. M. Balladur stated at the time that France desired to see the creation of a peacekeeping force, *'proprement africaine... capable d'intevenir rapidment en Afrique pour des operations de maintenir de la paix sur mandat des Nations Unies'*.³ At the Franco-African summit in Biarritz that November, the subject of peacekeeping was again top of the agenda. Although President Mitterand mounted a vigorous defence of *Operation Turquoise,* his ambiguous stance on the atrocities committed by the French backed former government tended to add credence to the growing body of opinion that believed that the French had acted purely out of self interest to facilitate the flight of disreputable allies, rather than out of any humanitarian motivations. This particular impression was reinforced by the deliberate exclusion from the Biarritz conference of the new RPF government of Rwanda on somewhat spurious linguistic grounds.⁴ At that conference President Mitterand promised logistic and training support for an African peacekeeping force and indicated that he had also obtained similar pledges of support from other European and Scandinavian countries.⁵

Although Jacques Chirac's election as President did not immediately appear to herald any revolutionary changes in French policy towards Africa, events in the former Zaire and the recent election of a socialist Prime Minister in Paris, seem to have radically affected France's position on the continent. Despite apparently a more multilateral approach to the wider questions of peacekeeping in Africa,⁶ France has continued to try to intervene unilaterally where it feels its interests warrant it and it believes it has the capacity to do so.

At the root of France's current problems in Africa is an often officially denied but nevertheless quite tangible Franco-American rivalry on the continent. For example, in January 1996, the French effectively blocked an American plan for the deployment of a preventative peacekeeping force in Burundi, which might have forestalled some of the horrors that subsequently took place there. France was obviously concerned about further incursions of 'Anglo-Saxon' influence into its back-yard following the loss of Rwanda from the 'La Francophonie' in 1994.⁷

Worse was to come for the French in the autumn of 1996 with the start of Laurent Kabila's revolt against Mobutu's regime in Zaire (now the Democratic Republic of Congo). France clearly perceived this as an invasion by Rwanda and Uganda sponsored by the US. The French eagerly supported the idea of international intervention during October and November 1996, ostensibly for humanitarian purposes to alleviate the suffering of refugees, but perhaps more likely a ruse to enable them to prop up the collapsing Mobutu regime. It was made clear to the French by Kabila's ADFL forces and the Rwandans that the insertion of French forces in whatever guise would be met by force[8] and following their rough handling by the RPF in 1994, the French had no desire to endure the consequences of such a fight. The proposed UN intervention into Zaire was rendered pointless by the clearing of the refugee camps by the Rwandan-led ADFL just hours before its proposed deployment.[9] As the ADFL advance progressed steadily against Mobutu's disintegrating army, elements within the French military appeared to be behind the failed attempt to recruit Bosnian Serb mercenaries to prop up the Mobutu regime.[10] The French also appear to have been the driving force behind a summit arranged in Libreville on 7 May 1997 between Mobutu and conservative Francophone African leaders, where Mobutu hoped to obtain military assistance, to no avail as it turned out. Mobutu's subsequent fall from power has been a body blow to French prestige in Africa and further recent upheavals in Congo (formerly Congo-Brazzaville) and the Central African Republic have only added to France's discomfort. In both countries, instead of trying to impose a solution of its own, France has chosen to support multilateral peacekeeping operations. In the CAR, numerous attempts by France since May 1996[11] to end the conflict between President Patasse and mutinous soldiers met with only limited success and some sort of peace has only begun to emerge after the intervention of an African peacekeeping force. This move towards a more multilateral approach, especially in concert with its remaining African allies, was demonstrated in March 1997 by an exercise, held in Togo, involving 4,000 troops from France, Benin, Burkina Faso and Togo, centred around the deployment and management of a multinational humanitarian force.[12]

Events in Central Africa since the autumn of 1996 would appear to indicate a de facto French withdrawal from its former interventionist role in Africa. This has been further confirmed by the recent announcement of the socialist government in Paris, of substantial cuts in France's military presence in Africa and the closure of at least one of its bases there.[13] This is obviously going to affect the future of peacekeeping in Africa with France perhaps adopting a more multilateral approach in concert with its European and African allies. How significant these changes will be remains to be seen. Nevertheless a niggling rivalry persists between Paris and Washington and this does not bode well for a co-operative approach to meeting the needs of African peacekeepers.

The attitude of successive British governments has traditionally been in stark contrast to that of their French counterparts. Whereas the French have maintained a close relationship with their former colonies and other states on the continent, Britain has adopted a very low key approach to

Africa since withdrawing from the Empire. However Britain too is now advocating the cause of regional peacekeeping for Africa. The approach of the British government was initially set out by John Major during a speech to the South African National Assembly on 20 September 1994 when he said: '*We have in mind for example setting up regional peacekeeping cells. We need more people trained to mediate, more people trained to act as peace brokers*'.[14] The following week the Foreign Secretary, Douglas Hurd, went into more detail about these proposals, during an address to the UN. He suggested that there should be an expansion of certain African military staff colleges into peacekeeping skills centres for the training of personnel in the disciplines of peacekeeping, mediation and conflict resolution. He also called for the establishment in Africa, of UN logistics centres for the storage and maintenance of equipment and the training of local personnel in its use. These would be bases for rapid mobile logistics teams provided by UN member states and would also have a headquarters staff to try to remedy logistics weaknesses and provide advice to troop contributing nations.[15] This idea is similar to the type of bases established in Europe by NATO to facilitate rapid reinforcement and it also follows on from the type of logistic support provided by the British elements of UNAMIR II (Rwanda) and UNAVEM III (Angola).

The British Army in partnership with the Foreign Office has already started to provide peacekeeping training material to military colleges in Zimbabwe and Ghana.[16] As part of this policy of supplying training assistance to African states, Britain was heavily involved in an extremely significant peacekeeping exercise held by members of Southern Africa Development Community in Nyanga, Zimbabwe, in April 1997. Operation Blue Hungwe (Eagle), as the exercise was code-named, involved around 1,000 troops from eight SADC member states, including 290 from South Africa and was under the supervision of Maj. Gen. Nyambuya of Zimbabwe.[17] The Zimbabweans proposed the idea and acted as hosts largely as a result of their extensive experience of peacekeeping operations. A sixteen-man British Military Advisory and Training Team helped design and run the exercises and Britain contributed some £300,000 toward their cost.[18]

In addition Britain is co-operating with France in a joint commission on peacekeeping set up following President Chirac's visit in May 1996[19] and is also involved in an initiative by the Western European Union to assess the level of assistance, it might be able to provide to African peacekeeping operations.[20] Following on from these political developments, the RAF and the French air force conducted exercise Volcano 96 in November of that year to evaluate their ability to co-operate in such operations.[21] It is not only the larger, historically connected European countries that are becoming involved. Recently two Irish military officers visited Zambia to explore the possibility of establishing a UN peacekeeping wing at the Zambia Military Academy.[22]

The US government, in what might be seen as a natural extension of its policy of opposition to UN-led peacekeeping operations, has expressed continuing support for various efforts designed to establish African peacekeeping structures. For example on 19 September 1994, Congress passed the African Conflict Resolution Act.[23] This provides for $25 million of assistance for the OAU's conflict resolution capability, for sub-regional organisations engaged in peacekeeping activities, such as ECOWAS, for the promotion of demobilisation programmes, the training of Africans in conflict resolution and the funding of NGOs involved in mediation in Africa.[24] In October 1994 the Deputy Secretary of State, Strobe Talbot, suggested, whilst in Zimbabwe, that the US might be prepared to supply transport planes to a Southern African regional organisation, in order to give such an organisation a rapid response capability.[25] Again, in December 1994, whilst visiting Ethiopia, Anthony Lake, the President's National Security Advisor, pledged $1.5 million for the OAU's Peace Fund and indicated his support for a unified operations command at the OAU headquarters in Addis Ababa.[26] All these offers of assistance fit in with the current US policy of avoiding direct military involvement in peacekeeping operations in Africa. American forces have been involved in Africa recently both in Liberia and the Central African Republic. However, in both cases, their role was strictly limited to the protection of US lives and property. Nor should anything be read into the US involvement in Bosnia. This has gained a certain amount of domestic US support precisely because it is no longer a UN operation but effectively a NATO one and follows on from a US brokered agreement.

The image of dead US servicemen being dragged through the streets of Mogadishu is so burned into the public's and policy-maker's minds in the US that it seems highly unlikely that US ground forces would be committed to a peacekeeping operation in Africa. Notwithstanding the fact that the Somalia fiasco was as much the result of US political and operational failings as anything else, the UN has been burdened with the blame for that failure of US arms and Africa made into a continent to be avoided where at all possible. It is clear that any future US assistance to African peacekeeping operations will be limited to the political, financial and logistical spheres. This final point was made explicitly clear in July 1996 in the immediate aftermath of Pierre Buyoya's coup in Burundi when there was much discussion of military intervention. At that time, a State Department spokesperson made it clear that although the US was prepared to offer communications, logistics and transport assistance to an intervention force either UN or African-led, the US government was '*not prepared to contribute troops to any kind of UN operation in Burundi.*'[27]

This policy of supporting peacekeeping efforts by Africans themselves without becoming involved on the ground militarily, was pushed one stage further in the autumn of 1996 with the launching of the proposal for an African Crisis Response Force (ACRF). The idea, as later enunciated by the Secretary of State, Warren Christopher, was not for a standing force, as such, but for states in sub-Saharan Africa to earmark units up to a total force of about 10,000 men, who could be available for deployment in times of crisis. It was proposed that the force would be led by Africans and operate under the auspices of the UN. The US would provide $40 million towards its establishment and $20 million towards the cost of its deployment.[28]

A series of US diplomatic missions were sent to Africa and Europe in September and October of 1996 to drum up support for this plan. General Jamerson, the Deputy Commander in Chief of US Army forces in Europe visited the OAU headquarters in Addis Ababa and George Moose, the Assistant Secretary of State for African Affairs, led a team to Europe and to ten African states to enlist their support.[29] Finally Warren Christopher made a much publicised trip to Africa in October 1996, with promotion of the ACRF as its main purpose. Reaction to the proposal was mixed. Britain, Canada and a number of other western nations offered financial assistance[30] but other European countries, particularly France, thought the idea too vague.[31] The European Union felt that there were problems with the fact that the plan was an American one and had not come via the OAU or UN.[32]

In Africa itself there was general support for the idea of US assistance for African peacekeeping operations but the nature of the planned ACRF caused concerns for many African leaders.[33] These centred around the command and control of the force and its finances. President Mandela, while not opposing the plan, believed that there was a need for a more significant element of African control over its use.[34] The Americans were perhaps suspected of wanting a force that could be used in lieu of their own troops and the idea of UN control was viewed with considerable scepticism following the failures of UNAMIR in Rwanda. The Nigerians were particularly scathing in their criticism of the ACRF, perhaps piqued at not being included on the list of states approached by the US for troop contributions.[35] On the financial front, the OAU while welcoming any such assistance pointed out that the real problems began with the costs of maintaining such a force in the field. While addressing a conference of African military officers in Zimbabwe, attending a two week peacekeeping course, the OAU's Assistant Secretary General, Ahmed Hagag, pointed out that the UN operation in Rwanda had cost US $1.5 billion, a figure Africa could not hope to approach.[36] Despite commitments from Mali[37], Ethiopia, Uganda and Senegal, to support the ACRF, Warren Christopher's trip could not immediately be termed a success. At the end of it, the Franco-American rivalry came out into the open. The French Minister for Foreign Co-operation, Jacques Godfrain, was sarcastically critical of the Clinton Administration's belated interest in Africa. This drew a response from Washington along the lines that the days of former colonial powers regarding parts of Africa as their private domain were long over. In view of subsequent developments in Central Africa, these were prophetic words indeed.[38]

However the idea of an American-supported African peacekeeping force was not dead. In January 1997, General Jamerson returned to Africa to discuss with Senegal plans for such a force.[39] Now retitled the African Crisis Response Initiative (ACRI), the idea still centres around a force of about ten battalions from seven African states. It received a boost in July 1997, with the despatch of 120 Green Berets from Fort Bragg in two detachments of 60 each to Uganda and Senegal to train a nucleus of local troops in peacekeeping techniques in order that they can pass this knowledge on to their colleagues. It is proposed to include Ethiopia, Malawi, Mali, Tunisia and Ghana in the programme at a later date.[40] Response to this initiative within Africa, particularly from the OAU, has been confused but Uganda has stated openly that it would only commit troops to a peacekeeping operation if it was under the auspices of the OAU.[41]

Amongst African countries themselves there has been a great deal of discussion and debate over peacekeeping, conflict prevention and intervention. Unfortunately this has not been translated into a great deal of positive action. The OAU established a Conflict Resolution Mechanism and a Peace Fund to help finance its work.[42] However this immediately brought it face to face with its most persistent problem, that of money. Few member states have been paying their regular OAU contributions[43] and obtaining money for the new fund has been difficult despite contributions from the US and the UN Development Programme.[44]

The financial handicaps of the OAU were highlighted at two conferences on peacekeeping which were held in January 1995. The first was held in Cairo and attended by representatives from African and Western nations.[45]

The second was held in Harare and was co-hosted by the Zimbabwean Defence Minister, Moven Mahachi, and Britain's Chief of the Defence Staff, Sir Peter Inge. This conference drew the conclusion that the state of the OAU's finances made the creation of a standing OAU force impractical. Instead it was suggested that member states should earmark units to be made available for peacekeeping duties and the OAU ought to establish a number of logistical supply bases to meet their logistical requirements.[46] This opposition, on grounds of practicality, to standing forces, extends further to sub-continental groupings. In its defence White Paper the South African government voiced its opposition to the establishment of such a force by the members of the Southern African Development Community (SADC).[47]

Controversy has also arisen over the location of skills and training centres that could form the basis for a future headquarters for African peacekeeping. The Egyptians have announced the establishment of a training centre in Cairo[48] and the Ethiopians have expressed a desire to be at the forefront of an African peacekeeping force.[49] Meanwhile Britain and France appear to favour the Zimbabwean Staff College as a centre of excellence.[50] The question of the location of any force headquarters was a topic of some debate at the Franco-African summit in Biarritz. Here some observers got the impression that a number of African leaders were motivated by the potentially lucrative advantages of playing host, while others of a more despotic disposition were disinclined to have such a force in their domains.[51]

The same Biarritz conference was also preoccupied by questions of membership. Some wanted a purely Francophone force while others argued that reasons of credibility would require the inclusion of such Anglophone states as Ghana and Nigeria.[52] This debate reflects the arguments over the composition of the ECOMOG force in Liberia and has echoes in the more recent discussions about a potential East African intervention force in Burundi. Tanzania appeared to take the lead on this with some support from Uganda and Ethiopia but with Kenya expressing grave reservations.[53] These questions of regional political rivalry seem destined to bedevil attempts at peacekeeping throughout the continent.

A great deal is expected of South Africa now that it has lost its pariah status but although the South African Defence White Paper foresees a role for South African forces in peacekeeping operations, it adopts a very cautious approach based largely on the grounds of a lack of training and the continuing realignment of South Africa's armed forces.[54] The South Africans also appear to be rightly cautious about being dragged into intractable problems in other African states. The Defence White Paper lays down a number of conditions to South African participation in peacekeeping operations. These conditions lay great emphasis on political and public support, both domestic and international, clarity of mandate for the force and the need to act in concert with allies.[55] The pressure to become involved counterbalanced by a reluctance to actually commit troops has led to some apparently contradictory statements from South African politicians over potential involvement in Burundi. President Mandela seemed to rule out the involvement of South African forces only for the deputy Foreign Minister to suggest that they might be committed.[56] In reality it appears that for the time being that the actual involvement of South African troops in peacekeeping operations will be limited to operations closer to home and then more than likely only as part of a force operating under the auspices of the SADC. This organisation with its recent establishment of a defence and security organ appears to be evolving into the prime organisation for conflict resolution and crisis management in the sub-continent.[57] It remains to be seen whether or not it will develop the political and military structures necessary to make rapid peacekeeping intervention a practicality, but the peacekeeping exercise 'Blue Hungwe' in April 1997 indicates the serious intentions of the SADC members to develop such a capability. Such speculation is not idle given the tensions in Zambia, the border dispute between Namibia and Botswana and the recent significant increase in the capability of the Botswanan armed forces.[58] When added to the continuing problems of Angola and the potential for internal strife throughout the sub-continent, then the need for a conflict management and peacekeeping structure has never been greater.

Developments in 1996 and 1997 have provided a mixed bag of results for African efforts at peacekeeping and conflict resolution. The peaceful elections in Liberia in July 1997 appear to have brought the long running ECOMOG operation a significant measure of success. The elections brought a landslide victory for ECOMOG's fiercest opponent amongst Liberia's warring factions, Charles Taylor.[59] Whether or not this success with the electoral process will presage a durable peace is dependent upon many factors. Not least amongst these is Taylor's attitude toward his defeated opponents and also their reaction to electoral failure. Notwithstanding these concerns for the future, ECOMOG is being hailed as an African peacekeeping success story.[60]

However although one might optimistically state that significant steps have been taken in Liberia, towards a peaceful and democratic future, the reverse is unfortunately the case with its neighbour, Sierra Leone. Here the spill over conflict from Liberia appears no nearer a resolution. The Sierra Leone Army and their theoretical enemies, the RUF, combined in a coup on May 25th 1997, to oust the democratically elected President, Ahmed Tejan Kabbah.[61] The new junta are opposed by a majority of the Sierra Leone population and are locked in conflict with both ECOMOG forces, Guinean troops and the local Kamajor militia.[62] The Nigerian military attempted unsuccessfully to reverse the coup by force in its immediate aftermath and in August 1997 ECOMOG, with the support of the UN, effectively imposed a blockade of Sierra Leone.[63] It has long been believed that the so-called war between Sierra Leone's previous military regimes and the RUF was in fact more a mechanism for the leaders of both sides to divide up Sierra Leone's mineral wealth between themselves, with the civilian population being the losers as usual. The 'battles' between the army and the RUF appeared more like carefully choreographed theatricals where every care was taken to avoid deadly combat. The only forces effectively and successfully fighting the RUF were the private army of Executive Outcomes and the Kamajor militias.[64] In the short term any attempts to broker or enforce a peace in Sierra Leone will, as ECOMOG has found out, be fraught with problems.

In Central African Republic violent mutinies by disaffected army units, against the government of President Patasse, led to French military intervention in both 1996 and 1997.[65] However the French were unable to establish a permanent peace and in January 1997, after an agreement between the two sides, an African peacekeeping force began deployment. The Inter-African Mission to Monitor the Implementation of the Bangui Agreements, (MISAB), is composed of some 750 troops from Burkina Faso, Gabon, Mali, Chad and Senegal. Around 50 of the French troops in Central African Republic appear to be earmarked to provide limited logistical support to MISAB, although the overall role of the French forces in Central African Republic is not entirely clear. The force is provided by those countries who act as guarantors to the agreement between President Patasse and the mutineers and is supported and endorsed by the OAU and the UN. Despite regular flare ups of violence since its deployment, MISAB is making some progress toward disarming the mutineers and restoring peace.[66]

In Congo a civil war has raged since June 1997 between various rival political militias. The two main protagonists are President Pascal Lissouba and former President Denis Sassou Nguessou.[67] The conflict is ostensibly about the Presidential elections scheduled for 1997 but in reality it is a naked power struggle between two ambitious men and their supporters that has turned Brazzaville into a new Mogadishu. There are regional connotations to this conflict with Sassou Nguessou apparently receiving support from Kabila's new regime in Kinshasa and the Angolan government, while Lissouba is allegedly an ally of UNITA's Jonas Savimbi.[68] The UN has agreed to send a peacekeeping force to Congo, with offers of troops from Botswana, Senegal and Bangladesh and led by a Senegalese officer. An embattled President Lissouba has even offered money to fund the force, however the continued fighting has made its deployment impossible and the situation in Congo remains the most pressing current challenge to Africa's peacekeepers.[69]

African military capacities

It is realistic to expect that all branches of any given state's armed forces might be called upon to contribute to any peacekeeping operation and so we have taken into account not only the army but also the navy, air force, and where appropriate the gendarmerie, when calculating the size of an African state's military establishment. However since most African military establishments are dominated by the army, for convenience sake we will use that term as representative of all the military services.

Perhaps the most pertinent point to make is that the armies of most Sub-Saharan African states are small, both in absolute terms and as a percentage of the population.[70] The vast majority of countries have armies numbering less than 50,000 men. Nineteen states have armies less than 10,000 strong, a further five have between 10,000 and 20,000 men, and ten have forces between 20,000 and 50,000. Only five states have armies in excess of 50,000 strong and of these, three, Angola, Sudan and Ethiopia, either are or have recently been, engaged in civil wars.

The total military manpower pool available is thus a little in excess of one million.[71] However due to a variety of political and military reasons not all these troops would be able to be called upon for peacekeeping missions at the present time. Obviously for reasons of involvement in actual or nascent civil wars, it would be prudent to exclude all or large sections of the armies of Angola, Sierra Leone, Sudan and Uganda from the calculation of forces available. In addition restructuring following a change in political or military circumstances would limit the availability of forces from Mozambique and South Africa. Their particular circumstances would exclude the armies of Rwanda and Burundi from active participation in peacekeeping operations and the forces of Liberia and Somalia have already been discounted on the grounds of their effective non-existence. Finally, Nigeria, as a result of its involvement in Liberia, internal political difficulties and current international pariah status, would be unlikely to contribute to future continental peacekeeping operations. All of the above reduces the manpower pool to around 630,000.[72] The suitability of many of those troops theoretically available for peacekeeping, to that task, has to be open to question. This is due to the high level of politicisation of African armies and their frequent use as organs of internal repression. Effective peacekeeping requires a number of delicate skills which it is not unreasonable to suggest that certain armies would need a great deal of time, training and a radical overhaul to acquire.

Apart from size, the other major factors affecting the capacities of African armies are those of logistics and transport. The crucial purpose of having a peacekeeping or intervention force is the ability to deploy it where it is needed, when it is needed. Once it has been deployed there is a consequent requirement to supply such a force with all the paraphernalia of modern military operations. Given the, at best inadequate, nature of Africa's road and rail communications and taking into account the geographical factors of distance and difficulty of access, the burden falls upon air and, to a lesser extent, sea transport. It is not surprising to find, given the expense, that there is a dearth of such equipment available from amongst the resources of Africa's own armies.

On paper the total of some 300 locally available transport aircraft looks impressive. Closer examination reveals that only about 40 of these are of the necessary size for rapid deployment of the number of troops likely to be required. The total figure of 470 available helicopters again looks impressive but many of these have a limited carrying capacity. In addition it has to be remembered that these resources are scattered amongst the armies of the continent and collecting them together would be a major organisational headache in itself. On top of this there is a major question over their serviceability and the availability of trained personnel to operate them.

To put this in perspective, Britain by comparison has over 90 heavy transport aircraft and around 180 medium lift helicopters. France also has a sizeable airlift capacity. Nevertheless both these countries have had to resort to hiring civilian aircraft or requesting the assistance of others when moving significant numbers of troops by air. The most recent example being the French use of Ukrainian-owned planes when moving forces into the Central African Republic in May 1996. It is sobering to reflect that the only nation with a truly strategic airlift capacity, the USA, has a fleet of over 800 transport aircraft and nearly 2,000 transport helicopters.

Quite obviously, given the prohibitive cost, it is both unrealistic and impractical for African states either individually or even collectively, to buy a significant number of such aircraft. In this particular area any African peacekeeping force is going to remain reliant on external assistance. Both Britain and France operating together and through the auspices of the WEU, have made proposals to offer such assistance but nothing concrete has yet emerged. As previously mentioned the USA has also indicated a willingness to make transport aircraft available under certain circumstances. One possible option for any African peacekeeping force would be to follow the recent French example and lease aircraft from the countries of the former Soviet Union where significant resources remain available and with whose equipment the personnel of many African armies are familiar.

In the area of shipping, Africa's militaries lack any significant sealift capacity beyond a number of landing craft of questionable serviceability. The shortfall would have to be met by leasing from the commercial sector[73] and or assistance from outside powers.

Some logistical and transport problems might possibly be overcome through the prepositioning of equipment in strategic locations. This has certain advantages in terms of speed of deployment and, as shown earlier, has proponents from both inside and outside the continent. There are however certain drawbacks such as the necessity for permanent staffs to maintain the equipment and train its users and the questions of who pays for it and to whom does it ultimately belong? It is quite feasible for some equipment to be communally owned through membership of a defence or security organisation.[74] This would need to be agreed upon at a political level and the current organisational structures on the continent would need to be amended accordingly.

Given the almost certain centrality of the OAU to any African peacekeeping structure, the involvement of a number of North African countries cannot be discounted. Algeria, because of its domestic problems and Libya because of its isolated international status, need to be left out of the equation. Nevertheless that leaves Morocco, Tunisia and Egypt as potential participants in peacekeeping operations with previous experience as such. They possess between them armies numbering 670,000 men and have a useful airlift capacity.[75]

This brief survey of the continent's military resources shows that although the manpower resources for peacekeeping forces exist to a certain extent, the logistical and transport resources do not and that reliance on external assistance in this respect will remain a crucial fact of life.

Conclusions

Given the nature of the problems that might require intervention by the states of Sub-Saharan Africa in the affairs of their fellows, it is clear that those states need to be able to conduct the full range of operations from, on the one hand, traditional style peacekeeping, to, at the other extreme, peace enforcement. The essential prerequisite is therefore the establishment and maintenance of the political will to intervene. Operations launched without this securely in place are doomed to failure.

There is a demonstrable need for proper organisational structures at both the continental and sub-continental level into which peacekeeping operations can be fitted and which can operate as the fora for the achievement and consolidation of the aforementioned political will. These organisations need to include a clear political chain of command to which the military are answerable and which can react to developments in what are often complex and continually changing crises. These organisations need to provide the administrative and financial bases around which forces can be organised and funded. This needs to be done in advance. For example the earmarking of forces for peacekeeping duties helps with rapidity of deployment. A list of suitable commanders can avoid unseemly squabbling and helps with their training and preparation. There is no overemphasising the importance of proper funding.

On a political level, the mandate of the force needs to be agreed upon by the participants and clearly enunciated to those affected. This avoids contributing nations operating to their own agendas and misinterpretation of the force's role by those with whom it is intervening. The unfortunate experience of the Inter-African Force in Chad in 1982 highlights the importance of this point. Here lack of clarity over the mandate led to confusion on all sides as to the role of the IAF and the divergent interests of the contributing states led to it becoming something of a fiasco. In addition the relationship between the intervening force and the belligerent parties needs to be clearly defined and wherever possible the consent of those parties obtained.

On the military front, Africa has a wide range of experience in all types of peacekeeping and non-peacekeeping interventions. For example 22 African countries have made 95 individual contributions to 21 separate UN operations. If this experience could be pooled into permanent structures there is no reason why the mistakes of the past cannot be avoided in the future. In practical terms individual countries need to earmark those forces which they intend to make available for peacekeeping operations. Troops need to receive specific training appropriate to the complexities of peacekeeping and command and control structures set up. Political structures would need to establish permanent military staffs where the differing practices between militaries could be harmonised to facilitate future co-operation. In addition logistical supply bases with training facilities would be a great advantage.[76] That steps are already being taken in the direction of improving co-operation between African militaries was shown by the recent peacekeeping exercises held by the members of SADC in Zimbabwe in April 1997, referred to earlier in this chapter. Part of the umbrella exercise, Blue Hungwe, was a command and control exercise featuring some 70 officers of the SADC Command Battalion. The 36 hour long Exercise Blue Tsuro was held at the Zimbabwe Staff College and included training in UN peacekeeping doctrine, command procedures and strategies.[77]

It should be clear from what has been said earlier in this chapter, that there exists a wide gulf between what is desirable for the successful operation of peacekeeping and associated missions by African states and what is actually in place. If the more developed countries in the world, particularly those in Europe and North America, are not prepared to get involved on the ground in Africa, then it is to a certain degree incumbent upon them to provide the kind of assistance African forces require to carry out these operations. A certain amount of help has been offered, some such as training programmes is concrete if not extensive, but much of it exists only as offers of possible assistance. This is not good enough. Real help and in particular, real money needs to made available. The consequences for Europe of a failure to act can only be increased pressure from migrants fleeing Africa's conflicts to say the least. The consequences for ordinary Africans can only be fatal.

However one has to temper this criticism by pointing out that Africa needs to quickly establish the organisational structures to whom concrete offers of help can be made. It might seem a tall order to ask Africa to develop the kind of organisations that have taken decades to evolve elsewhere, but Africa can learn from the experience of others, adapt their ideas to its own circumstances and avoid their mistakes.

Because of the cost involved, Africa remains dependent on external assistance in the areas of transport, logistics and finance. That assistance nearly always comes with a price tag, more often than not a political one. The sooner the states of Sub-Saharan Africa get themselves organised, the sooner they will be able to pool what resources they have and learn from their collective past experiences. They will be able to make better use of what assistance they can obtain and hopefully gradually reduce their dependence on external help. However until the political decisions on organisation are taken, Africa will remain more dependent on others than it needs to be and the notion of Africans keeping or enforcing the peace on their own continent, will remain merely a notion.

Notes

1 Speech by President George Bush at Maxwell Air Force Base, Alabama, on 13.04.91.
2 Speech by President Bill Clinton to the UN General Assembly on 27.09.93. Albright, M.K. (1993) 'Building a Consensus on International Peacekeeping', a statement before the Senate Foreign Relations Committee on 20.10.93, reproduced in the Department of State's *Dispatch*, Vol. 4, No. 46.
3 Le Monde, 30.07.94.
4 Africa Research Bulletin, November, 1994, p. 11639.
5 West Africa, 21-27 November, 1994, p. 1987.
6 Independent, 22.05.96.
7 The Guardian, 29.01.96.
8 President Bizimungu of Rwanda quoted in the Financial Times, 09.11.96. Rwandan Foreign Minister Gasana quoted in Liberation, 06.11.96.
9 Interview with Paul Kagame, Rwandan Defence Minister, in the Washington Post, 09.07.97.
10 Independent, 08.01.97 and 09.01.97, Le Monde, 08.01.97.
11 Independent, 22.05.96.
12 Panafrican News Agency (PANA), 17.03.97, 'Benin, Burkino Faso, France and Togo plan joint war games'.
13 West Africa, 28.07.97-03.08.97, p. 1196 and p. 1199. PANA, 30.07.97, 'Gabon, France discuss military bases'.
14 'Britain and South Africa: a fellowship for the future', a speech given by John Major to the South African National Assembly in Cape Town, 20.09.94.
15 'Thoughts for the Anniversary', a speech given by the Foreign Secretary, Douglas Hurd, to the UN General Assembly on 29.09.94.
16 Interview with Lt. Col. P. R. Wilkinson (author of the British Army's manual 'Wider Peacekeeping') at Coventry University on 23.02.96.
17 PANA, 05.04.97, 'African peacekeeping force exercise launched'.
18 The Guardian, 17.04.97.
19 Independent, 22.05.96.
20 Declaration of the WEU Council of Ministers meeting in Birmingham, 07.05.96.

21 RAF Yearbook 1997, p. 88, published by the RAF Benevolent Fund Enterprises.
22 Zambian News Agency, 07.07.96.
23 West Africa, 13-19.03.95, p. 381. Africa Research Bulletin, October, 1994, p. 11629. US Congressional Record, Vol. 140, Nos. 129-131, 19.09.94.
24 Africa Research Bulletin, October, 1994, p. 11629.
25 Ibid, p. 11629.
26 Africa Research Bulletin 1994-1995, p. 11698.
27 Nicholas Burns, State Department spokesperson, quoted by Africa News Service, 26.07.96.
28 PANA, 03.10.96., 'US Commander pledges to assist OAU peace efforts', and Reuters, 09.10.96, 'US: Support for Africa Crisis Force Building', and the Daily Nation, Nairobi, 10.10.96.
29 PANA, 03.10.96, 'US Commander pledges to assist OAU peace efforts', and the Daily Nation, Nairobi, 10.10.96.
30 PANA, 16.10.96, 'Lagos not impressed by US proposal for African force'.
31 Independent, 05.10.96.
32 PANA, 14.10.96, 'EU supports South African stand on African Peace Force'.
33 The Guardian, 12.10.96, and Independent, 06.11.96.
34 PANA, 13.10.96, 'South Africa not against African Peacekeeping Force'.
35 PANA, 16.10.96, 'Lagos not impressed by US proposal for African force'.
36 PANA, 14.10.96, 'OAU cool on US idea of an African force'.
37 All African Press Service, 28.10.96, 'Mali commits troops to ACRF'.
38 Independent, 19.10.96.
39 PANA, 06.01.97, 'Discussions on African Reaction Force'.
40 The East African, 07.07.97, 'Peace Force for Africa', and PANA, 20.08.97, 'US Troops training Ugandan Trainers', and US Department of State, 30.07.97, 'US Officials describe African Crisis Initiative'.
41 New Vision, Kampala, 01.08.97, 'US trains for peace', and the East African 07.07.97, 'Africans strive for pact on proposed US peace scheme'.
42 Africa Research Bulletin (1994), p. 11640.
43 West Africa, 21-27.11.94, p. 1987.
44 Africa Research Bulletin 1994-95, pp. 11640 and 11698.
45 Africa Research Bulletin, January 1995, p. 11707.

46 Ibid, p. 11707 and West Africa, 30.01-05.02.95, p. 152.
47 'Defence in a Democracy', draft White Paper on National Defence for the Republic of South Africa, 21.06.95.
48 West Africa, 30.01-05.02.95, p. 152.
49 Africa Research Bulletin (1995), p. 11698.
50 The Independent, 22.05.96.
51 West Africa, 21-27.11.94, p. 1987.
52 Ibid, p. 1987.
53 'Burundi talks start behind closed doors', Nando.net, 18.07.96 (Internet news service).
54 South African Defence White Paper, see Note 25 above.
55 Ibid.
56 'South African peacekeepers may go to Burundi', The Mail and Guardian, Johannesburg, 23.07.96.
57 'SADC to hold summit as tension mounts', Panafrican News Agency, 27.6.96.
58 'Defence force rapidly expanding', The Mail and Guardian, Johannesburg, 04.04.96.
59 PANA, 23.07.97, 'Taylor's party sweeps Liberia poll'.
60 PANA, 24.07.97, 'Liberian elections crown Africa's efforts'.
61 The Guardian, 26.05.97.
62 The Observer, 01.06.97, and Independent, 03.06.97, and West Africa, 28.07.97-03.08.97, pp. 1214-1215.
63 PANA, 07.08.97, 'Economic blockade of Sierra Leone now in force'.
64 West Africa, 28.07.97-03.08.97, pp. 1214-1215.
65 The New York Times, 07.01.97, 'French forces continue operations in Central Africa Republic' and The Guardian, 06.01.97 and Independent, 07.01.97.
66 All Africa Press, 30.06.97, 'Fighting in Central Africa complicates situation in region' and PANA, 30.07.97, 'Togo sends new contingent to Bangui'.
67 West Africa, 28.07.97-03.08.97, p. 1196 and pp. 1206-1207.
68 The Mail and Guardian, Johannesburg, 13.06.97, 'Congo sinks into anarchy'.
69 PANA, 10.07.97, 'Senegal names commander of multinational force in Congo', and PANA, 11.07.97, 'UN to deploy peacekeeping force in Congo', and United Nations, 15.08.97, 'UN asks for immediate end to Brazzaville fighting'.
70 All figures in this section are taken from *The Military Balance 1994-1995*, published by Brasseys for the IISS.
71 Excluding Liberia, Somalia and Rwanda, the total is 1,012,970.

72 The precise figure is 630,720.
73 For example, the British policy of STUFT (Ships Taken Up From Trade) used in both the Falklands and Gulf Wars.
74 The NATO E-3 Sentry AWACS planes operated by multinational crews.
75 47 transport planes, 32 of them 4-engined types and 172 transport helicopters.
76 'Commander tells generals to communicate on personal level', Zambian News Agency, 31.07.96, and 'Southern African generals meet', The Post of Zambia, 31.07.96.
77 PANA, 08.04.97, 'Southern Africa military exercise continues', and PANA, 07.04.97, 'SADC command battalion officers meet'.

4 Peacekeeping in Africa, 1990-1996: the role of the United States, France and Britain

Mats Berdal

Introduction: a failure of expectations

In 1992, Chester Crocker, US Assistant Secretary of State for African Affairs under President Ronald Reagan, published his own account of the US role in securing a peaceful transition from South African rule to independence in Namibia and the simultaneous withdrawal of Cuban forces from Angola.[1] It was the story, he wrote, 'of how Southern Africa's own thirty years' war was finally ended, setting the stage for the recent, dramatic turn away from apartheid and one-party dictatorship and toward democracy and political reconciliation in this vast region'.[2] Crocker's confidence was widely shared in Western policy-making circles in the late 1980s and early 1990s. It was also around this time that the promotion of 'good governance', economic liberalisation and 'accountability', both in the economic and human rights field, became prominent themes in American, British and French policy pronouncements on Africa.[3] Optimism about the future was also evident in the peace and security field and derived, above all, from the fact that Cold War competition for political influence and military assets was no longer *the* defining framework for the policies of external powers vis-à-vis the continent.[4] This fundamental change in context, it was argued, would allow for a new, more innovative and disinterested approach to African conflicts.

The success of the United Nations Transition Assistance Group (UNTAG) in Namibia in 1989-90 appeared to justify this sanguine view. The Namibian operation, which had grown out of the settlements that Chester Crocker helped negotiate, was seen as foreshadowing a new pattern of external involvement in two ways. First, with the debilitating impact of Cold War rivalry finally removed, outside powers would now be in a position to co-operate in efforts to address African conflicts and facilitate transitions to democratic rule. Second, UNTAG also appeared to suggest that innovations in 'traditional' peacekeeping - a distinctive form of third party intervention governed by the principles of consent and minimum use of force - opened up new avenues of action and pointed to new modes of involvement by external powers. This, indeed, was also the point of reference for much of the academic peacekeeping literature which in the early 1990s stressed the obsolescence of 'classical peacekeeping', calling instead for more intrusive and forceful options to be considered.

By late 1996, however, the optimism to which the US, Britain and France had all, to varying degrees, subscribed in statements about Africa, had been profoundly undermined. The comparative success of the UN mission to Mozambique (ONUMOZ) and the peaceful transition to multi-racial democracy in South Africa in 1994 have both been dwarfed by the tragedy of events in Angola, Rwanda, Burundi, Liberia and Sudan. Indeed, since the publication of Crocker's upbeat reflections on peacemaking in Southern Africa, large parts of the continent have experienced wars, accompanied by economic and social dislocation, on a scale unsurpassed by the independence struggles and drawn-out proxy wars of the Cold War era. More than 300,000 people are thought to have died as a direct result of the resumption of civil war in Angola in late 1992, and at least 800,000 people lost their lives between April and June 1994 in the genocide against the Rwanda's Tutsi minority and moderate Hutus.[5] An estimated 150,000 people have died since Liberia's collapse into civil war in 1989. Accurate figures, though certainly in the thousands, are even more difficult to obtain for Burundi, Somalia and Sudan where fighting continues with little immediate prospect of lasting settlement.

It is against this background of shattered hopes and failed policies, that US, British and French peacekeeping policy and involvement in Africa after the Cold War must be considered. This chapter explores three sets of questions.

First, what has been the actual content of peacekeeping policy in each of the three countries? Although a distinct 'peacekeeping' policy in relation to Africa cannot easily be separated from other aspects of policy towards the continent, certain themes and concerns are evident. In the US, an initial commitment to focus on African issues has been replaced by reluctance to become directly involved and a preference for 'African solutions to African problems'. Above all, an initial willingness to explore the scope for enforcement action under Chapter VII of the UN Charter has been decisively rejected. In the case of Britain, limited resources have been a chief determinant of policy. As with the US, the underlying thrust of British policy in Africa has been to 'help African states to help themselves', though, unlike the US, Britain has focused more on the mobilisation of 'existing resources and know-how' than on the infusion of additional resources from outside.[6] French policy in Africa remains the most difficult to disentangle and cannot easily be separated from the history and nature of Franco-African relations since decolonisation. More importantly for the purposes of this chapter, French peacekeeping policy cannot be treated in isolation from the instability and the wars that have plagued Central Africa in the 1990s.

Second, to what extent has the end of the Cold War resulted in a more coherent approach to African conflicts by outside powers? The picture which is emerging in this respect is certainly not as unambiguous as many had hoped in the early 1990s. While East-West rivalry is no longer an issue, a more complex pattern of competition, involving a greater number of actors driven by a wider range of motives, appears to be emerging. Specifically, this chapter considers the growing signs of tension between France and the US. This tension, which has been most evident in relation to Central Africa and which is exacerbated by the greater saliency of economic competition, is increasingly complicating the task of developing a coherent policy towards conflict in parts of Africa. While the extent of 'great power competition' can easily be exaggerated (especially when compared to the Cold War era), its potentially destabilising effects have been enhanced by other developments in recent years. Chief among these is the growing involvement of private and semi-private security firms in Africa. Their relationships both to external powers and commercial interests have added a new dimension to discussions of peacekeeping policy in the Africa. The linkages in this area are still poorly understood and present a particular problem for researchers.

The final question to be examined follows logically from the previous discussion: in what areas of peacekeeping policy can France, Britain and the US, given the various constraints that govern policy in each country, still make a significant contribution in Africa. The chapter identifies four key areas in which a co-ordinated approach can be envisaged and where outside support, both financial and technical, will continue to be required. These are: electoral support; repatriation of refugees/displaced persons and humanitarian assistance; demining; and disarmament, demobilisation and reintegration into civil society of soldiers after prolonged periods of war. Progress in these areas is a necessary, though clearly not a sufficient, ingredient for the resolution of the many conflicts that continue to plague parts of the continent. Indeed, while the focus of this chapter is on peacekeeping policy, its chief conclusion is that the supposed failure to develop the 'potential of peacekeeping' in the early 1990s is only part of the reason (and I would argue not the most important) why progress in resolving African conflicts has been so very limited. The misguided attempt to combine peacekeeping and enforcement in one location undoubtedly contributed to the debacle in Somalia in late 1993. UNAVEM II's efforts to steer Angola through elections in 1992 were critically undermined by the acute lack of resources devoted to the operation. Yet, in the long-run, peacekeeping or even enforcement, can only be successful as part of a broader strategy based on a comprehensive understanding of the nature and functions of conflict.

Peacekeeping policy and practice

The United States

The sense of optimism which permeated academic and policy debates about 'Africa after the Cold War' in the early 1990s was both stronger and more genuinely felt in the US than was the case in either Britain or France. In part, this was because the effect of removing the Cold War prism through which the continent had been viewed for so long was most striking in Washington. It was also related, however, to the belief that new forms of outside involvement offered unique opportunities for addressing conflicts no longer fuelled by global rivalry.

These hopes, however, were short-lived. US peacekeeping policy in Africa in the 1990s is characterised by a swing from initial enthusiasm to extreme weariness and caution about any direct involvement on the continent. Indeed, it was the US experience in Africa - specifically the involvement of US troops in Somalia in 1992 and 1993 - which contributed most directly to what the then Ambassador to the UN Madeleine Albright, in May 1994, pointedly described as 'a period of recalibrating our expectations'.[7] Because the US, unlike Britain and France, also attempted to formulate an overall policy for peace support operations - eventually codified as Presidential Decision Directive - 25 (PDD-25) in May 1994 - and this process was powerfully influenced by experiences in Somalia and by the administration's generalised reading of the nature of conflict in Africa, it is necessary to examine the shift in US policy under President Clinton more closely.

Bill Clinton, while still only a presidential hopeful, committed himself to reversing the policies of preceding Republican administrations with regard to the UN. In April 1992 he called for a 'rapid deployment force' at the UN to conduct operations such as 'standing guard at the borders of countries threatened by aggression, preventing mass violence against civilian populations, providing humanitarian relief and combating terrorism'.[8] It was against the background of such ideas, that the new President, in February 1993, ordered an 'inter-agency review of [the] nation's peacekeeping policies and programmes in order to develop a comprehensive policy framework suited to the realities of the post-Cold War period'.[9]

Significantly, the administration also promised a 'substantially new' relationship with Africa.[10] In a keynote speech in May 1993, then US Secretary of State Warren Christopher explained that the administration's 'new relationship towards Africa [would] differ in important respects from the approach of the past 12 years.' At the same time, however, he wished to 'salute' the former President for 'launching Operation Restore Hope - a military mission of mercy in Somalia'.[11] And, more significantly, Christopher went on to argue that 'now we need to apply these lessons [of the international community's response to Somalia] in Sudan'.[12]

It was the administration's own encounter with Somalia, however, which over the next six months were to lay down the true parameters of its peacekeeping policy in Africa. Not only did the operations in Somalia bring out the strength of domestic political constraints on US foreign policy; it also concentrated the minds of the US military, specifically with regard to the vexed issue of 'enforcement' and, more generally, the difficulties and dangers of intervening in intrastate conflicts. For all these reasons, but also because the British and French military drew important lessons from UNOSOM II's hapless experience, the American involvement in Somalia merits closer scrutiny.

Somalia: combining peacekeeping and enforcement

As noted above, President George Bush's decision to launch 'Operation Restore Hope' in December 1992 had been welcomed by the incoming Democratic administration. That operation, however, was conceived as a strictly limited one by the American Unified Task Force (UNITAF) Commander: to end starvation by protecting food and medical convoys; to provide security in the 'hardest hit' areas and to prepare for a transition to a UN peacekeeping operation.[13] The Clinton administration accepted in early 1993 that the continuing precariousness of the humanitarian situation in Somalia, the abundance of weapons, and the general state of anarchy still characterising many aspects of Somalian society, required a more forceful mandate for the UN forces preparing to take over from UNITAF. Consequently, UNOSOM II, which formally replaced UNITAF on 4 May 1993, was 'endowed with enforcement powers under Chapter VII of the Charter' and became the 'first operation of its kind to be authorised by the international community'.[14]

The task which the UN set for itself in Somalia, and to which the US signed up both as a major troop-contributor and Security Council member, was ambitious. According to the Secretary-General's plan of action, UNOSOM II would assist 'the Somali people in rebuilding their shattered economy and social and political life, re-establishing the country's constitutional structure; achieving national reconciliation, [and] recreating a Somali State based on democratic governance'.[15] Clearly, these objectives could only be achieved with the support of the Somalis themselves, and it was essential, therefore, to ensure that military operations were subordinate to and closely co-ordinated with a broader political process aimed at addressing the root causes of conflict. This in turn meant that the third party, neutral and impartial status of UNOSOM II would have to be preserved.

The fact that this did not happen was largely due to the direction which the US-led operation took after the death of more than 20 Pakistani soldiers on 5 June 1993 at the hands of 'forces apparently belonging to the United Somali Congress (USC/SNA)'[16] led by Mohamed Farah Aydeed. The enforcement provisions of UNOSOM II's original mandate and the wording of Security Council Resolution 837 which condemned the attack on the Pakistani contingent, were interpreted by the US leadership in Mogadishu - notably by Admiral Jonathan Howe, the Special Representative of the Secretary General in Somalia and Major General Thomas Montgomery, the Deputy Force Commander who, significantly, wearing his US hat also retained direct command of the US Quick Reaction Force (QRF) which operated outside the UNOSOM structure - as requiring a significant escalation in the use of force and the targeting of the top hierarchy of the SNA loyal to Aydeed. The new phase of operations began on 12 June 1993 with a series of night and daytime attacks by US attack helicopters and gunships of the QRF in an effort to destroy SNA weapons sites and Radio Mogadishu.

A critical turning point in UNOSOM II's history was reached on 12 July when US forces launched an attack on the house belonging to an important clan elder (Abdi house), described by the US commanders as 'a major SNA/Aydeed militia command and control centre, serving as a militia meeting site, staging area and rally point'. The attack was estimated by the ICRC to have killed more than 50 Somalis and injured a further 170, including key religious and clan elders.[17] The operation was profoundly damaging in terms of undermining the overall objectives of the operation. The high casualty figure in this attack stemmed from the fact that, unlike previous military action by the QRF, *no* warning had been given before the attack. The aim had been quite simply to 'eliminate the SNA command centre and its occupants'[18]; consequently the policy of prior notification designed to minimise collateral damage had to be abandoned in favour of preserving the element of surprise.

By this time the US-UN forces had been drawn irretrievably into the clan warfare of Somalia, though other troop-contributors, notably France, were highly critical of the US approach. 'The dynamics of war', as a Commission of Inquiry set up by the UN later aptly described it, reached its tragic climax on 3 October, when 18 American soldiers were killed and 84 wounded in a firefight which also killed hundreds of Somali civilians. After this, the relationship between US forces and Somalis in Mogadishu deteriorated further, to the point where US forces had, by late 1993, become completely estranged from the local population. Indeed, the final withdrawal of US troops in late March 1994 was vividly portrayed by the *Washington Post* as a 'guns-cocked withdrawal'.[19]

PDD-25 and US peacekeeping policy in Africa

As a result of events in Somalia, the contents of a broad-ranging Presidential Policy Review of peacekeeping policy, ordered in 1993 and finally presented in May 1994, differed markedly from the earlier pronouncements. An important objective behind the review had been to identify criteria that would provide the basis for making decisions about whether or not the US should support and participate in multilateral peace operations.[20] The essence of the policy when US participation is being considered can be summarised as follows:

- the objectives of an operation must be clearly defined, in 'America's own national interest' and assured of 'continuing public and Congressional support';

- the commitment of US troops cannot be 'open-ended' and consequently an 'exit strategy' must be in place before troops are deployed;

- operations involving US forces must have 'acceptable' command and control arrangements.

Even a brief survey of the African conflicts in which the UN and/or regional organisations have assumed a peacekeeping role, let alone those in which no significant action has been taken by the international community, highlights the inherent difficulties of applying these criteria. A narrow definition of 'national interest', strict adherence to the principle of 'no open-ended commitments' and the requirement for continuing public and Congressional support, are bound to limit the scope for direct peacekeeping involvement in Africa. Addressing an African audience in 1995, a senior member of the US administration, stressed that while the US had to 'make highly disciplined choices about when and under what circumstances to support, extend, or participate in peacekeeping operations ... the PDD is not prescriptive, but a device for policy makers to analyse proposals on a case-by-case basis'.[21] Yet, while PDD-25 may not be prescriptive in a strict sense, there are two additional 'lessons' from Somalia which the US administration has effectively internalised and which ensure that even if decisions are made on a 'case-by-case' basis, a commitment of US troops on a peacekeeping or enforcement mission in Africa is highly unlikely. The first of these is simply that the threshold for an 'acceptable' level of casualties in operations other than war is very close to zero. The second lesson is that public and Congressional support for these kinds of operations is very hard to generate and, even more so, to sustain over a period of time. In the case of Africa, the 'constraining' role of public opinion is reinforced by what Peter Schraeder sees as a 'lack of knowledge about Africa [that] is especially acute at the level of mass public' and which, in turn, is 'reinforced by the nature of US media programming and the safari tradition of US journalism'.[22]

One of the chief conclusions reached by the US military in its 'after action' analysis of events in Somalia was, rather more sensibly, that 'peace enforcement' was difficult to distinguish from war-fighting and that, in the future, to confuse peacekeeping and enforcement in one location was a recipe for disaster.[23] In the charged domestic atmosphere of late 1993 and early 1994, however, the criteria of PDD-25 and the unspoken assumption that casualties were not acceptable, meant that the chances that US personnel would be involved, either in a peacekeeping or enforcement capacity, on the ground in an African context were very remote. For this reason, unquestionably the 'most serious casualty of the American failure in Somalia was Rwanda'[24], since the administration's profound reluctance to become engaged in *any* capacity, enormously complicated its ability to respond to the many signs of impending disaster in Rwanda in the early half of 1994. The administration's refusal even to acknowledge the scale of the tragedy became source of acute and justified embarrassment when the State Department in June 1994 appeared to be downplaying reports of genocide in Rwanda in the face of arguments from human rights groups that the 1948 Genocide Convention provided a legal basis for immediate intervention.[25] Perhaps even more telling was the fact that at the White House press briefing called to launch PDD-25 on 5 May 1994, a time when the genocide was at its height, there was hardly a mention of Rwanda.[26]

Policy initiatives since 1994: 'African solutions to African problems'

In spite of domestic criticism, notably from the Congressional Black Caucus, about the absence of a coherent Africa policy in the wake of the genocide in Rwanda, the basic parameters underlying PDD-25 continue to shape US peacekeeping thinking about Africa.[27] On a visit to several African countries in December 1994, Anthony Lake, President Clinton's Assistant for National Security Affairs and an Africa specialist, was short on new initiatives and spoke, significantly, of the need to confront 'the reality of shrinking resources and honest scepticism about the return on our investment in peacekeeping and development'.[28]

Since then, the persistence of conflict and the danger of further eruptions of mass violence, most notably in Burundi, have nevertheless forced the administration to recognise that it cannot disengage altogether. A corollary to the retreat from direct involvement has therefore been an increased emphasis on encouraging 'African solutions to African problems' through the strengthening of regional and sub-regional groupings. This was a central theme of the only trip which the US Secretary of State, Warren Christopher, made to sub-Saharan Africa in October 1996, shortly before the US presidential elections. Addressing the Organisation of African Unity (OAU), Christopher proposed the creation of an African Crisis Response Force (ACRF), consisting of some 5,000-10,000 troops drawn from various African countries and 'reinforced by training, equipment, logistical and financial support' from the US and other donor countries.[29] The concept envisages the force to be a 'fully inter-operable, fully trained African-led and manned capability ... composed of a headquarters element, support units and up to ten African battalions'. Its mission, in the words of Christopher, would be to 'protect innocent civilians, ensure the delivery of humanitarian aid, and help resolve conflicts in Africa and beyond'.[30] Mindful of Congressional hostility to the UN, the Clinton administration's initiative does not, unlike British and French proposals, envisage a major role for the UN in peacekeeping in Africa. To underscore American commitment to the force, the administration has earmarked $20 million for the project.

Neither the visit of Warren Christopher, nor the concrete proposal he presented, has done much to change the perception of American disengagement from Africa. While welcomed in principle by some countries (Mali, Ethiopia and Tanzania), others, including South Africa and SADC countries, deeply resent the fact that the proposal emanates from outside the region and bypasses the UN altogether. They also fear that the proposal signals a 'further writing off the continent with a grand-sounding plan for which no real funding or interest would follow' and that, even if it were to become operational, it would only 'ensure that African troops would do the work and take the risks'.[31] This is indeed an important motivation behind the proposal and, as such, reflects domestic political reality in the US and is consistent with the underlying thrust of PDD-25. As one senior official associated with the Secretary of State's 1996 visit candidly admitted ' "there is absolutely no political appetite at home" for sending any US troops to Africa for any cause'.[32] Thus, when the US agreed to airlift African peacekeeping troops in Liberia in February 1997, the administration was typically emphatic in stressing that 'US military men and women will not be involved in peacekeeping'.[33]

Britain

British peacekeeping policy *vis-à-vis* Africa in the 1990s has been shaped by limited resources and a relatively low order of priority given to African issues (in sharp contrast to France) in British foreign policy. In terms of direct involvement, the tradition - dating back to the early 1980s and based in part on the experience of the British-led Commonwealth Monitoring Force (CMF) in Zimbabwe in 1979-80 - of using small-scale military assistance missions to help with training, monitoring and verification tasks has continued in Namibia, Mozambique and South Africa.[34] Thus, in late 1993, the training centre at Nyanga in eastern Zimbabwe was used to train 540 instructors, drawn from the Mozambican Army and RENAMO, for the new unified army that was formally constituted after multiparty elections in 1994. Follow-up training for the new army within Mozambique has since been provided by Britain, along with France and Portugal. In South Africa, the British Military and Assistance Training Team (BMATT) has acted effectively as a 'referee' in the integration process of former SADF and ANC and 'homeland' forces, certifying that agreed procedures and standards are applied in an even-handed fashion to all parties.[35] Elsewhere, British peacekeeping deployments have been short-term and focused principally on the initial provision of logistic support prior to the deployment of UN peacekeepers. This was the case with the three-month deployment of 600 troops to Rwanda in August 1994 (Operation Gabriel) to prepare for the deployment of UNAMIR II, as well as with the logistics battalion sent to Angola before the full deployment of UNAVEM III in 1995.

Such direct commitments notwithstanding, if a central theme in British peacekeeping policy towards Africa can be identified, it is that of 'helping the Africans to help themselves'. This is to be done by encouraging the UN to support the Organisation of African States (OAU) to establish 'a coherent structure of support systems running from early warning and preventive diplomacy right through to humanitarian and peacekeeping deployment on the ground'.[36] In order to strengthen the OAU, both physical resources (finance, equipment, logistic infrastructure and, above all, transport) and expertise in the form of training and doctrine development are required. With regard to resources, Britain has emphasised multilateral channels, urging the UN to establish 'logistic basing centres ... with rapid mobile logistics teams, earmarked by member states, to help maintain peacekeeping equipment in good running order, and give training'.[37] According to the 'Africa initiative' presented by Foreign Secretary Douglas Hurd to the UN General Assembly in September 1994, these centres would also have their own 'headquarters staff to identify and remedy logistic weakness ... and advise on existing and potential troop contributors'.[38]

Britain has been much more directly involved at the conceptual level and has actively engaged African countries in a *discussion* about the requirements of conflict prevention and peacekeeping in Africa. Indeed, the Foreign Secretary's initiative stressed the need not for a 'new machinery', but for a 'framework within which existing resources, capability and know-how can be mobilised'.[39] To this end, Britain has sponsored a series of seminars and workshops in Africa to discuss, as one summary report put it, 'both the principles and the practical priorities and scope for action at various levels'.[40] If this sounds vague, it has nevertheless, by drawing in representatives of African military establishments, promoted a professional dialogue and, if nothing else, delineated the scope for more practical steps to be taken. Perhaps more importantly from a British point of view, it has also served as a forum for disseminating British thinking on peacekeeping doctrine, the area where

British influence has been most keenly felt in recent years, even though disagreements persist about its applicability to contemporary conflict.

In developing that doctrine, the aforementioned experience of UNOSOM II played an important role. To Charles Dobbie, the principal author of 'Wider Peacekeeping' finalised in 1995, events in Somalia demonstrated:

> ...what seems likely to happen in theatre if a peacekeeping force crosses the impartiality divide from peacekeeping to peace enforcement. If perceived to be taking sides, the force loses its legitimacy and credibility as a trustworthy third party, thereby prejudicing its security. The force's resources will then become ever more devoted to its need to protect itself. It actually joins the conflict it was there to police and is likely to become embroiled in activities that are irrelevant to the overall campaign aim. Such a situation will almost certainly result in the loss of popular support, a loss of control and uncontrolled escalation upwards in the ambient level of violence which will heighten political tension and foreclose opportunities for resolving the conflict. To cross the impartiality divide is also to cross a rubicon. Once on the other side, there is very little chance of getting back and the only way out is likely to be by leaving the theatre.[41]

France

Examining the history of post-colonial military involvement in Africa by Britain, France and Belgium, Alain Rouvez notes how the 'lack of political motivation to make the necessary efforts to preserve a role in even selected parts of the overstretched British Empire, combined with Britain's military policy of committing itself to the allied defence of Europe, would deprive Britain of the will and the array of instruments necessary to play a role similar to that of France in sub-Saharan Africa'.[42] There is little doubt that the depth of French interest in Africa (specifically, though not exclusively, its Francophone part) - whether it is measured in cultural, economic and military terms or by the degree of high-level policy attention given to it - is far greater than that of Britain. Partly for this reason the 'policy stance of the UK in Africa appears far clearer than that of France, for whom a multitude of conflicting policy interests continue to complicate relations with former colonies on the continent'.[43] This fact also complicates the study of French peacekeeping policy and military involvement more generally in Africa in the 1990s, which cannot be discussed without reference to developments in Central

African and the growing perception within French decision-making circles that the US and Britain are encroaching on a traditional sphere of French interest. The validity of this view and its impact on attempts by external powers to formulate a coherent policy towards the continent is therefore discussed more fully below.

Meanwhile, it may be noted that if Somalia was the defining moment for US policy in Africa, the tragedy of Rwanda between April and June 1994 has haunted French policy-makers, influencing both concrete proposals pertaining to peacekeeping as well as doctrinal thinking within the military.

In the wake of the Rwandan genocide, France proposed the establishment of a 5,000 strong 'rapid deployment force capable of quelling large-scale ethnic strife, protecting civilians and seeing that humanitarian aid reaches victims'.[44] The plan, which envisaged a multilateral approach involving the UN, the OAU and the West European Union (WEU), has been effectively shelved, ostensibly for financial reasons though suspicions about French motives, whether in this case justified or not, also seem to have contributed to the plan's demise.

In terms of doctrine, the failure of the international response to the unfolding tragedy in Rwanda in 1994 led the French military to question what is still at the heart of the British doctrine of 'Wider Peacekeeping': that no credible category, middle-ground or spectrum of military operations exist between 'peace-keeping' and 'peace-enforcement'. While still highly critical of the US army mode of operation in Somalia, especially its excessive reliance on superior firepower as means of minimising US casualties, the French military has identified 'peace-restoring operations' (restauration de la paix) as a third category for which its armed forces have to be prepared. The declared aim of such operations would be to restore security for civilian populations in conditions of civil war and mass violence by using coercive measures under Chapter VII, though without formally designating an aggressor or prejudging the political outcome of the conflict in question.[45] While the French position has generated some professional debate - the British army, for example, has begun to examine the requirements of a 'peace enforcement' doctrine as distinct from 'wider peacekeeping' - lingering suspicions about French motives, not least from African countries, have not been dispelled by the France's role in the Rwandan tragedy and, especially, by the practical consequences of 'Operation Turquoise' (whose effect as a 'peace-restoring operation', whether intended or not, was *also* to create a safe area for Hutu militia members).[46] It is necessary, therefore, to turn to this aspect of French 'peacekeeping' policy in Africa more carefully.

II American-French tensions over policy in Africa: a new scramble?

An important source of optimism about the place of Africa in the post-Cold War international order in the early 1990s was the belief that 'great power rivalry' - which in one form or other has been a feature of outside interest and policy towards the continent since its very first encounter with the European state system - would no longer be an obstacle to addressing Africa's own needs and problems. This initial enthusiasm regarding the scope for 'great power' co-operation, however, has crumbled; indeed, mutual suspicions between France on the one hand, and the US and Britain on the other, is greater than it has been for a very long time. A major factor behind the worsening of relations has had to do with different perceptions and policies in Central Africa between 1993 and 1997. French officials, most notably the protégés of the late Jacques Foccart and others 'in the imperial tradition'[47] of French post-colonial Africa policy, have expressed deep concern about the motives and policies of the US and, to a lesser degree, Britain, in Francophone parts of Africa. There can be no doubt that some of these concerns, especially about the long-term strategy and the supposed coherence of US and British policy, are exaggerated. Indeed, as David Styan has perceptively noted, they reflect a 'persistent tendency to legitimate French actions in Africa elsewhere against a notional - and usually nefarious - "Anglo-Saxon" other'.[48] In his survey of British policy in Africa, Styan stresses that whatever else might be said about British policy, it 'bears little resemblance to the image imputed to it by some French policy makers. In particular it is not "Anglo-Saxon", if this implies a unity of purpose between the United Kingdom and the US'.[49] The tendency in French policy-making circles dealing with Africa to conflate US and British policy and motives appears, at times, almost instinctive; as if Britain, whether she is acting in Europe, within NATO or in some other international arena, is invariably going to act in collusion with the US or, worse still, as a 'Trojan horse' of US influence.[50]

It would nevertheless be wrong to ascribe existing tensions simply to mutual misperceptions and inflated rhetoric. Real differences do exist and these are likely to inhibit the development of common approaches to peacekeeping on the continent. Two related issues merit special attention. In the first place, traditional differences between French policy and those of other great powers, especially with regard to Francophone sub-Saharan Africa, have been powerfully exacerbated by tensions over policy in Central Africa since the early 1990s. Secondly, there are growing signs of economic rivalry, especially between the US and France, in those parts of Africa that have been plagued by war and conflict.

'Anglo-Saxon' encroachment and the crisis in Central Africa, 1993-97

Since the granting of independence, France has consistently viewed its former colonies in sub-Saharan Africa as 'a natural French preserve - *domain réserve* or *pré-carré* - off limits to other foreign powers, whether perceived as friends or foes', and has tended to show 'a deep suspicion of the motives and actions of these powers in Africa'.[51] What Guy Martin has described as a 'French version of the Monroe doctrine' has been underpinned by close personal relationships between French and African leaders; a preferential economic area (the Franc zone); a series of bilateral defence and military co-operation agreements; a substantial military presence in Africa and, not least, a manifest willingness to intervene when deemed necessary.[52] The principal threat to the exclusive nature of this relationship has always been seen as coming from 'Anglo-Saxon' interests, and it is against this background that French actions in Central Africa since 1990 are best understood. Indeed, in terms of explaining 'France's interest' in Rwanda, the dominant view is that the country lies 'along with its troubled "twin" Burundi, on the linguistic and political faultline between Francophone and Anglophone east Africa.'[53] According to Gérard Prunier, the key to understanding French policies lies in the 'Fashoda syndrome' which he sees as still 'very much part of French political thinking' and according to which 'the whole world is a cultural, political and economic battlefield between France and Anglo-Saxons'.[54] In such a world, the invasion by Rwanda of rebels based in Uganda (Rwandese Patriotic Front, RPF) 1990 was naturally seen as a 'test case - an obvious "Anglo-Saxon" plot to destabilise one of "ours", and one we needed to stop right away if we did not want to see a dangerous spread of the disease'.[55]

The policy decisions that emanated from this, were to have disastrous consequences. Between 1990-93 France sent both military equipment and, at one stage, 700 of its own soldiers to assist the Forces Armées Rwandaises (FAR) and President Juvénal Habyarimana against the Rwandese Patriotic Front (RPF). Within hours of President Habyarimana's death in a plane crash on 6 April 1994, the pre-planned massacres of Rwanda's Tutsi minority in the country began. But French support to the FAR did not stop with onset of the genocide. When an international embargo was imposed against Rwanda on 17 May 1994, at least five French shipments of arms to the genocidal regime were later documented by *Human Rights Watch*.[56] Moreover, although formally authorised by the Security Council, *Operation Turquoise* - launched by the French military between 14 June and 21 August 1994 and which provided a security zone for Hutu civilians in the south-west of the country - was not only a disinterested humanitarian effort but looked to many, as the *Economist* chose to report it, the creation of a 'safe area on to which the toppled Rwandan government could fall back'.[57] As with previous French interventions in Africa, the operation appeared to confirm Alain Rouvez perceptive comment that 'the fine line between a purely humanitarian intervention and a regime-stabilisation operation is sometimes difficult to draw'.[58] This view has since been reinforced by clear evidence that Hutu militias and FAR inside the refugee camps established along the Zaire (now the Democratic Republic of Congo) border were rearmed by Zaire with French collusion between 1994-96.

Intense suspicions and deep-seated differences over policy continued to bedevil relations between France and the putative 'Anglo-Saxon' bloc after the Banyamulenge rebellion in eastern Zaire that began in the autumn of 1996. The formation and sweeping progress of the Alliance of Democratic Forces for the Liberation of Congo-Zaire (ADLF) under Laurent Kabila did nothing to ease French suspicions.[59] The fact that many of the Banyamulenge rebels had been trained by or had previously fought alongside the RPF against the FAR in Rwanda and that the ADLF advance in Zaire depended on continous support from Uganda and Rwanda (whose current governments have been firmly supported by the US), only confirmed French suspicions about 'Anglo-Saxon' encroachment.

Although Mobutu Sese Seko's odious regime in Zaire received more US aid than most African countries between 1961 and 1990, American support to Mobutu was formally withdrawn in 1991.[60] As the Central African crisis widened, the US administration called on President Mobutu Sese Seko to step down.[61] In 1994, the French re-established links with Mobutu and the persistent calls by the French for a 'humanitarian intervention' force in eastern Zaire in early 1997 were turned down both by Britain and the US, no doubt in part because it was seen as a French attempt to throw a lifeline to an old and discredited ally.

By early 1997, reports and rumours (the two have been difficult to separate) were rife about direct US support, through covert and semi-covert networks, to Laurent Kabila's rebel alliance in Eastern Zaire.[62] While the extent and the precise nature of American support has been difficult to ascertain, it is worth noting, as a more general consideration, that US decision-making with respect to Africa has become more fragmented after the Cold War, with the result that policy outcomes reflect the 'established organisational missions' of those bureaucracies with a specific interest in Africa: State Department, the Defence Department and the CIA.[63] Each of these have historically tended to pursue particular interests or missions in Africa and co-ordination among them has often been lacking. On the ground this has frequently led to situations where not only the UN has had little understanding of US policy but also where different branches of the executive have been unaware of the policies and activities of others.[64] The US certainly has a long history of covert involvement in sub-Saharan Africa, using for example, air bases in Zaire in the mid-1980s to provide military assistance to UNITA in Angola.[65]

Growing economic rivalry and commercial competition

The post-Cold War period has also brought with it a deeper long-term challenge to France's exclusive economic relationship to its *chasse gardée*. As Peter Schraeder notes, the abandonment by Washington of 'ideologically based policies in favour of the pursuit of economic self-interest' has already 'heightened economic and political competition between the United States and other Western powers, most notable of which is the rising French-US conflict within the financially important telecommunications and petroleum industries of Francophone Africa'.[66]

Influential US officials, including former Assistant Secretary of State for African Affairs, Herman Cohen, and the late Commerce Secretary Ron Brown, have indicated that the 'US can no longer afford to accept France's determination to maintain its privileged *chasse gardée* within the economic realm'.[67] At the same time, the economic importance of Africa to France remains considerable, not least because of its dependence on key imports of strategic raw materials for its high-technology industry.[68]

Confirming French suspicions about US economic assertiveness was the purchase agreement signed in April 1993 between Occidental Petroleum Corporation (OXY) and the Congolese government giving the American company petroleum interests in three offshore blocks operated by Elf Aquitaine and AGIP for $150 million. The episode was seen by French officials as 'yet another inadmissible intrusion of US capitalism into a region considered as an exclusive French preserve'.[69] American suspicions about France's determination to maintain exclusive access on the other hand, appeared to be confirmed by the Government of Cote d'Ivoire's decision in January 1997 to disqualify a consortium allied to *AT&T* (US) from bidding for the national telephone company; a decision which had the effect of leaving *France Telecom* as 'favourite to clinch the deal'.[70] If indeed the decision was politically motivated, it would be in line with President Jacques Chirac's 'outburst', made on a visit to Gabon in July 1995 shortly after coming to power, against 'the Anglo-Saxons [who] dream of pushing France out of its position in Africa without paying a price'.[71]

Adding to French concerns about economic intrusion into its domain, has been a material change in the source of French power and economic influence. In January 1994, following the Franco-African summit in Dakar, the Communauté Financière Africaine (CFA), shared by 14 countries and pegged to the French franc since 1948, was devalued by 50 per cent. This effectively brought an end to the franc zone as a 'preferential and monetary trading area', and as one long-time analyst of the region has noted, this, for France, is likely to 'result in a gradual (but substantial) loss of political, diplomatic and economic power and influence in Francophone Africa'.[72] In spite of the French commitment to remain actively involved on the continent, not only external competition but financial and economic considerations at home will act as a growing constraint on French policy. Increasingly, calls are being made by 'reformers' (led notably by former Prime Minister Alain Juppe) for a reassessment of the costs and practical value of the exclusive nature of relations to Francophone Africa.[73] The long overdue devaluation of the franc was seen by some as victory of this more pragmatic line and an indication that France's African allies would have to take greater responsibility for their own economic restructuring. In terms of France's ability to project military power, the reductions in defence spending (including manpower) announced by the administration of Jacques Chirac has already led to a gradual draw-down in the number of French troops deployed in Africa, even though the logistical structure required for rapid deployment has been maintained (France's long-range transport capability, however, is still an area of weakness and vulnerability).[74]

Impact of great power rivalry on peacekeeping policy

There is clearly a danger of overstating the extent to which French, American and British interests and policies in parts of Africa diverge and have given rise to destructive suspicion or, worse still, active competition. Nevertheless, any discussion of great power co-operation in the field of peacekeeping, as well as in the whole range of activities that come under the loose heading of 'peace-building', is incomplete without a reference to this broader context. Indeed, there are clear signs that tensions and mutual suspicions are already undermining attempts to develop more coherent policies. The US proposal for an 'African Crisis Response Force' discussed above has not been welcomed by France which views it simply 'as a formula for diluting Paris' strong influence on the continent'.[75] Indeed, France was reported to have boycotted a meeting to discuss the US proposal held in New York in May 1996, called in part to examine how it might be co-ordinated with the French proposal for a similar force made in the wake of the Rwandan genocide.[76]

It is clear from the discussion thus far that the 'great powers', with the partial exception of France, will continue to exhibit a marked reluctance to intervene directly either in a peacekeeping or an enforcement mode in Africa. One consequence of this is already beginning to become apparent: the growing role of commercially-driven security firms on the continent. While many of these firms are relatively small, the very weakness and fragility of many African states enhance their ability to shape the course of events, as the activities of *Executive Outcomes* in Sierra Leone have demonstrated.[77] The role of commercial or private security firms may prove, therefore, far more significant than their actual resources would tend to suggest, especially in those cases where they are operating on behalf of a state or alongside powerful local economic actors (such as mining companies). What was reported to be a British intelligence document detailing the activities of *Executive Outcomes* in sub-Saharan Africa indicated why its apparent successes may be a cause for concern:

> It appears that the company and its associates are able to barter their services for large shares of an employing nation's natural resources and commodities. On present showing EO will become ever richer and more potent, capable of exercising real power, even to the extent of keeping military regimes in power.[78]

Against this it needs to be stressed that private sector involvement does not invariably have to be destabilising. Indeed, a number of companies have been engaged in 'wider' peacekeeping tasks which, for reasons discussed above, the armed forces of major powers have been reluctant to carry out. These have included mine-clearance and repairs of basic infrastructure such as bridges, roads and harbours damaged by war.

The precise interaction of commercial and state interest in conflict zones in Africa is beyond the scope of this chapter, though it clearly merits further research.[79] What is certain is that growing private sector involvement in African conflict zones, whether for benign or destabilising purposes, is a trend that is likely to intensify.

III The scope for constructive engagement

While the direct involvement of Britain, France and the US may be limited by domestic constraints, scarce resources, political and economic rivalry, none of these countries are in a position to disengage altogether from addressing conflicts and wars on the African continent. Finding an appropriate role for each of them may start by recognising that their continued involvement and co-operation remain vitally important also in the field of peacekeeping and that there are distinct areas where the constraints discussed above ought not to preclude a more active role on their part. The final section of this chapter considers briefly four such areas, all of which fall within a 'wider' definition of peacekeeping as, fundamentally, still a consent-based set of activities. These are:

- technical and security assistance for the organisation, monitoring and verification of elections;

- logistics support and security assistance for the repatriation and resettlement of refugees/displaced persons and related humanitarian tasks;

- technical assistance, training and financial support for de-mining;

- logistics support, financial and technical assistance for disarmament, demobilisation and reintegration of soldiers after civil wars, including training of unified armed forces after conflict;

Although the UN has been involved in all these categories of operations, the degree to which Britain and France but, above all, the US participate actively in them, will make a critical difference to long-term success.

i. Electoral support Assistance in the organisation of national and local elections has become an increasingly important and, indeed, highly effective area of UN activity in the 1990s. In the course of 1994 alone the UN undertook electoral support activities in more than 20 countries, many of them in Africa.[80] It is an interesting feature of peacekeeping in Africa in the 1990s that *outside* assistance in this area, which used to generate acute fears of intrusion in the domestic affairs of African countries, has been widely accepted. In 1989 UNTAG monitored elections in Namibia organised by South African authorities and in 1994 ONUMOZ helped organise elections in Mozambique. The logistic and security challenges which such operations entail usually require the involvement of external powers with air-transportable engineering, communications and logistics capabilities. It was the failure to provide precisely these kinds of assets that did so much to undermine UNAVEM II's activities in Angola in the 1992.

ii. Repatriation of refugees/displaced persons and humanitarian assistance The provisions made for repatriating refugees displaced internally or to neighbouring countries as a result of internal conflict, have become an integral part of peacekeeping operations in Africa. The scale of such operations are usually formidable, and they always involve major financial and logistical commitments on the part of overstretched UN agencies and struggling NGOs. The limited capacity of local infrastructure to deal with refugee flows and humanitarian disasters gives the mobile elements of military forces from powers such as France, Britain and the US, a key role in providing basic services such as food, water, primary medical care and temporary shelter.

iii. Demining activities The indiscriminate resort to low-cost and low-tech mine warfare has become an endemic feature of contemporary warfare. An estimated 110 million land-mines are scattered throughout more than sixty countries world-wide. Angola, Somalia, Mozambique, and Sudan are all among the worst-hit cases.[81] Even when a durable cease-fire is agreed among parties to a conflict, anti-tank and anti-personnel mines continue to claim their deadly toll of casualties for many years after the cessation of hostilities. Moreover, land-mines also inhibit the economic and social reconstruction of war-torn areas long after the fighting has stopped. International organisations, including the UN, have only just begun to address seriously a problem which is bound, sadly, to remain a high priority for decades.[82] A particular responsibility for action in this field must rest with major powers, both for the development of more effective demining techniques and for the promotion of regulatory frameworks aimed at controlling the manufacture of and trade in mines.

iv. Disarmament, demobilisation and reintegration of soldiers after wars Disarming, demobilising and reintegrating soldiers that have been engaged in armed conflict for extended periods of time, are major challenges faced by a number of war-torn countries in Africa. The circumstances that have given rise to these kinds of operations vary from country to country. In Angola and Mozambique they grew out of so-called 'comprehensive political settlements' aimed at ending internal conflicts. In another set of cases, responsibility for demobilisation and military reform has been assumed by governments victorious in civil war or otherwise not under direct military threat. The most comprehensive initiatives in this respect have occurred in Uganda, Ethiopia and Eritrea. Whatever the circumstances, the issue of how best to ensure that ex-combatants are effectively integrated into society is, perhaps, the single most important one facing African countries over the next five to ten years. The record of outside assistance in this area - including weapons control measures, reintegration schemes for demobilised soldiers and support for the creation of new unified military and police forces - is generally poor. Such support, however, will continue to be required. The specific contribution of France and Britain, both of whom have maintained close links to military establishments in Africa, should be to use their own military forces and civilian expertise more effectively to train and monitor the functioning of new military and police forces.[83] The US is in the best position to provide and co-ordinate financial assistance both bilaterally and through international financial institutions such as the World Bank and the IMF.

This list is clearly not exhaustive, nor do any of these tasks address what may be described as 'root causes' of conflict. Nevertheless, the history of peacekeeping in Africa in the 1990s, strongly suggests that the efficiency with which these are carried out is a necessary condition for progress in other areas. Moreover, as noted above, these are also areas where the constraints on external involvement that have become so evident in recent years may hopefully prove less acute. As such they meet the critical test of being, not only theoretically desirable, but practically and politically feasible.

Conclusion

It was noted at the outset of this chapter, that the success of the Namibian operation in 1989-90 was seen by many as presaging a new era; one that would finally allow for long-running African conflicts to be 'resolved' and for outside attention to be more appropriately focused on the challenges of development and economic growth on the continent. The Namibian peacekeeping experience was contrasted with that of the UN operation in Congo (ONUC) (now the Democratic Republic of Congo) from July 1960 until June 1964, the only other time the UN had been involved in a military capacity in Sub-Saharan Africa. On that occasion, the competitive engagement of the superpowers did indeed undermine the operation, threatening in the end to fatally weaken the UN as a whole. Yet there were also other aspects of the Congo experience which figured much less prominently in the debates about peacekeeping in the early 1990s, but which might otherwise have tempered some of the more sanguine views about future prospects. In fact, not only did the Congo operation threaten to bring about the virtual collapse of the organisation, it also pointed to some of the problems which the UN was to encounter, on a much larger scale, after the Cold War. In the Congo, the UN intervened in an *internal* conflict and even though the Secretary-General at the time, Dag Hammarskjold, initially stressed that the peacekeeping principles of consent, minimum use of force except in self-defence and strict impartiality had to be applied, the UN found it difficult not become embroiled in the civil war. As Inis Claude perceptively observed:

> ... the *local* task of ONUC was predominantly that of helping to curb and reverse the tendencies toward internal political disruption and social and economic disintegration within the Congo - an enormous task made doubly difficult by the ambiguity implicit in ONUC's mandate to intervene without interfering, to uphold order without enforcing orderliness, to assist the government without taking sides in controversies regarding the location of governmental authority, and to prevent civil war without becoming involved in efforts to suppress dissident and secessionist movements.[84]

Some of these dilemmas have also been present during 'peace support operations' in Somalia and elsewhere in Africa in the 1990s. While the global context has changed, difficulties inherent in the deployment of peacekeepers in the *local* context of a civil or intra-state war have not.

The sources of failure in recent years do not, however, lie in the field of peacekeeping alone. At a deeper level, the UN and its member states need to overcome three major impediments to more effective action in the future: first, their inability to re-examine the nature and functions of conflict, especially how the benefits that powerful groups and interests derive from conflict contribute to its perpetuation; second, to establish a clearer link between short-term considerations related to peacekeeping, relief and security on the one hand, and the long-term requirements of 'peace-building' on the other; and, finally, to sustain commitments over an extended period of time, both in terms of policy focus (and high-level policy attention to African conflicts has proved to be particularly short-lived) and the allocation of resources.

Notes

1. Chester A. Crocker (1992), *High Noon in Southern Africa: Making Peace in a Rough Neighbourhood*, New York: W.W. Norton & Company.
2. Ibid., p. 17.
3. See the discussion by Larry Diamond of important policy statements made in 1990 by Herman Cohen, Assistant Secretary of State for African Affairs under President Bush, British Foreign Secretary Douglas Hurd, and, most dramatically, by President François Mitterand at the Franco-African summit at La Baule in France. Larry Diamond (1995), 'Promoting Democracy in Africa: US and International Policies in Transition', in Harbeson, J. W. and Rothchild, D. (eds), *Africa in World Politics: Post-Cold War Challenges* (2nd Edition), Boulder, CO: Westview Press, pp. 256-259.
4. For a brief and useful overview of extent to which global rivalry with the Soviet Union and considerations extraneous to Africa (e.g. the need for communication facilities, airports and airfields) determined the policies of the US during the Cold War, see Diamond (1995), 'Promoting Democracy in Africa', pp. 250-251.
5. Mel McNulty (1996), 'France, Rwanda and the genocide: a review of the literature', in *Modern and Contemporary France*, London: Longman Ltd. p. 501.
6. 'Speech by the Foreign Secretary, Mr Douglas Hurd, to the 49th General Assembly of the United Nations, New York, 28 September 1994', FCO Information Department, p. 4.
7. Statement of Madeleine Albright, US Permanent Representative to the UN, Hearing Before Subcommittee on International Security, International Organisations and Human Rights of the Committee on Foreign Affairs, House of Representatives, 103rd Congress, 17 May 1994, p. 8.
8. Quoted in Elaine Sciolino (1993), 'US Narrows Terms for its Peacekeepers', *New York Times*, 23 September.
9. The Clinton Administration's Policy on Reforming Multilateral Peace Operations (Executive Summary), May 1994, State Department.
10. 'Clinton's Policymakers Turn to Africa', *International Herald Tribune*, 19 May 1993 and 'The United States and Africa: A New Relationship', Address by Secretary of State Warren Christopher before 23rd African-American Institute Conference, Reston Virginia, 21 May 1993, US State Department.

11 Christopher (1993), 'The United States and Africa', 21 May.
12 Ibid.
13 For a fuller discussion of the UN/US operations in Somalia in 1992 and 1993, see Mats Berdal (1996), *Disarmament and Demobilisation after Civil Wars*, Adelphi Paper 303, Oxford: OUP/IISS, pp. 25-32. For the broader context of international involvement see Samuel Makinda (1993), *Seeking Peace from Chaos: Humanitarian Intervention in Somalia* London: Lynne Rienner Publishers for the International Peace Academy, and James Mayall and Ioan Lewis, 'Somalia' in the Mayall, J. (1996) (ed) *New Interventionism*, Cambridge: Cambridge University Press.
14 S/25354, 3 March 1993, paras. 58 and 101.
15 Report by the Secretary General, S/25354, 3 March 1993, para. 91.
16 Security Council Resolution 837 (1993) (my emphasis).
17 'Report of UN Commission of Inquiry to Investigate Armed Attacks on UNOSOM II Personnel which Led to Casualties Among Them', S/1994/653, 1 June 1994, p. 30.
18 Ibid., p. 30, paragraph 153.
19 'US to Leave Somalia With Its Guard Up', *The Washington Post*, 8 December 1993.
20 The Clinton Administration's Policy on Reforming Multilateral Peace Operations (Executive Summary), May 1994, State Department, pp. 4-5.
21 'The Role of the US in Peacekeeping', M. Lemmon, Deputy-Assistant Secretary for Regional Security Affairs, Paper delivered at conference on South Africa and Peace-keeping in Africa, 13-14 July 1995, Institute for Defence Policy, Johannesberg, p. 7.
22 Peter J. Schraeder (1996), 'Removing the Shackles? US Foreign Policy Toward Africa After the End of the Cold War', in *Africa in the New International Order: Rethinking State Sovereignty and Regional Security*, edited by Edmond J. Keller and Donald Rothschild, Boulder, CO: Lynne Rienner Publishers, p. 189.
23 See Kenneth Allard (1994), *Somalia Operations: Lessons Learned*, Washington, DC: National Defence University Press, pp. 63-66. This insight was later codified in the field manual for OOW.
24 Interview with Elizabeth Lindemayer, New York, May 1995.
25 See 'US position protested', *International Herald Tribune*, 13 June 1994.
26 White House Briefing, Subject: Policy on Multilateral Peacekeeping Operations, May 5 1994, USIS Reference Center. It was, of course,

telling in a double sense: administration officials did not raise the Rwandan situation and the press corps failed to ask about it.
27 For criticism from members of the Congressional Black Caucus see 'Administration is faulted over conference on Africa', *The New York Times*, 27 June 1994, section A, p. 9.
28 Quoted in 'Africans told to expect less from the US', *The Washington Post*, 16 December 1994, section A, p. 46.
29 'Remarks by US Secretary of State Warren Christopher at the Organisation of African Unity', Addis Ababa, 10 October 1996, US State Department (Office of the Spokesman).
30 Ibid.
31 'Africa Hears Indifference in a US Offer to Help', *The New York Times*, 20 October 1996; 'SADC reserved over US proposal for African crisis force', Agence France Presse, 13 October 1996, and 'African trip not helping perception of neglect by Clinton administration', *Dallas Morning News*, 11 October 1996.
32 'Christopher's Africa trip stirs hopes, fears for complicated continent', *The Washington Post*, 16 October 1996, section A, p. 15.
33 'US planes will airlift African peacekeepers', *Washington Times*, 12 February 1997.
34 Alain Rouvez (1993), 'French, British and Belgian Military Involvement', in *Making War and Waging Peace: Foreign Military Intervention in Africa*, edited by David R. Smock, Washington, DC: US Institute for Peace, p. 42.
35 'Integration and Demobilisation in South Africa', *Strategic Comments*, No. 6, July 1995.
36 'Speech by the Foreign Secretary, Mr Douglas Hurd, to the 49th General Assembly of the United Nations, New York, 28 September 1994', FCO Information Department, p. 4.
37 Ibid., p. 5.
38 Ibid.
39 Ibid.
40 Report on 'Conflict Prevention and Peace-keeping in Africa' based on discussions and seminars held in Accra (November 1994), Cairo (January 1995) and Harar (1995), ND.
41 Charles Dobbie, 'Wider Peacekeeping - A Peace Support Operations Doctrine' (Presentation Script), ND.
42 Alain Rouvez (1993), 'French, British and Belgian Military Involvement', in *Making War and Waging Peace: Foreign Military Intervention in Africa*, edited by David R. Smock, Washington, DC: US Institute for Peace, p. 38.

43 David Styan (1996), 'Does Britian have an African Policy?', *L'Afrique Politique 1996*, Paris: Karthala. For the 'deeply confused' state of policy- arrangements under President Chirac see, 'Low key in Ouaga', *Africa Confidential*, Vol. 37, No. 25, p.4.
44 'France looks for ways to keep its African influence intact', *Janes Defence Weekly*, 23 October 1996, p. 17.
45 'Principles for the Employment of Armed Forces under UN Auspices (draft)', 10 March 1995, outlined at conference on Peacekeeping Doctrine, Helsinki July 1995. See also, 'Supplement to an Agenda for Peace, Aide-memoire by France', A/50/869, S711996/71, 30 January 1996, UN Document.
46 Explaining the rationale behind 'peace-restoring operations', the French government explicitly referred to *Operation Turquoise* as an example of such an operation. Ibid., ('Aide-memoire by France').
47 'End of an Affair?', *The Economist*, 12 August 1995. The chief representative of this tradition at present is Jacques Godfrain at the Ministry of Cooperation. The Ministry is often referred to as the 'Ministry for Africa'. Prunier, *History of a Genocide*, p. 101.
48 David Styan (1996), 'Does Britain have an African Policy?', *L'Afrique Politique 1996*, Paris: Karthala.
49 Ibid. See also David Styan, 'Il n'y a pas d'anglo-saxons en Afrique; mirrors and myths in the reform of France's African policy', Paper prepared for conference on 'L'Afrique, les Etats Unis et La France', organised by CEAN/Graf University of Bordeaux, 22-24 May, 1997. Styan argues persuasively in this paper that 'the idea that there are common, coherent US and British policies in Africa - which somehow share 'Anglo-Saxon' roots' has very little basis in fact. He further warns that 'simplistic, static and ahistorical stereotyping, by journalists and policy makers, is a dangerous distraction from the real debates over policy reform'. Yet, he also observes that one cannot simply 'dismiss such ideas as being irrelevant, arising from simplistic journalism which has no bearing on policy'. I am most grateful for being given permission to quote from this excellent paper.
50 It needs to be stressed here that such views are less prominent outside the circle of advisers and policy-makers responsible for Africa policy. This circle is, however, influential and traditionally much closer to the centre of power, i.e. the President, than their counterparts in the British and US executive branches of government.
51 Guy Martin (1995), 'Continuity and Change in Franco-African Relations', *The Journal of Modern African Stuides*, 33, 1, p. 5.

52 Since Jacques Chirac came to power in 1995, French troops have already been sent to Africa on two occasions in order to put down internal rebellion; in the Comoros in October 1995 and in the Central Africa Republic in May 1996. Defence and technical agreements, it should be noted, have also been concluded with countries outside the 'traditional sphere of influence', most notably Burundi, Rwanda, Zaire and Zimbabwe.
53 Mel McNulty (1996), 'France, Rwanda and the genocide: a review of the literature', in *Modern and Contemporary France*, London: Longman Ltd, p. 499.
54 Gérard Prunier (1995), *The Rwanda crisis 1959-1994: History of a Genocide*, London: Hurst & Company, p. 105.
55 Ibid., p. 106.
56 *Rearming with Impunity: International Support for the Perpetrators of the Genocide*, Human Rights Watch Arms Project, Vol. 7, No. 4, May 1995, pp. 6-7.
57 'France and Africa: Dangerous Liaisons', *The Economist*, 23rd July 1994, p. 19.
58 Alain Rouvez (1993), 'French, British and Belgian Military Involvement', in *Making War and Waging Peace: Foreign Military Intervention in Africa*, edited by David R. Smock, Washington, DC: US Institute for Peace, p. 36.
59 In December 1996, for example, the US ambassador to Zaire, Daniel Simpson, was quoted in the local press as stating that 'France was no longer capabable of imposing its will in Africa and that it continued to support decadent regimes'. Quoted in 'France - Africa', *African Research Bulletin,* Volume 33, Number 12, 1996, p. 12494.
60 Michael Clough (1992), 'The United States and Africa: The Policy of Cynical Disengagement', *Current History*, Vol. 91, No. 565, May, p. 195.
61 'Christopher's Africa trip stirs hopes, far for complicated continent', *The Washington Post*, 16 October 1996, section A, p. 15.
62 A particularly interesting connection has been the presence of the Military Professional Resources Incorporated (MPRI) a Virginia-based military 'consultancy' firm with very close links to the US Pentagon in Angola where it has been involved in talks with the government about training its armed forces. The MPRI was deeply involved in training and preparing the revamped Croatian Army for its successful and bloody Krajina offensive in 1995.
63 For a most perceptive discussion of this particular 'trend' in US foreign policy towards Africa after the Cold War, see Peter J.

Schraeder (1996), 'Removing the Shackles? US Foreign Policy Toward Africa After the End of the Cold War', in *Africa in the New International Order: Rethinking State Sovereignty and Regional Security*, edited by Edmond J. Keller and Donald Rothschild, Boulder, CO: Lynne Rienner Publishers, p. 195-96.

64 Interviews with senior UN officials in New York, March 1997. As Chester Crocker recalls, this was certainly also a feature of decision-making in the 1980s. See Crocker, *High Noon in Africa*, pp. 282-283.

65 See Larry Diamond (1995), 'Promoting Democracy in Africa: US and International Policies in Transition', in *Africa in World Politics: Post-Cold War Challenges* (2nd Edition), edited by John W. Haberson and Donald Rothchild, Boulder, CO: Westview Press, pp. 250-51.

66 Peter J. Schraeder (1996), 'Removing the Shackles? US Foreign Policy Toward Africa After the End of the Cold War', in *Africa in the New International Order: Rethinking State Sovereignty and Regional Security*, edited by Edmond J. Keller and Donald Rothschild, Boulder, CO: Lynne Rienner Publishers, p. 201. The same point was made by the late Commerce Secretary Ron Brown in February 1996, addressing business representatives from West Africa in Abidjan. See for this and other sources of French fears of US encroachment, 'Pré carré revisited', *Africa Confidential*, Vol. 37, No. 16, pp.4-5.

67 Peter J. Schraeder (1996), 'Removing the Shackles? US Foreign Policy Toward Africa After the End of the Cold War', in *Africa in the New International Order: Rethinking State Sovereignty and Regional Security*, edited by Edmond J. Keller and Donald Rothschild, Boulder, CO: Lynne Rienner Publishers, p. 201.

68 Guy Martin (1995), 'Continuity and Change in Franco-African Relations', *The Journal of Modern African Studies*, Vol. 33, No.1, pp. 9-12.

69 Guy Martin, 'Continuity and Change in Franco-African Relations', p. 16. OXY actually sold its royalty stakes in the all three oilfields in 1996 (for $215 million), though it still holds exploration rights in two blocks. 'Occidental Petroleum Sells State in Oilfields to Congo', *New York Times*, 31 July 1996.

70 'Africa-France, US', *Africa Research Bulletin*, Vol. 34, No.1(Economic, Financial and Technical Series), 1997, p. 12882 and 12901. According to the *Africa Research Bulletin* 'France and the US are shaping up for a battle of business supremacy in West and Central Africa' and that the 'stakes are getting larger' because governments have embarked on extensive privatisation programmes, including in the areas of telecommunication and railways.

71 Quoted in 'End of an affair?', *The Economist*, 12 August 1995.
72 Guy Martin, 'Continuity and Change in Franco-African Relations', p. 20. For the significance of the franc devaluation, see also 'France and Africa: Dangerous Liaisons', *The Economist*, 23rd July 1994, pp. 19-21.
73 'End of an affair?', *The Economist*, 12 August 1995. See also 'France's African Adventure: Plus ça change?, *Strategic Comments*, Vol. 2, No. 5, June 1996, which speaks of 'traditionalists' versus 'pragmatists', with the latter group seeing sub-Saharan Africa as a burden undermining the focus on and commitment to European issues.
74 'France set to withdraw 7000 troops from Africa', *Janes' Defence Weekly*, 16 December 1996, p. 4. French military presence in Africa is currently about 8,800 troops dispersed in six countries (CAR, 1,300; Chad, 800; Côte D'Ivoire, 700; Djibouti, 3,900; Gabon, 600; Senegal, 1500), *The Military Balance 1996/96*, London: OUP for IISS, 1996, p. 56.
75 'Africa Hears Indifference in a US Offer to Help', *The New York Times*, 20 October 1996, section 4, p. 4.
76 'French, Upset, Hint at Politics in Africa Visit by Christopher', *International Herald Tribune*, 10 October 1996, p. 7 and 'France looks for ways to keep its African influence intact', *Janes' Defence Weekly*, 23 October 1996, p. 17.
77 See Jeremy Harding (1996), 'The Mercenary Business', *London Review of Books*, 1 August, pp. 3-9. Because of its very visible involvement in places such as Sierra Leone and Angola, EO has received rather more public attention than other companies operating in parts of Africa. See also 'Corporate dogs of war who grow fat amid the anarchy of Africa', *The Observer* 19 January 1997. See also David Shearer, *Private Armies and Security in Africa* (forthcoming Adelphi Paper, IISS/OUP).
78 Quoted in *African Research Bulletin*, Volume 34, No. 1, 1997, p. 12527.
79 See in particular forthcoming Adelphi Paper (IISS) on the 'Role of Private Security firms in Africa' by David Shearer.
80 A/50/60, S/1995/1, 3 January 1995 (Supplement to An Agenda for Peace).
81 For the scale of the problem in Africa, 'Landmines: Africa's Deadly Legacy', *Africa Confidential*, 19 November 1993, Vol. 34, No. 23, pp. 1-3.
82 See A/49/357 'Assistance in Mine Clearance: Report by the Secretary General', 6 September 1994.

83 For a much fuller discussion of these issues see Mats Berdal (1996), *Disarmament and Demobiliastion after Civil Wars*, Adelphi Paper 303, London: OUP for IISS.
84 Inis Claude, Jr. (1984), *Swords into Plowshares: the problems and progress of international organisation, 4th edition*, New York: McGraw-Hill, Inc, p. 317.

Acknowledgements The author would like to thank David Keen, David Styan, Dominique Jacquin-Berdal and David Shearer for their very helpful comments on various drafts of this chapter. He also wishes to extend special thanks to Ellen Peacock for her research assistance during the preparation of this paper.

Part Two
CASE STUDIES

5 Zimbabwe's peace settlement: re-evaluating Lancaster House

Norma Kriger

> ...where their [peace settlements] recipes for dealing with the last war are seriously flawed, they help create the conditions for the wars of the future. Peace then becomes the father of war.[1]

The Lancaster House peace settlement has been widely applauded by academics and diplomats as having ended successfully the war of independence. This essay, a revisionist perspective, seeks to show the darker side of the settlement. By defining the conflict as an anti-colonial war which pitted supporters of continued white minority rule against united African nationalist guerrilla forces, the peacemakers deliberately suppressed the dimension of the war which had to do with the two guerrilla forces' rivalry. Consequently, though the settlement altered the political landscape for domestic actors, the competition between armed nationalist contenders for power persisted as the settlement was being implemented. By setting the stage for this continued rivalry, as well as ongoing guerrilla indiscipline and threats to public order, the settlement became a cruel accomplice of the next round of warfare and other threats to domestic order. Locating competing African nationalist struggles for power as an integral part of the conflict for black majority rule rather than artificially separating them from the anti-colonial or revolutionary aspects of the struggle also exposes the limitations of evaluations of the Lancaster House settlement which either celebrate its success at ending colonial rule or deplore its perpetuation of imperialism and capitalism. Neither assessment takes into account how the settlement did nothing to terminate certain war-time conflicts even as it changed the circumstances in which those contests would play themselves out. More generally, settlements that seek to settle complex intrastate wars by suppressing some of their dimensions are likely to be harbingers of further war rather than contributors to peace. Simplifying multilayered conflicts may facilitate peacemaking and remove conflicts from the international arena but it does not necessarily bring domestic peace.

This chapter begins with a description of the actors at Lancaster House, their major internal and external feuds, and the key compromises reached. It then documents how war-time competition among the two African nationalist parties with guerrilla armies continued during the implementation of the settlement, setting the stage for post-war violent conflict between the two political and military rivals. The failure of the settlement to address these war-time political dynamics forms the basis of my reassessment of Lancaster House as an important contributor to the post-independence violence between these two parties and armies.

The Lancaster House settlement

Presided over by the British chair, Lord Carrington, the Lancaster House conference which began on 10 September 1979, and ended some three and a half months later, represented yet another attempt to solve the conflict in Rhodesia. Like its predecessors, the conference ignored an important element of the inter-African nationalist dimension of the conflict and focused only on its colonial aspect. The structure of the delegates reflected this interpretation of the conflict. There were no international organisations or foreign diplomats pushing for a more complex definition of the conflict. In brief, there was an international consensus, as in the previous settlement initiatives, to label the conflict as being over colonialism and to ignore its entanglement with African nationalist inter-party competition.

Apart from the British delegation, there were only two other teams. Prime Minister Muzorewa's delegation represented Muzorewa's UANC and Ian Smith's Rhodesia Front, an uneasy mixture of African nationalist and white minority interests. Muzorewa had nationalist credentials but had lost out in power struggles to control the exiled guerrilla movements. Along with another African nationalist, Ndabaningi Sithole, Muzorewa had then negotiated with Prime Minister Ian Smith and two African chiefs and participated in designing a new constitution which provided for universal suffrage elections and an African parliamentary majority. Held in April 1979, the elections resulted in Muzorewa becoming the first African Prime Minister. White minority rule had been removed from parliament but the new constitution provided for reserved parliamentary seats for whites. Importantly, whites still controlled state institutions - the army, civil service, judiciary and police - which meant that they continued to make decisions about the execution of the war. Also, the war continued because the two guerrilla parties, ZANU and ZAPU, had not participated either in devising the new constitution or in the elections. For these reasons, the international community, excluding South Africa, denied recognition to the Muzorewa regime. Consequently, the country's fourteen year illegal status, begun with the white minority regime's declaration of unilateral independence from Britain in 1965, remained unchanged.

The other delegation attending the conference was the Patriotic Front (PF), composed of the two rival parties, ZANU and ZAPU, each with their respective guerrilla armies, ZANLA and ZIPRA. The deep rifts dividing ZANU and ZAPU were no secret. Nkomo had been the leader of several nationalist organisations since the 1950s, and of ZAPU since 1962. In 1963 several leaders, including Mugabe and Sithole, broke away to form ZANU, dividing what had till then been a single nationalist party. Behind the split was a growing disenchantment with Nkomo who was cast as too conservative, too willing to compromise, and too engaged in international diplomacy at the expense of grass roots indigenous political organisation. In 1963 and 1964, ZANU and ZAPU became embroiled in violent competition which resulted in them being banned. Both parties established themselves in Zambia, and began to build guerrilla armies. Though their leaderships were ethnically mixed, Ndebele-Kalanga people going into exile from Matabeleland were more likely to go to ZAPU-run camps and Shona speakers from the rest of the country to ZANU bases. In late 1975, with front line state support,[2] the two guerrilla armies came together under a military leadership drawn from both armies. This attempt at unity presented a massive challenge. Apart from the lines of cleavage already mentioned, the two armies' military strategy and tactics had been affected by their chief international military supporters, China for ZANLA, and the Soviet Union for ZIPRA. The attempt at military unity collapsed as ZIPRA and ZANLA guerrillas clashed in external training camps and inside Rhodesia. From supporting military unity, the front line states shifted to promoting political unity. In 1976 the two rival parties were pressed to form a political front, the PF, to attend the Geneva conference. For ZANU, the front line states offered as an incentive the release of its political and military leaders who had been detained in Zambia because of their alleged involvement in the assassination of ZANU's external leader Herbert Chitepo. In subsequent international negotiations, the two parties constituted a single delegation, but the issues dividing the rivals only deepened.

As the war intensified, it became apparent that Nkomo was infiltrating only a small percentage of his large army amassed in Zambia and Angola. ZANU and other observers believed that Nkomo was holding forces in reserve to demolish ZANU and its ZANLA guerrillas after independence, while leaving the battle for independence to ZANLA troops. Also, it became known that ZIPRA was converting many of its forces into a conventional army in 1979. Whether true or not, the perception that ZIPRA was planning to annihilate ZANLA rather than overthrow the colonial regime and its Muzorewa successor was reinforced. Secret talks between Nkomo and various actors only added to ZANU suspicions. To get ZANU to the negotiating table in 1979, and as a member of the PF, required tremendous pressure from its regional patron, Mozambique, and other front line states. ZANU believed that its army, given more time, would win the war and it preferred military victory to negotiating a settlement, especially with ZAPU, an arch rival, as its ally. However, Mozambique was suffering from repeated Rhodesian raids on ZANLA camps and wanted to end the war. ZAPU was more inclined to negotiate, as it historically had been, and needed less pressure from its regional patron, Zambia, which was also being punished for offering external bases.

At the conference, each team had some unity of purpose. Predictably, the Muzorewa team divided along racial lines on the merits of white monopoly control of state institutions and reserved parliamentary seats for whites. However, the team was united in its desire to preserve the existing regime's control during the transition period when elections would take place. Muzorewa and his delegates fully expected that their arch rivals, the guerrilla parties, would not remain in the talks and that Britain would negotiate a separate peace with them. The PF claimed, as they had in previous international negotiations, that their troops had won the right to share in or dominate state institutions during the transitional period. For both ZANU and ZAPU such control or participation would serve as an insurance scheme against Rhodesian manipulation of the process and would maximise their electoral prospects. For Britain, the most unified team, the central purpose of the conference was to try to bring about 'authentic' African majority rule - that is, to remove those aspects of the constitution which prevented Africans from exercising power - and to include the guerrilla parties in the exercise.[3]

The participants agreed first to a new constitution which provided for African majority rule by removing the entrenched monopoly power of the white minority. At the same time, the white minority's property, public sector jobs and pensions, and representation in parliament were given constitutional protection. An agreement on arrangements during the transition was reached next. It provided for a British Governor who would assume full executive and legislative authority, who could call on the forces of either the Rhodesian government or the guerrillas to help the police impose law and order should the cease-fire seem in jeopardy, and who would govern with the help of the existing Rhodesian administration. His chief task was to organise and hold elections and to ensure that the campaign and the elections were free and fair. The settlement provided for a Commonwealth Observers' Group to evaluate the campaign environment and the conduct of elections. Lastly, the conference worked out the details of a cease-fire agreement, which was signed on 21 December 1979. The cease-fire would become effective at midnight on 28 December 1979. A Commonwealth Monitoring Force drawn from the United Kingdom (1,100 servicemen), Australia (150), New Zealand (74), Kenya (50), and Fiji (23) would monitor, but not enforce, a cease-fire. For this reason, monitors - subsequently increased to 1,500 - were to carry only light personal weapons. Cross-border movements by the armies were to stop as soon as the cease-fire was signed; from 29 December 1979 the guerrillas were to assemble with their arms at designated rendezvous places where they would meet monitors who had been accompanied by a guerrilla liaison officer. By 4 January 1980 the guerrillas had to be in assembly places where they would live with the monitors or be held in violation of the cease-fire. A Cease-fire Commission composed of representatives from each army and chaired by the Governor's military adviser, General Acland, was to investigate reported breaches of the cease-fire. Despite agreement that there would be no institutional remodelling during the transition, Britain recognised that some planning for the future of the three military forces would need to occur during the interim administration and it offered unspecified assistance.

Governor Soames, along with his military adviser, General Acland, and General Learmont, the commander of the Commonwealth Monitoring Force, and a small staff, arrived in Salisbury on 12 December 1979, before the cease-fire had actually been signed. This was a deliberate British attempt to pressure the Patriotic Front (PF) into accepting the cease-fire arrangements, with which they were dissatisfied. It was a classic example of Carrington's frequent use of the threat of reaching a separate settlement with Prime Minister Muzorewa alone if the PF refused to accept British proposals. Governor Soames had to hold elections by a specific date, but he also had to give the parties enough time to campaign. Elections were set for 27-29 February 1980. Mugabe's party decided to contest the election on its own, and ended the coalition with Nkomo's party at the outset of the campaign. The Commonwealth Observer's Group was asked to give its assessment of the election prior to the announcement of the results. Like other observer groups, it declared the election had been as free and fair as possible given the circumstances in which it had been held. On 4 March 1980 election results were announced. Mugabe's party, now renamed ZANU-PF, won 57 out of the 80 common roll seats, giving it a majority in the 100 member legislative assembly. Mugabe announced that he would form a coalition government, and allocated cabinet positions to white supporters of Ian Smith and to Nkomo's party. At the request of newly elected Prime Minister Mugabe, Governor Soames stayed on in the country until the new government formally took office on 18 April 1980.

Continued military and political competition

The settlement did not end competition between ZANLA and ZIPRA for military and political advantage though it did change the context, introducing the British as a potential resource. A party representing the Ndebele-Kalanga minority, ZAPU's best chance of winning the election was to co-operate in implementing the settlement with the British Governor and the Rhodesian administration on which he depended. Nkomo hoped he might win enough seats in a hung parliament to be instrumental in forming and possibly leading a coalition government.[4] With its electoral base among the Shona who represented 80 per cent of the African population, ZANU's main concern was to ensure that this ethnic group voted for it rather than for Muzorewa, who was being lavishly supported by the South African government and the intimidatory tactics of his auxiliaries in the Rhodesian forces. Sithole and other lesser competitors were also seen as having the potential to make inroads on the Shona vote which ZANU sought to secure. Defying the settlement provisions would most enhance ZANU's political ambitions, though this strategy of resistance ran the risk of Britain disqualifying it from electoral participation - an outcome on which ZAPU, Muzorewa's UANC, and Smith's Rhodesia Front party all counted. The different approaches of the two competing nationalist parties are also apparent in their response to British initiatives to begin the process of military integration by placing a Rhodesian police and military presence in the assembly places and commencing joint ZIPRA and ZANLA training under the Rhodesian military and Commonwealth Monitoring Force.

ZANU-PF and ZANLA challenged the settlement provisions that cross-border movements stop after the cease-fire and that all guerrillas be in assembly points by a specific date. The numbers of ZANLA fighters who did not assemble and who entered Zimbabwe illegally after the cease-fire give some idea of the extent of ZANLA violations. Perhaps as many as two-thirds of all ZANLA's 30,000 guerrillas entered illegally from Mozambique after the cease-fire, taking advantage of the two-week late deployment of the seven teams which were supposed to monitor the borders.[5] Even though Governor Soames extended the period of assembly by forty-eight hours to assist the guerrillas in meeting the assembly deadline, thereby infuriating the Rhodesian forces who were anxious to declare the unassembled guerrillas in violation of the cease-fire and therefore fair game, many guerrillas did not assemble. In 1989 Emmerson Mnangagwa, ZANLA's chief of intelligence, claimed that 9,000-10,000 guerrillas, 40 per cent of all ZANLA forces, may have remained outside the assembly points during most of the pre-election period;[6] Mugabe admitted some 4,000 stayed outside the assembly points[7] - a figure that the British believed at the time.[8] General Walls carped that ZANLA sent to the assembly points only a 'few old men and women ... their mujibas [young male civilian helpers] ... with a few ant-eaten old muskets and a few rusty old weapons that couldn't possibly have been the terrorists' weapons ... and meantime the terrorists mingled with the population and made damn certain which way they were going to vote'.[9]

ZANLA's violation of the settlement was an assertion of its power which had several purposes. ZANLA commanders' orders to their most seasoned fighters to go to the rural areas to maintain its army's logistical structures and to campaign for the election was intended to ensure that ZANLA could compete at least on an equal footing with the Rhodesian forces whose mobility the settlement did not constrain. Pouring large numbers of guerrillas into the countryside would make a public display of ZANLA power, serve electoral objectives, and still leave enough fighters in assembly places so that elements of ZANLA appeared to be adhering to the settlement. Also, should the cease-fire collapse, those fighters outside the assembly places would be able to resume the war and would escape annihilation which Mugabe's party (and Nkomo's) feared might occur in the assembly places.[10] These violations of the settlement did intensify existing British and Rhodesian mistrust of ZANLA and ZANU-PF. ZANU-PF rightly claimed that the settlement provided that the guerrilla forces had de facto equality with the Rhodesian forces during the interim administration, and therefore that Governor Soames could and should have called on ZANLA forces who were abiding by the settlement to help the

Rhodesian police discipline its dissident colleagues.[11] But the British had never regarded de facto equality of the forces during the cease-fire as anything but a meaningless concession, and in the words of the British Ministry of Defence report, 'it was fairly obvious that the treatment of the two sides would be unequal.'[12] By focusing on Soames' exclusive use of Rhodesian forces to impose law and order, ZANU-PF sought to portray Soames as partial and to delegitimise his authority.

In general, ZAPU and ZIPRA adopted a different approach to the settlement. Rather than assertively challenging the British ZAPU hoped to win their favour by demonstrating its forces' commitment to the settlement, and to benefit from Rhodesian and British prejudices against ZANU-PF and its forces. There were no serious ZIPRA cross-border breaches and most ZIPRA abided by the assembly provisions. All but one per cent of ZIPRA guerrillas were ordered to enter the assembly places. According to Dabengwa, ZIPRA chief of intelligence, those instructed to stay outside were primarily political commissars who 'remained in certain areas ... looking after some strategic arms that were left outside the assembly camp ... (acting) as a liaison between the camps and the population and the rear base in Zambia ... (and) spell(ing) out ... our ideas ... '.[13]

The different approaches of ZANLA and ZIPRA were evident too in their responses to two British initiatives to begin to plan for military integration of the three forces. The first British scheme to move towards integration involved removing the Commonwealth Monitoring Force as administrators of the assembly places and replacing them with Rhodesian forces. For General Acland, it was obvious that the Rhodesians, 'possessing the paraphernalia of government and administration, would have to take over the running of the Assembly Places from the Commonwealth Force'.[14] However, little progress was made in getting the military representatives of the three armies to move towards this end. In so far as monitors at particular assembly places were able to work out arrangements with local security forces and police to engage in joint patrols, such progress was always overturned by the intervention of the Rhodesian military and police hierarchy.[15] The issue of transferring camp administration to the Rhodesians became more urgent after General Acland, fearing for the safety of the monitors, decided to withdraw them from the assembly places before the election results were announced.[16] The next day, 19 February 1980, Acland appealed to the Cease-fire Commission, composed of two representatives each of the Rhodesian army, ZANLA and ZIPRA, to personally seek authority from Walls, Mugabe and Nkomo for an initiative to resolve the problem of the looming administrative vacuum in the camps.[17] The Cease-fire Commission representatives returned a day later without the approval of their respective military leaders. With the election just six days away, Acland presented his plan for handing over the administration of the assembly places to the Rhodesians. 'The Cease-fire Commission was to have the full authority to order the Rhodesians to produce an immediate presence of effective and adequate size to take over from the Monitoring Force in each Assembly Place and the PF guerrilla commanders were to accept, and co-operate with, such a presence'.[18] From 22-25 February 1980 the Cease-fire Commission, either as a whole or in two halves, visited every assembly place with the Acland's message that '... while a country can have any number of political parties, it cannot, if it is to remain at peace, have more than one Army'.[19] The plan was to move in Rhodesian police, an army liaison officer, and then soldiers.[20]

Once again, ZIPRA camps co-operated whereas ZANLA camps resisted. ZIPRA's receptivity to Acland's message is portrayed by a monitor at a ZIPRA camp. When top political leaders, touring the assembly places for a second time to preach reconciliation and the need for integration, arrived at Romeo assembly place, a joint patrol of ZIPRA forces and the Grey Scouts, a much detested cavalry unit of the Rhodesian army, were apprehending and disarming 'dissident terrorists' - that is, ZIPRA guerrillas.[21] The experience with ZANLA camps was much different. 'ZANLA camps were a much more tricky affair' as 'ZANLA were much more deeply suspicious of RSF motives and progress was slow'.[22] The British Ministry of Defence report regarded this exercise as 'the greatest single contribution to the maintenance of peace in Zimbabwe' and described each assembly place prior to the start of voting as 'a comparatively happy mixture of monitors PF, RSF [Rhodesian Security Forces] and BSAP [British South Africa Police]'.[23] This upbeat assessment belied the fragility of the arrangement - in a very short time each guerrilla group would control its own assembly places without any Rhodesian presence - and was impervious to the significance of the recurrent pattern of ZANLA resistance and ZIPRA co-operation. Beneath these different ZANLA and ZIPRA responses to the Rhodesians were the divergent strategies of each in their continued contest for power over each other.

The other British effort to begin military integration before handing power to a newly elected government was to embark on joint training schemes for ZIPRA and ZANLA under the authority of Rhodesian forces and Commonwealth Monitoring Forces. Britain's decision to use Rhodesian trainers reflected its commitment to the new constitution in which the Rhodesian forces were the constitutional forces, and therefore could be expected to control training in the post-independence period. Just prior to the election General Acland secured agreement from General Walls, head of the Rhodesian forces, Nkomo and Mugabe for joint training of 600 ZIPRA from Lima assembly place and 600 ZANLA from Foxtrot assembly place. But joint training never did take place. Instead, each army's candidates were trained by Rhodesians and monitors in separate camps. Still, General Acland regarded the experiment as 'an important psychological gesture because the guerrillas who went to the camp laid down their arms and for the first time expressed their trust in the Rhodesian army'.[24]

British self-congratulations aside, the training experiment exposed ZIPRA and ZANLA opposition to sharing power, and their mutual distrust of the Rhodesians. Rhodesian commanders continued to assume that the future army of Zimbabwe would change only cosmetically, with a few black officers absorbed among the whites, and regarded the guerrillas as grossly inferior irregular forces which naturally would have to disband as soon as the elections were over. A British monitor (recently in the limelight when his wife left him for Prince Charles) described the Rhodesian military hierarchy's notion of integration as: 'We'll produce the sergeants. You produce the men. Our men will shout at your men.'[25] ZIPRA was willing to use the more favourable disposition of both Britain and Rhodesian forces towards it to get a head start in the competition for power with ZANLA. In contrast, ZANLA openly resisted British schemes because it distrusted their motives and those of the Rhodesians and believed it could better secure its goals without co-operating.

Both ZANLA and ZIPRA publicly made much of the importance that they be treated equally, but their ideas on integration excluded their opponents. Presenting ZAPU as eager to co-operate, Nkomo repeatedly urged an immediate start to military integration with the Rhodesian army and made this appeal at campaign rallies.[26] On 10 February 1980 he told a rally that the nucleus of a Zimbabwean army composed of Rhodesian security forces and guerrillas - something he said he had been calling for since his return - would start taking shape 'within the next few days'. Mischievously overlooking Britain's vague commitment to initiate integration during the interim administration, Nkomo claimed Britain now favoured what it had rejected at Lancaster House. Interviewed years later, ZIPRA's intelligence chief, Dabengwa, claimed ZIPRA had been anxious to proceed with military integration and eager to compete on the basis of ability for places in the new army of Zimbabwe.[27] To this end, ZIPRA had provided its crack battalion, never tested in battle, but trained by East

Germans in conventional warfare. According to New Zealand monitors who were in charge of the ZIPRA battalion at Lima assembly place, these soldiers 'had effective discipline and their drill and basic soldier standards appeared to be reasonably high'.[28] But ZIPRA had hidden agendas. Nkomo saw his army as superior to ZANLA's 'ragamuffin forces'[29], as did the British;[30] competition based on merit would enable ZIPRA's numerically smaller forces to dominate a new army. Also, ZAPU and ZIPRA officials' public support for military integration and the equal treatment of ZIPRA and ZANLA contradicted their private hopes. The British Ministry of Defence report describes how the pro-Nkomo bias of the Soames' administration and the Rhodesian army led to a ZIPRA battalion receiving the offer of training first.[31] Also, ZIPRA guerrillas went to Essexvale, an established training centre near Bulawayo for the Rhodesian army whereas ZANLA was to be trained at Bravo assembly place, which was emptied for that reason, but on Rhodesian advice, they were taken to Rathgar, a white-owned farm in Mtoko district. 'Rathgar was a hopeless place for a training camp because not only was there little water and no sanitation, but there was no training area. A massive amount of work had to be done in the place before it became habitable.'[32] When ZANLA complained that its forces were being discriminated against, 'although publicly Nkomo had to say that they should be treated equally, privately he made it quite clear that he hoped they would not and furthermore he was averse to ZANLA sharing the same camp'.[33] Similarly, Nkomo's public appeals to Governor Soames to collect all arms from the combatants for use by the future army[34] were an instance of public posturing to win points with the British and had nothing to do with his private support for the guerrillas bearing arms as an insurance mechanism.

ZANLA also opposed any power-sharing with ZIPRA and saw Britain as a biased actor rather than a valuable resource in its competition with ZIPRA. According to the British Ministry of Defence report, Rex Nhongo, who had become head of ZANLA after the death of Josiah Tongogara in an alleged car accident in Mozambique on 26 December 1980, 'was heard on more than [one] occasion to say that there would only be one army and it would be composed of people from the ZANLA Army and that the ZIPRAs and the whites would not figure in his plan'.[35] ZANLA felt that militarily it had earned the right to comprise the forces of the newly independent government since it had provided the overwhelming number of guerrillas inside the country whereas ZIPRA had held back large numbers of its troops. Robert Renwick, a key political advisor to Lord Carrington during the negotiations, believes that Mugabe would never have allowed his guerrilla forces to be tampered with till the outcome of the election was clear because he was convinced that the British would rig the election against him.[36] Presumably, too, he feared British bias in favour of ZIPRA over ZANLA in a military integration exercise. Reflecting ZANLA's negative attitude to military integration and its suspicions, those guerrillas whom it sent for training for a new integrated army were its least experienced.[37]

The experiences of ZIPRA and ZANLA forces in the two mixed assembly places - Kilo and Juliet - is indicative of the obstacles to them sharing training camps. The monitors separated the encampment of the forces but still incidents occurred in each. A Juliet assembly camp monitor came upon a ZANLA group patrolling, against the rules, outside the camp. Frightened, the ZANLA team fled leaving behind their weapons which he picked up and took to the monitors' camp in the assembly place. That afternoon when monitors went to the ZANLA section of the camp, six were taken hostage and surrounded by 1,200 ZANLA guerrillas angrily demanding their weapons back. According to the monitor commanding the assembly place, who was among those taken hostage: 'Our biggest surprise came when ZIPRA, alarmed by our actions, stood to also and offered to help defend our camp against ZANLA'.[38] At Kilo assembly place, there was a mortar and RPG attack on the ZANLA camp on the night of 19 February 1980, with ZANLA and ZIPRA blaming each other. The following morning, the assembly camp commander and three other monitors who had set off to try to find out what had happened were 'ambushed' by '30 extremely irate ZANLA' who accused them of having engineered the attack.[39] Just before the election the assembly place was split up and the ZIPRA and ZANLA contingents were dispersed to other, 'one faction' camps.[40] For the monitors, mixed assembly camps, despite their separate quarters for ZANLA and ZIPRA guerrillas, 'were very much more difficult to control. There was continued acrimony and bad blood between the two factions.'[41]

ZIPRA's co-operative strategy toward implementing the settlement and military integration should not be taken to reflect softer ZIPRA than ZANLA attitudes to the Rhodesian law and order forces. The common behaviour of those ZIPRA and ZANLA guerrillas who failed to assemble by the extended cease-fire deadline and who opted for amnesty to avoid being in violation of the cease-fire shows how much both guerrilla forces despised the Rhodesians and sought to assert their military superiority. The amnesty provisions, governed by pre-existing Rhodesian emergency rules, required that the guerrillas go to a police station and give up their arms. According to the British Ministry of Defence report, the assembly period under the amnesty was 'the most testing time' for the monitors with ZANLA and ZIPRA. Each team of monitors had a guerrilla leader whose job was to explain the amnesty rules to guerrillas who resisted giving up their arms. One monitor described how his ZANLA liaison officer battled to get a group of guerrillas to disarm.

> It took him five hours to explain the terms of the amnesty and why they had to be disarmed and even then we had to agree to a pride-salvaging compromise whereby the guerrillas were allowed to carry their weapons while they walked the twelve kilometres to where the buses were parked; the guerrillas would not accept the loss of face involved if they had had to walk through the Tribal Trust Lands, to be seen by all the Africans to have been disarmed.[42]

Often the persuasive powers of the liaison officer failed, and senior ZANLA and ZIPRA officers from Salisbury had to be flown to the scene to give clear orders to the guerrillas. The British Ministry of Defence report says of the guerrilla commanders that 'even they themselves jibbed at giving unpopular orders' and goes on to discuss how 'Rex Nhongo, the ZANLA commander, would argue for hours in his stuttering, illogical way that ... it would be ignominious for the "victors" to be disarmed. Many of these negotiations lasted more than 48 hours whilst really bolshy bush leaders refused flatly to hand over their arms.'[43] ZIPRA as much as ZANLA also harboured fears that the Rhodesians would bomb the assembly places, turning them into death traps.[44]

There were also limits to ZIPRA's strategy of co-operation. On the question of hiding arms, ZANLA and ZIPRA leaders both employed identical strategies. Both parties hid arms, not just in case the cease-fire collapsed and they needed to resume the war against the Muzorewa government but also as an insurance policy against whatever new political dispensation would emerge from the election. ZANLA commanders Tungamirai and Chinenge described the guerrilla armies' practice of 'tactical deceit' so that they could return to war if the cease-fire and elections failed: each army revealed no more about its numbers, weaponry, and contingency plans than it thought necessary for the success of the cease-fire.[45]

ZANU's strategy of resistance ultimately did not interfere with its electoral victory. The Commonwealth Observers' Group and other observers' groups declared the election as free and fair as it could have been under the circumstances, and believed that neither ZANLA nor Rhodesian auxiliary intimidation affected the election outcome.[46] This international effort to affirm the election result did not reverse the sentiments of high-ranking ZAPU and Muzorewa officials that ZANU-PF's intimidatory tactics had paid off. Senior Muzorewa officials could hardly claim their security force auxiliaries, part of the Rhodesian army, had been well-behaved but ZAPU could point to how ZIPRA had respected the settlement whereas ZANLA had openly defied it. John Nkomo, a high ranking ZAPU politician, believed that '[W]e cannot rule out the possibility that the elections were rigged.'[47] Senior ZAPU politician Cephas Msipa believed that the elections were less than free and fair in the rural areas, that the people were tired of the war, and that 'to end the war maybe they voted ZANU(PF) because they had more people in the field'.[48] Years after the election, Joshua Nkomo still believed it to have been a sham.

> After the count, the used ballot papers were flown especially to Britain, not to be stored as historic documents, but to be burned. It's hard to believe that that would have been done if there was nothing to hide. I could not believe it and still do not believe. Even the known and massive intimidation campaign could not have achieved that. That the first elections in free Zimbabwe failed to reflect the people's will is something of which I am sure.[49]

Similarly, asked if he thought the 1980 election had been free and fair, Muzorewa said in 1989:

> Definitely not. Everybody knows that including the Commonwealth Observers. Someone has to convince me that we actually lost the votes. But to say the least, I don't believe we lost the election but we lost the verdict. There's no way we could have gone from 65 per cent of the vote [in 1979] to three seats. The British thought that the best way to stop this [war] was to let the people with the guns in [to power].[50]

These domestic sentiments, notwithstanding international observers' declarations, meant that the first independent government's legitimacy was questioned from the outset by its most important rivals.

Re-evaluating Lancaster House

Analysts of the Lancaster House settlement and its implementation have almost uniformly praised it as a resounding success. In accounting for the success of the conference, some have focused on Carrington's strategy and tactics at the conference,[51] others on regional and international pressures on the key domestic actors to end the conflict.[52] On the success of the settlement's implementation, there has been some debate about the effectiveness of Governor Soames[53] but most have agreed on the importance of the CMF, the COG, and the will of the domestic actors,[54] while some have also emphasised the contribution of a well-designed cease-fire plan, and the fact that it was part of a broader settlement which solved the central issue of conflict.[55] A few observers have lamented the success of the settlement, which they attribute to the power of international capital and imperialism to produce a constitution which inhibits radical socio-economic and political change.[56] At the heart of the difference between those who praise the settlement and those who condemn it are different understandings of the objectives of the war. The settlement's celebrators define - as did Britain, the PF and the international community - the central conflict in the war to be about ending colonialism and transferring power from the white minority to an elected black majority; its detractors define the conflict to be a revolution to effect political and economic change. To the celebrators, the settlement represents a rupture with the past because it ended the anti-colonial war. To its critics, the settlement is the main reason for continuities in colonial and post-colonial political and economic inequalities. Neither set of analysts criticise the settlement for its failure to address African nationalist struggles; nor do they see the settlement as an important link bridging war-time and post-war problems of law and order.

Jeffrey Davidow's widely read *A Peace in Southern Africa*, an openly celebratory account of the Lancaster House settlement, is worth discussing in some detail. Davidow's celebration of the settlement does not challenge its fundamental premise that its objective was to end the conflict between Muzorewa and the PF. Consequently he is able to attribute to the settlement a brief peace and to divorce the post-independence ZIPRA-ZANLA conflict from the settlement. Davidow begins by asking whether each of the three players (the British, Muzorewa's team, and the PF), allowing for the divisions in the Muzorewa and PF teams, obtained outcomes that met their basic goals. Davidow replies that Britain rid itself of a fifteen year conflict honourably. Despite claiming to take into account the disunity within the PF, Davidow proceeds to treat it as a unified actor even when it had dropped such pretence. 'The Patriotic Front obtained, through the electoral process made possible by the conference, what it had been denied on the battlefield, effective political control.'[57] By treating ZANU and ZAPU as if they had both won the election, Davidow is able to avoid assessing the conference outcomes for an electoral loser, ZAPU. He does acknowledge the defeat of Muzorewa's delegation, but asserts it 'gained a clear shot at international responsibility, the lifting of sanctions, an end to the war, and independence - goals, which though less important than perpetuating themselves in power, were nevertheless major objectives.'[58] But these were only major objectives for Muzorewa's team if it continued in power. After discussing the costs to each delegation, Davidow concludes: 'There were debits, undoubtedly, but few of the participants, except perhaps the most die-hard Smith supporters and inconsolable Muzorewa loyalists, would argue that they outweighed the credits of peace, independence, return to the world economy, and, for Britain, extrication from a vexing problem'.[59] This evaluation ignores the fact that leading members of ZAPU and Muzorewa's UANC saw the election result as illegitimate because of ZANU's use of intimidation. Moreover, key ZAPU and ZIPRA conference participants, to say nothing of the rank and file ZIPRA and ZAPU members, would be hard-pushed to describe their post-war experiences as peaceful.

Davidow's book is unusual in that not only does it offer his evaluation of the settlement's success but it also examines criticisms of the settlement - albeit that all but one appear as emanating from unnamed phantoms - in order to come to its defence.[60] This provides an opportunity to see how seldom even those who criticise the settlement have not condemned its premise that the PF represented a viable negotiating partner. Davidow identifies and dismisses three criticisms. Firstly, to those who complain that the settlement ignored the reality of Zimbabwe's tribal divisions and thus failed to construct institutional or constitutional mechanisms that would prove more equitable and enduring, he replies that none of the African leaders at Lancaster House were interested in such structures. One might counter that had ZAPU and ZANU appeared as opponents at the negotiating table - and it is unclear that the critics he is repudiating argue that they should have - ZAPU might have promoted the protection of African minority rights. A second criticism is that the settlement unfairly limited the freedom of action of the new Zimbabwean government in effecting radical socio-economic and political changes - the view of those I have called the detractors of the settlement. To these critics, Davidow responds that the negotiated settlement presented necessary compromises. I would argue, however that the constitution was respected for as long as it was precisely because it did not inhibit the new leaders who have displayed little interest in redistributing as opposed to amassing personal wealth. Thirdly, some have seen Carrington's directive approach, especially over the constitution, as creating an agreement which is highly fragile; they have argued that bargaining between Muzorewa and the PF would have produced a more durable agreement. Davidow responds that the Lancaster House agreement has held up relatively well, and that the tensions between Nkomo and Mugabe forces would not likely have been ameliorated by more direct negotiations between the PF and Muzorewa in London. Davidow believes that what distinguishes his assessment of the settlement from that of its critics is that he measures its effectiveness in terms of its ability to obtain the immediate objectives of the participants whereas they measure the settlement in terms of its contribution to longer-term effectiveness or stability. However, at least both the second and third criticisms, Davidow's responses to all three objections, and his own account, accept the basic conference structure of the delegates, and thereby, of the anti-colonial dimension of the conflict at the expense of the inter-African nationalist struggles for power, especially between ZANLA and ZIPRA.

Conclusion

In my account, the settlement appears not as the harbinger of peace but as a major contributor to the next round of warfare in which ZANLA decimated ZIPRA and its ZAPU support structures and to other specific problems of law and order. This different evaluation of the settlement and its implementation stems from my focus on how the settlement was premised on a deliberate myth about the political and military unity of the PF. Failure to address African nationalist inter-party competition as an integral part of the conflict meant that the settlement merely created a new playing field for the continuation of the deadly contest for military and political power. This battle for power, in which ZANLA and ZIPRA adopted different strategies, was evident in their approach to the settlement and to British initiatives to begin to integrate the military during the cease-fire. The settlement's creation of assembly places did nothing to solve existing problems of guerrilla indiscipline, but it did concentrate in poorly bounded camps over 20,000 guerrillas with their arms and under their respective commanders who themselves lacked the necessary leadership qualities to control their rank and file. With the power of numbers and arms, the guerrillas in the assembly places could, and did, use violence and threats to destabilise the cease-fire to obtain the resources they desired. The settlement did improve an aspect of guerrilla-civilian relations by removing the burden of feeding and clothing the guerrillas from impoverished rural civilians.

More generally, this re-evaluation of the Lancaster House settlement cautions against assessing success or failure too narrowly in terms of settlement provisions which themselves may be flawed because they address only a limited dimension of a complex intrastate war. Equally problematic are assessments which downplay the violation of settlement provisions. International observers may be more willing to overlook unfair electoral practices, as they did in Zimbabwe, on the grounds that the results would have been no different in the absence of intimidation and violence. However, local actors engaged in struggles for power may not perceive electoral victors who rely on intimidation so benignly. At a minimum, settlements should be held to be successful only if they remove not only the original cause of the conflict but other subsequent war-related conflicts. If the causes of the war or goals of participants are too narrowly construed, as they were at Lancaster House, the settlement is likely to contribute to further war. Academics engaged in comparative analyses of settlements and their outcomes must be careful not to accept uncritically peacemakers' self-interested definitions of complex wars.

Notes

1. Kalevi J. Holsti (1991), *Peace and War: armed conflicts and international order 1648-1989*, Cambridge University Press: Cambridge, p. 353. Holsti also burdens peace settlements with having to anticipate and devise means to cope with future issues.
2. The front line states were Mozambique, Zambia, Angola, Botswana and Tanzania.
3. A few analysts believe that Britain's chief interest in the conference was to ensure a Muzorewa electoral victory. See Anthony Verrier (1986), *The Road to Zimbabwe 1890-1980*, Jonathan Cape: London.
4. Susan Elizabeth Rice (1990), 'Commonwealth Initiative in Zimbabwe, 1979-1980: Implication for International Peacekeeping', Oxford University, PhD history thesis, p. 304.
5. Susan Elizabeth Rice (1990), ibid., p. 83, pp. 200-201. According to Rice, senior ZANLA officers consistently gave the total number of ZANLA guerrillas as 30,000 but offered radically different estimates

of how many were inside the country on the day of the cease-fire. Both Brigadier Gurdon, CF Chief of Staff and ZANLA's chief of intelligence, Emmerson Mnangagwa, claim that no more than 30 per cent of ZANLA troops were inside the country before cease-fire day.

6 Rice (1990), p. 161.
7 Verrier (1986), p. 295, notes that Mugabe admitted that 4,000 ZANLA forces did not assemble but remained in the eastern part of the country; Mashonaland East, Manicaland, and Victoria Provinces.
8 Interview with British Ambassador Robin Renwick, British Embassy, Washington DC, 17 June 1994.
9 Rice (1990), p. 162, citing General Walls, Rhodes House Library Mss.
10 Rice (1990), pp. 160-1.
11 Rice (1990), pp. 153-6, p. 247.
12 *Report of the British Ministry of Defence on the Commonwealth Monitoring Force*, p. 21, V84/B04. Obtained from UK Ministry of Defence.
13 Rice (1990), p. 161, citing an interview with Dabengwa on 30 November 1989.
14 Major-General J. H. B. Acland (1980), 'The Rhodesian Operation', *Guards Magazine*, Summer, p. 48.
15 *Report of the British Ministry of Defence on the Commonwealth Monitoring Force*, pp. 129-130, V84/B04. Obtained from UK Ministry of Defence; Captain Barry Radford (1980), 'Zipcon Tangent', *Globe and Laurel: The Journal of the Royal Marines*, 89, 2, March/April, p. 72; Captain J. B. A. Bailey (1980), 'Operation Agila - Rhodesia 1979-80', *British Army Review: The House Journal of the Army*, 66, December, p. 24; Rice (1990), p. 116.
16 *British Ministry of Defence on the Commonwealth Monitoring Force*, pp. 152-3. There is some irony in the British withdrawing their monitors at the crucial moment and persuading the Rhodesians to do the job they considered too dangerous for their own forces.
17 *Report of the British Ministry of Defence on the Commonwealth Monitoring Force*, pp. 12-13, pp. 106-8, p. 113, p. 123.
18 Major-General J. H. B. Acland (1980), 'The Rhodesian Operation', *Guards Magazine*, Summer, pp. 48-9.
19 Major-General J. H. B. Acland (1980), 'The Rhodesian Operation', *Guards Magazine*, Summer, pp. 48-9.
20 *The Herald*, 'First step to a new army', 27 February 1980, p. 3.

21 Captain S. J. L. Roberts (1980), Irish Guards, 'Romeo, Romeo wherefore art thou Romeo ... Over', *Guards Magazine*, Summer, p. 79.
22 Lt. Colonel R. J. Rhoderick-Jones QRIH (1980), 'The Commonwealth Monitoring Force in Rhodesia - December 1979 to March 1980', *The Gauntlet*, p. 73.
23 *Report of the Ministry of Defence on the Commonwealth Monitoring Force*, p. 115.
24 Major-General J. H. B. Acland (1980), 'The Rhodesian Operation', *Guards Magazine*, Summer, p. 49.
25 Susan Rice (1990), pp. 171-2, citing Parker-Bowles' comments on Rhodesian attitudes to military integration during interview on 25 May 1989.
26 e.g. *The Herald*, 'Law and order up to police - Nkomo', 13 February 1980, p. 3.
27 Susan Rice (1990), p. 171, citing interview with Dabengwa on 30 November 1989.
28 Lt Colonel D. W. S. Moloney (1980), Commander of the New Zealand Contingent of the Commonwealth Monitoring Force, *Final Report of the New Zealand Contingent*, 19 May, p. 5.
29 Interview with Robin Renwick, British ambassador to the US, Washington DC, 17 June 1994.
30 e.g. see *Report of the British Ministry of Defence on the Commonwealth Monitoring Force*, p. 153.
31 *Report of the British Ministry of Defence on the Commonwealth Monitoring Force*, p. 135.
32 *Report of the British Ministry of Defence on the Commonwealth Monitoring Force*, p. 135.
33 *Report of the British Ministry of Defence on the Commonwealth Monitoring Force*, p. 134.
34 Rice (1990), p. 246.
35 Letter from David Moloney, head of New Zealand Contingent to Commonwealth Monitoring Force to former Ambassador to New Zealand, 1995 (exact date not available).
36 Interview with Ambassador Robin Renwick at the British Embassy, Washington DC, 17 June 1994.
37 Interview with Colin Gordon, British monitor in charge of training at Rathgar, England, August 1994.
38 Captain H. B. Margesson (1980), 'Rhodesia: Operation "Agila", December 1979-March 1980', *The Men of Harlech: The Journal of the Royal Regiment of Wales 24th/41st*, May, p. 26.

39 Captain Nick Beyts (1980), 'Assembly Point "Kilo" ', *Globe and Laurel*, 89, 2, March, p. 74.
40 Major J. N. Alford (1980), 'The Gunners in Rhodesia', *The Journal of the Royal Artillery*, 107, 2, September, p. 100.
41 Lt.-Col. Peter Treneer-Michell (1980), 'Rhodesia/Zimbabwe - Operation Agila 1979-80', *The Royal Green Jackets Chronicle*, p. 103.
42 Lt. H. G. Morgan-Grenville (1980), p. 55.
43 *Report of the British Ministry of Defence on the Commonwealth Monitoring Force*, pp. 72-3. Rhodesian police evidently took advantage of their powers in terms of the emergency rules, sometimes engaging in brutal interrogations and holding guerrillas beyond the thirty day limit.
44 Rice (1990), p. 58, citing interview with Ariston Chambati, a ZAPU member of the PF delegation at Lancaster House, on 4 December 1989.
45 Rice (1990), p. 102, citing interviews with Tungamirai and Chinenge on 5 December 1989 and 20 November 1989.
46 Rice (1990), p. 358. Acknowledging deficiencies in the process, the Commonwealth Observers' Group believed they were not sufficient to thwart free expression.
47 Rice (1990), p. 308, citing interview with John Nkomo on 7 December 1989.
48 Rice (1990), p. 308, citing interview with Msipa on 16 November 1989.
49 Joshua Nkomo (1984), *Nkomo: the Story of my Life*, London, Methuen, pp. 209-210.
50 Rice (1990), pp. 308-309, citing interview with Muzorewa on 12 December 1989.
51 Jeffrey Davidow (1984), *A Peace in Southern Africa. The Lancaster House Conference on Rhodesia, 1979*, Westview Press: Boulder; Stephen John Stedman (1991), *Peacemaking in Civil War. International Mediation in Zimbabwe, 1974-1980*, Lynne Rienner publishers: Boulder; Rt. Hon. Lord Soames (1980), 'From Rhodesia to Zimbabwe', *International Affairs*, 56, 3, Summer, pp. 405-419.
52 M. Tamarkin (1990), *The Making of Zimbabwe: Decolonization in Regional and International Politics*, Frank Cass and Co Ltd: London; Sir Anthony Parson (1988), 'From Southern Rhodesia to Zimbabwe: 1965-1988', *International Relations*, 9, November, pp. 353-361, makes the same point as Tamarkin without really analysing the Lancaster House negotiations.

53 e.g. Rice (1990); Verrier (1986), *The Road to Zimbabwe 1890-1980*, Jonathan Cape: London, takes a critical view of the Soames' interregnum arguing he was biased in favour of the Muzorewa government and its security forces and against ZANU and ZAPU. Verrier takes a much harsher view of British politicians, diplomats and administrators than Rice does, arguing that even during the negotiations the British conspired to ensure a Muzorewa electoral victory and the initial cease-fire plan was designed to ensure such an outcome.

54 Rice (1990); Verrier (1986); Henry Wiseman and Alistair M. Taylor (1981), *From Rhodesia to Zimbabwe. The Politics of Transition*, Pergamon Press: New York; John MacKinlay (1990), 'The Commonwealth Monitoring Force in Zimbabwe/Rhodesia 1979-80' in Thomas G. Weiss (ed) *Humanitarian Emergencies and Military Help in Africa*, Macmillan in association with the International Peace Academy, Chapter 3, pp. 38-60.

55 John MacKinlay (1990); Wiseman and Taylor (1981); Rice (1990), p. 355.

56 Ibbo Mandaza (1986), 'The Post-White Settler Colonial Situation' in Ibbo Mandaza (ed), *Zimbabwe. The Political Economy of Transition 1980-1986*, Codesria Book Series, Chapter 1; Mariyawanda Nzuwah (1980), 'Conflict Resolution in Zimbabwe: Superpower Determinants to the Peace Settlement', *Journal of Southern African Affairs*, 4, 4, October, pp. 389-400.

57 Davidow (1986), p. 97.
58 Davidow (1986), p. 97.
59 Davidow (1986), p. 98.
60 Davidow (1986), pp. 98-100.

6 Chad

Simon Massey and Roy May

> It [the Chadian Affair] glaringly reveals the growing discrepancy between what is said and what is believed, between the absolute 'will' and relative 'ability', between declared intentions and actual results.[1]
> (OAU Secretary-General, Edem Kodjo, 1981)

In 1967, Ali Mazrui declared that, '*Pax Africana* asserts that the peace of *Africa* is to be assured by the exertions of *Africans* themselves'.[2] This has remained an unfulfilled ambition. However, Mazrui now contends that the goal of 'African solutions to African conflicts' is currently being discussed with more conviction than at any time since the independence period.[3] Any future blueprint for pan-African security must take cognisance of the experience of the OAU's ineffectual peacekeeping operation in Chad in 1980 and also the, more ambitious, but equally futile Inter-African Force (IAF) which intervened in the Chadian civil war from November 1981 to June 1982. As far as the OAU's role is concerned, there have been analysts who, damning the enterprise with faint praise, deem the IAF's greatest success the simple fact that it managed to deploy. More trenchant criticism has focused on the patent shortcomings of the operation at both a theoretical and institutional level. It is hard to escape the damning observation that the IAF deployed, ostensibly in support of a legitimate regime recognised by the OAU, and withdrew as that government was being ousted by rebel forces.

The idea that Africa should take the lead in policing its own conflicts has been advocated since the early 1960s and the OAU's initiative in sending a peacekeeping force to Chad was widely applauded by interested commentators. The feeling within the OAU Secretariat was that the organisation had evolved sufficiently to move from a static period of norm creation, to a more dynamic era in which pronouncements on conflict resolution could be translated into action. This noble aspiration proved premature. The timing was not auspicious. With the Cold War entering end game, the prospect of an all-African force preserving its absolute autonomy was unrealistic. As the planned intervention left the committee room for the operations room, the crippling paucity of funds and logistical resources became apparent. As the OAU succumbed to the inevitability of bilateral *extra*-continental funding for the troop-contributing states, so the likelihood of tacit conditionality increased. At a more fundamental level, the formation of the IAF heralded a shift away from the basic tenets of OAU doctrine - absolute territorial integrity coupled with non-interference in the internal affairs of member states. The attempt to realise an intervention for which there was no basis in OAU philosophy or ethos, resulted in the IAF following a schizoid mandate whose complexion altered as the operation progressed.

The background to civil war

The narrative of Chad's post-independence history has become monotonous through repetition. A backdrop of unceasing civil strife has been interspersed with cyclical external interventions. Reasons for the conflict overlap in a complex web of ethnic, religious, economic and political motivation.

On an elemental level, ill-will between the 'Goranes' Muslim ethnic groups, especially the Toubou, of northern Chad and the Christian Sara people of the south was exacerbated and entrenched by a negligent colonial administration. By 1965, President François Tombalbaye had exploited the advantages bequeathed to him by the French to consolidate oppressive Christian Sara dominance. In response to growing resentment a rebellion coalesced behind FROLINAT (*Front de Libération Nationale de Tchad*). A tripartite offensive in the northern BET (Borkou, Ennedi, Tibesti) provinces was launched. Even at this early stage, the encroachment by neighbouring and external states into the conflict that would inhibit the OAU's peacekeeping effort was already apparent. Of FROLINAT's original three battalions, the *Forces Armées du Nord* had Libyan support, whilst the *Forces Armées Occidentales* (later known as the *Mouvement Populaire pour la Libération du Tchad*) had the implicit support of Nigeria. For his part, Tombalbaye increasingly relied on French *forces d'intervention* (1968, 1969-1972) to guard his regime.

From 1968 onwards, Chad came to epitomise a collapsed African state. To paraphrase Jackson and Rosberg, Chad's juridical cart was now before its empirical horse.[4] In April 1975 Tombalbaye was assassinated in a *coup d'état* by a man whom he had formally incarcerated, General Félix Malloum. In view of FROLINAT's *de facto* jurisdiction over much of the country, the new administration (the *Conseil Supérieure Militaire*) pursued a policy of national reconciliation. However, by this juncture the CSM was faced by a fragmenting FROLINAT. The movement was ideologically multi-faceted - in Buijtenhuijs' terms more à la carte than à plat unique.[5] Moreover, the sociology of the conflict had always extended beyond the crude dimensions of a North\South or Christian\Muslim dichotomy. Around a hundred distinct language groups, frequently split into several sub-groups, exist amongst a population of only 5 million people.[6] Furthermore, *intra*-group relations, especially in the bellicose north, were highly prone to segmentation. The factionalism of the civil war underscored this inclination to find allies amongst neighbouring sub-groups, rather than amongst an inclusive ethnic, religious or linguistic group.[7] In this respect the Chadian conflict fits the 'warlord model' with its stress on, 'regional centres of power based on personalised rule and military force, and the consequent prevalence of a politics of conflict and war'.[8]

The internal pressures towards factionalism were intensified by Tombalbaye's death. In the absence of an integrating ideology, FROLINAT had depended on the battle against the oppressive regime for its cohesion. The period between 1976 and 1978 saw increased international concern over Libya's expansion from bases in the contested Aouzou Strip in northern Chad. Despite substantial logistical aid for the Chadian government, the essential ineptitude of the national army resulted in the deployment of French troops in 1978. At the same time, Qadafi's continued incursion in the north and his meddling in factional politics led to a pivotal schism within FROLINAT. Anti-Libyan elements under Hissène Habré, retaining the name *Forces Armées du Nord*, joined a short-lived coalition government with Malloum's CSM under a 'fundamental charter'. The remaining majority of FAN under Goukouni Oueddei, having regrouped as the *Forces Armées Populaires*, maintained a strong territorial and military position. As the Habré-Malloum coalition began to collapse, a process of recurring disintegration occurred. The result was a proliferation of factions of which two proved to be especially significant - the remnants of the national army and *Gendarmerie* regrouped as the *Forces Armées Tchadiennes* under Colonel Wadal Kamagoué in the south and Ahmet Acyl's *Forces d'Actions Communes*, or New Vulcan Army, in the north and centre of the country. Together with FAN and FAP, these would be the players whose prevarications and shifting alliances would frustrate the OAU's efforts at mediation in the coming years.

Regional and sub-regional mediation

In keeping with the strict interdiction on interference in the internal affairs of member states, the OAU remained passive in the face of the continual civil conflict between 1965 and 1977. The OAU first approached the issue, at Malloum's invitation, prior to the OAU summit meeting in Libreville in July 1977. The request for mediation was restricted to the question of Libya's continued occupation of the Aouzou strip in northern Chad. This area between Chad and Libya had been occupied by Qadafi's troops since 1972. Libya's claim was based on the unratified Laval-Mussolini Accords of 1935, and a secret agreement between Tombalbaye and Qadafi by which the Chadian President hoped to trade territory in return for a Libyan undertaking to withdraw his support for FROLINAT. In addressing the Aouzou Strip dispute, the OAU's response was sincere, but ineffectual. A six member *ad hoc* committee managed to negotiate what was to become a series of cease-fires that seemed impressive on paper, but were ignored in the field. Despite a specific Charter commitment to seek the peaceful settlement of disputes (albeit with an emphasis on *inter*-state conflict rather than civil war), the OAU's resources to achieve this aim remained meagre. The Commission for the Conciliation, Mediation and Arbitration created in 1963 was moribund, and the Defence Commission met rarely and had never intervened in a dispute. The OAU relied on *ad hoc* committees and the initiatives of statesmen and OAU officials to defuse conflicts. Prior to 1977, the Presidents of Libya, Sudan and Nigeria had offered their services as peace emissaries to Chad. In each case their credentials as *bona fide* honest brokers in the conflict were intrinsically limited.

In the event, inhibited by its own Charter and confined by the decrepitude of its conflict resolution mechanisms, the OAU resorted to offering ancillary support to the diplomatic efforts of the, partial but powerful, regional hegemon - Nigeria. In response to an appeal from the Sudanese, the Nigerians called for a meeting of representatives from all warring factions at Kano on 11 March 1979. Only four attended: Goukouni's FAP, Habré's FAN, Kamagoué's FAT and the Nigerian-sponsored MPLT. Kano I established a transitional government of national unity (GUNT) that was to prepare for the election of a coalition government that reflected the factional composition of the country. The Accords were to be monitored by an independent commission chaired by

Nigeria, whilst the cease-fire, and the demilitarised zone around N'Djaména, was to be secured by replacing the French garrison with a neutral force comprising of Nigerian troops. Only the Nigerian deployment materialised. This accomplished little. Some commentators commended Nigeria's initiative as a timely and necessary response to an increasingly violent conflict with important humanitarian and regional security dimensions. However, most of the players in the conflict, including France, treated the Nigerian approach with extreme scepticism. Indeed, Nigeria's short-lived experience in N'Djaména proved to be a portent of the OAU's future peacekeeping efforts in Chad. Lacking any real mandate, other than vague plans to police the cease-fire, the Nigerian troops, both underfunded and undermanned, responded in a petty, heavy-handed fashion to the provocations of the factions in the capital. When Nigeria accepted a request to withdraw its troops in June 1979, N'Djaména remained highly militarised and ready for war.

Nigeria was learning that it would take more than troops - or more troops - to unravel Chad's factional quagmire. Further meetings at Kano in April and Lagos in May sought to expand the basis of negotiations by including five factions absent from the March talks. However, Nigeria became increasingly exasperated at efforts by Habré and Goukouni from within the GUNT to entrench their own positions at the expense of other factions, especially those of Acyl and Kamagoué, by ignoring the wider terms of the Kano I agreement. At this point the OAU decided to play a more direct part in the negotiation process. Nigeria's call for a punitive economic boycott against land-locked Chad was taken up by the OAU at the summit meeting in Monrovia in July 1979. In keeping with its more robust stance, the OAU denounced the current composition of the GUNT as unrepresentative and denied its representative a seat at the summit. The conference supported the continuation of the Lagos process, whilst envisaging a wider role for Secretary-General Edem Kodjo and, for the first time, discussing funding for a potential peacekeeping force under the auspices of the OAU.

The first OAU intervention

Lagos II realised comprehensive participation by all major factions (including FAN, FAP, FAT and FAC) and the neighbouring states of Benin, Congo, Senegal and Liberia. A major feature of the conference was a shift in the onus for instigating mediation towards the OAU. For Nolutshungu, this effort, 'to minimize the element of bilateral conflict between Nigeria and Chad,'⁹ resulted in an obfuscation of where responsibility for mediation lay. In an effort to 'Africanise' or 'de-Gallicise'¹⁰ the conflict, the OAU chose to place the abstraction of African unity over the pragmatic reality of Nigeria's unique position as the natural instrument for intervention in the region. Otherwise, much of the substance of the agreement mirrored the accords of Kano I. A significant modification was the supercession of Nigeria by the OAU as the fulcrum for the independent monitoring of the cease-fire and as the organising body for a neutral force. In contrast to the unilateral intervention by the Nigerians, the new Force would comprise troops from states that were non-contiguous with Chad - Guinea, Benin, and Congo. The GUNT was to be reconstituted with Goukouni as President, Kamagoué as Vice-President, Habré as Minister of Defence and Acyl as Minister of Foreign Affairs. However, these were to prove essentially fictitious positions in a government which existed in name only. Further, the agreement called for those French troops still in Chad to withdraw. However, events on the ground emphasised the gulf between rhetoric and reality. The goodwill upon which Lagos II depended was absent. The intended demilitarisation of N'Djaména secured only token compliance from the factions. Moreover, despite the commencement of the French withdrawal, the construction of the replacement all-African Force was becoming a painfully slow process. Henceforth, the impotence of the OAU would loom larger in the designs of the factions than its exhortations to make peace, or its stated support for the transitional government. For the GUNT, as well as for FAN, the OAU would be seen as just another external actor amongst many others that might be played according to expedience.

Although deriving its mandate from Lagos II, rather than directly from the OAU, the troops that eventually arrived in January 1980 were recognised as the OAU Neutral Force. The obstacles were the same as those facing the Nigerians a year before, writ large. Only the Congolese detachment of 550 men deployed. Finance, supposedly provided through a special OAU fund collected from all member states, amounted to less than $250,000. When Algeria was not recompensed by the OAU for airlifting the Congolese to N'Djaména, they invoiced Brazzaville.¹¹ Once more, the Force on the ground faced immense problems of logistics and manpower. A working command structure was never properly established. One element of the monitoring commission, the GUNT, was irreconcilably split and another, Ethiopian Force Commander Major Gebre-Egziabher Dawit, was absent during most of the operation. Most significantly, the inadequate Force was asked to fulfil a mandate that required them to uphold the cease-fire, keep the roads open for civilian traffic, disarm the population, restore order and bring the factions together into an integrated national army.[12] Following the ignominious evacuation of the Force on 26 March 1980, Secretary-General Kodjo travelled to N'Djaména to conduct a secret post-mortem. His report stressed the negative impact of the absence of Beninoise and Guinean contingents. However, the exasperated tone of the document only serves to stress the OAU's institutional and logistical inadequacies in the face of rapidly degenerating circumstances. Whilst acknowledging the OAU's culpability in not pre-arranging a working budget for the operation, Kodjo placed most of the blame on the failure of the warring factions within the GUNT to fulfil the conditions of Lagos II. Kodjo's reasoning tended to be circuitous. The Congolese troops were unwilling to leave barracks in order to help with the demilitarisation of N'Djaména without the support of Benin and Guinea's forces. These were disinclined to deploy whilst the capital remained militarised. N'Djaména remained militarised since Habré's Ministry of Defence refused to convene the requisite committee charged with demilitarisation.[13] For their part, the Congolese felt stung to react to the withering criticism of the Force's performance. Habré had accommodated the Force in deplorable conditions without running water or sanitation. They suffered casualties and lost a man in cross-fire.[14] The Congolese delegate at the UN denounced the 'slanderous campaign' of 'hate-filled and defamatory articles' by the West's 'blinkered press'.[15] In the light of their unrewarding and unappreciated exertions, the decision of Congo (as well as other small country troop-contributors - Benin, Togo and Guinea) to withdraw from future interventions was understandable.

The second OAU intervention

For the rest of 1980 the OAU always seemed to be a step behind events on the ground or, in Massaquoi's words, 'forced to feebly follow the changing guards, and attempt to pick up the pieces afterwards'.[16] Heavy fighting continued in the capital and the centre of the country between FAN and the GUNT, as well as between elements in the GUNT and Acyl's Libyan-backed FAC. The OAU Secretary-General's assessment was bleak and forthright: 'Le Tchad est en passe d'être détruit et les parties parviendront à cette fin plutôt triste si elles continuent d'agir commes elles le font'.[17] General Gnassingbe Eyadéma convened two meetings of the *ad hoc* committee in Lomé during October and November which called for the abortive Lagos II Neutral Force (Guinea, Benin and

Congo), plus Togo, to be redeployed in full. However, ironically, it was the successful Libyan incursion into Chad in late 1980 in response to a request from Goukouni for support against Habré's FAN, and the joint communiqué declaring a potential 'merger' between Chad and Libya, that galvanised the OAU into firmer action and created the strategic conditions for the IAF to deploy.[18] Still more important, Qadafi's acceptance of Goukouni's demand for Libya's withdrawal in October 1981 left the OAU as the last, best repository of trust amongst the greatest number of players in the conflict. If the financial and logistical obstacles could be surmounted, the geopolitical circumstances were conducive to another OAU intervention.

A further meeting of the *ad hoc* committee in Lomé in January 1981, endorsed by the OAU summit in Nairobi in June, had nominated Benin, Congo, Guinea and Togo as countries to supply manpower for the IAF. However, it became clear that if the Lagos II condition - that troop-supplying states should not border Chad - was maintained, then the Force would never deploy. All the potential contributors were wholly ill-equipped in terms of personnel, logistics, finance and experience. Promises of future financial support were patently illusory given the state of the OAU's resources and were belied by the experience of the first OAU Force in 1980. Even the initial cost of deployment was beyond the capacity of these countries. Thus, by the time of the formal establishment of the IAF in Paris on 14 November, the Lagos stipulation on non-contiguity had been abandoned. Influence within the operation shifted from the small states to US-sponsored Zaire (now the Democratic Republic of Congo), French-sponsored Senegal and Chad's neighbouring giant, Nigeria. A parallel meeting in Lagos of foreign ministers from the proposed troop-contributing states, chaired by Kenya, set a modest target of 5,000 troops with 2,000 men coming from Nigeria and 600 men from each of Benin, Guinea, Togo, Zaire and Senegal.

The usurpation of the Force by the major regional players and their sponsors left few concrete incentives, beyond altruistic considerations, for the small states to further tax their exchequers. Togo had long been assumed to harbour pro-FAN sympathies. Certainly, Habré's second-in-command, and future Foreign Minister, Idriss Miskine, was fulsome in his praise for the 'sympathy expressed towards our cause...especially by the founding President of the Togolese People's Assembly'.[19] For the remaining radical states, Benin and Guinea, the choice of Paris as venue for the signing of the Memorandum of Agreement intimated an unsettling neo-colonial dimension to the operation. Sekou Touré's characteristically robust advocacy of subsidiarity within regional conflict management, delivered to the UN General Assembly in October, had stressed the necessity for the putative IAF to be strictly neutral, whilst condemning the presence of non-African forces on the continent.[20] Thus, notwithstanding heavy financial constraints, unease about the 'French Factor' added another compelling reason for Benin and Guinea to rescind their offers of troops.[21]

The final composition of the Force was determined at the Kinshasa meeting on 27 November. The size of the IAF had contracted to 3,275 troops, out of which 2,000 were Nigerian. Nigeria supplied a Force Commander with experience in UN peacekeeping operations, Major General Geoffrey Ejiga. The chief of staff was to be Zairean, whilst Senegal was to control the air detachment and intelligence. At the top of the command structure on the ground was the OAU's special representative Major Gebre-Egziabher Dawit of Ethiopia. Finally, Kenya would lead an observer group whose other members were to be Algeria, Gabon, Guinea-Bissau and Zambia.

Issues of sovereignty and intervention

The right to national sovereignty and the concomitant principle of non-interference in the internal affairs of another sovereign state were twin issues lodged in the back of the minds of those involved in the Chadian peace process. Yet, these most sacred of OAU tenets were rarely deliberated during the crisis and then only in terms of, 'opaque distinctions between "internal" and "external" [sovereignty], "intervention" and "disinterested mediation"'.[22] This studied indifference gives testament not only to an acceptance that the *locus* of Chadian sovereignty was uncertain, but to a determination on the part of the Secretariat and the membership to avoid the dilemma in this case. Thus, Chad became the arena for OAU innovation. In a reversal of roles, the UN served as a forum during the crisis, whilst the OAU sought to free itself from its juridical fetters and expand its political capacity as an instrumental player in the conflict.

In view of the entrenched doctrine of non-interference, many commentators felt that the Chadian intervention's most astonishing feature was that it happened at all. The debate which informed the construction of the OAU had polarised political opinion amongst Africa's emerging leaders. National sovereignty lay at its core. By the time of the OAU's inaugural summit at Addis Ababa on 22 May, 1963, conflict generated during the transition to independence, notably in Algeria and Congo-Leopoldville, had supplied both the radicals of the Casablanca group and the conservative Monrovia bloc with substance for their respective images of Africa's future. The question was whether Africa would acquiesce to the inviolability of the Berlin Conference boundaries or concertina history by circumventing the imposition of the Westphalian paradigm on the continent and accepting the intrinsic limitations to sovereignty of a *supra-national* authority? Fear that a redrawing of boundaries along ethnic lines could lead to secessionist and irredentist chaos, together with an impulse to legitimise states that were not coterminous with their many nations proved potent stimuli. The conservatives triumphed. African unity was relegated from a putative, concrete institutional entity to a mere aspiration.

The template for future pan-African discourse was cast by Haile Salassie's welcoming speech at Addis Ababa. Pragmatism and caution underscored the essence of the address, whilst the radical camp was mollified by empty rhetoric. Nkrumah was isolated. The grand pan-African project - 'political union based on defence, Foreign Affairs and Diplomacy...a Common Citizenship, an African Currency, an African Monetary Zone, an African Central Bank...a Common Defence System with an African High Command'[23] - was rejected. Unity was reduced to co-operation and action was replaced by consultation. The compromise earned the OAU condemnation from both sides of the ideological divide. A pan-African response to *intra*-African crises was derided by conservatives such as Félix Houphouet-Boigny as manifestly chimerical. Amongst the radicals the new organisation was, 'a toothless, clawless lion in a decorated cage'.[24]

Thus, from a political standpoint, the OAU was hamstrung as an effective regional institution for conflict management and resolution from the onset. The exercise in self-emasculation was given standing in international law through Article III of the Charter of the OAU[25] and subsequent resolutions of the organisation's Assembly of Heads of State and Government. The preamble to AHG/Res.16(1) in accepting that, 'the borders of African states on independence constituted a *tangible reality*',[26] implicitly adopted the Roman Law concept of *uti possidetis juris*. This doctrine, which had underpinned state formation in Latin America, aimed to preclude a welter of post-independence boundary disputes. AHG/Res.16(1) reinforced article 3 of the Charter in that it emphasised the sovereign equality of member states, non-interference in the internal affairs of other member states and respect for the territorial integrity of states.

Did the draughtsmen of the OAU Charter designedly frame a document with less scope for robust conflict resolution than its immediate predecessor, the UN Charter? One of their number, T.O. Elias, has asserted that whilst the Charter sought to prevent interference by member states in other member states' affairs during a period of state formation, there was no intention to limit the range of measures open to the OAU in addressing conflict.[27] The relative competence of the OAU and the UN in conflict management was coloured by Article 52(2) of the UN Charter, which requires states to use regional conflict mechanisms before reference to the Security Council.[28] Having asserted its primacy amongst African regional organisations for conflict management,[29] the OAU jealously guarded the right to, 'try Africa first'. Nonetheless, the OAU Charter makes no mention of either consensual deployment of armed forces in order to implement a truce agreement along the lines envisaged by Chapter VI of the UN Charter or an uninvited armed intervention in order to restore and enforce a peace as sanctioned by Chapter VII of the UN Charter. Explicit proposals for conflict resolution modalities concentrated on peacemaking through diplomacy. Yet, the Commission of Mediation, Conciliation and Arbitration instituted by Article XIX never operated in a dispute between states, still less in, more contentious, *intra*-state conflicts. In response to these institutional flaws, OAU conflict management practice was forced to develop within the organisation, rather than by the organisation. In the years up to the escalation of the Chadian civil war in 1979, conflict management practice was typified by mediation undertaken by heads of state acting collectively, *ad hoc* committees in which individual initiatives were subject to ratification by the whole committee and conference diplomacy.[30]

In keeping with the assumed intent of Article III, informal mediation was generally restricted to *inter*-state conflict and boundary disputes. So, why did events in Chad provoke an effective sea change in OAU methodology and a redefinition of principles? Former UN Secretary-General, Boutros Boutros-Ghali, has warned that ethnic, secessionist conflict and concomitant state fragmentation present the most immediate dangers to security in Africa.[31] Ethnic conflict can spread within a state and also directly, or by contagion, into neighbouring states and, potentially, into regional conflict. However, the OAU had assiduously avoided any interference in the long-running civil wars in Burundi and Sudan, or the secessionist struggle in Ethiopia.[32] In lieu of positive grounds, the general absence of serious objections by the member states, and the temporary unity created by the Qadafi-factor, might be advanced as motives for the intervention. Certainly, from the OAU Secretariat's standpoint, there was a sense that Chad was placing the organisation's limitations in stark perspective. Secretary-General Kodjo recognised that its credibility was seriously threatened. As he told the assembled Heads of State - '[Chad] dictates a change of conception of our machinery, a renovation of principles and action'.[33]

During the 1970s, support for an African defence force had shifted away from the radical camp towards a clutch of moderate, Francophone states such as Ivory Coast, Senegal, Zaire and Gabon.[34] The deployment of the IAF in Chad had a precursor in the five nation Force that replaced French and Belgian troops in southern Zaire after Shaba II. Although, in view of the conspicuous support of France and Belgium,[35] the Shaba Force was formed outside the aegis of the OAU, it secured tacit support from the General Secretariat. Whilst the relative success of this Force served to convince sceptics that an *inter*-African Force was viable, the operation exposed the negative political and logistical factors that would undermine the Chad intervention.

Outside the conservative Francophone states, there existed a strong feeling that opportunities for neo-colonial interventions should be averted. A key proponent of this policy was Nigeria. The rhetoric was idealistic and uplifting - African solutions to African problems.[36] African peacekeepers should intervene in internal conflicts in order to deter vulnerable states from being driven, in Olesegun Obasanjo's words, 'into the laps of extra-African powers for defence and security'.[37] Clearly, Nigeria was being deliberately disingenuous. Their objective was as much to *replace* French influence in the region as to *check* it. Nonetheless, the anti-colonial rhetoric was sufficient to elicit the potential participation of radical states such as Congo, Benin and Guinea in the IAF. For their part, conservative Francophone states were typically receptive to the advances of the new Mitterrand government, which they received first hand at the Franco-African summit held in Paris in November 1981.

Consequently, self-interested endorsement averted any problems of legitimacy that might have arisen for the OAU interventions in Chad. In the case of the IAF, although it was acting within a legal vacuum, at least the OAU could point to a Memorandum of Agreement between the GUNT and Chairman Moi and Secretary-General Kodjo.[38] Any relief that the potentially vexed issue of 'sovereignty' had been avoided was soon dissipated. The most critical failing of the intervention would be contradictory interpretation of the IAF's mandate. If the GUNT represented the sovereign government of Chad, and, in signing the Memorandum of Agreement with him, the OAU implicitly supported Goukouni, what was the role of the IAF in the conflict?

The mandate

> Any intervention force must have a realistic mandate, clear goals, a firm strategy and a timescale for withdrawal.[39]

So says a senior British official referring to a proposed intervention force for the crisis in the Great Lakes region in 1996. The advice was equally as pertinent in November 1981. The document signed by the GUNT and the OAU in Paris on 14 November established the conditions under which the IAF was supposed to operate. The following meeting in Nairobi offered the chance to rectify some of the principal ambiguities in the Paris document. It didn't. The vital sections are contained in Paragraph 3 of OAU Resolution AHG/Res 102;103 (XVIII), variously known as an 'Agreement between the GUNT and the OAU regarding the status of the peacekeeping force in Chad' and the 'Nairobi Accords'. It stated:

a) The OAU, 'reaffirms its support to the GUNT and requests that all member States of the OAU support this Government in its efforts to maintain peace and security in the country and abstain from interfering in the internal affairs of the country'.

b) The peacekeeping force 'will ensure the defence and security of the country whist awaiting the integration of Government Forces'.

c) 'The OAU decides to provide the GUNT with financial and material means to enable it to train quickly a National Integrated Army for the gradual replacement of foreign troops in their national territory.'[40]

It appeared that the OAU aspired to achieve two conflicting goals by simultaneously endorsing the government and remaining neutral in the conflict. Whilst the underlying perspective of the mandate assumes that the IAF would act as a 'standard' Chapter VI peacekeeping force, there are also shades of Chapter VII compulsion. Thus, the mandate begged two questions. Would the OAU support the GUNT as the sole responsible authority in Chad? If so, to what extent would the IAF act to uphold that authority?

During the period covered by the Paris and Nairobi negotiations and the IAF's deployment there was an assumption, based on the authoritative Lagos II Accords, that the GUNT constituted the legitimate government of Chad. The prime catalyst for the construction of the IAF had been a shared objective amongst the OAU members to see Libya out of Chad.

Goukouni (and Qadafi) obliged. In return there was an expectation that OAU recognition of the GUNT would become entrenched and irrevocable. Goukouni admitted frankly, 'In view of the attitude of African brothers and due to extra-African pressure, we were forced to demand the withdrawal of Libyan forces from our soil, to enable those countries which are fearful about Chad because of the presence of Libyan forces to have confidence in us'.[41] Any such confidence proved short-lived. The messages from the OAU and the IAF were confused. Early in the operation, the OAU representative, Major Dawit, had foreshortened the bounds of IAF support for the GUNT in discounting a repetition of the UN experience in the Congo, which he perceived as being a collaboration by an international organisation with a government to crush a rebellion.[42] Conversely, communiqués from Force Commander Ejiga struck a more muscular note. As late as February 1982, he spoke of, 'crushing any attempt at infiltration by FAN into the zones occupied by his forces'.[43]

This led to the question of engagement. The Nairobi Accords required all member states (including those in the IAF) to support the GUNT in its efforts 'to maintain peace and security'. This aim endured even when individual states sought to emphasise their even-handedness. Senegal's Abdou Diouf stated that the Force was not there to, 'wage war against any of Chad's factions, but to restore peace and maintain security there'. In response, *West Africa* magazine posed a rhetorical question. If the GUNT was the repository for the rule of law, and the IAF was bound to support the GUNT, how do the peacekeepers react to an attack on the legal authority?[44] The nuances between offensive and defensive action in a conflictual cauldron such as Chad were slight and precarious. Even so, as late as December, the upper echelons of the OAU in Addis Ababa were apparently willing to countenance a compromise scheme in which IAF units would substitute for GUNT forces in non-combat roles, thereby freeing government troops for front-line action.[45] This fell short of Goukouni's expectations - 'We do not need troops massing here increasing our difficulties, if they are not going to ensure the defence and security of the country...they should fight, otherwise their presence makes no sense'.[46]

It is now accepted that there must be an unambiguous appreciation by all involved in a conflict as to what type of peacekeeping is being undertaken. Clearly, this certitude was lacking in Chad. In the wake of the IAF's withdrawal, the OAU stressed that they had always conceived of the intervention as being, in essence, more political than military. The retrospective definition of the IAF unequivocally emphasised its function as a peacekeeping force based on the UN Chapter VI model as deployed in

Cyprus and the Lebanon. An accepted definition of 'peacekeeping' stipulates, 'the stationing of neutral, lightly armed troops as an interposition force following a cease-fire to separate combatants and promote an environment suitable for conflict resolution'.[47] The cease-fire element of such an operation was absent in Chad. A pre-requisite for the legitimisation of peacekeeping, as opposed to peace-enforcement, interventions is the notion of consent based on a desire by the major warring parties for peace. The IAF deployed without the express agreement of a major player in Habré. Even Goukouni's consent was grudging. For FAN's part, Idriss Miskine outlined the ground rules, with just a hint of menace, at the start of the operation - 'We belong to the OAU. We recognise its judicial and moral role. We expect the force will stay strictly neutral. But we will fight it if we are attacked.'[48] Without a truce to uphold, the IAF perforce adopted the role of *force d'interposition*. The rigidity of such a buffer depends on the availability of manpower and logistics, as well as political will on the part of its sponsors. However, it does not preclude a robust response if any party threatens a mandate to 'maintain peace and security'. Indeed, an intervention force is unlikely to retain respect and legitimacy, unless it shows itself willing to employ the judicious use of force at key moments during the deployment. Whilst Goukouni was naive in expecting the IAF to act as a strident 'peace-enforcement' force, there was some justification in the accusation that the IAF neglected its mandate.

For the GUNT, the meeting of the OAU Standing Committee on Chad (Benin, Cameroon, Congo, Guinea, Libya, Niger, Republic of Central Africa, Sierra Leone, Senegal, Sudan, Chad and Togo - plus troop or observer-contributors Nigeria, Zaire, Algeria, Gabon, Guinea-Bissau and Zambia) in Nairobi on 11 February 1982 shattered any vestigial illusion that the IAF might defend the government. Until that date the most charitable interpretation of the OAU's strategy was impotent procrastination. Resolution AHG/Cttee/Chad/Res.1(III) cleared any ambiguity by stating - 'the Inter-African Force is a neutral force whose role is to maintain peace and ensure the formation of an integrated Chadian Army without favouring any political faction whatsoever'. The Resolution went on to call for a series of wholly unattainable political objectives - a cease-fire by midnight 28 February, national reconstruction talks in March, the drafting of a new constitution and elections for May. It also set the deadline for the withdrawal of the IAF at 30 June 1982. The Standing Committees' political demands took the operation's abrogation of the sacrosanct principle of non-interference in the internal affairs of a member state a step further. The call for elections was egregiously hypocritical coming from a committee whose members exercised precious little democratic process themselves. It was also specious. Calls for an instant democratic solution to a profoundly undemocratic fratricidal conflict that had endured for thirteen years went beyond wishful thinking. The response of the major protagonists was predictable. Goukouni quit Nairobi describing the meeting as an 'absurd scenario', and denouncing the OAU's treachery.[49] For his part, Habré saw the *volte-face* as, 'an enormous victory for the Chadian people and the OAU'[50] (for which read 'for FAN').

The inadequacy of *inter*-African and *extra*-African funding for the IAF was cited as the prime reason for the curtailment of the operation. However, there were clear signs that many members of the *ad hoc* committee, the OAU Secretariat, the field commanders and governments of troop-contributing states and their foreign sponsors had recognised that they had underestimated Habré and overestimated Goukouni.[51] In contrast to Goukouni's increasingly ineffectual histrionics, Habré's forces had consolidated their positions in the north and east, whilst adopting the tone of a government-in-waiting. Regardless of its rationale, the committee's decision had a devastating effect on Goukouni's legitimacy as President. With the GUNT relegated to the position of a faction in the conflict, there was a rapid deconstruction of the coalition. Recognising a *fait accompli*, and moving to reposition in anticipation of a realignment of forces in the country, Kamagoué and Acyl declared their forces neutral. By the end of May only Goukouni's FAP was left to defend N'Djaména from FAN. However, the capital was spared further destruction with the rout of Goukouni's troops at Massaguet. Habré took N'Djaména in less than three hours on 7 June.

The Standing Committee's claims to have reemphasised the political dimension of the peace process rewrote the operation's history. There had always been a military aspect to the Force's deployment. FAN had only been prevented from taking the capital through the intervention of Libya. Prior to the OAU intervention, Ahmed Acyl had pointed out acerbically, 'Si l'armée libyenne se retirait, nous ne tiendrions pas dix jours ici. Ce n'était pas nos combattants qui avaient chassé Hissein Habré de N'Djaména'.[52] In Libya's absence, the deployment of the IAF clearly recognised the need for the balance of military strength within Chad to be redressed if the status quo was to be maintained. Diplomatic initiatives could have been made whilst Libyan troops maintained stability. Few outside the GUNT expected the IAF to take the battle to FAN. However, the total ineffectualness of the Force, far from advancing a political solution, doomed the GUNT to defeat. The equation between 'force' and 'consent' was wrong. The IAF, with negligible capacity for engagement and a lack of political will, needed a high level of consent from all combatants if a traditional peacekeeping methodology was to prove viable. It was asking for miracles for the actual scenario - low consent and low capacity for force - to prove anything other than unsustainable.

It is hypothetical, but instructive, to speculate how the IAF would have acted had it had a greater military capacity? In the face of adverse criticism of the IAF, Ejiga, together with many of the Nigerian commanders sounded a wounded note in his epitaph for the operation. Most blame was placed on the lack of funds and leadership from the OAU. However, Ejiga claimed that the IAF had fulfilled the limited aims of the mandate to 'pacify, make appeals and persuade'. As Nolutshungu indicates, these limitations were not stressed at the stage when the GUNT was being asked to accept an OAU force in place of the Libyans. Having, for once, come off the fence and intervened in the internal affairs of a member state, did the OAU have the moral right, when the intractability of the operation became apparent, to insist on its 'neutrality'? Indeed, the Force Commander apparently perceived the mandate as not entirely passive - 'the force also had the mandate to put an end to hostilities and to force the parties in conflict to confine themselves to their respective positions to permit negotiations, if the OAU resolutions had been accepted by the parties in their entirety'.[53] This implies that the ambiguities in the mandate would have been less of a problem in either the unlikely event that the two major factions had been more open to negotiation, or the IAF had been properly funded, manned and armed.

External influences

Even the UN, an international organisation well versed in the vagaries of intervention, falls prey to pressure from external agencies. The OAU was (and still is) immature and untutored in peacekeeping operations. As an international body, what the OAU said in Addis Ababa or in any of the succession of conferences about the Chad crisis was divorced both from the dynamics of the conflict and their chosen modality for its resolution - the IAF.

The OAU's lack of salience or administrative wherewithal left it as just another actor in its own operation. The extra-continental protagonists, notably France and the US, treated the OAU as a necessary evil, rather than as the instigator of the mission. Likewise, regional actors, including members of the IAF worked to their own agenda. The layers of confusion and intrigue multiplied as the OAU acted as a conduit for self-interested international political realism played out on the Chadian stage.

a) France

Chad's size and vulnerability mark it as emblematic of the relationship which exists between France and its former African colonies. France in Africa has always been a *quid pro quo*. As May and Charlton assert - 'Both the extensiveness and the intensity of the ties of "sentiment" and "interest" - cultural, economic, strategic and geopolitical - that continue to tie France to Africa ensure that the concept of dependence increasingly cuts two ways'.[54] By 1979, French economic interest in Chad was subordinate to French prestige. France perceived Africa as the cornerstone of its claim to be a great power. For Nolutshungu, 'a kind of domino theory seemed to apply'.[55] If France could not preserve leverage in one state, then its credibility in the others would be diminished.

France's policy in Chad following the fall of Tombalbaye has been described as weak and vacillating. Indeed, any French Legionnaire based in N'Djaména would have been well advised to reserve his copy of *Le Monde* to see which faction he might be fighting next week. However, France had always pursued a cautious policy in Chad. Whilst it did not create the internecine factionalism that pervades the country, it was partially culpable for entrenching existing antagonisms. Paris was ever wary of arbitrating in quarrels between clans and their perfidious leaders or attempting to exert control beyond the southern *Tchad utile* and the garrison towns. This policy survived Chad's independence. The majority of the country escaped the pro-consul-like tendencies of the Elysée Palace's 'Monsieur Afrique', Jacques Foccart. The concern was not really about who ruled in N'Djaména, but how to prevent the sort of external interference that Libya was exercising? To that extent, armed intervention was a blunt weapon which France had not hesitated to use. In 1981 circumstances dictated otherwise. The transition from a Gaullist to a Socialist administration occupied minds at the *Quai d'Orsay*. In office, Mitterrand was unwilling to launch his government's African policy in such precarious conditions. His election manifesto, *Projet Socialiste*, had promised an end to French militarism in Africa and specifically called for the 'indépendance du Tchad'.[56] Moreover, whilst previous *forces d'intervention* had been invited to intercede, an uninvited intervention would have put France outside international law.[57] A further complication was the strong economic link - oil and arms - between France and Libya. French troops were already disengaging following the Lagos II Accords.

In the absence of its accustomed military presence, the prospect of an OAU-sponsored intervention, potentially open to manipulation, offered a risk-free opportunity to maintain an interest in events. However, the policy was not without its detractors amongst French officers in Chad and the conservative press. In the midst of the IAF negotiations, Chad-based agents of the SDECE (Documentation and Counter-espionage Service) narrowly failed to draw France into a full scale attack on Libya by fabricating a *coup d'état* in N'Djaména and a supportive reinvasion by the departing Libyans.[58]

The often delicate relationship between Nigeria and France was key to the impetus to assemble the IAF. The sincerity, or otherwise, of the apparent *rapprochement* between the two rivals for regional supremacy was hidden beneath the usual veils of diplomatic verbal camouflage. Nolutshungu hints at collaboration between the two states in efforts to secure US support for the IAF during the North-South summit at Cancún, Mexico in October 1981.[59] *Some* prominent Nigerians, at least, appeared less enamoured of the French role in negotiations. Commenting on the choice of Paris as the venue for the agreement establishing the Force, Vice-President Alex Ekwueme charged that, 'the OAU has sold itself cheaply to France and degraded the true meaning of African Unity'.[60] Notwithstanding, French diplomatic pressure was central to the IAF's metamorphosis from possible to probable. For Sesay, the Paris meeting was final proof that France was, 'indeed the brain behind its [the IAF's] formation'.[61]

France's performance during the Force's deployment fell far short of its promise. Early expansive guarantees to underwrite the majority of the operation's costs[62] vanished with Qadafi's surprise departure. The bulk of French assistance to the IAF was channelled through logistical supplies and support to the Senegalese battalion. A commitment to bolster Goukouni's GUNT made at the Franco-African summit in Paris also failed to live up to expectations. The dispatch of 25 tonnes of Kalashnikov rifles and ammunition 'seized' by French forces in actions in Chad and The Central African Republic[63] was a poor replacement for Goukouni's former shield - 14,000 Libyan soldiers. Further harsh lessons in *realpolitik* followed. A week after Libya's withdrawal, GUNT representatives met French Foreign Minister Claude Cheysson with an invoice for £110m, including £43m to rebuild the Chadian army. At the time the French, 'cast an anxious eye over the Chadians' shopping list'.[64] Aid increased, but only by a 'trickle'.[65] Kelley notes that, whilst France remained Chad's single largest donor of ODA, when French ODA to Chad is compared with total French ODA there was a decrease between 1980 and 1982.[66] France's rolling, but ultimately pragmatic, policy in Chad was always liable to forsake Goukouni's GUNT as being 'too divided, too weak and too incompetent'.[67]

b) United States

Given the IAF's terminal financial and institutional problems, the OAU must have counted itself unjustifiably ill-fated when the Chadian civil war captured the attention of the CIA. It was historical coincidence that the escalation of the civil war, and Libya's involvement, coincided with the accession to the Presidency of Ronald Reagan. Convinced that Libya was merely a surrogate for Soviet policy, Reagan targeted Qadafi's regime. When the CIA isolated Qadafi's overextension in Chad as his weak link, the civil war became a focal point of Reagan's anti-Libyan offensive.

The State Department developed a two pronged strategy. The idea was, in Nolutshungu's words, 'to give a positive and constructive rationality to a White House attitude without subtlety in its emotional character and one-sidedness'.[68] On the one side the US supported the French approach with warm words. There was to be logistic support for the IAF and non-lethal aid for the GUNT. In its execution this policy was more honoured in the breach than the observance. The $12m passed by Congress to finance the Nigerian contingent (NICON) was loaded with conditions. ODA for the GUNT was conditional on the withdrawal of the Libyan troops. In 1980 the State Department had intervened to prevent Unicef from distributing US-donated corn soya milk in Chad.[69] In 1981, the sum total of US ODA to Chad amounted to $160,000. This amount increased following the Libyan departure, but in a piecemeal fashion with a heavy concentration on emergency food relief.

One element of the peacekeeping mission which consistently received support was the Zairean contingent (ZACON). This battalion became the subject of much adverse speculation within the IAF. The new US Director of Central Intelligence, William Casey, had been an old friend of Zairean President Mobutu Sesi Seko since the CIA's involvement in the assassination of Patrice Lumumba.[70] There existed a widespread assumption that ZACON was acting as a proxy force for US interests. The Zairean troops proved remarkably ineffective and uncooperative. Their premature deployment and unwillingness to leave N'Djaména seemed suspect. Kupolati recalls ZACON receiving a disproportionate share of US food and logistic supplies.[71] The Zaireans provided one facet of an American fail-safe strategy. ZACON acted as a passive unit who could be counted upon to stymie any unforeseen demands for the IAF to physically defend the GUNT.

For Goukouni the plan was yet more sinister and extensive. Speaking in exile, he accused the US of coordinating both the Zaireans and, more significantly, the Nigerians in a plan to 'gain the confidence of the GUNT and then to betray it'.[72] Prior to Nairobi III, the Nigerians' demeanour had suggested positive support for the GUNT and an apparent determination to resist any FAN aggression. According to Goukouni, this was a bluff. Following the OAU's demand at Nairobi III that the GUNT negotiate with FAN, both NICON (at Mao and Moussoro) and ZACON (at Ati) demanded that the GUNT forces retreat from jointly occupied positions. Once yielded, these zones were then ceded to FAN without any opposition.

It is debatable whether Goukouni's accusation of complicity between the US, Nigeria and Zaire was true, sprang from his growing paranoia or was the result of an imploding peacekeeping operation. Better documentation exists for the US' secondary strategy.[73] CIA files show that President Numeiri of Sudan had urged the CIA to support Habré. In response, covert supplies were sent to FAN camps in Sudan with Haig's stated purpose being to 'bloody Qadafi's nose' and 'increase the flow of pine boxes back to Libya'.[74] With an eye on possible human rights questions in Congressional oversight committees, the Directorate of Operations expressed qualms at the supply of lethal aid to FAN. Casey's response was forthright - 'God damn...did they want a note from Habré's mother? Habré was a brutal, calculating survivor. Didn't they read their own reports. Where was the realism?'[75] America expended about $10 million on Habré. This relatively small amount of aid, nonetheless, was sufficient to sustain the FAN at a time of crisis. $10 million financed the FAN's push to N'Djaména and, in the process, '[undermined] the one test that the French, Libyans, the OAU and Goukouni's government had agreed upon, the establishment of an OAU peacekeeping force'.[76]

c) Nigeria

Nigeria had no vital economic interests in Chad. The rationale for Nigeria's central role in the mediation and peacekeeping effort was based on geopolitical, strategic and humanitarian concerns. The Nigerian Director-General for African Affairs at the time has offered a variety motives for Nigeria's prominent role in the IAF.[77] The prime reason was the need to bolster Nigeria's hegemonic interests in the region, and counter internal and external rivals, by playing a leading role in the intervention. Likewise, Nigeria had a vested security interest in ensuring a stable, and friendly, government in Chad. Finally, contrary to a cynical realist reading of international affairs, were Nigeria's efforts based on an altruistic sense of duty to a sister African state in trouble?

A natural rivalry existed between Nigeria and regional competitors, Libya and France. The former had been implicated in fostering internal unrest in Borno and Kano states.[78] Moreover, Nigeria's regional hegemony was clearly challenged by Tripoli's expansionist policies in Chad. The prospect of an indefinite Libyan presence in Chad, still less the proposed 'merger' of the two countries, was unacceptable to Lagos. The only real external competitor in the region was France. As an Anglophone state surrounded by Francophone states, Nigeria had always felt compelled to fight its corner against persistent French influence. Clearly, if IAF troops, with Nigeria in the vanguard, could succeed in bringing stability to Chad it would be a huge boost to Nigerian prestige in the region.

Whilst these geopolitical considerations coloured Nigerian policy, the diplomacy was never cut and dried. Strong anti-colonial elements within Nigeria felt a degree of sympathy with Qadafi's stance against 'Western imperialism'. However, at the same time, the growing audacity of Libya's expansionist policy in Chad led others to be persuaded that Nigeria and France should seek to coordinate their respective policies regarding Chad. The lack of a 'concrete national objective' left Nigerian foreign policy open to, what Nolutshungu has called, 'a certain vagueness and whimsicality'.[79] Lacking either a crystal ball or a perspicacious Foreign ministry, Presidents Olesegun and Shagari embarked upon a Chadian policy in which hope triumphed over expectation. Nigerian involvement in the IAF lent the OAU's operation a credibility, both political and financial, which the 1980 intervention had lacked. However, Nigerian commitment depended on a clear and quick solution to the conflict for which they could take credit. Nigeria was never wedded to the GUNT or to any of the OAU's stated goals for the mission. As soon as the IAF's intrinsic institutional shortcomings became apparent, Nigeria began the process of pulling out.

d) Other regional actors

A major problem for the OAU operation was the extent to which so many states saw Chad as an opportunity to exercise a varying measure of regional policy, whether at their own behest or as surrogates for external powers. Always an amorphous term, Chad's size and position has dictated that its 'region' has been defined broadly. Clearly, for many states in the region, security considerations prevailed. The fear of the exportation of violence and instability by contagion was ever-present. Moreover, regional leaders were well aware that persistent institutional chaos in Chad threatened the tacit 'compact', based on the juridical norms of the international states-system, through which the precarious viability of many African states was maintained.[80]

Given the extent to which its material resources were stretched, the OAU was highly reliant on unity of political purpose from its members if the IAF was to succeed. However, two strategically vital states - Sudan and Egypt - far from supporting the operation, actively undermined it. FAN camps along the Sudan/Chad border and equipment transported to Habré's men along the 'Sadat trail'[81], were supposedly covert. However, the very active nature of Sudanese and Egyptian backing for Habré against Goukouni, as an integral part of their anti-Libyan strategy, was an open secret. On 22 April 1981, the GUNT's representative at the UN delivered a letter charging that, 'Egypt and the Sudan were threatening it [Chad] with armed aggression'.[82] The *Guardian* stated in November 1981 that Sudan's President Numeiri was, 'doing nothing in practical terms to discourage Habré's remorseless drive to regain the eastern part of Chad'.[83] This underestimated the position. Without the assistance of Sudan and Egypt (and US aid channelled through the two countries) Habré would probably never have managed to regroup and launch his assault on N'Djaména. The financial burden of sponsoring FAN was significantly eased by massive increases in US military aid - in the case of Sudan from $30m to $100m and for Egypt from $550m to $900m.[84] Throughout the peace process OAU demands that member states refuse the use of their territories as sanctuaries for 'dissident Chadian groups' had remained unequivocal.[85] The willingness of Egypt and Sudan to arm and accommodate FAN chronically subverted the OAU's salience as a body capable of preserving a true unity of purpose amongst its own members in the midst of a peacekeeping intervention undertaken under its auspices.

Whilst Senegal acted as a stalking horse for French interests in the operation, Zaire played the same role for the US. However, at the same time as currying favour with America's new President, Mobutu took the opportunity to increase Zaire's visibility in the region. The intervention also offered the opportunity for Mobutu to employ a favoured ploy, deflecting international criticism of domestic policies by promoting Zaire as a valuable strategic asset. The surprise deployment of its elite, French-trained, Paratroop Brigade contained more than a hint of vainglory. The shine was taken off this *coup de théâtre* when the much-vaunted contingent showed a tendency to merely shadow the Nigerian troops and to be so ill-equipped that their field hospitals boasted doctors, but no drugs or operating tables.

Finance and logistical aid

The most basic, but most formidable obstacle which the IAF faced was financial. Chronic under funding became an increasingly important determinant during the operation, leading to the decision to disengage at Nairobi III in February 1982. By 1980, the OAU was already the most populous regional organisation in the world, yet also the poorest. Plainly, the OAU's parlous financial position, mirrored the increasingly dire economic standing of the continent. The annual budget since 1963 has never exceeded $30m per annum.[86] In the fiscal year 1980/1981 only $3m out of $17m was collected.[87] Moreover, as Sesay has pointed out, unlike other regional bodies, the OAU has no single state or group of states that has the will or ability to underwrite initiatives in extraordinary circumstances.[88] Furthermore, in a case of poverty breeding contempt, the OAU's cumulative financial plight could be said to bring the organisation's international salience into question. In Chad, the simple arithmetic was devastating. The OAU costed the operation at $162,900,000m per annum.[89] In the first two months following the deployment of the Zairean battalion, they collected £280,000 from member states.[90] Such a shortfall undermined all aspects of the operation, and doomed the Force to failure.

Primarily, OAU penury threatened its ability to establish unconditional neutrality in a complex conflict like Chad. Ideally, after the Paris and Nairobi meetings, funding for the operation would have flowed directly from the Organisation to the Force. In the event, the OAU were forced from an early stage to allow individual troop-supplying states to seek bilateral aid.[91] This arrangement proved equally inadequate, whilst having the added disadvantage of further *extra*-African influence being brought to bear. The foreign aid policies of both France and the US were being reassessed following respective changes in government. Despite, an avowed anti-aid stance by President Reagan, veiled diplomacy at the North-South summit at Cancún, Mexico in October 1981, resulted in the two main non-African players joining regional actors in a combined strategy to thwart Libyan ambitions. In fact, as Massaquoi has contended, the West's interest in funding peace-keeping troops waned considerably following Qadafi's withdrawal in November.[92]

Nigeria used informal channels to indicate requirements for keeping its troops in Chad to the US, French, British and West German embassies in

Lagos.[93] For the consumption of the international community the Reagan administration obtained Congressional approval for $12m non-lethal aid. Following objections that the Nigerians proposed paying their troops too much, and a dispute over apportionment between Nigeria and Zaire, only $6.6m was used.[94] Greater resentment was engendered over apparent American partiality over their distribution of logistical largesse. Whilst, the IAF received a minor contribution of a Class 12 ferry and six small boats, the irresolute Zairean contingent was frequently resupplied by US planes.[95] Certainly, the widespread assumption that the US saw the fall of the GUNT as its ultimate unofficial goal was not disabused by the level of American funding that the IAF received.

For the French the final *compte* was always going to be more costly. Since May 1980, France had been saving the estimated $1m a day that it had been expending to keep its *force d'intervention* in Chad. Subventions to balance the Chadian budget had also become less regular. In terms of the IAF, the French concentrated their funds on Senegal and Zaire. Apart from transport and logistic costs for the Senegalese detachment, France bolstered its own forces in the region in order to guarantee rapid reinforcement in the event of an attack from Libya. As previously shown, French aid to the GUNT fell significantly short of Goukouni's expectations. Nonetheless, French logistical support during the operation (including the consignment of confiscated Kalashnikov rifles) amounted to considerably more than that supplied by the British - five Land Rovers and a consignment of berets for Nigeria.

Funds in place at the start of the operation were barely sufficient to deploy the Force. Initially, Senegal, Zaire and Nigeria, assumed that their commitment would be limited to supplying troops. It very quickly became apparent that neither the OAU nor bilateral sponsors would contribute the sort of finance, arms or logistics to support the IAF for the duration of its mandate, still less beyond. The immediate effect was to dissuade Guinea, Benin and Togo from proceeding. Of the three remaining troop-contributors, Nigeria was the most exposed. Unwilling to accept the conditions attached to US logistic support, the Nigerians soon realised that they would have to meet their own expenditure. The eventual cost of NICON would be $43m. It must be assumed that the issue of funding narrowed the political options open to the contingent's planners in Lagos. Following Nairobi III, the Nigerians' prime military concern was to effect a successful phased withdrawal from Chad.

The possibility of applying for UN support in the event of the OAU being unable to maintain any potential peacekeeping force had been foreseen at the Freetown summit in 1980.[96] By mid-January there was increasing speculation that the OAU was preparing a request for funds from the UN.[97] Several factors mitigated against such a rescue plan. The UN had never supplied funds for an intervention which was not under its direct and complete control. The majority of the OAU (with notable exceptions being Cameroon and Senegal) favoured an all-African force with the UN component being restricted to finance. It seemed unlikely that UN Secretary-General Kurt Waldheim would support such an unprecedented arrangement. Most importantly, there was no support for funding from any of the three Western members of the Security Council.[98] The US in particular, having expended time and money in covert promotion of FAN, were unwilling to risk a resuscitation of the IAF which might occur if the OAU were given an injection of funds. As ever, the OAU conspired to reach the worst solution. A voluntary fund organised by the UN was doomed to failure, whilst leaving the justifiable image of the OAU as impotent and dependent.

Deployment and 'command and control'

As with the other accepted fundamental prerequisites of successful peacekeeping, the IAF failed to establish a workable system of command and control. This deficiency was the more surprising given the protracted period of negotiation over the redeployment of an OAU force after the disengagement of the first OAU Force in March 1980. Indeed, the delay in the deployment of the IAF was both an integral technical problem for the Force and an indictment of the administrative inadequacy of the OAU Secretariat. Despite a succession of decisions authorising the creation of the Force, no troops arrived in N'Djaména before 14 November 1981. In the interim, FAN profited by securing its positions and moving into the town of Oum Hadjer and, eventually, Abéché.

The first sign that command of the IAF would lack cohesion was the premature deployment of the Zairean contingent (ZACON). Since troops were already on the ground Nigeria decided to postpone a second planning meeting set for Kinshasa on 19 November until 27 November. Thus, detailed analysis of the mandate and the military response in terms of operational tactics and rules of engagement during the initial deployment remained vague. Additionally, Ejiga's original plan to assemble the full Force at the Nigerian base at Maiduguri, and enter Chad as a body was stymied from the outset. Tactical confusion was further aggravated by the non-arrival at the Kinshasa meeting of representatives from Togo, Benin and Guinea, imposing an immediate change in the proposed pattern of deployment. The backbone of the Force, the Nigerian contingent (NICON), did not arrive until December. Ejiga set up his headquarters in N'Djaména on 2 December. The Force had, through financial necessity, been reduced from a proposed 11,500 troops to one of 3,275. The result was a logistical impasse. The IAF was expected to cover an area of 500,000 square miles or 100,000 square miles per battalion.[99] The country had been split into seven zones. The GUNT reserved control of the front line in the east covering Abéché and Bilitine and the Kanem region in the west. The other zones were to be occupied by the five battalions of the IAF by 16 December. Only NICON 1 deployed on time. ZACON 2 did not materialise at all. Mobutu's Paratroops in ZACON 1 refused their arranged deployment to BET, staying in N'Djaména until reluctantly moving to share Ati in central Chad with NICON 2. The Senegalese contingent (SECOND) were deployed in the south, although they never occupied the area around Am Timmam in Salamat province. This left some of the south, much of the east and all of the north beyond any intervention from the IAF.[100]

Such large troop/territory ratios severely stretched supply lines and tested command and control capabilities. The harsh terrain, poor transport system, basic communication network and high temperatures would have taxed a better equipped force. The IAF entered Chad without any central supplies. Each contingent was dependent upon their own government and any bilateral support they could negotiate. Distances and terrain dictated a need for extensive air mobility. The senior Senegalese air detachment officer only ranked Lieutenant Colonel. More significantly, he controlled no IAF aircraft. Each contingent relied on the relative capacities of their home air force, and such bilateral support as they could muster, to supply air transport. The Force lacked sophisticated independent communications. The radios and transmitters they possessed frequently broke down in the heat and dust. Fuel was scarce owing to the high consumption rate and evaporation.[101] As a serving officer in the Force noted the, 'OAU peacekeeping effort in Chad suffered all the disadvantages of an ill-planned, ill-equipped and under-funded venture while enjoying none of the known advantages of a multi-national force of the United Nations'.[102]

The IAF suffered from a severe credibility deficit. Without reinforcements and reorganisation there was no possibility of the Force fulfilling the deterrent role vacated by the Libyans. Clearly the IAF would have been hard pushed to engage any of the battle-hardened factions. According to Ejiga's Operational Order No.1, the principal directive of the mandate, 'to maintain peace and security', would be achieved using basic peacekeeping practice - patrols, road blocks, check points, cordons and searches. Even these limited ambitions would be circumscribed by a tenuous chain of command and control. The structures in place were unfit to cope, either on a command or liaison basis, with the number of actors in theatre. For an operation, one of whose aims was to demonstrate a unanimity of purpose on the part of the pan-African organisation, there was a propensity for each link to act as an independent entity. Insofar as the various contingents and observer groups had cause to interact, there appears to have been a harmonious working relationship.[103] The real problem lay with the inability of the Force Commander to maintain a common purpose and strategy against the interference of the contingents' home governments. As Nolutshungu points out, 'the operation belonged to the OAU in name only; in reality it was a Nigerian, Zairean and Senegalese operation'.[104] Kupolati has castigated the system whereby direct communication between Secretary-General Kodjo and Force Commander Ejiga was replaced by an unorthodox connection between Force Headquarters and the current OAU Chairman, Daniel Arap Moi, in Nairobi. The interests of the Secretariat were left to Kodjo's representative, Gebre-Egziabher Dawit, described by Kupolati as, 'a hard working gentleman', who 'did not seem to know many atimes what was going on in Addis Ababa'.[105]

Conclusion

The OAU's response to the Chadian crisis showed prescience in recognising a need for an effective response to *intra*-state conflict on the continent. Civil strife has been consistently cited as one of the most serious impediments to development, as well as a shameful illustration of the scale of human suffering in much of Africa. The IAF provided a cautionary example of the inherent difficulties in mounting a peacekeeping intervention. A chastened OAU have taken over a decade to digest the lessons of the experience. In the interim they have avoided intervention as a modality for the resolution of the civil conflicts that have proliferated since Chad (including the continuing war in Chad itself). If the intervention had a virtue, it was that since there were shortcomings in every facet of the operation, the experience has been able to fully inform the debate over the future of African peacekeeping. The IAF suffered from problems - mandate, resources, command and control, pressure from external actors - that are common to all peacekeeping operations. The IAF's most distinctive feature was its departure from the OAU's intrinsic proscription against interference in the internal affairs of member states.

However, the OAU's total inexperience, the poverty of its member states and the want of an institutional framework for peacekeeping interventions all marked the IAF's problems as peculiarly profound and intractable.

For France and the OAU Secretariat, Goukouni's signature on the Memorandum agreed in Paris in November 1981 was a Trojan horse. They could claim that any objections based on the fundamental principle of non-intervention had been legally satisfied. Nevertheless, the stipulation persisted as a constraint on action throughout the mission, just as the absence of a doctrinal framework for peacekeeping condemned the IAF to organisational disjuncture. The OAU Secretariat, progressive politicians such as Julius Nyerere and Olusegun Obasanjo, academics and jurists have frequently called for an amendment to the Charter that would dilute the absolute prohibition on intervention. Obasanjo has asked, 'why does sovereignty confer absolute immunity on any government who commits genocide and monumental crimes of destruction?'[106] Solomon Gomes, the OAU's Special Affairs Officer at the UN, sees the end of the Cold War as opening a 'window of opportunity'. He detects a new dynamism within the organisation's conflict resolution capacity concomitant with an 'opportunity for the desensitization of governments long obsessed with sovereignty and noninterference'.[107] In that vein, the Mechanism for Conflict Prevention, Management and Resolution, adopted in 1993, has been lauded as a concrete step towards a more resolute approach to conflict resolution on the continent. Yet, has the contradiction between state sovereignty and non-intervention on one hand and humanitarianism and regional security on the other been resolved in favour of the latter? The OAU and its Mechanism has been conspicuously inadequate in the series of catastrophes in the Great Lakes region of Central Africa. Plans for an all-African peacekeeping force have been made outside the aegis of the OAU and have been stymied from the onset by the same problems that befell the IAF - a lack of resources and potential troop-contributors following divergent agendas. In a further evocation of the Chadian operation, the Canadian-led multi-national Force proposed by the UN in November 1996 became the focus of power games between *extra*-African powers. France has been accused of hoping to use the Force to halt the 'Anglo-Saxon expansionism'[108] of Laurent Kabila's rebels in eastern Zaire, whilst the US has been counter charged with preventing a humanitarian intervention for cynical, political reasons.[109] Still confined by its own rules governing non-intervention, the OAU - derided as 'le dernier pompon' to aggravate the crisis - could only react, as in Chad, with well intentioned diplomacy and proposals for a nebulous buffer force whose mandate has best been described as 'politique-fiction'.[110] For, whilst idealists outside government or within the OAU see the potential to surmount the sovereignty conundrum, those in power in African states consistently reaffirm their adherence to the norm. Thus, as Gene Lyons and Michael Mastanduno point out, 'it is undoubtedly premature to declare that international society has moved beyond Westphalia and has overcome the idea of state sovereignty'.[111] A statement from Presidents Mobutu and Moi following talks about the Great Lakes crisis stressed that 'national sovereignty, territorial integrity, inviolability of national boundaries and citizenship issues were not negotiable.'[112]

Have the other obstacles that beset the IAF been addressed with greater success? Finance became a critical stumbling block in Chad. The OAU's budget deficit is even more dire now than it was then. Few states meet their existing commitments, still less pay contributions to the Mechanism's Peace Fund. Michel Djiena Wembou has noted that, 'il apparaît clairement que l'OUA fera face à des redoutables difficultés financières dans la mise en oeuvre de ses décisions dans le domaine de la gestion et du règlement des conflits'.[113] The point has been underlined by the current OAU Secretary-General, Salim Ahmed Salim - 'People make very, very nice sounding declarations of commitment of support for the OAU, but there are many countries, many member states who do not really live up to their obligations'.[114]

The OAU's persistent fiscal shortfall has thrown the potential for African conflict resolution capacity building into the mire of *extra*-continental financial and logistical assistance. Dependency on Western financial aid and logistical support seems as inevitable and as fraught with danger as it was in Chad. The principal protagonists have remained the same as well. Whilst neither the US nor France want to pay to high a price in Africa, both in terms of cash and lives, there remains an abiding desire to retain influence in the region. Political change and domestic financial constraints has seen Russia switch, at least in the short term, from seeing the continent less in strategic, and more, in economic terms. The initial response from the US was a policy of retreat from intervention, both overt and covert, in African affairs. However, the partial replacement of communism by Islamic fundamentalism as the State Department's chief bogey, coupled with electoral influence of the black caucus, has dictated a recent reassertion of US foreign policy in Africa. French interest on the continent, whilst it always endures, has become stretched in the 1990s. The cost of maintaining 8,000 soldiers in Africa (including 800 in N'Djaména), and the current professionalisation of French armed forces have encouraged a limited reassessment of future African policy. Traditional interventions, such as *Opération Almandin* in the Central

African Republic in 1996, are henceforth to be considered 'exceptionnelles'.[115]

Mindful to wrap their proposals in suitable politically correct, anti-neo-imperialist rhetoric, both the US and France have come to the same solution - peacekeeping based upon all-African forces supplied and maintained by the West. The shades of Chad are apparent. As with Chad, the Western powers' input is firmly based on considerations of national interest. The result has seen France and the US swapping insults with the French accusing the Americans of pursuing a short-term agenda and the Americans denouncing the French as neo-colonialists.[116] The specifics of the proposed Force have barely been considered. Issues which were important in Chad such as the training of troops, supply of equipment and weapons and the formation of effective command and control, have been subsumed by general politicking. As with the IAF, *intra*-African tensions have influenced the debate. Regional hegemons have reacted cautiously to current initiatives. Lagos has stated that any standing force which sought to ignore Nigeria was doomed to failure.[117] Conversely, Mandela's South Africa has rejected pressure to assume the task of regional policeman.[118] For Jack Spence, future foreign policy decisions 'will be based on an estimate of potential profit in a secure political order'.[119] A prudent promotion of preventive diplomacy, based on South African neutrality, seems more likely than extensive interventionist peacekeeping.[120]

The OAU's experience in Chad proved an inauspicious debut into the complex process of peacekeeping intervention. The IAF's failure led to a long period of self-contemplation which has obscured positive aspects of Africa's potential for conflict resolution. Africans possess good skills for reconciliation. Mazrui has alluded to a 'limited memory of animosity' as 'an important cultural resource, a valuable traditional *more*, for future conflict-resolution'.[121] All-African interventions must avoid the enforced 'mission cringe' which marred the IAF operation. The OAU must ameliorate its salience as the continent's conflict resolution body of first resort before it attempts intervention. Future IAFs must be wholly credible to all involved in the conflict if they are to succeed. A reoccurrence of the Chad intervention could demolish the possibility of a valid *Pax Africana*.

Notes

1   Quoted in Legum, C. (ed), *African Contemporary Record,* Africana: NY, 1980-1981, A38.
2   Mazrui, A.A. (1969), *Towards a Pax Africana: A Study of Ideology*

and Ambition, Weidenfield and Nicholson: London, p. 203.
3   Mazrui, A.A., 'External Marginalisation; Internal Democratisation', Paper presented to Conference on the Marginalisation of Africa, African Studies Centre, Coventry University, 16-17 December, 1996.
4   Jackson, R.H., and Rosberg, C.G. (1982), 'Why Africa's Weak States Persist: The Empirical and the Juridical in Statehood,' *World Politics,* Vol. 35, No. 1, October, pp. 1-24.
5   Buijtenhuijs, R. (1978), *Le Frolinat et les révoltes populaires du Tchad 1965-1976,* Mouton Publishers: The Hague, p. 345.
6   Foltz, W.J., 'Reconstructing the State of Chad,' in I.W. Zartman (1995), *Collapsed States: The Disintegration and Restoration of Legitimate Authority,* Lynne Rienner: Boulder.
7   Magnant, J-P. (1986), *Terre Sara, Terre Tchadienn,* L'Harmattan: Paris, p. 261.
8   Charlton, R., and May R. (1989), 'Warlords and Militarism in Chad', *Review of African Political Economy,* Nos. 45/46, p. 12.
9   Nolutshungu, S.C. (1996), *Limits of Anarchy: Intervention and State Formation in Chad,* Univ. Press of Virginia: Charlottesville, p. 133.
10 Ibid., p. 133.
11 Pelcovits, N. (1983), 'Peacekeeping: The African Experience,' in H. Wiseman (ed.), *Peacekeeping: Appraisals and Proposals,* Pergamon Press: NY, p. 277.
12 Ibid., p. 277.
13 See 'Rapport secret d'Edem Kodjo, Secrétaire Général de l'OUA après son voyage d'information à N'Djaména (8-9 avril 1980)' in G.J., Ngansop (1986), *Tchad: Vingt Ans de Crise,* L'Harmattan: Paris, pp. 203-207.
14 Ibid., p. 204.
15 See UN General Assembly Plenary Debate A/36/PV.20 (274).
16 Massaquoi, B.J. (1991), 'Conflict Resolution: The OAU and Chad,' *TransAfrica Forum,* Winter, p. 96.
17 Ngansop, op. cit., p. 207.
18 Pittman, D. (1984), 'The OAU and Chad,' in Y., El-Ayouty, and I.W. Zartman, *The OAU After Twenty Years,* Praeger Press: NY, p. 311.
19 See UN General Assembly Plenary Debate A/27/PV.30 (16).
20 See UN General Assembly Plenary Debate A/36/PV.24 (104-107).
21 Sesay, A. (1989), 'The OAU Peacekeeping Force in Chad: Some Lessons for Future Operations,' *Current Research in Peace and Violence,* p. 192.

22 Nolutshungo, op. cit., p. 116.
23 Kwame Nkrumah, quoted in Esedebe, P.O. (1982), *Pan-Africanism: The Idea and Movement 1776-1963*, Howard University Press: Washington D.C., pp. 223-224.
24 Ihonvbere, J.O., 'Pan-Africanism: Agenda for African Unity in the 1990s', Paper presented to All-African Student's Conference, Peter Clark Hall, University of Guelph, Ontario, 27 May 1994.
25 See, *Charter of the OAU. Article III*; The Member States, in pursuit of the purposes stated in Article II, solemnly affirm and declare their adherence to the following principles:
    1 the sovereign equality of all Member States;
    2 non-interference in the internal affairs of States;
    3 respect for the sovereignty and territorial integrity of each State and for its inalienable right to independent existence;
    4 peaceful settlement of disputes by negotiation, mediation, conciliation or arbitration...
26 Shaw, M. (1986), *Title to Territory in Africa: International Legal Issues,* Clarendon Press: Oxford, p. 185.
27 Elias, T.O. (1972), *Africa and the Development of International Law,* Dobbs Ferry Press: New York, p. 127.
28 Andemicael, B., and Nicol, D. (1984), 'The OAU: Primacy in Seeking African Solutions Within the OAU Charter', in El-Ayouty and Zartman, op. cit., p. 102.
29 Wallerstein, I. (1966), 'The Early Years of the OAU: The Search for Organisational Preeminence', *International Organisation*, v. 20, pp. 774-787.
30 Mwagiru, M. (1996), 'Who Will Bell the Cat? Article 3(2) of the OAU Charter and the Crisis of OAU Conflict Management', < http://snipe.ukc.ac.uk/international/papers.dir/mwagiru.html >, 5 July 1996.
31 See also, Shehadi, K.S. (1993), 'Ethnic Self-determination and the Break-up of States' *Adelphi Paper*, No. 283, December, pp. 9-10.
32 Sesay, A., Ojo, O., and Fasehun, O. (1984), *The OAU After 20 Years,*Westview: Boulder, p. 40.
33 Quoted in Legum, C. (ed), *African Contemporary Record,*Africana, NY, 1980-1981, A38.
34 Zartman, I.W. (1985), *Ripe for Resolution: Conflict and Intervention in Africa,*Oxford University Press: New York, p. 144.
35 Somerville, K. (1990), *Foreign Military in Africa,* Pinter's Publishers: London, p. 103.
36 See Cleaver, G., and May, R. (1995), 'Peacekeeping: The African

Dimension,' *Review of African Political Economy*, No. 66, p. 496.
37   Quoted in Pecovits, op. cit., p. 265.
38   Ajibewa, A.I., 'Regional Organisation and Conflict Resolution in West Africa: Learning and Lessons from the Chadian and Liberian Conflicts', unpublished PhD, University of Lancaster.
39   *Guardian*, 14 November 1996, p. 13.
40   OAU Resolution AHG/Res 102/103 (XVIII).
41   Quoted in Ajibewa, op. cit., p. 19.
42   See *West Africa*, 30 November 1981, p. 2820.
43   Quoted in Nolutshungu, op. cit., p. 164.
44   *West Africa*, 23 November 1981, p. 2757.
45   Nolutshungu, op. cit., p. 164.
46   *West Africa*, 28 December 1981, p. 3028.
47   Diehl, P.F., 'Operations Other than War (OOTW): Mission Types and Dimensions', <http://www.ccsr.uiuc.edu/People/gmk/Projects/UNCMCW/Documents/OOTW.html>, 20 September 1996.
48   Quoted in *Guardian*, 20 November 1981, p. 6.
49   Quoted in *Africa Research Bulletin*, 1-28 February 1982, p. 6335.
50   Ibid., p. 6336.
51   See *West Africa*, 22 February 1982, p. 495.
52   Quoted in Dadi, A. (1987), *Tchad: l'Etat retrouvé*, L'Harmattan: Paris, p. 195.
53   Quoted in Nolutshungu, op. cit., p. 170.
54   May, R., and Charlton, R. (1989), 'Chad: France's Fortuitous Success', *Modern and Contemporary France*, Vol. 37, p. 3.
55   Nolutshungu, op. cit., p. 11.
56   May and Charlton, 'Fortuitous Success', op. cit., p. 8.
57   Buijtenhuijs, R. (1995), 'French Military Interventions: The Case of Chad', in A.Kirk-Greene and D.Bach, *State and Society in Francophone Africa since Independence,* Macmillan: London, p. 222.
58   *Guardian*, 19 November 1981, p. 7.
59   Nolutshungu, op. cit., p. 161.
60   Quoted in Sesay, 'Some Lessons', op. cit., p. 192.
61   Sesay, A., 'The OAU Peacekeeping Force in Chad: What are the Lessons for the Future', Paper presented to 30th Annual Convention of the International Studies Centre, London, 28 March-1 April 1989, p. 13.
62   *Economist*, 31 October 1981, p. 57.
63   *West Africa*, 2 November 1981, p. 2555.
64   *Guardian*, 14 November 1981, p. 4.

65 *Economist*, 14 November 1981, p. 55.
66 See Kelley, M.P. (1986), *A State In Disarray: Conditions of Chad's Survival*, Westview Press: Boulder, p. 97.

Year	France ODA to Chad (a)	Total ODA (b)	% a/b
1978	$43,167,000	$242,944,000	17.8
1979	$29,720,000	$277,675,000	10.7
1980	$15,043,000	$319,216,000	4.7
1981	$22,389,000	$384,068,000	5.8
1982	$24,989,000	$302,281,000	8.3
1983	$18,680,000	$144,099,000	13.0

Source: Comité Permanent Inter-Etats de Lutte Contre la Secheresse dans le Sahel, Club du Sahel, *L'Aide Publique au developpement dans les Pays Membres du CILSS*, Annual Reports 1975-1983, Club du Sahel/OCDE: Paris.

67 Nolutshungu, op. cit., p. 306.
68 Ibid., p. 309.
69 *Guardian*, 14 November 1981, p. 4.
70 Woodward, B. (1987), *Veil: The Secret Wars of the CIA*, Simon and Schuster: London, p. 268.
71 Kupolati, R. (1993), 'The Nigerian Contingent in the Organization of African Unity Peace-keeping Operation in Chad', in Vogt, M.A., and Ekoko, A.E., (eds) *Nigeria in International Peacekeeping*, Malthouse Press: Lagos, p. 152.
72 See Nolutshungu, op. cit., p. 171.
73 See May and Charlton, 'Fortuitous Success', op. cit., p. 9.
74 Woodward, op. cit., p. 96.
75 Ibid., p. 157.
76 Wright, V., quoted in Lemarchand, R. (1985), 'The Crisis in Chad', in Bender, G.J., et al., *Africa Crisis Areas and US Foreign Policy*, University of California Press: Syracuse, p. 249.
77 See Jolaoso, O. (1991), *In the Shadows: Recollections of a Pioneer Diplomat*, Malthouse Press: Lagos, pp. 202-209.
78 Kelley, op. cit., p. 72.
79 Nolutshungu, op. cit., p. 121.

80 See Kelley, op. cit., p. 80.
81 See Sesay, 'What are the Lessons?', op. cit., p. 20.
82 Letter from GUNT to UN Secretary-General and the President of the Security Council, 22 April 1981, UN Document S/14455.
83 *Guardian*, 30 November 1981, p. 5.
84 *Africa*, December 1981, p. 18.
85 See *Final Communiqué of the Conference of Lomé* (14 January 1981), OAU Document AHG/104(XVIII) Annex V.
'...CALL UPON all member countries especially those with common borders with the Republic of Chad, to refuse their territories to be used by extra African powers and dissident Chadian groups as sanctuaries or bases for mounting armed attacks against the Republic of Chad...'
86 Sesay, A., 'What are the Lessons?', op. cit., p. 21.
87 Ojo, O. (1988), 'The OAU and Conflict Management: The Case of Chad', *International Problems (Tel Aviv)*, Vol. 27, Pt. 3-4, p. 38.
88 Ibid., p. 21.
89 *Keesing's Contemporary Archives*, 3 September 1982, p. 31678.
90 *Guardian*, 15 February 1982, p. 9.
91 Ndiaye, T.M. (1992), 'Conflict Prevention and Conflict Resolution in the African Context', in *Disarmament: Topical Papers,* No. 12, p. 104.
92 Massaquoi, op. cit., p. 41.
93 *Times*, 7 December 1981, p. 6.
94 Pittman, op. cit., p. 316.
95 Kupolati, op. cit., p. 152.
96 See AHG/Res.101 (XVII).
97 *Guardian*, 21 January 1981, p. 5.
98 Nolutshungu, op. cit., p. 163.
99 Kupolati, op. cit., p. 148.
100 Ibid., p. 146.
101 For the logistical constraints on the IAF see, ibid., pp. 150-151.
102 Ibid., p. 151.
103 Ibid., p. 153.
104 Nolutshungu, op. cit., p. 169.
105 Kupolati, op. cit., p. 149.
106 Quoted in Gomes, S. (1996), 'The OAU, State Sovereignty and Regional Security', in Keller, E.J. and Rothchild, D., *Africa in the New International Order: Rethinking State Sovereignty and Regional Security,* Lynne Rienner: Boulder, p. 41.
107 Ibid., p. 43.

108 *Africa Confidential*, 29 November 1996, pp. 1-4.
109 *Libération*, 3 March 1997, p. 7.
110 Ibid.., 3 March 1997, p. 7.
111 Lyons, G., and Mastanduno, M. (1995), 'State Sovereignty and International Intervention: Reflections on the Present and Prospects for the Future', in Lyons, G. and Mastanduno, M. (eds), *Beyond Westphalia: State Sovereignty and International Intervention,*John Hopkins University Press: Baltimore, p. 265.
112 'Integrated Regional Information Network Emergency Update No.73 on the Great Lakes (Tuesday 7 January 1997), <http://www-jha.sps.cam.ac.uk/DHA/dha75.htm> 17 January 1997.
113 Djiena Wembou, M.C. (1994), 'A Propos du Nouveau Mécanisme de l'OUA sur les Conflits', *Revue Générale de Droit International Public*, Vol. 98, Part 2, p. 385.
114 'Can This Man Help?', *BBC Focus on Africa*, p. 19.
115 *Libération*, 7 October 1996, p. 10.
116 See 'Washington and Paris in a Tiff Over Africa', *Africa News Service*, 17 October 1996.
117 'Lagos Not Impressed by US Proposal for an African Force', *Pan-African News Agency*, 16 October 1996.
118 *Independent*, 21 November 1995, p. 17.
119 Spence, J.E. (1997), 'On Becoming "Just Another Country"', *The World Today*, March, p. 69.
120 See *West Africa*, 28 October 1996, p. 1670.
121 Mazrui, A.A. (1994), 'Africa: In Search of Self-Pacification', *African Affairs*, Vol. 93, No. 370, p. 41.

7 Somalia

Peter Woodward

The general image of Somalia is that of an African state which of its own volition had plunged into anarchy by the early 1990s, when along came the UN like a knight in shining armour in 1992. But alas in the murky world of Somalia, slaying the dragon(s), let alone rescuing the maiden(s) proved more difficult than anticipated; and the knight was unexpectedly burned before riding off again and leaving the Somalis, dragon(s) and maiden(s), to their own violent devices. Reality is rather more complex of course, not least the fact that the UN had been contributing to developments in Somalia for over 40 years, and was thus no newcomer to its complex problems.

Somalia is, or more accurately was, as artificial a state as any other in Africa. While the mainly pastoral Somali clans had common cultural and religious traditions, there had been no experience of indigenous state formation, and it was the imperial division of the continent in the late nineteenth century that put Somalis in a number of states. Britain, France and Abyssinia all absorbed swathes of Somali-occupied territory into their colonial and imperial states, while the largest area and number came under Italian rule. It was Italy's defeat in World War II which made its former Somali territory the responsibility of the UN Trusteeship Council at the war's end. But there were few covetous glances at it, and in 1950 it was returned as a trusteeship to Italy to be prepared for independence ten years later, for such was the flow of international and UN politics at the time.

Like most former European colonies independence brought liberal democracy, and as in most of the rest of Africa that gave way to authoritarian rule, in this case via the military coup of Siad Barre in 1969. Few tears were shed, and indeed for a while it seemed that Barre might bring Somalis together for development in the 1970s more than the fractious politicians of the previous decade. The UN Development Programme (UNDP) certainly seemed to think so, becoming one of a number of donors which invested generously in rural development in particular.

However the hopes of the 1970s were to be a false dawn, especially after Barre sought to take advantage of the turmoil of the Ethiopian revolution to capture Somali-occupied territory in eastern Ethiopia in 1977. Defeated the following year by Ethiopia's newly Soviet-backed army, the clan-based resistance to Barre began which was to grow through the 1980s and eventually lead to his downfall in 1991. Somalia's defeat in 1978 also opened a new chapter in UN involvement, for hundreds of thousands of refugees poured into the country from Ethiopia (estimates ranged from six hundred thousand to two million). It gave Somalia the highest concentration of refugees to indigenous population (five million) in the world. The UN High Commission for Refugees (UNHCR) was swiftly involved, and by the early 1980s was spending US$70 million per annum. The impact of the refugee camps was most important. They were a major source of foreign exchange; numerous jobs were provided for educated Somalis; and the rations distributed eked out into the poor Somali communities in which they were situated. As Somalia deteriorated politically in the late 1980s Barre took military conscripts from the camps, looted refugee supplies and extorted protection money, much in the manner of which the 'warlords' were to be accused when the UN Operation in Somalia (UNOSOM) began in 1992. Yet in spite of this background of involvement the UN from 1992 was to appear to have learned little: perhaps one of its characteristics as an international organisation is a lack of, or an unwillingness to draw upon, a collective memory on the part of the various roles and agencies already experienced in Somalia.

UNOSOM

The events that were to lead to the decision to undertake UNOSOM date from the downfall of Barre in January 1991. The violent overthrow of one autocrat and his replacement by a new ruler would have been of no particular significance in much of contemporary Africa, but in Somalia's case it led instead to anarchy. Barre had been opposed for several years by a number of clan and sub-clan based militias. The collapse of the Somali state, and coincidentally the downfall of Mengistu in Ethiopia, had released a mass of arms and the civilian population was awash with guns.

The eight main militias identified after Barre's downfall were commanded by emerging leaders swiftly labelled 'warlords' as they competed for power. In addition to these militias, generally of 2-3,000 men, there were numerous smaller bands, often of youngsters who appeared beyond any form of authority.[1]

While the 'warlords' appeared to be essentially political rivals, amongst whom efforts at conciliation and mediation proved unsuccessful, many of the other armed men were little more than bandits. Barre's men had increasingly looted, and their example was continued in the vacuum left behind. Continuing commercial activity, especially the trade in the popular narcotic, *qat*, attracted violence, as did the agricultural areas of the south. Soon refugees were pouring into Kenya and Ethiopia. Foreign aid organisations had long been working in Somalia, and as the crisis deepened, so the need for emergency relief rose as well. The international community responded to what was depicted as 'famine', but the relief itself became a target. Supplies arriving at the port of Mogadishu in particular came under attack, and the relief agencies found themselves forced to hire protection from among the armed groups that threatened them.

It was as this situation intensified that the UN was drawn in. Somalia was very much in mind when the UN Department of Humanitarian Affairs was established in 1991; and Under Secretary-General James Jonah arrived in Mogadishu in January 1992 to assess the situation. His task was to facilitate the flow of aid, but he also appeared to make some headway towards a cease-fire between two of the leading warlords contending for power in Mogadishu, Mohamed Farah Aideed and Ali Mahdi. He even suggested a UN force to separate the warring factions, but the suggestion was still-born. However, under Security Council Resolution 751 of 24 April 1992, it was agreed to establish a United Nations Operation in Somalia (UNOSOM), to enable humanitarian relief to be carried out.

An experienced Algerian diplomat, Mohamed Sahnoun, was sent to take charge of UNOSOM, and soon evolved his own approach. He tried to develop relations with the leading 'warlords', and not just Aideed and Ali Mahdi (though the former in particular was highly suspicious of the UN). Any attempt to deploy UN forces Sahnoun thought should have their agreement and co-operation. He also endeavoured to encourage other elements in Somali society, such as clan elders, and women's representatives. In an effort to deflect the concentration of attention on Mogadishu, and rivalry for control thereof, he proposed dividing the country into a number of zones for the delivery of relief, each to be supplied by different routes. These were to be around Bassosa, Berbera, and Kismayo, as well as Mogadishu. In addition to relief, the zones would become centres for regional reconciliation, which would involve local leaders such as clan elders, as well as the 'warlords' whose importance would be slowly eroded in a process that would require time.[2]

But later in 1992 the situation soured. Sahnoun became increasingly frustrated with UN headquarters in New York and expressed his criticism publicly. He felt that in practice his policy of regionalism was being undermined by UN agencies concentrating their presence in Mogadishu to the neglect of other zones, partly due to lack of staff to work outside the capital. He was also critical of other aspects of the agencies: the headquarters in New York were overly bureaucratic; there was a lack of co-operation between agencies; while some agencies were failing to fulfil the commitments that they had made. Furthermore the 500 troops sent by UNOSOM to assist with humanitarian facilities arrived late and soon proved to be too few. For his part Secretary-General Boutros Boutros-Ghali felt that Sahnoun was acting too independently, and some suggested favouring Aideed in the Mogadishu area.[3] The clash between the two former friends led to Sahnoun's resignation, and his replacement by an Iraqi diplomat, Ahmed Kittani, a much less flexible personality who did as New York told him. At the same time the situation on the ground appeared to be worsening once more. Relief aid came under more attacks, and reports indicated that the levels of famine and disease were rising fast. A major humanitarian crisis appeared to be looming once more, in spite of the efforts of UNOSOM, which in its existing form was widely regarded as inadequate.

UNITAF

Developments in Somalia were having a growing impact in two places in particular. In New York Boutros Boutros-Ghali reviewed the options. Existing operations under Resolution 775 would permit the deployment of a further 2,400 UN peacekeepers, but this was thought to be an inadequate number in the deteriorating situation. On the other hand, total withdrawal of UN forces was seen as a retreat that would have disastrous consequences in the worsening security situation. Thirdly there could be a show of force in Mogadishu, the main area of violence, but this might only provoke the well-armed main faction leaders, and not help elsewhere in the country. Fourthly, there could be a countrywide operation at the behest of the UN but led by a member state, and the US had indicated its willingness to act in this role. A fifth option was for an enlarged UN force to take-over from the existing UNOSOM operation, but this was thought beyond existing UN capacity.[4] In reality Boutros-Ghali himself was becoming ever keener on armed intervention by the UN. In part it was because he judged it the only way to deal with what appeared to be a deteriorating situation on the ground; and in part because he had greater ambitions for the UN internationally in the wake of the end of the Cold War.[5]

Meanwhile in Washington the rivals for the White House in the forthcoming presidential elections were also moving in the same direction. The press coverage of the deteriorating situation was causing American politicians to take Somalia more seriously than any concern for national interest required; and George Bush in particular, the incumbent candidate, had long prided himself on being a foreign policy president. After his success in the Gulf War in particular, he was much given to speaking of a New World Order, a concept however which remained largely undefined. Moreover he was frustrated with perceived lack of European action in former Yugoslavia and sought to show by the example of decisiveness in Somalia what could be achieved in a disintegrating state. Though there were doubting voices about the need for armed intervention and the objectives, Bush was moving in that direction even before his electoral defeat. And once he had lost to Bill Clinton, intervention was one last chance to demonstrate his decisiveness in foreign policy, and show America what it was losing. Clinton was understandably more cautious, but it was difficult to deny the humanitarian pressure, and in the campaign he had tried to spoil Bush's foreign policy achievements by doubting his morality in the face of situations such as those in Bosnia and Somalia. Faced with the new moral maze Clinton too gave his agreement to US leadership of Operation Restore Hope. As it moved towards a commitment in principle, the US was also reviewing what it meant militarily. One possibility was greater US support for a traditional UN peacekeeping operation. A second was the organisation by the US of an international force, but without US ground troops. Thirdly US troops could take the lead in an international operation, as had been the case in the liberation of Kuwait. With faction forces seeming so much weaker than those of Iraq, Bush chose the third option, with the proviso that it would also be a short operation, after which there would be a handover to the UN once more.[6]

The alliance of the UN secretariat and the US was followed on 3 December 1992 by the passage of UN Resolution 794 which called for the establishment of a safe environment for humanitarian aid in Somalia. It was a double first for the UN. The intervention would take place without the permission of the government of the member state of the UN involved, for though Somali faction leaders claimed to rule, none was recognised internationally as the legitimate ruler. Furthermore it was to be a Chapter VII operation, by which the Unified Task Force (UNITAF) would be required to *make* peace among the disputing parties rather than simply *keeping* the peace between them.

Television cameras were already set up on the shore to record the arrival of the first UNITAF forces on 9 December 1992. Eventually they built up to 38,000 troops (three quarters from the US), who were deployed to take control of the southern ports of Mogadishu and Kismayu and ensure that relief could get through to the urban and rural distribution centres. Originally Bush had spoken of this being completed by 20 January, but this optimistic timetable was extended to 120 days; after that UNITAF would withdraw to be replaced by UNOSOM II, which would then be responsible for peacekeeping and further UN operations.

In terms of improving the supply of aid UNITAF did have initial success. Its problems soon turned out to be political. On the UNITAF side differences soon appeared with regard to dealing with the militias. Boutros-Ghali thought that a secure environment for relief necessarily required a commitment to disarm the gunmen, but Bush and the US commanders on the ground thought that this was neither necessary to ensure relief, nor practicable. It was not deemed necessary since it was a humanitarian operation to permit aid to flow to Somalis, and not a strategic exercise to take over Somalia. It was not thought practical since it was not clear how much disarmament would be necessary, especially since arms were so widespread in the country; large scale disarmament might result in clashes and casualties on both sides which would be politically damaging; and such a large operation would be very expensive. The possibility of guns for food was contemplated, but with so many weapons was also deemed impractical. This position on disarmament was to cause friction between the UN and UNITAF, especially when Boutros-Ghali and Kittani were still actively, if somewhat ambiguously, involved in Somalia.[7] Furthermore elsewhere in the country, especially while the Australians were in Baidoa, more progress on disarmament was achieved.[8] Though the US eschewed systematic disarmament, when the crime situation again deteriorated sharply in January 1993, and a number of NGO relief operations were suspended, there were intermittent ad hoc seizures of arms in Mogadishu. However the uncertainty and inconsistency surrounding the UN and UNITAF on disarmament from the outset served to alarm the Somali factions more than they secured the environment for relief. This was particularly damaging when the US

Special Envoy, Robert Oakley, was trying to take a political approach towards the 'warlords'. Initially the leading figures in Mogadishu, Aideed and Ali Mahdi, had welcomed UNITAF's arrival. Conferences involving them and 13 other leaders from elsewhere in the country were held in Addis Ababa in January and March, and Oakley hoped that if agreement could be fostered then there could be a voluntary beginning on disarmament, demobilisation, and the reintegration of the militias into Somali society.[9] But tensions surfaced. Politically the 'warlords' rivalries remained intense, with Aideed in particular appearing determined to prevent Ali Mahdi from being recognised as interim leader. Militarily Aideed was particularly unwilling to hand over weapons, though Ali Mahdi did initially surrender some armoured trucks known as 'technicals'. The outcome of resistance to disarmament by SNA in particular was some heavy but brief clashes in the capital.

Although UNITAF was not supposed to be involved in the establishment of a fully fledged UN trusteeship, Boutros-Ghali was keen to see it contribute to political and economic recovery. As he put it at the time: 'Efforts are also required to create the political conditions in which Somalia can begin to resolve its political problems and rehabilitate its economy'.[10] Though the US was keen to avoid such a role (apart from trying to reconcile faction leaders), the rising crime at the beginning of 1993 encouraged UNITAF to make some efforts to restore a semblance of law and order. Police were trained and some began to be deployed, as well as a few courts being opened. There was also some encouragement of local elders to try and restore an element of authority which had been much weakened by the militia conflicts. However in total these efforts had little effect in Mogadishu in the long term.

All these moves were in any case only beginnings. UNITAF may have claimed to have established a somewhat safer environment for relief (which was principally what it was for), but that was all that it had achieved. UNITAF was coming to an end less because the situation had improved sufficiently to ensure greater security in the future, than because its limited time span was running out. Boutros-Ghali for one claimed that UNITAF's work was incomplete, but the UN-US alliance which had started the operation was now essentially the voice of the US, and by the end of March UNITAF was being wound down.

UNOSOM II

In theory UNOSOM had never stopped and UNITAF was simply an additional short term measure. But in reality UNOSOM had been sidelined, and with UNITAF's withdrawal a new operation, UNOSOM II, was established. The major difference in aim was that under UN resolution 814 of 26 March 1993, UNOSOM II was specifically intended to give greater emphasis to disarmament than had been the case under the more ambiguous UNITAF. The confrontation with the Somali militias which the American leadership of UNITAF had sought to avoid was now to take place. Yet though there was to be a tougher line, it is claimed that there was in fact no proper UN planning of how to tackle the whole disarmament issue.[11] This may have been due partly to Boutros-Ghali who was reluctant to delegate the planning and handling of operations. (He had also had been forced by demonstrators to cut short a visit to Mogadishu which some thought may have influenced his judgement.) Furthermore the absence of Kittani, who was away for medical treatment in the early weeks of UNOSOM II, did not help the development of policy. In March he was replaced by an American, Admiral Jonathon Howe.

The main protagonist on the Somali side in the unfolding conflict was Mohamed Farah Aideed and his Somali National Alliance (SNA) in south Mogadishu. Aideed saw himself as the real destroyer of Siad Barre and consequently the rightful leader of a new Somalia. He was rightly suspicious that UNOSOM II would not share this evaluation, and he soon accused it of favouring his rival claimants, with whom UNITAF had tried to arrange pacts in the past. Since Aideed's claim lay in his military capacity, the new UNOSOM II mandate of disarmament was another major challenge, and one to be tested to see if UNOSOM II was any sterner than the first feeble UNOSOM force of the previous year had been. A successful challenge to the UN would also strengthen the SNA's position. Furthermore it was noticeable that with 20,000 troops, UNOSOM II was substantially smaller than the UNITAF force which had not attempted systematic disarmament. Weapons which the SNA had moved out of Mogadishu at the time of UNITAF's arrival were smuggled back in; and SNA's Radio Mogadishu was used to whip up civilian hostility to the UN.

Tension rose in the weeks after UNOSOM II's deployment as its patrols tried to find weapons' dumps, and conflict came to a head on 5 June when 24 Pakistani troops and scores of Somalis were killed in a single clash. From then on it became open warfare. UNOSOM II was to place its highest priority on capturing Aideed, and a price of US$25,000 was placed on his head. Heavy weapons and even helicopter gunships were deployed on the UN side, but to little effect. The use of violence was making the UN look like the biggest 'warlord' of all, and with the help of SNA radio propaganda the population of south Mogadishu in particular was turning against the UN. UN forces were scarcely able to leave their quarters, even in vehicles (particularly since they were short of armoured personnel carriers after UNITAF withdrew). Firepower and aerial domination were proving unable to defeat the SNA on the ground, or to capture Aideed. Realisation of this emerging bloody deadlock was driven home by a clash between the SNA and US troops on 3 October, which left 18 American dead and countless Somali victims, in one of the largest battles ever involving UN peacekeeping forces. Political opinion in the US, already concerned by events, was now outraged and demanded that something be done to clarify UNOSOM II's objectives, and the US role in particular.

President Clinton's response, announced without consultation with the UN, was confusing. US forces in UNOSOM II would be strengthened: but they would also be pulled out entirely by 31 March 1994. The impression was thus created that the US would be involved in one last effort in Somalia, but would then wash its hands of UNOSOM II. Furthermore Clinton announced that there would be a greater involvement of neighbouring states in peacemaking, a move which was generally welcomed since the neighbours had long offered their services but hitherto been neglected by the UN and the US. At the same time the return to the kind of talks between factions attempted by Oakley at the start of 1993 meant abandoning the demonising and pursuit of Aideed. Contact with Aideed was restored, and in December he was even flown to one meeting in Addis Ababa in a US plane (having refused a seat on a UN flight as unsafe)! For his part Aideed had responded by producing his own thoughts on the future of Somalia which linked local Somali politics - 'the most democratic people in the world' - with a national system of non-clan based parties which would compete on the basis of proportional representation in order to ensure stable coalition governments.[12]

While the Americans prepared to leave as scheduled, the political initiative was passed to the UN, the factions and to neighbouring states that sought to broker peace. But nothing substantial had been achieved by the time that the Americans had finally pulled out, or even a year later in March 1995 when the remaining UN forces were withdrawn. They had spent much of the intervening period shut in their compounds scarcely able to move out around Mogadishu and surrounding areas. Meanwhile the factional rivalry in Mogadishu and southern Somalia continued with occasional outbreaks of heavy fighting.

UNOSOM II was not only a military and political debacle for the UN, it was also damaging operationally. Even the military operations had shown up major problems of co-ordination. The pull out of UNITAF had placed a heavy burden on Pakistani forces in UNOSOM II in south Mogadishu for which they were ill-prepared and equipped. It also became clear that US troops remaining with UNOSOM II were taking their orders from Washington rather than the UN commander on the ground (even though for continuity the deputy commander was an American, General Montgomery), and their apparent example was taken up by other countries. The French were accused of unilaterally withdrawing their forces from Mogadishu to avoid taking casualties. While the Italians, who as the former colonial power felt a special affinity for Somalis, were alleged to be bribing SNA supporters to obtain a quiet life for their troops.

UN operations were being so dominated by what had become a military confrontation with the SNA that other aspects of its work were being neglected. In particular humanitarian work, supposedly the original reason for intervention, was reduced. It was also claimed that there was less need for disaster relief outside Mogadishu at least, but such claims only heightened the questioning of the whole UNOSOM II operation. Efforts at further promoting the restoration of some basic attributes of a state also appeared beyond the capacity and resources of the UN. Work did continue, especially after the ending of confrontation with Aideed, but it was always limited and fragile in the face of the continuing factional rivalry which remained the dominant characteristic of politics in southern Somalia.

A further major weakness of the UN lay in its bureaucratic incompetence and waste. There was little effective co-ordination of the military, political, humanitarian, and institution-building sides of the UN's work. Combined with the embarrassments caused to the US militarily, this aspect of the UN's shortcomings in Somalia was a major contribution to the growing criticism in the US government of the Secretary-General. In his defence it would be argued that there were some efforts to improve the bureaucracy, and that with a number of operations simultaneously across the world the UN was underfunded (partly due to US deficiencies in payment) and understaffed.

After UNOSOM II

At the time of the UNOSOM II pull out in 1995, Somalia was comparable to conditions before UNOSOM in 1992. The two major faction rivals for control of the largely destroyed capital of Mogadishu were still those of Aideed and Ali Mahdi, with the latter proclaiming himself president (a claim recognised only by Libya and Sudan). There was still a UN presence, and its civilian personnel, as well as those of the remaining NGOs, were as constrained in their activities as they had been for much of the time since Barre's downfall in 1991, with or without foreign troops. There were continuing efforts to facilitate political reconciliation between the factions, but the latter appeared as implacable as ever, and deadly clashes occurred from time to time. There was one notable development when on 1 August 1996 Mohamed Farah Aideed died following a violent incident. Some thought that his SNA was already weakening following the defection of his main financial backer, Osman Ato, to Ali Mahdi Mohamed, and the development of fresh clan and sub-clan rivalries within it. Aideed had not prepared a successor, and the announcement that his son Hussein Maalim Aideed, a young man of 31 who had spent much of his life in the US (and, initially unrecognised by the American authorities, had arrived with UNITAF as an interpreter), would take over might herald further decline. A weakened SNA could lead to a consolidation of power around Ali Mahdi and the SSA which has been less belligerent and shown considerable interest in developing a climate for business activities in the past.

Away from southern Somalia, the situation in the country had long been less violent. In the central and north-eastern areas, away from the intensity of Mogadishu, local faction leaders, especially the Somali Salvation Democratic Front (SSDF) emerged to participate in the management of stateless society. They were joined in this by clan and sub-clan leaders, particularly of the Mijerteyn; as well as by influential Muslim figures. The balance and stability varied from one area to another, but there was not the intensity of rivalry and violence of the south.

However, the most remarkable transformation had been in the region of former British Somaliland in the north-west. It had suffered terribly in the unsuccessful uprising of 1988, but after Barre fell, the Somali National Movement (SNM) assumed full control. In May 1991 President Abdel Rahman Ali 'Tour' announced the formation of the state of Somaliland, and repealed the Act of Union which had joined the former British and Italian administered territories in 1960.

There were predictably faction, clan and sub-clan tensions but Somaliland did not descend into the violent anarchy of the south. In part this seemed due to the devolution of power with local leaders being actively involved in administration. Traditional processes of mediation and dispute settlement were revived, as well as *guurti* (councils of elders) that could arbitrate between clans on sensitive subjects such as grazing and water rights. This local involvement in political life culminated in a national *guurti* or conference at Boroma which lasted from February to May 1993. Amidst criticism of the new 'national' government the local representatives voted for a new leader, former prime minister Mohamed Ibrahim Egal, to replace Ali 'Tour'. Alongside this new state with its considerable reliance on local leaders, a vibrant commercial dynamic was growing including a good deal of trade with neighbouring countries.

Yet internationally Somaliland remained unrecognised, and an important factor in that was the attitude of the UN. From the outset of UN involvement, Secretary General Boutros-Ghali in particular had opposed recognition. (As Egypt's Deputy Foreign Minister he had backed Barre in the repression of the north in 1988.) Sahnoun had hoped to bring Somaliland back into the regionalised fold of a re-built Somalia, but after he had gone the UN was seen as actively hostile to the self-proclaimed new state. Other countries followed suit, including neighbouring states much involved in Somalia such as Ethiopia and Djibouti. It all appeared to stand in sharp contrast with the readiness of the international community to recognise the independence of Eritrea, formerly part of Ethiopia, following its referendum in 1993. The lack of international recognition deprived Somaliland of official aid, though some NGOs resumed work there. It also left some Somalis in the south hoping that in some way the former regions of the country might be brought together once more in the future.

Conclusion

Almost from the outset of operations, and certainly from UNOSOM II, Somali has gone down as one of the worst ever UN interventions anywhere in the world. As indicated at the start, Somalia was not unknown territory either for the UN, or the US, which was to become the major operational arm. As a former UN Trust Territory, and a US client in the Second Cold War as it affected north-east Africa in the 1980s, there was no lack of experience of the country. Yet the first line of criticism is that in spite of that experience opportunities for that desirable alternative to intervention, 'preventive diplomacy', had been missed. Mohamed Sahnoun has argued the case for three wasted opportunities.[13] The first was in 1988 when the uprising in the north was met by savage butchery from Barre. (Though the US did subsequently cut military aid, there was little public criticism.) The second came in 1990 when intellectuals in Mogadishu sought reform through the presentation of a manifesto. The third chance was the failure of the reconciliation conference in 1991. On none of these occasions was there sufficient international concern and pressure; indeed the international response was more to cut and run, as with UN personnel in the north in 1988, than to engage positively in 'preventive diplomacy'.

Once there was international recognition of the scale of the problem of Somalia there was little criticism of the decision to embark on UNOSOM in 1992, but much of the way it was handled. In particular the public clash between the Secretary General Boutros Boutros-Ghali, and UN Special Representative Mohamed Sahnoun, did much to undermine confidence. While Sahnoun was not above criticism, there was wide support for his ideas for targeting intervention regionally, and trying for local support including 'traditional' authorities. Even in the Security Council the permanent members were all critical of the clash that led to Sahnoun's resignation, and some sympathy was expressed for the criticisms of the UN bureaucracy that he had made.

Later in 1992 the circumstances leading to UNITAF were to be called into question. In particular the famine situation, and the losses on relief due to armed robbery which were set as high as 80 per cent. It has been argued that the losses had never been so high as cited, and that famine was declining rather than increasing before UNITAF was deployed. There were also criticisms that the decision to deploy UNITAF involved two private agendas, irrespective of conditions in Somalia. Boutros-Ghali wanted to demonstrate the UN's role in forcible intervention as a contribution to the New World Order; while outgoing President Bush welcomed a last opportunity to combine decisiveness and humanitarianism in US foreign policy. The reasons for undertaking UNITAF thus appeared to take precedence over what it might actually do, and the conditions to obtain before it should finally leave.

Indeed the uncertainties over UNITAF's role were not confined to the circumstances in which it should leave, but began as soon as it had arrived. There was no doubt that in the short term the flow of relief aid was improved. The issue was whether the supply of such a large force for such a limited objective was really all that had to be done to contribute to the establishment of a secure environment in the longer term. The central question was disarmament. The UN, in the person of the Secretary-General, believed that disarmament was an imperative for relief and reconstruction. The US military and the US Special Representative believed that it was dangerous and unnecessary and that a conciliatory approach to the 'warlords' could reduce tension. In reality this turned out to be confusing and capable of manipulation. To Somalis who saw the 'warlords' as a cancer it seemed unbelievable that a force of 38,000 well-armed foreigners could not at least make inroads into disarming the much smaller and less well-equipped militias. Events outside Mogadishu, such as in Baidoa, appeared to indicate that much more could have been done. Instead UNITAF talked to all the 'warlords' when it could have detained them and then allowed them to return to their armed groups, whose weapons were only intermittently and ineffectively raided.

UNITAF appeared to think that it could be above the political fray, when in fact it was a part of the political scene to be manipulated by Somali players. Faction leaders manoeuvred to seek to win apparent preference from it, or to demonise it to enhance their own support. And UNITAF was trying to play a reconciliatory role which would certainly require time, when it itself had a tight timetable. 'Warlords' knew that it would leave, and that some differences at least would emerge when UNOSOM II took over.

The sense of a missed opportunity became much greater once UNOSOM II was in place. Now that there was a more determined effort to pursue disarmament, the 'warlords', especially Aideed, had had several months to adjust to what was in effect military occupation and he was able to hit back to embarrassing effect against UNOSOM II forces. While it was trying to do more than UNITAF, UNOSOM II had fewer forces; and displayed marked fragmentation and signs of national rather than UN command. There were also a number of accusations of abuse of Somalis' human rights during the course of UN operations, and in 1997 charges were made against French and Italian troops.

At the same time there was much to be criticised in the UN itself. The active involvement of the Secretary-General himself was seen by many as unfortunate. He was personally associated with Egypt's backing of the former Somali dictator Siad Barre who had contributed so much to his country's debacle. Widely criticised for sacking Sahnoun, that decision also led to the concentration on Mogadishu to the detriment of a more regionalised approach; which alienated Somaliland in particular. UN headquarters remained overly bureaucratic, while on the ground in Mogadishu there sometimes seemed to be a lack of expertise and co-operation amongst a staff who for much of the time were confined to their bunkers.

Though the US role was supposed to be diminished under UNOSOM II, in fact it remained central, and it was Clinton, rather than the UN, who dramatically changed direction in the autumn of 1993. While following the final withdrawal of US troops in 1994, UNOSOM II was a listless operation in its final year. Not only was there a continuing resemblance in the conditions in Somali between arrival and departure, but also a sense that any hope of international intervention to help the people of that failed state was now finally dashed.

The UN's experience in Somalia in turn fed back into broader thinking about the organisation, and the international community's responsibility in humanitarian crises. Somalia did not serve to extinguish the view that there should be greater readiness to act in such cases. The emergence of a more widespread consensus internationally on human rights, especially after the collapse of the Soviet Union, was the main approach for justifying intervention where state breakdown was creating humanitarian crises. But while this did not diminish, the UN's performance did lead to new questions about its capability to act. One outcome was a loss of confidence in the organisation and its ability to reform itself, especially in the US. Some saw the international community's reluctance to act in Rwanda as linked to the operational debacles of Somalia. At the same time it was hoped that regional organisations might shoulder a greater responsibility, in spite of the lack of resources in the case of such groupings in Africa, the continent in which the prevalence of state breakdown and humanitarian crises has been greatest in recent years. (Indeed there have been suggestions of Western financial aid to regional peacekeepers). Somalia's impoverished neighbours have been involved in its experiences, sometimes controversially, and after UNOSOM II finally departed, were left as continuing players on the sidelines of the country's continuing struggles.

Notes

1 Said S. Samatar (1991) *Somalia: a nation in turmoil*, Minority Rights Group: London.
2 Mohamed Sahnoun (1994) *Somalia: the missed opportunities*, US Institute of Peace Press: Washington, p. 27.

3   Patrick Gilkes (1994) 'Descent into chaos: Somalia, January 1991-December 1992' in Charles Gurdon (ed) *The Horn of Africa*, University College London Press: London, p. 53.
4   Sahnoun (1994), pp. 53-4.
5   Boutros Boutros-Ghali (1992) *An Agenda for Peace*, United Nations: New York.
6   John L. Hirsch and Robert B. Oakley (1995) *Somalia and Operation Restore Hope*, US Institute of Peace Press: Washington, p. 47.
7   In theory the US was still present in Somalia throughout UNITAF, causing some vagueness about roles. Hirsch (1995), p. 51.
8   Robert Patman (1997), 'Disarming Somalia: the contrasting fortunes of United States and Australian peacekeepers during United Nations intervention, 1992-1993', *African Affairs*, 95.
9   Hirsch (1995), p. 105.
10 Quoted in Adam Roberts (1993) 'Humanitarian War' in *International Affairs*, 69, 3, p. 441.
11 Hirsch (1995), pp. 102-114 passim.
12 Mohamed Farah Aideed and Satya Pal Ruhela (1993) *The preferred development in Somalia*, Vikas: New Delhi; Satya Pal Ruhela (ed) (1994) *Mohamed Farah Aideed and his Vision of Somalia*, Vikas: New Delhi.
13 Sahnoun (1994), pp. 3-12.

References

Clarke, W. S. (1995) *Humanitarian Intervention in Somalia: Bibliography*, US Army War College: Pennsylvania.

Drysdale, J. (1994) *Whatever Happened to Somalia: A Tale of Tragic Blunders*, HAAN: London.

Laitin, D. D. and Samatar S. S. (1987) *Somalia: Nation in Search of a State*, Westview: Boulder.

Lewis, I. M. (1980) *A Modern History of Somalia: Nation and State in the Horn of Africa*, Longman: London.

Lewis, I. M. (1993) *Understanding Somalia*, HAAN: London.

Makinda, S. L. (1993) *Seeking Peace from Chaos: Humanitarian Intervention in Somalia*, Lynne Rienner: Boulder.

Samatar, A. (1994) (ed) *The Somali Challenge: From Catastrophe to Renewal?*, Lynne Rienner: Boulder.

8 Peacekeeping in Mozambique

Sam Barnes

The successful implementation of the General Peace Agreement (GPA) signed by the Government of Mozambique and Renamo in October 1992, bringing to an end a sixteen-year war which displaced more than one third of the country, 15 million persons and destroyed the economic and social infrastructures, must be attributed to a range of factors. This chapter will limit its focus to the official period of the United Nations Peacekeeping Mission (ONUMOZ), October 1992 through March 1995. However, actions and initiatives taken by the UN and its agencies, bilateral aid organisations, NGOs, regional actors, Mozambican institutions and individuals before and after this period were also significant in creating and maintaining a political and social environment conducive to peace-building and peacekeeping.

ONUMOZ's presence may be seen as decisive and necessary, but it is important to view it as part of this broader dynamic that contributed to the consolidation of peace in Mozambique. An important feature of ONUMOZ's role was the interplay and reinforcing nature of the 'hardware' of peacekeeping (military and political) with the 'software' of peacekeeping (humanitarian assistance, demobilisation and reintegration programmes). The relative smoothness of the Mozambican transition from war to peace resulted from this multiplicity of forces which, operating concurrently with the UN peacekeeping operation, ensured that the overall process could advance.

The United Nations and the international community were given an expansive role and mandate by the GPA. The direct costs of the ONUMOZ operation were some $565 million, while the humanitarian programme accounted for an additional $532 million obligated in the ONUMOZ period.[1] The international community contributed $59.1

million for the elections, while the Government provided $5.4 million. In addition, there were two political trust funds; one Fund for Renamo to transform itself from a military organisation to a political party which received $13.6 million and another for all registered political parties which benefited from donations of $1.88 million. All this makes the Mozambique Peace Process one of the most costly, with $1.1 billion contributed by the international community during a 30 month period. Another interesting point is the balance of the 'peacekeeping' dollar to the 'peace-building' dollar. For each ONUMOZ dollar, at least one more was spent on humanitarian programmes and support for the electoral process. This underscores the importance of the dynamic between the formal peacekeeping operation, and the complementary programmes which create and sustain an enabling political and social environment to consolidate the peace.

UN involvement was first pushed by the mediators and Renamo during the peace negotiations. The Mozambique Government was very sensitive to sovereignty issues and favoured a much more limited UN role. However, succumbing to pressures from the international community and responding to the political necessity to deliver on the peace promises, the United Nations was awarded a role in almost all aspects of the process. This 'mandate' became the explanation for a further intensification in this period of the international communities' efforts to control policy and programme implementation resulting in further weakening and decapacitisation of national institutions.

Background to the war

Mozambique gained independence from Portugal in 1975, after more than twenty years of armed struggle led by the Frente de Libertacao de Mocambique (FRELIMO). The new country's strong political commitment to anti-colonial and anti-racist struggles coupled with its declared Marxist-Leninist allegiance gained it the immediate wrath of neighbouring minority-ruled South Africa and Rhodesia. Mozambique offered support and bases for the Zimbabwean freedom fighters, resulting in direct attacks against Mozambican territory by the Ian Smith UDI government in Rhodesia. By 1977, Rhodesian covert support and training of the Resistencia Nacional Mocambicana (MNR - later known as RENAMO) expanded in an effort to destabilise the young and fragile Mozambican government. After Zimbabwean independence in 1980, the Rhodesian Central Intelligence Organisation 'divested' itself of the MNR and handed it over to the South African Military Intelligence which assumed the 'controlling interest in all external operations'.[2]

While the Mozambique Government maintained contacts and discussions with the South African Government throughout the 1980s in an effort to stop South African support for the Renamo forces, the conflict continued to devastate the Mozambican countryside. The conflict was viewed externally as a by-product of South Africa's destabilisation of its neighbours and so therefore Mozambique gained the support of the UN and international community as it was perceived as the victim. The first direct negotiations took place in July 1990 in Rome, facilitated by the Sant'Egidio community.[3] A partial cease-fire on the economically vital Limpopo and Beira Corridors was accepted in December 1990. The two parties, the Mozambique Government and Renamo, accepted an Agenda for the Negotiations in May 1991, specifying the areas which would require agreement; the law on political parties, the electoral system, military issues, guarantees, a cease-fire and a donors' conference. The discussions crawled along for another sixteen months while both internal and external pressures increasingly pushed the two parties to accelerate the negotiation process.

Concurrent to this, Mozambique was not only moving from war to peace, but was in the process of transforming from a single-party state to a multi-party electoral system; from a socialist economy to a capitalist market system within the framework of structural adjustment programmes and resulting pressures from the World Bank and IMF; and from an extremely centralised state administration and planning to more decentralisation and deconcentration of state power. A new constitution was approved in November 1990, which established the multiparty state with direct elections for President and members of Parliament. These changes were important for the negotiation process.

The UN had virtually no role in the negotiations. The Italian mediators were those that provided the continuity to the process, while several individual Mozambicans and international figures exerted their influence at key moments. The UN was brought in as an official observer in June 1992, in order to work with the mediators on the role of the UN in verification of the agreement. A 'non-paper' was sent by Secretary-General Boutros Boutros Ghali to President Chissano on 19 August 1992 which outlined the specific mechanisms for verifications of the military aspects of the peace agreement as well as the organisational mechanisms and requirements of a UN Security Council Operation. Finally, on 4 October 1992, the GPA was signed by the Government of Mozambique and Renamo, and the transitional process formally began.

Setting up the framework for peacemaking

All parties recognised early on that the humanitarian component was going to be key to the Mozambican peace process. Protocol III, signed in March 1992 by the Representatives of the Government and Renamo in the Rome negotiations included a chapter (IV) on *The return of Mozambican refugees and displaced persons and their social reintegration*.[4] This chapter stated that these groups would not 'forfeit any of their rights ...for having left their places of residence' and 'shall be registered and included in the electoral rolls...in their places of residence'. It went on to indicate that the Government and Renamo should draw up a draft agreement for assistance to these groups, and the United Nations should be involved in the drawing up and implementation of such a plan. A clear link was made between the return and resettlement of externally and internally displaced Mozambicans and the electoral process, as envisaged by the evolving peace agreement.

By this time, the drought in Southern Africa was putting additional pressures on the peace negotiation process, as both Government and Renamo were having severe difficulties in feeding their civilian populations. The United Nations, ICRC and humanitarian organisations operating in Mozambique were pressuring for humanitarian safe zones or corridors. The UN-SADCC Appeal for the Drought Emergency in Southern Africa (DESA) estimated that 3.1 million Mozambicans were in need of immediate relief assistance, of which at least 500,000 were in Renamo-controlled areas to which there was no access.

By June 1992, pressures from the UN, ICRC, US and Italy to include humanitarian issues in the peace negotiations were increasing. At the same time, Renamo - looking ahead to elections as part of the peace agreement - was losing population to government areas where relief food could be more easily found. Finally in early July 1992, both Government and Renamo agreed to a proposal by an Italian mediator for a meeting with humanitarian agencies to discuss mechanisms to ensure the delivery of relief to all areas of Mozambique. These meetings in Rome resulted in the *Declaration on the Guiding Principles for Humanitarian Assistance* signed by the two parties on 16 July 1992.

The Declaration agreed that assistance could go to all Mozambicans and that the United Nations would preside over a Committee which had responsibility for the co-ordination and supervision of all humanitarian operations undertaken under the agreement. This placed humanitarian assistance co-ordination firmly within a peacekeeping context in which neutrality and impartiality were part of the modus operandi. It became increasingly evident that maintaining a peace in Mozambique would be closely linked to the effectiveness of the humanitarian programme.

In some previous peacekeeping missions, humanitarian co-ordination had been outside the mission with responsibility held by the UNDP or a lead agency (UNHCR, WFP, UNICEF). Though the agencies preferred this arrangement, it often led to problems in ensuring that humanitarian and political priorities and programmes were mutually reinforcing and consolidating to the process. There was a growing recognition and lobby in New York for more effective integration of the various aspects of peacekeeping. The United Nations Department of Humanitarian Affairs (DHA) had been created within the Secretariat upon the request of member states, to respond to these criticisms. An USG for Humanitarian Affairs was named in April 1992, and ONUMOZ was the first major peacekeeping operation in which DHA could be included within the apparatus along side the Department of Peacekeeping and the Department of Political Affairs. USG James Jonah and USG Abdulrahim Farah, both familiar with the pressing humanitarian needs of Mozambique, in a briefing note to the SG in August 1992, transmitted the view that the UN involvement in Mozambique should be integrated and that the humanitarian co-ordination component should be within the structure of the peace keeping operation.[5]

The General Peace Agreement (GPA) was finally signed on 4 October 1992 and stipulated a broad role for the United Nations in the overall supervision of the implementation of the GPA. The UN was to verify the cease-fire; to supervise and monitor the withdrawal of foreign troops, the separation of the two armies, their entry into assembly areas, their disarmament and eventual demobilisation; to observe the electoral process and provide technical assistance and material support for the Mozambican Government to organise and carry out the multi-party elections for President and members of Parliament. When the final structure of ONUMOZ was presented to the Security Council for Approval in December 1992 the interrelated and overlapping nature of the mandates were evident.

> Without sufficient humanitarian aid, and especially food supplies, the security situation in the country may deteriorate and the demobilisation process might stall. Without adequate military protection, the humanitarian aid would not reach its destination. Without sufficient progress in the political area, the confidence required for the disarmament and rehabilitation process would not exist. The electoral process, in turn, requires prompt demobilisation

and formation of the new armed forces, without which conditions would not exist for successful elections.[6]

The UN peacekeeping machinery, ONUMOZ, included within it military, political, electoral, humanitarian and administrative components, as well as a Technical Unit on Demobilisation (TU). Aldo Ajello, the Special Representative of the Secretary-General (SRSG), in charge of the ONUMOZ operation influenced the form of the final structure, but it was certainly consistent with the prevailing views within the Departments of Peacekeeping, Political Affairs and Humanitarian Affairs in New York. According to Ajello, 'there was an agreement from the beginning that UNOHAC, the humanitarian component would be within ONUMOZ. I would have refused to have it outside the structure'.[7]

UNOHAC had the responsibility for the co-ordination of all humanitarian assistance programmes for the internally displaced, returning refugees and the reintegration of demobilised soldiers, while the TU was responsible for the implementation of the demobilisation process. Both these units were led and staffed by civilians, who reported directly to the SRSG. This was the first time that it was recognised within a UN peacekeeping operation that demobilisation was not the sole domain of the UN military components. The military had the responsibility for the disarmament of the soldiers and the verification of the process, but the technical unit assumed responsibility for its overall organisation.

Another equally important characteristic of the Mozambique peace process was the fact that the GPA recognised the Mozambican Government, its institutions and its laws. The GPA was, in fact, approved by the Parliament and therefore became law. The GPA went further to state that 'the two Parties undertake to guarantee that the laws and legislative provisions of the Republic of Mozambique, ...shall be respected and guaranteed in all parts of the national territory..'.[8] This was particularly important when the re-establishment of the health and education systems in both Renamo and Government areas became a focus of reintegration programmes. In some areas that were under Renamo control, there was initial resistance to the reintroduction of the national health or education systems of the Mozambican Government. There were special provisions of the GPA which created a National Commission for Administration to oversee the integration of areas controlled by Renamo into the State Administration during the period between the GPA and the elections. This Commission's membership was constituted from the two parties without UN participation. It had limited success leaving several districts and localities with dual administrations at the time of the elections. However, the Commission agreed that five districts and 42 administrative posts were under Renamo control and appointed new administrators before it ceased to function in July 1994.[9]

The software of peacekeeping

This civilian side of peacekeeping, especially humanitarian assistance programmes, was the de facto advance guard of the peace process. The civilian populations, on both sides, needed to gain confidence in the newly found peace, if the plans for elections were to move forward. The first result of the GPA for many Mozambicans in the country side was the provisioning of food and other relief items, once the cease-fire went into effect on 15 October 1992. Before the signing of the peace agreement, over seventy percent of the 3.1 million tons of food aid beneficiaries could only be reached by militarily protected convoy or air lifts. Supplies were limited and irregularly delivered. Despite the humanitarian Declaration in July 1994, few gains had been made in securing access to civilians in Renamo-controlled areas until the cease-fire.

Since a UN Special Co-ordinator for Emergency Relief Operations (UNSCERO) had been named at the time of the first UN Emergency Appeal in 1987, there was an in-country UN co-ordination body with five years of experience liaisoning with Government, donors and relief organisations. All major operational UN agencies (UNDP, WFP, UNICEF, UNHCR, WHO, FAO, UNFPA, UNIDO, UNDRO/DHA) had programmes and over 50 NGOs were engaged in operations in the humanitarian area at the time of the signing of the peace agreement.[10] $1.5 billion had been pledged to Mozambique in the six emergency appeals (1987-1992) for food and non-food relief, emergency health care, water supply, seeds and tools and support for spontaneous returnees from neighbouring countries. All this combined to create a strong foundation for a rapid humanitarian intervention after the GPA.

The political and military components of ONUMOZ came on board slowly. The first military cease-fire observers arrived in February 1993, four months after the cease-fire came into effect. The military contingents, placed on the key corridors, took up positions between April and August 1993. With 6,000 ONUMOZ soldiers on the ground in August 1993, UN blue berets became a part of the peacekeeping dynamic. However, the fact that before their arrival, there were few significant violations of the cease-fire and that confidence in the security situation increased, must be attributed to political factors rather than UN military presence. The

Mozambican President and the Renamo President repeatedly stated that they would not go back to war. But more important, the soldiers were tired of fighting and the Mozambican people wanted peace. Tens of thousands began to move back to their homes immediately after the cease-fire. By January 1993, there were already an estimated 200,000 internally displaced persons (IDPs) that had resettled and 190,000 refugees that had returned (principally from Malawi to Tete province). As the cease-fire was maintained, confidence increased and the movements speeded up in 1993, especially of the IDPs. Resettlement was in part conditioned by the confidence that support would be received (i.e. food, seeds and tools, water supply, health care) when they reached their destination. Fortunately, due to the Mozambican Government and the international community's long history of collaboration during the war period in responding to the grave humanitarian crisis, there could be an immediate response.

The humanitarian programme

The humanitarian programme concretised the peace for many rural Mozambicans. So as to fulfil the principles of the Rome Declaration, that assistance should be available for all needy Mozambicans, emphasis was placed on getting relief to civilians in Renamo areas and isolated Government-held areas that were previously inaccessible. Impartiality and neutrality emerged as important characteristics in the assessment of need and the delivery of assistance. First and foremost was the delivery of food to sustain the populations and agricultural seeds and tools for the planting season which coincided with the signing of the peace agreement.

Immediately, the ICRC, WFP, UNICEF and WHO expanded their operations into the Renamo areas and facilitated the entry of international NGOs, already working in the country, to complement their work. At the time of the signing of the GPA, only ICRC was working in Renamo areas. Renamo was suspicious of the international NGOs, since they had been exclusively working on the government side. They were unfamiliar with the 'requirements' of needs assessments, control and monitoring of distribution. The ICRC and UN personnel witnessed delays in the delivery of needed relief, due to the refusal by Renamo officials in some areas to allow international relief workers into affected areas to assess the needs, or because of difficulties between relief agencies and Renamo in agreeing on distribution modalities.

The GPA stipulated a Donors' Conference (held in December 1992) to finance the electoral process, emergency programmes and reintegration programmes for the IDPs, returning refugees and demobilised soldiers. The UN and the Government with Renamo prepared the 'appeal' for financial support which totalled some $403 million. $300 million was immediately pledged. Later, UNOHAC refined and expanded on the needs and presented a Consolidated Humanitarian Assistance Programme to a follow-up conference in June 1993, totalling some $560 million. These programmes were multi-sectoral, and though they included the necessary food aid, clothing and basic necessities, moved away from truly a 'relief' mode to include the rebuilding of basic services in the rural countryside. In addition, mine clearance and support for the reintegration of demobilised soldiers were added to the list of priorities along with agriculture, health, water supply, road repair, education and area-based integrated rural revitalisation programmes By the end of the ONUMOZ period, further revisions had been done, placing the needs at $775 million.

Before the GPA, Mozambique had become dependent upon international aid for up to 80 per cent of its imports. Donors were already 'calling the shots' and increasingly channelling funds through NGOs, bilateral or UN agencies rather than governmental or national institutions. Decision-making on key policy issues was being taken over by those that were paying for the programmes - the international community. Therefore, it is not surprising that in the context of the GPA and with the presence of ONUMOZ, that the donors expanded their influence and 'defined' the programmes that emerged.[11]

The largest donors, in humanitarian and well as long term development programmes, were the United States, European Community, the Netherlands, Sweden, Italy, Norway, Denmark, UK, and Switzerland. The SRSG realised that the Ambassadors of this group would be important to the political process. He, therefore, held meetings with this group each week in his office, to get their endorsement and financial backing. As a consequence a co-ordinated stance could be presented to the two parties to the GPA - Government and Renamo, when faced with political roadblocks.

The role of the donors in the humanitarian programme was more contentious. At the time, several key donors were not in agreement with the inclusion of UNOHAC within ONUMOZ, thereby removing UN humanitarian co-ordination from UNDP.[12] The Maputo field offices of the UN agencies had recommended to DHA in October 1992 that UNDP not continue as the lead in humanitarian co-ordination during the peacekeeping phase, and that a new structure be set up for this phase in which all agencies would be a part.[13] However, during the ONUMOZ period these same agencies (WFP, UNHCR, WHO) never accepted UNOHAC's (and DHA's) co-ordination mandate in relation to their operational areas.[14]

UNOHAC's role, as initially stated in the Report of the Secretary-General on ONUMOZ of December 1992 and at the Rome Donors' Conference the same month, was to co-ordinate the various humanitarian assistance programmes in liaison with Government, Renamo, donors and implementing agencies; to gather and disseminate information on humanitarian needs, programmes, donations; to manage a UN Trust Fund established to support reintegration activities. The Government did not want to lose its pre-GPA co-ordination authority to UNOHAC, though clearly Renamo would not have participated in a Government-run body. Donors continued to define their priority areas and used a neutrality or impartiality argument to sideline government ministries (especially health, water, education) and replace them with NGO implementers.

Expanded assistance to Renamo areas

A Technical Committee chaired by the UN, set up to implement the Humanitarian principles of the Rome Declaration, continued under UNOHAC to bring together representatives of the Government, Renamo, UN agencies and NGOs to discuss needs, populations movements, problems areas and approve distribution plans, so as to guarantee transparency and neutrality. Within the first six months after the GPA; 16,000 tons of food, 2,000 tons of seeds, and more than 130,000 units of relief supplies were distributed to civilians in Renamo-controlled areas. This type of co-ordination started out on a central level, but as UNOHAC decentralised and opened up offices in each province it became evident that relief programmes and reconstruction priorities were best discussed and co-ordinated at the provincial level.

In June 1993, the first provincial Humanitarian Assistance Committee (HAC) was held in the much divided central province of Sofala. Other provinces started up shortly after. These forums were useful in promoting contacts among the two parties and feeding a reconciliation agenda. They also provided opportunities for Renamo and Governmental authorities to solve problems and determine priorities together. There was a lot of name calling at first, and in several provinces the Governors forbid provincial authorities to attend meetings with Renamo representatives. These blockages would be transmitted to the central offices of UNOHAC, whereby contact would be made with higher level governmental authorities to pressure their provincial colleagues. At the same time, literally thousands of contacts were being made at the level of districts and localities, where Renamo and Government would have to work together to facilitate food aid deliveries from one area to another, to organise a vaccination campaign with 'government' health department nurses working in a Renamo controlled area or to identify land mines placed by both sides so that vital land routes could be opened up.

By the end of the ONUMOZ mandate, total food distribution to what were then called ex-Renamo areas reached 116,000 tons to 75 districts in all ten provinces. Thirty-five NGOs were involved, and most of the civilian population was no longer at risk. Twenty different organisations worked to expand the seed and tool distribution to civilians in Renamo areas in 45 districts so that agricultural recovery programmes could begin. Total seed distribution in the ONUMOZ period included 2.1 million families who received 56,000 tons of seeds and more than 8 million agricultural hand tools.[15]

The dependence upon relief food diminished over the period from the signing of the GPA to the post-election period, signalling the move from a relief to a development framework. In 1992, WFP reported 3.8 million Mozambicans in need of food aid (650,000 mt), due to the effects of the war and the drought. By 1993/94 crop season this had dropped to 1.8 million persons, while by 1994/95 it further reduced to 1.5 million. The 'peace factor' was important; providing the security for crops to be planted and harvested; stored for family consumption and surpluses to be transported to emerging local markets for sale.

Reconstruction and rehabilitation

Rapidly, it became evident that rural reconstruction would have to be activated so as to create the minimal conditions for the massive influx of population. In 1993, 2.1 million IDPs resettled while another 400,000 refugees returned bringing the total to 600,000 by January 1994. In 1993, there were political delays in both the demobilisation process and the approval of the election law for the multi-party elections as stipulated in the GPA. The GPA had stated that the elections would take place within one year. By mid-1993 it became clear that this would not be possible, and the timetable was changed requiring elections by the end of October 1994. These delays had a greater impact on the return of refugees than the resettlement of the IDPs.

From UNHCR's perspective, the repatriation of Mozambican refugees was a complicated process; involving six countries and over 1.7 million persons returning. Despite the various indications throughout 1992, that a peace agreement was imminent, UNHCR was very slow in responding to the peace context. It was only in March 1993 that a repatriation plan was developed, staff capacity increased slowly throughout 1993, and the Reintegration Programme for the returnees was only approved in December 1994 (after elections were held). UNHCR centralised the power for the Mozambique repatriation programme in Geneva.

The UNHCR Offices in the asylum countries, especially Malawi, had built up large bureaucracies which they did not want to cede to the country of origin office, Mozambique, which logically should have had the lead role in determining the repatriation and reintegration strategies. In Cambodia, a Special Envoy had been named, who had exceptional powers and reported only to the High Commissioner. In Mozambique, the Mozambique office was treated almost as a distant cousin, until more than a million refugees had already returned, most of them spontaneously, by 1994, and then the support programmes had a larger profile.

Reconstruction programmes, supported by HCR, USAID, EU, UNOHAC Trust Fund, and other bilateral donors and UN agencies, began to take off towards the end of 1993. The Mozambique Government had a National Reconstruction Plan, developed by the line ministries, but it suffered from the lack of clear prioritisation and was limited in its ability to address the problems in ex-Renamo areas. International NGOs implemented most of the reconstruction programmes during the ONUMOZ period, and in the immediate post-election period. Of the $160 million obligated for agriculture, health, education and area-based programmes as defined in the UNOHAC Consolidated Humanitarian Assistance Programme, 60 per cent went to NGOs. By and large, the projects had a 'bricks and mortar' orientation which rebuilt schools, health posts, opened water sources or repaired rural roads or bridges. Unfortunately, their sustainability was often undermined by the NGOs' lack of co-ordination with local authorities to ensure, for example that teachers or health workers would be available to staff the newly rehabilitated facilities; or limited technical expertise on the part of the NGOs resulting in shoddy building practices. Donors, in part, should bear responsibility for improper control and monitoring. However, at the same time the 'boom' in reconstruction activity did contribute at a critical phase to a 'peace momentum'. The question is raised whether the expediency of moving quickly, was truly necessary to build confidence and consolidate peace. This is difficult to measure, but the fact that reintegration and reconstruction programmes existed within the context and framework of a peacekeeping operation highlights its importance for the peace process.

Demobilisation before elections

As the soldiers from the two sides began to move into their Assembly Areas between November 1993 and April 1994, the refugee flow back to Mozambique accelerated. The Electoral Law was finally approved by all parties in December 1993 and formally came into effect in January 1994. Demobilisation began in April 1994 continuing through September. Voter registration was carried out from June through September, while elections were 27 to 29 October.

The demobilisation process and the start-up of reintegration support programmes for the 92,000 demobilised soldiers from the two armies were determinant for the peace process. The Cease-Fire Commission (CCF), chaired by the UN, and composed of Government, Renamo, Portugal, Italy, France, UK, USA, Botswana, Nigeria, Egypt had to approve the location of the assembly areas, the procedures for cantonment as well as troop movements and conduct within the assembly areas. The assembly areas were approved and opened up in phases, the first twenty in November 1993, then fifteen more in December 1993, while the final fourteen sites only became operational in late February 1994. The SRSG had to negotiate with the two sides to finally get agreement.

The GPA had also set up a Commission on Reintegration (CORE), again, chaired by the UN, to undertake the planning, organisation, supervision and monitoring of programmes for the economic and social reintegration of demobilised soldiers. The GPA, recognised that this group must have special attention if they were to be effectively 'neutralised' as soldiers and integrated as civilians. The GPA also stated that the resources for the programmes should come from the international community. Given the slow pace of the political process which defined and determined demobilisation, the international community did not place importance on this group until mid-1993. In fact, at the donors' conference in December 1992, the final resolutions stated the programmes for demobilised soldiers, returning refugees, IDPs and affected populations should be integrated, not giving preference to any single group. The group of donors also proposed that the CORE expand its scope, as defined by the GPA, to include displaced persons and returnees. This attitude set back the planning for reintegration programmes for demobilised soldiers.

As the process of demobilisation slowed down, and the soldiers themselves surfaced as a disruptive and unruly group; blocking roads, detaining hostages and vehicles, attacking or looting UN, NGO or Government offices or warehouses; the donors and the SRSG began to realise that visible programmes for the demobilised soldiers were needed for the process to advance. The broader area-based programmes would not have the capacity to absorb the soldiers in the short or even medium-term.

UNOHAC had been working, with the two parties through the CORE mechanism, to develop a strategy which had an economic focus and included training and vocational kits, credit, employment programmes and counselling and referral services. The donors perceived these programmes as being weighted towards longer term reintegration, while what was needed was a 'quick-fix' that would assist in the social reintegration of the demobilised soldiers since the economic reintegration was not feasible or possible in the foreseeable future given the state of the Mozambican economy. The SRSG Aldo Ajello, was also critical of UNOHAC's approach as being driven by the 'culture of development' rather than the 'culture of peacekeeping'.

The Dutch Ambassador came up with a proposal that was quickly endorsed by other European donors, for a cash subsidy for all soldiers so as to extend the Government six month severance pay to a two year subsidy programme. This was quickly endorsed by the SRSG as he saw that it could be used to persuade the two parties to move more soldiers into the assembly areas and to speed up the demobilisation process, a precondition for the elections. In late January 1994, this Reintegration Support Scheme (RSS) was formally announced and over $20 million immediately pledged by the donors.

The package of programmes to support the social and economic reintegration of the demobilised soldiers that eventually emerged covered three phases of the process; the demobilisation phase; the reinsertion phase; and the actual reintegration phase. While in the assembly areas, there was an 'Information and Social Reintegration Programme' which trained Mozambican monitors from the two sides to work in the assembly areas to inform the soldiers through a civic education programme of the terms of the GPA, health education (especially AIDS and family planning), the rights and duties of demobilised soldiers and information on their entitlements, literacy classes, sports and cultural activities in the assembly areas. The disabled soldiers were provided with special support by NGOs specialising in working with the disabled.

Due to the delays in reaching political agreements on the composition of the new unified defence force (FADM), and decisions regarding which soldiers would be demobilised and the demobilisation calendar, many soldiers were in the camps for several months. In an analysis of unrest among demobilising or demobilised soldiers over the period January through September 1994, of 317 incidents, 60 per cent occurred in assembly areas while Government and Renamo soldiers were awaiting demobilisation. Once the benefits of demobilisation, especially the cash payment for two years, became known to the soldiers, 97 per cent wanted to be demobilised.

The reinsertion phase starts upon demobilisation and covers the period when the demobilised soldier and his family dependants are to be transported to their chosen destination until the ex-combatant has settled in his home area. Support for this phase, given to the soldier in the assembly areas included transport for the ex-soldiers to their chosen district, civilian clothing, a seed and tool kit, a two-week food-for-home ration and three-months' severance pay provided by the Government. Once they were in their home district, each soldier received three months' food ration for himself and family members transported to the district, another three-month pay check from the government, and after four months started receiving the RSS subsidy for another 18 months. Demobilised soldiers resettling in rural areas were also eligible for relief food and seed and tool distributions that were part of the humanitarian support programme for all resettling Mozambicans. Since between April and September, more than 92,000 soldiers were demobilised, these programmes were instrumental in the social pacification of this group in the critical pre- and post-election period.

An Information and Referral Service was set up in each province to assist soldiers in clarifying doubts on their benefits and referring them to appropriate training or employment programmes. In order to support the economic reintegration of the demobilised soldiers medium term programmes were set up which provided vocational and entrepreneurial training and supplied kits for self-employment. To complement this a Provincial Fund was set up in each province to provide small grants to projects which employed soldiers.

These specifically targeted programmes for the 92,000 demobilised soldiers continued until the end of 1996 and consumed almost $95 million, more than $1000 per person; of which $83 million was donated by the international community and $10.5 million was provided by the Government. Although clearly the returning refugees (1.7 million) or resettling internally displaced (3.2 million) far outnumbered the demobilised soldiers, they were not as volatile a group and so the per capita contribution that directly or indirectly benefited the returnees and IDPs was less than $100 in the ONUMOZ period.

Conclusions

The peace process in Mozambique was very dependent upon the humanitarian assistance programme, including support for the demobilised soldiers; to stabilise civil society so that a new smaller unified army could be formed, multi-party elections could be held, and an elected government, accepted by the parties to the conflict, could take office. The elected President, Joaquim Chissano, took office on 9 December 1994. The last ONUMOZ contingent left in January 1995.

Though the peacekeeping mandate ended in early 1995, the United Nations, through its agencies, and the international community continued to provide massive foreign aid to Mozambique, as they had before ONUMOZ's entry into the country. The withdrawal of ONUMOZ was typical of the 'culture of peacekeeping', treating it as a military and logistical operation rather than examining the various components and determining whether transitional approaches might be required. This was particularly true in the case of UNOHAC, with donors, UN agencies and government critical of the lack of a handover process to ensure continuity, especially at the provincial level, where UNOHAC's co-ordination mechanisms were most effective. The provincial offices closed down one month after the elections, so as to comply with the UNOHAC close down date set by ONUMOZ, 31 December 1994.

Humanitarian crises do not get resolved from one day to the next by political events, such as an election. Peacekeeping operations, increasingly, must consider the humanitarian needs if the operation is to be successful. Yet the political parameters and the time frame of humanitarian action is different than that of a security council intervention. Humanitarianism must straddle both the peacekeeping and the developmental frameworks. To work, it must be inside the operation in terms of policy, but outside the operation in terms of implementation - which was effectively what happened in Mozambique.

Notes

1   There was approximated $200 million paid out by the international community in the 1994 to 1996 period for support for reintegration,

especially by UNHCR, EU and USAID. This was a continuation of programmes started in the ONUMOZ period. The humanitarian component of ONUMOZ tracked all contributions to humanitarian assistance during its mandate. Post-ONUMOZ, there was no single UN agencies keeping such information, so the figure is an estimate by the author based on information from individual donors.

2   Flower, K. (1987), *Serving Secretly: Rhodesia's CIO Chief on Record*, Galago Publishing Ltd: Alberton, RSA, p. 262.
3   Two recent books present an analysis of the Mozambique peace negotiations, focusing on the role of mediation. Cameron Hume (1994) *Ending Mozambique's War: The Role of Mediation and Good Offices*, United States Institute for Peace: Washington DC, is the American view, as Hume was the deputy chief of the US Mission at the Vatican during that time. Roberto Morozzo della Rocca (1994) *Mozambico: Della guerra all pace, Storia di una mediazione insolita*, Editioni San Paulo: Turino, provides an inside look at the role of the church, the Italian Government and the Sant'Egidio community.
4   United Nations (1995) *The United Nations and Mozambique*, Department of Public Information, United Nations: New York, Document 12, 'General Peace Agreement for Mozambique', pp. 105-128.
5   Interview by the author with Taye Zerihoun, United Nations Department of Political Affairs, New York, on 17 April 1995.
6   *The United Nations and Mozambique*, Document 26, Report of the Secretary-General on ONUMOZ, p. 152.
7   Interview by the author with Aldo Ajello, United Nations, New York, on 3 April 1995.
8   *The United Nations and Mozambique*, Document 12, p. 119.
9   Ibid., p. 46.
10 UNSCERO, *Mozambique Emergency Programme: Closing Report 1991-1992*, Maputo, Mozambique.
11 There are a number of good sources on the influence of aid and the donor community in Mozambique. They include Abrahamsson, H. and Nilsson, A. (1995) *Mozambique: The Troubled Transition: From Socialist Construction to Free Market Capitalism*, Zed Press: London, Hanlon J. (1991) *Mozambique: Who Calls the Shots?*, James Currey: London, and Hanlon, J. (1996) *Peace without Profit: How the IMF Blocks Development in Mozambique*, James Currey: London.
12 It is interesting to note that the American Ambassador, Dennis Jett, one of the more vociferous in his criticism of UNOHAC's role, reflecting in 1995 on a piece that the US Embassy had written in 1994

stated, 'Rereading it a year later, I find little that needs to be changed. One point that could be clarified is the relationship of (PKO) to humanitarian relief efforts. There is a definite need for the PKO to co-ordinate such efforts, but to the extent possible implementation of them should be left to other organisations that can do so more efficiently', in Ambassador Dennis C. Jett (1995) 'Lessons Unlearned - Or Why Mozambique's Successful Peacekeeping Operation might not be Replicated Elsewhere', *Journal of Humanitarian Assistance*, American Embassy, Maputo, Mozambique, posted at 5 December.

13 Department of Humanitarian Affairs, Office of the Director and Deputy to the Under-Secretary-General, *Report of DHA Mission to Mozambique, 6-10 October 1992*, Geneva, 16 October 1992.

14 See Antonio Donini (1996) *The Policies of Mercy: UN Humanitarian Co-ordination in Afghanistan, Cambodia and Mozambique*, published by the Watson Institute, Brown University.

15 For details on the Mozambique humanitarian programme under ONUMOZ, see United Nations Department of Humanitarian Affairs, *Final Report: Consolidated Humanitarian Assistance Programme: 1992-94*, December 1994.

References

Abrahamsson, Hans and Nilsson, Anders (1995), *Mozambique: The Troubled Transition*, Zed Books: London.

AWEPA (1995), *Report of AWEPA's Observation of the Mozambique Electoral Process: 1992-1994*, African-European Institute: Amsterdam.

Donini, Antonio (1996), *The Policies of Mercy: UN Co-ordination in Afghanistan, Mozambique and Rwanda*, Thomas J. Watson Jr. Institute for International Studies Occasional Paper 22: Providence, R.I.

Jett, Dennis, C. (1995) 'Lessons Unlearned: Or Why Mozambique's Successful Peacekeeping Operation might not be Replicated Elsewhere', *Journal of Humanitarian Assistance*, posted 5 December 1995, WWW.

Mazula, Brazao (ed) (1996), *Mozambique: Elections, Democracy and Development*, Maputo.

Moore, Jonathan (1996), *The UN and Complex Emergencies: Rehabilitation in Third World Transitions*, United Nations Research Institute for Social Development: Geneva.

United Nations (1995) *The United Nations and Mozambique, 1992-1995*, Department of Public Information, United Nations: New York.

United Nations (1996) *Elections in the Peace Process in Mozambique: Record of Experience*, UNDP/DDSMS: New York.

UNHCR (1996), *Rebuilding a War Torn Society: A Review of the UNHCR Reintegration Programme for Mozambican Returnees*, Maputo.

Vines, Alex (1996) *Renamo: From Terrorism to Democracy in Mozambique?*, James Currey Ltd: London.

Acknowledgements

The author would like to acknowledge the support of the MacArthur Foundation during the research for this chapter.

9 Angola: the search for peace and reconstruction

Barry Munslow

Introduction

Angola is a land where diamonds co-exist with tears and where oil has not soothed troubled waters but rather fuelled the flames of conflict. A rich and abundant natural resource endowment has made the prize too tempting. The fight to control the country's wealth has been bitter, intense and protracted. It has been one of the worst and most intractable conflicts on the African continent. Peacekeeping initiatives have been stretched to the limits of tolerance. International leverage has been restricted. Rich pickings have made obtaining a unified international effort extremely difficult.

Effective peacekeeping in Africa requires a multipronged effort if it is to be sustainable. Reducing and finally eliminating the armed conflicts between contending parties is only one part of the equation. In addition the means have to be assured to enable people to sustain their livelihoods. If human survival is left in question then the seeds of further conflict may be nurtured and will grow in fertile soil. The central arguments put forward in this chapter concern firstly the lessons to be learned from the mistakes which led to a lost opportunity for peacekeeping in Angola in the early 1990s, and the most recent, but still troubled, efforts to repair the damage and start anew. Secondly, it is important to build development into the peace making process to create the conditions for peace to be sustained. In Angola, establishing the conditions for macroeconomic stabilisation, an end to hyper-inflation and the accompanying redistribution effect from the poor to the rich has not to date been tackled with any seriousness. This failure remains a potent destabilising force.

Elusive peace

This large country with enormous natural resource potential and a relatively small population, has been sorely afflicted in recent history by civil war, global cold war struggles and a regional battle against the maintenance of white supremacy in South Africa. The current sorry state of the country and the potential future opportunities for effective development have been shaped by these and other forces. Poor political leadership on all sides of the conflict has served to worsen the current situation still further.

Angola's long period of conflict began in 1961 with the anti-colonial struggle against Portuguese rule. Following Portugal's withdrawal from Africa in the mid-1970s various nationalist groups fought for control backed by rival superpowers and regional interests. The MPLA supported by the Cubans and Soviets took power. UNITA aided by South Africa and the United States continued in armed opposition, with the confrontation in the country massively escalating in the 1980s before finally receding with the end of the Cold War.[1] A peace agreement was signed by the rival parties at Bicesse in May 1991.

Hope of peace

It was encouraging to see the economic regeneration that occurred during the following seventeen month period of peace. People began to return to normality, cultivate their fields and build up their businesses. Political parties emerged and entered a democratic election process.

In the eventual National Assembly elections the ruling MPLA party won 53.74 per cent of the vote and the UNITA opposition 34.10 per cent. In the Presidential elections, Jose Eduardo dos Santos (MPLA) won 49.67 per cent and Jonas Savimbi (UNITA) 40.07 per cent of the vote. Because the Presidential winner did not poll over 50 per cent, under the election regulations a run-off ballot was required between the two leading candidates. But before these final niceties of the electoral arrangements could take place everything else went horribly wrong. That the war recommenced was not the result of a rigged election - the UN declared the result to be generally free and fair - rather it was the outcome of an unfortunate combination of circumstances. Angola's experience is essential if lessons are to be learned about how more effective peacekeeping can take place.

The crucial problem seemed to be that UNITA was determined to take power at any price, irrespective of election results and they were not sufficiently warned off such a strategy by their external supporters. Furthermore, the United Nations peacekeeping and electoral supervision mission had insufficient finance and personnel for the task. The UN representative Margaret Anstee described her job as trying to 'fly a 747 with only enough fuel for a DC3'.[2] It also highlighted the inadequacies of the UN to cope with the new responsibilities being placed upon it and the need for a drastic overhaul and streamlining of procedures.

Although the peace agreement was signed in May 1991, it was not until March 1992 that troops from the rival armies began to enter the 49 designated assembly points. Instead of the two months originally envisaged to place all of the troops into the assembly points, it took almost five times as long even to begin the process - a fatal flaw as it turned out. A second difficulty was that less than two thirds of the expected 160,000 troops actually entered the assembly areas. The reasons were various: inaccurate initial numbers, soldiers simply going home being fed-up with not receiving pay or adequate food and troops being deliberately kept back. Troops should have been assembled in good time, been demobilised properly and been given an economic stake in the future peaceful development of the country. It was essential that a single unified army be created well before elections took place. This would have effectively disarmed the parties to the conflict. However, certain international pressures, particularly from the US, obliged the election to go ahead before all the conditions of the peace agreement had been implemented.

The reasons for the return to war were essentially that the demobilisation process and integration of the two armies had not advanced sufficiently far to give all sides the sense of confidence that it would succeed. To be effective, tangible indicators of success were required in the form of retraining programmes and jobs for demobilised soldiers and effective joint military training facilities for the newly integrated Angolan Armed Forces (FAA). Guaranteeing the peace is the essential first stage for a return to normality. It remains the number one priority in the current Angolan context.

The UNITA offensive was very effective initially and the troops occupied most of the country and many of the provincial capitals. President dos Santos brought in a new military leadership, mortgaged off an unknown amount of the country's next few years of oil revenues to finance major arms purchases and to bring in military technical assistance (primarily from South Africa through Executive Outcomes, a private company using former South African Defence Force troops). The Angolan government proceeded to launch a highly successful counter-offensive. UNITA found itself defending fixed military positions, with declining external support, leaving itself out-gunned. The main pressures which brought the two sides together to reach a new peace agreement following a further two years of war were UNITA facing further military setbacks and the MPLA government being heavily squeezed financially. UNITA could still fight a small guerrilla bush war, the MPLA government can still mortgage yet more distant oil revenues at crippling commercial rates of interest; the important point is that each of the two sides saw sufficient advantage in at least being seen to be making a peace agreement which would be rewarded with international support.

New peace initiatives

Under the Lusaka Protocol of 20 November 1994, a power sharing agreement was made giving UNITA four cabinet ministers and seven deputy ministers, administrative control over three provinces (but not Huambo, the seat of UNITA's power) and dozens of municipalities. The power-sharing is intended to last until new elections are held.

There is a high level of mistrust on both sides which will continue for a long time. On the one hand there is a whole history of rivalry between the two parties going back to the mid-1960s. Next, on the side of the MPLA, there is an understandable mistrust because UNITA did not abide by the results of the 1992 democratic election which the UN judged to be free and fair. On the side of UNITA, mistrust deepened because when the 1994 peace agreement was ready to be signed, the MPLA government initiated a final offensive into UNITA's capital in Huambo and took the city. UNITA regard this as an act of bad faith.

The international community had set up a United Nations Angola Verification Mission (UNAVEM) which went through various phases, to assist the peace process, on the basis of the Bicesse Peace Accords of 31 May 1991, the Lusaka Protocol (which brought in UNAVEM III) and the relevant Security Council resolutions. The deployment by the UN Secretary General of the peace force was dependent upon an effective cease-fire. The timetable established was unrealistic, but it served to put pressure on the parties. It is perfectly clear what the necessary stages had to be. The priority was troop disengagement, quartering and demining. If UNITA maintained its army intact then it could defy the democratic process and the international community once more.

Only one priority task should have existed - consolidating the peace process by quartering and disarming the troops and creating a single unified national army. This would inevitably take a long period of time given the extent of the mistrust, and would require patience from the international community but above all a firmness of intent.

According to the Lusaka Protocol, 62,000 UNITA troops would be gathered into assembly areas and disarmed. Government and UNITA troops would be incorporated into a newly-designated Angolan Armed Forces which would number 90,000 troops. Remaining troops on both sides would be demobilised. By the end of 1996 the incorporation of UNITA troops into the Angolan Armed Forces had barely begun, yet UNAVEM began withdrawing its troops in February 1997.

Physical work had begun on only two of the proposed quartering areas by September 1995 one year after the signing of the peace accord. UNITA has been reluctant to send in its troops, it claimed, because it feared that UNAVEM would not protect them in the case of a FAA attack. Slowness in revealing maps of mines laid, to assist in the demining exercise was a further defensive mechanism. Political pressure as well as the provision of humanitarian aid were used to endeavour to encourage UNITA to open up its areas to allow freedom of movement and communication and at the same time to help persuade the government to take the necessary important gestures to allay UNITA's fears.

UNITA's 15,000 disabled and 1,500 under-age soldiers out of an army of 80,000 were the first batch earmarked to be demobilised. This was intended to build confidence for the next stage of troop integration.

For UNITA, it was the intentions of the FAA Generals that caused them concern. UNITA constantly protested that it could only proceed with the quartering when the camps were ready, but UNITA was continually coming up with new demands of what was required for the camps to be deemed 'ready'. UNAVEM had 7,000 troops to protect the camps in order to build confidence. The United Nations Humanitarian Assistance Co-ordination Unit (UCAH) oversaw the emergency co-ordination, with its activities intended to be taken over eventually by UNDP.

Towards the end of the 1995 there were the first positive political indicators of an improvement in the situation since the signing of the peace agreement. Savimbi and dos Santos appeared together at the international donor conference in Brussels in September 1995 and Savimbi declared that he had no intention of returning to war. The proof of his statement would only be measurable by whether he authorised the entry of all of his troops into the designated garrisoning points and their eventual incorporation into a national army. In December 1995 UNITA temporarily suspended the quartering of its troops with only a few hundred already in the camps, citing government offensives in Soyo region.

Delays continued in quartering troops throughout 1996. By the end of the year, however, Alioune Blondin Beye, the UN Secretary-General's Special Representative, was able to announce that 70,336 UNITA troops and police had registered in the quartering areas and 37,375 personal and crew-served weapons had been handed over of which about 60 per cent were in good condition.[3]

Some were worried by the accompanying statistics that 15,372 had deserted and a further 3,233 were 'absent' from the quartering areas. In many ways, however, this was the least of the problems. Large numbers had actually self-demobilised or were absent because they had been forcibly conscripted into the UNITA army in the first place or merely been civilians swept up to pretend they were UNITA soldiers whilst the real troops remained hidden. Not surprisingly they took the first opportunity to go home.

The UN recorded its concern about the high number of deserters and the low number of good operational weapons and high frequency radios handed in. More worrying still was the fact that the best UNITA fighting units were not in the camps at all but rather protecting UNITA's diamond and contraband interests in the Lundas (two northern provinces of Angola) and fighting alongside President Mobutu's army in the neighbouring Zaire (now the Democratic Republic of Congo) crisis to try to defend UNITA's rear base of support. In other words Savimbi was maintaining a military option. Yet the UN was sufficiently confident that the obstacles to the formation of a single national army and the extension of the state administration to the whole country had been removed that it approved the timetable for the integration of UNITA into a Government of Unity and National Reconciliation from early 1997.[4] The integration of UNITA generals and troops into a national army finally began at the very end of 1996.

Given the context it is hardly surprising that there were human rights abuses on both sides of the conflict. According to Human Rights Watch these included restrictions on freedom of movement, extra-judicial executions, conscription of child soldiers and the intimidation, detention and killing of journalists.[5] By early 1996, there was some evidence of improvement in the situation on the government side. It had freed all prisoners and held a high profile seminar on human rights. Yet fundamentally, as a UNAVEM person reported to Human Rights Watch 'the situation is too sensitive for serious human rights monitoring'.[6]

Humanitarian Situation

Over 300,000 Angolans were estimated to be living as refugees in neighbouring countries and some further afield. Most were settled in Zaire and Zambia, but around 12,000 were in Congo and 1,000 or more in Namibia.[7] Approximately two thirds of all refugees were located in Zaire. Only 15 per cent of the 200,000 lived in the three UN-assisted settlements. In Zambia only 30 per cent of the 100,000 refugees lived in assisted settlements, mostly in the 700 km^2 Meheba settlement in Northwestern province. Hence most refugees were self-settled and did not have any real contact with refugee assistance organisations.

By the beginning of 1996 almost 1.5 million Angolans were internally displaced. Exact figures are extremely difficult to calculate as many have moved several times in over a generation of warfare. It is simply impossible to tell how many people would remain where they were currently located, primarily in the coastal cities, or whether they will return to the interior. The first crucial test was how many would return in time to clear the ground and plant for the start of the agricultural season. Most of the displaced people live in insanitary shanties, abandoned buildings or makeshift camps. The extent of the problem varies from province to province. Cubal in Benguela province, for example, had 100,000 displaced persons in 1995.

There are various impediments to the relocation of refugees and internally displaced people. First, there is the uncertainty of whether the peace will really hold this time. Second, with the slow pace of troop demobilisation and with the two sides holding on to their areas of territorial control, free movement of people is not always possible. Third, there is the deadly legacy of mines. With anything up to 12 million or more mines having been laid, people are cautious about wandering around the countryside. The most likely scenario is a gradual return of displaced persons if there is no return to fighting and if there is some progress on reconstruction.

There appeared to be a significant institutional failure by UNHCR in Zaire who seemed to be unable, over several years, to provide the necessary data about the number of possible returning refugees (figures between 300 and 800,000 were mentioned) and where they wished to locate. The new president of Zaire, Kabila, publicly criticised the organisation and communication with the refugee organisations in Angola barely existed.

Role of the international community in peacekeeping

For the international community, the lessons of the failure of the 1992 peace initiative needed to be learned, and appropriate measures taken to ensure success given the new window of opportunity. In the words of the UN Special Representative for the former peace initiative, Dame Margaret Anstee,

> The inescapable and unpalatable truth is that the international community has never given enough support to the Angolan peace process. In the words of a former US Permanent Representative to the United Nations it was an operation 'done on the cheap' - at what terrible subsequent cost in lives and the sufferings of ordinary people...[8]

Clearly only adequate international levels of support can help ensure the success of the peace process.

In addition to improving the overall quantity of support to the new peace process, qualitative improvements were needed as well. To improve the political co-ordination of the donor community, UCAH asked for the formation of a co-ordinating group of ambassadors. All were agreed that there were problems in co-ordination. According to the chairman of the EU ambassadors, developing a common European position faced a number of conflicting interests.[9] If we were to delve deeper into what these conflicts might be we would soon find perhaps conflicting French and British spheres of interest and Portugal, the former colonial power, resenting the EU 'muscling' in.

Significant international support would seem to be required over a considerable period of time in order to help the peace process stick in Angola. This is of major importance not only for the people of Angola but for the well-being of the Southern African region and the Great Lakes region of Central Africa as a whole. Angola is a site of conflict with the terrible prospect of regional overspill. Supporting the difficult but necessary peace process in Angola through to the end, may take considerable resources, patience and active international political interventions, but the benefits could be long lasting. The challenge is how the international community can build from the least bad option towards a sustainable development future.

The challenges are threefold: whether UNITA can accept its military defeat and switch to a peaceful political rather than military field of confrontation; if the MPLA can raise its quality of leadership to defuse

UNITA's fears in the peace process and implement the multiple reforms required to ensure long term development and if the international community can respond with adequate targeted support and a co-ordinated response.

Neither peace nor war

Sadly the lessons appear not to have been drawn to make the latest round of peacemaking effective. As the stalemate dragged on into late 1997, certain things became clearer, indeed dramatically so. First, there was one completely overwhelming conclusion from the failure of the 1992 initiative which was the need to get the two rival armies integrated into one, with no 'wild card', heavily armed and well-trained body of troops left outside of the rule of law. Incredibly this has happened yet again in Angola. Benjamin Castello, Programme Director of Church Action in Angola, reported in September 1997: 'The military skirmishes in the provinces of Lunda North and South confirm the existence of two well-equipped armies. The evident re-arming and the troop movements throughout the country are compromising an already precarious peace process.'[10]

In essence, Savimbi had kept his best troops and arms out of the quartering areas. Surprisingly perhaps, the Special Representative of the UN Secretary General had allowed UNITA to bring in its 'soldiers' to the quartering areas without their weapons.[11] UNAVEM III also did not oblige the local opposing commanders to get together and communicate, this remained blocked by the two rival high commands.[12] Building peace relies precisely on such local initiatives.

By the end of August 1997, UCAH reported that in the quartering areas, 78,619 active troops had been registered of which almost 11,000 had been incorporated into the FAA, 67,686 were eligible for demobilisation, 25,000 had been demobilised and an equivalent number had deserted.[13]

Concern for the lack of progress with the peace process was such, and finally exhaustion with the constant delaying tactics of Savimbi had reached such a point, that the UN Security Council adopted resolution 1127 on 28 August 1997 that sanctions would be applied to UNITA from 30 September 1997, unless its military forces were demobilised and it co-operated in the extension of state control in the areas that it currently occupied and transformed its radio station into a non-partisan broadcasting facility.

In effect, the geopolitical transformation of central and southern Africa had deprived Savimbi of his South African and Zairian external bases of support. The US and other Western powers were now doing business with the existing President and the country was becoming an ever more profitable source of riches as deep off-shore oil technology had advanced to such an extent that huge new sources of petroleum wealth were being announced on a monthly basis. Savimbi now had only his diamond revenues to rely upon, purchasing his needs from the Russian Mafia with night flights coming into his airport from Petersburg, as irony upon irony piled up in the switching of partners. The US and South Africa were now supporting the MPLA and Russian (Mafia) support was going to Savimbi!

Peering into the future is always hazardous in Angola. Continuing tension seems certain between the two opposing leaders. Savimbi's support is dwindling not only internationally but within his own ranks as UNITA members of the national assembly and national army make themselves at home in Luanda and President dos Santos encourages a divide and rule strategy which is finding allies in a very authoritarian UNITA structure where the prospects of outright victory are diminishing rapidly. The Secretary General of UNITA defected in August 1997.

In essence, Savimbi's support now relies upon the revenue from his diamond resources in Lunda Norte and Lunda Sol provinces. He will fight to hang on to these and the government will fight to deprive him of these resources. Fighting is therefore quite possible, although it might be localised by province, including Savimbi's political base in Huambo province and well as in the Lundas.

Economic policies threaten peace and reconstruction

For peace to be consolidated, the economic turmoil in the country has to be resolved. This is profoundly destabilising in its own right as hyperinflation breeds unrest. Economic turmoil has been a constant. People are in a struggle to survive in the face of economic as well as military dangers.

The first big shock to Angola was the difficult transition to independence, involving the loss of nearly all skilled personnel with the Portuguese settler exodus. Then came the adoption of an inappropriate and heavily state centralised planning model. Whilst the model finally collapsed with the fall of the Soviet empire, its legacy lives on. Most of the country's economists, trained only in socialist economics, were unable to adapt to the subsequent changes. The Economics Faculty at the country's only university continued turning out ill-equipped central planning economists. Even when the syllabus changed in 1991, the lecturers had not themselves been retrained and were incapable of fulfilling their new role.[14]

The most serious economic policy problems concerned the maintenance of an administrative rather than a free market pricing policy, and in particular holding on to a fixed dollar exchange rate in spite of the complete production collapse and traumas of the fighting in the civil war. This continued to represent a major blockage to reform. Continuing for so long with administrative rather than price and market mechanisms for the allocation of resources precipitated the on-going gross macroeconomic distortions.

Constraints to reform and development

Single party rule, with a Leninist party model, created a tightly restricted ruling elite, a process exacerbated by the war against UNITA and South Africa. As the ruling MPLA party's Marxist-Leninist ideology collapsed with the ending of the Cold War individual interests rose in importance. Artificial constraints create scope for windfall profits for those with opportunities for self-enrichment.

Too often in African political culture, few distinctions are made between private and public goods. The existing circuits and mechanisms of corruption are the major barrier to serious structural reform of the economy. Many of the people commonly designated as big businessmen in Luanda are in fact state and party functionaries with privileged access to the 'esquemas' (schemes) which create fortunes for the small ruling elite. The concept of 'esquemas' in the popular culture and vocabulary used in Angola, denotes survival arrangements by building networks to resolve the day to day economic problems. Those who can get access to meat will liaise with those who can obtain vegetables, batteries and so on. It is a survival circuit in the context of an inadequate centrally planned economy. These schemes are both legal and illegal (*condonga*). As the deficiencies of the existing centrally planned system grew ever more apparent everyone was forced to adopt a dual survival morality and practice of engagement with the *candonga*.

Without economic reform there can be no development. From 1983 onwards, there has been a small but growing group of technically competent Angolan professionals who have urged reform and a move away from the inefficiencies of the existing system towards increasing reliance on market mechanisms, not least because the failures and absurdities of the system were becoming all too apparent. The first serious reform endeavour was the Economic and Financial Clean-Up initiative of 1987. This proposed a very gradual and phased transition towards a greater market orientation. The programme was announced with a great fanfare, but those people who had much to lose resisted it. The policy initiative ground to a halt, with those who had worked on it suddenly being looked on disfavourably. The politicians perceived that this would entail a shift of power from the state and therefore themselves to the private sector and they did not have private businesses at that time from which to benefit.

In 1989, Angola joined the IMF and World Bank and a Programme of Economic Recuperation (PRE) was launched, the Government's Programme of Action. The Central Bank and the World Bank discussed the remonetarisation of the economy with a liberalisation of prices. Whilst prices were indeed freed, wages were frozen. The civil service at all levels ceased to receive an effective salary and that has been the situation ever since. The Angolan state which functioned at only minimal levels of activity previously, henceforth ceased to function at all. Civil servants were increasingly absent altogether from government work, pursuing other jobs in order to earn a livelihood. Inevitably the opportunities for personal survival mechanisms to recompense the salary deficit were seized upon by everyone within the state structures who had the opportunity to benefit. The spiral of corruption increased dramatically. According to the World Bank, the capacity of macroeconomic management by the Government of Angola (GOA) will remain severely affected if measures are not taken to increase the salaries of public employees, as a national director in a ministry received on average in 1994 only $15 per month![15]

Major economic reform initiatives were announced every year but never seriously acted upon. All of the reform programmes stretching back to 1987 have met with a similar lack of success. In 1992 it was the Programme of Economic Stabilisation, in 1993 the Emergency Programme of the Government, then the Economic and Social Programme for 1994, followed by the Economic and Social Programme of 1995, and the 'New Life' programme of 1996.

The critical issue to understand is why these initiatives all failed. The answer lies in the petroleum wealth which allowed the government the liberty to resist internal and external pressures for change and the people in power who had a vested interest in maintaining the status quo. Two different exchange rates became the principal avenue of accumulation for a small inner political elite. Privileged access allowed dollars to be purchased from the Central Bank at the cheap official kwanza price, to be sold on the parallel market for the much higher black market price through diverse series of mechanisms.

A whole number of schemes were used for personal accumulation, based upon optimising access to the above system. The Ministry of Commerce, say, would inform the government that there is no rice available in Luanda and it urgently requires money to buy rice if urban unrest is to be avoided. The Central Bank is mandated to release the money. The Ministry of Commerce then says that there just so happens to be a ship with rice passing near the port of Luanda and if the Central Bank were willing to pay over the world market price they could get this cargo immediately instead of having a huge time delay. It is then authorised. But in fact the ship with the rice has been sitting in the port for months with the cargo of rice going mouldy! The country, therefore, allocates scarce foreign exchange resources to buy sub-standard food at well above world market prices which makes people sick. Or a certain sum is authorised for the purchase of a given quantity of rice, but only a proportion of this is actually imported, and the rest of the money allocated goes to private bank accounts abroad.

Huge profits were also facilitated by the absence of any effective customs service to monitor if goods supposedly purchased actually arrived. A conspiracy of silence permitted each to pursue their own 'get-rich-quick' schemes. No one was prosecuted.

The very high rate of currency inflation provides a further avenue of accumulation. People who had accumulated a lot of kwanza would go to a foreign exchange shop and offer a good kwanza dollar exchange price for that particular time as a promise to buy a certain amount of dollars. They then get a pledge from the government to pay the 'going' dollar price for certain goods at the time of purchase, and by manipulating the real time of purchase instead of the official stated time of purchase in their own favour, i.e. buying at an earlier cheaper exchange rate but claiming at a more expensive later one, they can reap the benefits of a dual exchange rate and high inflation. Because of the potential for personal accumulation through purchases of goods abroad, there has been no incentive to buy locally produced goods and thereby stimulate the Angolan economy. Most serious in this regard is the activity of the Ministry of Defence, which received the lion's share of the state budget. In most wars and conflicts there has been a positive spin-off for local industry, to produce the uniforms, food, soap etc. In Angola, everything was purchased abroad because there was cash to be made. There was no control over the military budget, the army had whatever they requested.

After the return to war following UNITA's refusal to accept its defeat in the 1992 democratic election, the future oil revenue earnings of the country for several years ahead were mortgaged to guarantee the purchase of arms.

Those outside of the immediate elite but who still benefit to some extent from the system are the urban middle class. In the 1991 price liberalisation, not all prices were liberalised. The most significant one not to be liberalised was the exchange rate, which allowed, as we have seen, for the continuing enrichment of the ruling elite. Other prices not liberalised were those which benefited the urban middle class: housing in the city, air fares, petrol, water, telephone and electricity. It was far more expensive to rent a house in the shanty towns without water, electricity, telephone or a sewerage system than it was to have a proper house in the city with all of these facilities.

The price distortions introduced by this administrative system of price allocation represented an effective transfer of resources from the poor to the rich. For this reason, it is essential to establish a macroeconomic stabilisation package. The ruling elite benefited massively from the existing situation. The government became sufficiently aware of its unpopularity to make some changes in 1996. The danger was that outside forces would be blamed for the economic chaos. The so-called 'Lebanese' were scapegoated in 1996, meaning foreigners who were traders in the informal economy. There were forcible expulsions of these selected foreigners. Looking to the future, the MPLA leadership could try to scapegoat UNITA for potential economic shortcomings.

The dual price exchange rate system has a grossly distorting effect upon the state budget. The receipts were registered at the official dollar/kwanza exchange rate but all expenditures had to be made at the parallel higher rate, as it was only at this rate of exchange that any goods were available. The distortions created in the state budget by the chaotic state of the economy are such that the total salary budget is but a tiny part of overall expenditure, even though hundreds of thousands of people are employed, because salaries are minute.

The state budgets have not been an effective policy tool as they were never adhered to by the various ministries. Angola has seen too many paper planning exercises of reform, which have failed to deliver the necessary remedies.

Because of these distortions and the absence of any systematic accounting or fiscalisation procedures in the customs, Central Bank or Ministry of Finance, it is impossible to obtain any clear overall picture of the economy. There has been a lack of transparency. Effectively there are hardly any revenues from general taxation or customs receipts. The government's revenue comes fundamentally from oil. Customs payments recorded represent only about a half of what the balance of payments data would suggest.

The agreements signed with the oil companies all involve banks abroad and not the Angolan banking system. Only in 1994 was the legislation changed on this. The oil companies are obliged to use official rates of exchange and were forbidden from buying their needs locally in dollars. This made purchasing anything from Angola prohibitively expensive, hence the potential positive effects on the Angolan economy from the petroleum sector were severely curtailed. All of the oil companies trade went abroad.

Angola's benefits from the oil industry come in two parts. The government oil company, Sonangol, has a percentage of any oil bloc production. There is also a government tax on the sale of the petroleum. However, Sonangol's payments did not always go to the Central Bank. The relationship between Sonangol, the Central Bank and the Ministry of Finance remained highly problematic as transfers were not transparent. This relationship was referred to by some as the 'Bermuda Triangle' as money entered only to disappear. The Presidency controlled the purse strings.

Economic indicators

There is no point in pretending that there is any clear or accurate statistical picture concerning the Angolan economy. There is limited value in providing a detailed analysis on the basis of misleading figures. Both by default and by design (by those who had much to gain by disguising the situation) there is very little really hard data to go on. Hence what follows should be seen as being primarily indicative.

Real GNP increased by 3.5 per cent in 1992 with the benefit of peace, but fell an alarming 26 per cent in 1993 with the resumption of war. Official figures suggest a recovery in GNP of 8.6 per cent in 1994. According to UNDP's *Human Development Reports*, Angola fell from a GDP per capita country ranking of 58 in 1990 to 161 in 1995. Its human development indicator rank fell from 94 to 164 over the same period. In terms of sectoral shares of GDP, petroleum has risen in importance from 18 per cent in 1991 to half of all GDP by 1995, given the production collapse in agriculture and the non-oil industry.

In terms of monetary policy, inflation was running at 496 per cent in 1992, 1,838 per cent in 1993, 972 per cent in 1994 and 3,783 per cent in 1995. Between early August and mid-September 1995 the parallel market rate for the dollar increased two and a half times as hyperinflation took hold. The money supply is totally out of control and highly destabilising both economically and socially. The government is simply printing money to cover its budget deficit. The rapid deterioration can be clearly seen in the parallel market kwanza per dollar exchange rate. This rose from 360,000 kwanzas to the dollar in September 1994 to 1.6 million by early 1995, to 8 million by September 1995. In an effort just to keep numbers manageable, new bank notes issued from the middle of the year simply drop off the last three noughts as the *novo kwanza* was substituted by the *kwanza readjustado* (readjusted kwanza). In reality, however, the dollar was worth 390 million kwanza or 390,000 *novo kwanza* in September 1997. This is no way to run an economy.

Aguilar and Stenman have provided the most up to date analysis of the economic situation in an aptly titled report *Angola 1996: Hyper-inflation, Confusion and Political Crisis*.[16] Hyper-inflation was the result of a desire to finance an ever growing budget deficit and at the same time reflected a lack of coherence and consistency in any form of economic policy. A pattern has emerged of a government policy being announced at the end of the first quarter of the year, inflation then falling, only for the policy to be abandoned in the third quarter and inflation to escalate once more.

Concerning fiscal policy, the government budget accounts are little more than a fictional exercise. No less than four budgets were approved by the Council of Ministers and National Assembly in 1994. Unclassified expenditure amounted to 30 per cent of total expenditures. The fiscal deficit for 1994 was 23.1 per cent of GDP, mainly accounted for by a sharp increase in defence spending, petrol subsidies, fraudulent payments with a breakdown in the expenditure control system and purchases of goods. Whilst subsidies amount to 22 per cent of total expenditure (11 per cent of GDP) the total salary bill is a mere 9 per cent of total expenditure (5 per cent of GDP). The 1994 Fiscal Accounts show that oil sector taxes represent 87 per cent of the tax revenues. As Aguilar and Stenman have commented, 'The budget is in principle entirely financed by revenues from the oil sector and by printing money'.[17]

Concerning the external balances, again the figures are extremely weak given a lack of capacity in the customs service and vested interests in a lack of transparency. Oil accounted for 96 per cent of exports in 1994. The country's balance of payment deficit has exceeded a billion dollars per year ever since 1990. This is financed by accumulating arrears.

According to the Economist Intelligence Unit earlier debt estimates are being revised down somewhat. These figures suggest a debt of just under US$12 billion by the end of 1995.[18] Total external debt stands at over three times the value of exports of goods and services. Portugal and Spain have agreed to reschedule bi-lateral debts and Denmark has written off its debt.

Russia is the largest creditor. It is owed around 60 per cent of medium and long term debt, mainly for arms purchases made in the latter part of the 1980s. Currently there are discussions about solving this problem through Angolan-Russian joint ventures.

Ending the war means consolidating the peace. A stable and secure economy is essential. The high degree of political instability and associated social unease was one factor in UNITA's overall calculations in the potential reward of delaying the peace process. There was some expectation of a popular uprising in the capital city in May 1996 and the police and army were facing delays in wage payments creating unrest. In the event the rumours of discontent came to nought given the fear of reprisals by the police and army. However, in response to these pressures, the President announced a major reshuffle in June. Interestingly, reliance on a continuing incompetence of the existing government provides a powerful incentive for UNITA to enter the democratic political process, as the next elections could reap the rewards.

The new peace process had three aims: to resettle displaced populations, reconstruct infrastructure and re-establish economic activities. Our central argument is that all of the above required a focused economic strategy to readjust the current gross economic distortions. Without far-reaching economic reforms, it will be very hard to consolidate the peace.

Long term investment prospects for the country are good given the rich natural resource endowment. The main attraction is the oil and diamonds. There is every prospect of oil production continuing to grow. Diamond production was more severely affected by the war, but peace is likely to improve investment and a channelling of diamonds through the formal sector of the economy rather than being smuggled abroad, as happens at present. Peace, a restoring of infrastructure and demining will in the longer term create a positive climate for investment in other sectors, depending upon implementing a successful programme of macroeconomic stabilisation.

Establishing priorities

The Government of Angola has a poor track record of implementing its stated plans, in part this has been because of the war, in part because there was a lack of political will to take the tough measures necessary. In principle the government's strategy can be derived from three major initiatives:-
- a prolonged macroeconomic reform programme
- a consolidated humanitarian appeal
- a programme of community rehabilitation and national reconciliation

Macroeconomic reform programme

Effectively, because of the oil, Angola was able to maintain its debt at reasonable levels throughout most of 1980s, yet the war, a collapsing oil price, subsidising an inefficient centrally planned economy and at least two mega debt inducing projects - the Capanda hydroelectric dam and former President Neto's mausoleum in Luanda - began to take their toll. Growing economic difficulties appeared to encourage reform efforts in a number of areas.

Angola's debt which stood at only US$2.8 billion in 1986 had reached nearly US$12 billion by the mid-1990s, of which an incredible four-fifths of the debt involved non-concessionary terms. Furthermore, as we have seen, several future years' oil revenues have been mortgaged for arms purchases. A worrying 45.5 per cent of the debt constitutes arrears on the principal and 12.3 per cent arrears on the non-payment of interest. Total debt service arrears in 1997 were estimated to be US$7.8 billion.

Debt restructuring is urgently required. The government's strategy is to negotiate the debt to the three largest bilateral creditors, eliminate arrears to international organisations and tightly control public sector short term foreign currency borrowing. In future, instead of mortgaging oil revenues, concessional terms will be sought. Finally Paris Club rescheduling is aimed for.

The main imperative for privatisation is the inability of the government to manage the economy. The only hope is to privatise and it will be those with privileged access through their state and party positions who will benefit. Government will try to limit its involvement in the economy to policy formulation and regulation, according to the stated intent, establishing an appropriate institutional and legal framework within which the private sector can work. By the end of 1994, only 192 out of 564 government enterprises had been privatised. Government has a stated commitment to bring the budget deficit under control. It remains to be seen whether the promised transparency and fiscal discipline will be translated from words into practice. There has to be a clear separation of commercial and national bank functions. Such an undertaking has been given for the National Bank of Angola. Little credibility exists concerning a determination to control the galloping inflation which has become a national scandal, causing a massive impoverishment of the weakest in society i.e. those without tangible assets.

This is a real test of the government's commitment to change as the elite have benefited so massively by the existing administrative allocation of pricing and trade. A unified exchange rate was finally introduced in 1995, which means effectively implementing a floating exchange rate.

The Minister of Planning led an important reform initiative in 1994, but in line with other reform initiatives before, it failed to be implemented. By 1995 lead responsibility for economic policy was given to the Ministry of Finance. Yet there were no less than four different ministers of finance within a two year period. The government continues to face a serious challenge of proving its long term commitment to a programme of reform.

The 1994 reform initiative was important because the government was very proactive in developing it. Conditions appeared favourable for reform. In 1993 inflation exceeding 1,800 per cent provoked severe popular discontent towards the end of the year. High inflation and grass roots protest combined with a low petroleum price to restrict the government's room for manoeuvre. It provided a window of opportunity for a rather ambitious programme to dramatically reduce inflation and the fiscal deficit. The programme started well in April 1994 but faced with strengthening opposition it collapsed by September of that year. The Minister of Finance who assumed the lead initiative for economy policy in early 1995 was regarded as broadly adopting the 1994 PES reform, albeit in somewhat watered-down form.

By 1996/97 it was clear that the problem was a lack of political will at the top to implement reform measures.[19] The technical arguments and the Angolan professionals with the skills and commitment to reform the economy were available. The problem was that every effort at policy reform over the past decade had been blocked. Yet at the same time no alternative viable strategy was being put forward.

The IMF at the end of 1994 laid out the lessons to be drawn from the attempt at implementing the Economic and Social Programme of 1994 (PES):

1 The budget has to be based on realistic hypotheses. The increase in receipts and cuts in expenditure must be examined in real rather than nominal terms.

2 Given the difficulties of cutting expenditures in real terms during the first year of peace, special attention must be given to ensuring that expenditures are protected for the prioritised sectors.

3 There is a lack of transparency in the transactions between the Treasury, Sonangol and the National Bank.

4 In the implementation of PES, sufficient attention has not been given to the problem of subsidies, particularly in relation to petroleum.

5 The fixing of the exchange rate was discredited by administrative interference.

The IMF at the end of 1994 laid out the steps that would have to be followed for the situation to change. They began by acknowledging that the negotiations were likely to be prolonged before an effective agreement was reached. Given the extent of the adjustment required and the difficulties facing the Angolan economy a number of urgent actions were requested of the Angolan government. These included the following:

1 A complete inventory of foreign exchange earnings from oil already committed for the future by the government with copies of the contracts.

2 Paying off all of the outstanding payments with the multilateral institutions.

3 Preparing a public investment programme with the World Bank for 1995 which is acceptable.

4 Restricting the commercial activities of the National Bank.

5 Transparency in the transactions between the Treasury, National Bank and Sonangol.

The World Bank has suggested that the priorities for structural reform should concentrate on the alleviation of extreme poverty, stimulate the development of the economy outside of the petroleum sector, rapid improvement of the human and social condition of the country, a continuation of the liberalisation of commerce and prices, establish a policy for the development of the private sector, modernising the financial sector, administrative reform, and revising public expenditure.

Whilst there are groups that resist reform measures there are others, especially at the technical level who support reform and a broad consensus exists concerning what needs to be done in line with the above mentioned IMF/World Bank proposals. In May 1995 the IMF team visited Angola and discussions were held with the Minister of Finance. Certain crucial issues were discussed and seemingly by October 1995, some progress was made on the initial issues, notably:

- On petrol prices, which are always highly sensitive, these increased three hundredfold. Previously it was more expensive to buy a litre of drinking water than to fill-up a car's petrol tank.

- Information was provided on future oil sales already committed to pay debts.

- Concerning the Bermuda Triangle, a consolidated petroleum account was established at the Central Bank.

- Better economic data was being provided more generally.

A shadow programme was established, known as a staff monitored programme. It was intended to last up to a year, starting from October 1995. No funding would be provided by the IMF although it would facilitate some World Bank support. It was a fairly soft programme which recognises the difficulties in cutting the budget deficit whilst the vital period of consolidating the peace was taking place.

There remains serious question marks over the extent of the effective co-ordination of this programme with the other two programmes discussed below. According to the World Bank, their FAS (Social Action Programme) will be in line with the Brussels programme of community reconciliation and rehabilitation. At present it appears that the three programmes are not sufficiently well co-ordinated with an effective sequencing of priorities. Also, at the time of writing there does not appear to be a sufficiently well co-ordinated international donor response which is sufficiently proactive in encouraging serious policy reform at the macroeconomic level.

This programme required one thing above all else in order to succeed - political will. Once again this was absent and the initiative fell.

Consolidated Humanitarian Appeal

The UN established a Humanitarian Assistance Co-ordination Unit (UCAH) in Angola in April 1993. Whilst UCAH focuses primarily on emergency issues and humanitarian needs its mandate was expanded to include demining, demobilisation and reintegration programmes. Since its operations began, a number of UN consolidated inter-agency appeals have been made for Angola.

This Consolidated Humanitarian Appeal is the building bloc upon which all else depends in the short to medium term. It has three targets:

- integration and demobilisation of the two main armies

- demining and restarting communications between the main economic centres of the country currently divided by the civil war

- providing for the emergency needs of Angola's long suffering people

As reported to the UN Security Council in early 1996, the slow development of the peace process in the previous year had its effect on the humanitarian assistance programme. 'With the quartering and demobilisation of troops behind schedule, very few refugees and internally displaced people have been able to return to and resume productive activities in their areas of origin or choice.'[20]

As a consequence, the Security Council Report emphasised the need for substantial humanitarian assistance in 1996 in particular to support demining, demobilisation and the resettlement of refugees and internally displaced persons.

There is no question that this had to be the number one priority for international community support. Upon this, all else depended and was of secondary importance. The total sum requested was US$ 281.5 million.

This is the essential funding priority and would remain so over the 1996 and 1997 period at least.

To open the way from emergency relief to long term reconstruction it was essential that in addition to the troop demobilisation, speedy progress was made on demining. With an estimated 12 million mines, Angola is one of the worst affected countries in the world. A World Bank commissioned report at the end of 1996 into the UN Department of

Humanitarian Affairs demining operations concluded that at the end of two and a half years the clearance operation had achieved 'virtually nothing'.[21] The report criticised the lack of understanding of the importance of demining for reconstruction. It found a complete breakdown in communication between the UN's Central Mines Action Office and the local Angolan Institute for the Removal of Explosive Obstacles. Finally, it noted that the management, training and planning structure for demining was unsustainable.

The situation was very different in relation to humanitarian relief in the war. Famine was averted. Of course quotas were overestimated, the two rival armies benefited as well, but overall a human tragedy was averted in terms of food availability.[22]

Community Rehabilitation and National Reconciliation Programme

With the support of UNDP the Government of Angola presented a Programme of Community Rehabilitation and National Reconciliation (CRNRP) at the international donors conference in Brussels in September 1995.[23] Key elements of the consolidated appeal were included in the CRNRP, as there was a funding shortfall in the appeal. Both President dos Santos and Jonas Savimbi were present at the meeting which sent important positive messages to the international community.

The Round Table resulted in pledges and indications of contributions of US$993 million which appear to exceed the target set, although some of this involved money previously committed. Donors made clear to the GOA that their continuing support for the CRNRP was dependent upon successful implementation of the reforms agreed upon with the IMF and World Bank and timely implementation of the peace accord.

The programme presented an overview of the crisis facing the country. As ever, caution is necessary concerning the accuracy of the figures. What is more important from the statistics is gaining an appreciation of the overall order of magnitude of the problems: one and a quarter million people internally displaced, 280,000 living as refugees abroad. People fleeing the war zones of the interior have contributed to an excessively high urban population growth rate, such that half the country's population are now urbanised. Massive social disruption has occurred with broken families, orphans, widespread armed banditry and crime and over 70,000 amputees. Under five child mortality, at 320 per 1,000 births, is twice the continental average.[24]

Destruction to the infrastructure matches that to the social structure. Roads, bridges, power lines, buildings, schools and health posts were destroyed, over ten million mines impede the free circulation of goods and people and agricultural production.

The aim of the programme is to nurture reconciliation, stability and development throughout Angola's eighteen provinces by supporting agricultural and small scale production, rehabilitation of basic services and infrastructure and resuscitating production and employment.

The aims of the programme were: to reintegrate refugees, displaced people and demobilised troops; promote the conditions for national reconciliation; to promote economic and social recovery in a decentralised manner and to lay the basis for sustained development and growth. Sensibly, the document stresses the linkages both with demining, rehabilitation and demobilisation and with macroeconomic stabilisation. However, it is not yet convincing that the necessary linkages and institutional co-ordination mechanism are in place to ensure this, either nationally or in the international community and more especially between the two sets of actors. At present there appears to be no overall co-ordinated response to the Angolan tragedy.

Conclusion

The destruction caused by 30 years of war between 1961 and 1991 was totally dwarfed in magnitude by the subsequent period of fighting from October 1992 to November 1994. Massive devastation of human life and the infrastructure of the country directly resulted from the failure to guarantee the peace process in the May 1991 to September 1992 period. It is essential that the appropriate lessons are learned from that experience and are applied in order to ensure that the new peace initiative is successful.

For many years this appeared to be a war between an MPLA government committed to a socialist trajectory and national independence fighting against a UNITA opposition combining a verbal commitment to a free market economy with an authoritarian political disposition, backed by an apartheid South African state.[25] This has turned into a contest between two groups struggling to control the petroleum and diamond resources of the country. The 'off-shore' oil and diamond enclaves have blinkered both partners to the conflict to on-shore agricultural potential.[26] At time of writing the final solution had not been found to guarantee UNITA a continuing flow of cash by allocating its front companies diamond concessions whilst allowing the government greater access to this lucrative resource.

The absolute priority for the international community as a whole and for the transitional programme of assistance, has been helping to consolidate the peace through the UCAH consolidated humanitarian effort. Achieving all other goals is dependent upon this, including poverty alleviation, sustainable development, human rights and supporting democracy. This means ensuring the integration of the two separate armies, disarming UNITA and supporting the coalition government between the two warring parties. The role of Savimbi remains decisive. He has turned down the offer of a joint vice-presidency. Demining, building bridges and the opening of roads is a necessary step to accompany this process and will also require support. The huge numbers of displaced people need help to begin producing once again in order to sustain their livelihoods.

Second in priority comes the programme of community rehabilitation and national reconciliation, but this needs to be co-ordinated with the macroeconomic framework to enable people to sustain their own livelihoods once the community rehabilitation and national reconciliation programme has ended. Poverty alleviation is required to support both the peace and macroeconomic stabilisation efforts. By early 1995, real wages had fallen to only 2 per cent of their 1991 level. In the absence of any effective salary, the civil service had ceased to function at all outside of the defence and petroleum sectors. If any form of government capacity is to be restored then this crucially depends upon structural economic reform. This is a necessary but not a sufficient condition for success. Once the above hierarchy and sequencing of priorities have made sufficient progress, continuing international assistance will then be required to help rebuild government capacity.

Notes

1. See O'Neil, K. and Munslow, B. (1995) 'Angola: Ending the Cold War in Southern Africa' in Furley, O. (ed) *Conflict in Africa*, Tauris Academic Studies: London.
2. Anstee, M. (1995) *Journal of Southern African Studies*, Vol. 21, No. 1, pp. 336-337.
3. *Angola News*, No. 38, December 1996/January 1997, p. 3.
4. Ibid.
5. Human Rights Watch (1996) *World Report 1996*, Human Rights Watch: New York.

6   Human Rights Watch Arms Project. Human Rights Watch Africa (1996) *Angola. Between War and Peace. Arms Trade and Human Rights Abuses since the Lusaka Protocol*, Vol. 8, No. 1, February.
7   US Committee for Refugees (1995) *If this Peace is Real: The Return Home of Uprooted Angolans*, December.
8   Anstee, M. (1995) op. cit., pp. 336-337. The title of her recent study of her time in Angola says it all, (1996) *Angola, Orphan of the Cold War*, Macmillan: London.
9   Interview with the Spanish Ambassador, the current chairman of the EU ambassadors, Luanda, September 1995.
10 Benjamin Castello, 'From the absence of war to a real peace', a presentation to the ACTSA Conference in Achieving Lasting Peace in Angola: The Unfinished Agenda', School of Oriental and African Studies, University of London, 4 September 1997.
11 Peter Simkin, former Director of the UN Department of Humanitarian Affairs operations in Angola, ibid.
12 Ibid.
13 UCAH (1997) *Report to the Joint Commission on the Status of Demobilisation in Angola*, 21-28 August 1997, UCAH: Luanda.
14 Interview with former top civil servant in planning and finance, September 1995.
15 World Bank (1994), *Aide Memoir*, 16 November.
16 Aguilar R. and Stenman, A. (1996) *Hyper-Inflation, Confusion and Political Crisis*, Department of Economics, Gothenburg University, SIDA.
17 Aguilar, R. and Stenman, A. (1995) *Angola 1995. Let's try again*, Department of Economics, Gothenburg University, SIDA, p. 13.
18 Economist Intelligence Unit (1996), *Country Report, Angola*, 4th Quarter.
19 An IMF *Aide Memoir* of 5 December 1995 already indicated that there was no political consensus within the government for economic stabilisation. Report of the Secretary-General on the United Nations Security Council, UN Angola Verification Mission, 31 January 1996, p. 7.
20 United Nations Security Council (1996) Report of the Secretary-General on the UN Angola Verification Mission, 31 January, p. 7.
21 One of the few international media organs to pick up this report was the British satirical magazine *Private Eye*, 24 January 1997, p. 15. Whilst this conclusion may overstate the problem, it should not be easily dismissed.

22 For one recent account, see Lanzer, T. (1996) *The UN Department of Humanitarian Affairs in Angola. A Model for the Co-ordination of Humanitarian Assistance?*, Nordiska Afrikan Istitutel: Uppsala.
23 Government of Angola (1995) *Programme of Community Rehabilitation and National Reconciliation*, First Roundtable Conference of Donors, Brussels, 25-26 September.
24 See UNICEF, (1995) *The State of Angola's Children Report*, UNICEF: Angola, p. 1.
25 See, for example, Minter, W. (1994) *Apartheid's Contras. An Inquiry into the Roots of War in Angola and Mozambique*, Zed Books: London and New Jersey.
26 Sogge, D. (1994) 'Angola: Surviving against Rollback and Petrodollars' in Macrae, J. and Zwi, A. (eds) *War and Hunger*, Zed Press: London.

10 Namibia[1]

Donna Pankhurst

Introduction

The role of the United Nations peacekeeping force in the build up to, process, and aftermath of the independence elections in Namibia has been held up as a successful model of UN intervention to keep the peace during a process of political transition, as the outcome was a largely free and fair election with comparatively few irregularities. However, a more nuanced assessment shows that the limitations of this process were also significant, and arguably affected the election results and some aspects of the subsequent political process of transition to independence. The chapter highlights the ways in which this model of the UN acting as supervisor, rather than administrator, of a political transition contains risks of failure and particularly of distorting election results.

Namibia's peacekeeping force in its transition to independence in 1990 was not the first such force, but headed a string of attempts by the UN to play a role in resolving conflict, maintaining peace, and monitoring the transformation of a political regime to a multiparty democracy at the end of the Cold War (swiftly followed by the former Yugoslavia, Cambodia, Somalia, Angola, and Mozambique, for instance). This particular site of Cold War politics and conflict had been very intense and meshed with the specific politics of decolonisation from South Africa, in what was often referred to as the last colony in Africa. The role of the United Nations Transition Assistance Group (UNTAG) therefore received quite a lot of attention beyond the specifics of Namibia's own circumstances and shed some light on the UN's competence, readiness and fitness to play a new post-Cold War role. Views on UNTAG's success or failure were to go on to influence ideas about, not only the potential of the UN as the world's police force, but also, in comparison, the appropriateness of the USA in playing such a role. As the USA itself played such an important role in bringing about the agreements between relevant parties which finally led to the transition to independence in Namibia, and the terms on which this was to be conducted, the connections are indeed complex, as we shall see.

UNTAG was charged with overseeing the three main processes of a Cease-fire, election of representatives to a Constituent Assembly (CA), and its acceptance of a constitution to mark the transition to independence. The agreements made on all of these processes had been negotiated over a decade and were never set out in a single document. In addition to the more usual military component of a UN peacekeeping force, distinguishing features of UNTAG included the use of civilian police monitors and election supervisors, and the central role of the UN Secretary General's Special Representative (UNSGSR) and his staff. The responsibilities of the civilian components of UNTAG came under considerable strain because of some of the particular features of the situation in Namibia, as we shall see, but there are nonetheless some general lessons offered by the effects which they and the UNSGSR can be seen to have had on the election processes and outcomes, which are not widely acknowledged.

There are also aspects of UNTAG's role which arose directly from the peculiarities of the long history of negotiations about Namibia's future, some of which, but not all, involved the UN directly, and the special relationship between it and the South West African People's Organisation (SWAPO) which had existed from 1973, in the General Assembly's recognition of SWAPO as the *sole authentic representative of the Namibian people*. Weighing up the significance of the particular political conditions of Namibia's transition against more general issues is of course not straightforward. In making these assessments, we begin with a review of the processes by which the plan for UNTAG's role in the transition was finally activated.

The status of Namibia before the transition[2]

Namibia was a colonial property of Germany until the First World War and was then mandated as a protectorate of South Africa by the League of Nations. It was the only League mandate territory that was not transferred to Trust status under the UN in 1947, and thence remained in an ambiguous legal situation. It never legally became a colony of South Africa, although it became so *de facto*. The UN itself pronounced the illegality of the regime from 1966 on, supported by the International Court of Justice in 1971, but nonetheless South Africa was to be allocated the role of administrator of the transition to independence as though it had in fact been the colonial power.[3] South Africa had had shifting ambitions for South West Africa, as Namibia was known, which included incorporation into its own state territory up to the 1960s, but from then on was under increasing international pressure to relinquish its hold and to facilitate a transition to independence. A nationalist movement developed in response to South Africa's intransigence, with the largest party being SWAPO, which sustained a two-pronged strategy of appealing to the international community for justice, particularly focusing on the UN, and engaging in armed struggle against South Africa until the peace process began in 1989. The diplomatic wing of this twin strategy was always necessary for the smaller partner in this David and Goliath fight, where the Whites in South Africa outnumbered the total population of Namibia, but itself became vastly complex because Namibia's struggle for independence always involved outside actors.

South Africa embarked on a regional strategy of destabilisation after the transition to independence in Mozambique and Angola (clearly identified as part of its *total strategy* from 1977 on), and Namibia became pivotal in the region's war and negotiations for peace. The South African Defence Force (SADF) used Namibia as a military base from which to conduct attacks on Angola's national army, the Angolan People's Liberation Army (FAPLA), and from which to give support to its rival Angolan movement and army, the National Union for the Total Independence of Angola (UNITA). Furthermore, as recruits to SWAPO's army, the People's Liberation Army of Namibia (PLAN) had, of necessity, to fight alongside FAPLA forces in order to protect their bases in Angola, as well as to prosecute their own war of resistance. In many ways the Namibian war for independence became part of Angola's war against South Africa. As the latter became a major site of Cold War politics, with the USSR and Cuba giving support to FAPLA and the USA giving support to UNITA, along with South Africa, so negotiations about the transition to independence in Namibia were to become very much an international affair.

The build up to implementation of the plan

Pressure from the international community brought South Africa to the negotiating table and signed an agreement on the transition to independence in 1976, UN Security Council Resolution 385 (UNSCR 385/76). This was a rather general agreement which spelt out a clear role for the UN in managing the transition, through the use of a special force,

UNTAG. It remained unimplemented and as a result of further talks, South Africa signed the better-known, but also short, agreement in 1978, UNSCR 435/78 which shifted the role of UNTAG to that of *supervision and control*. Research has yet to establish fully the motivations of the South African signatories to these agreements, as it seems that there was no intention at that time to implement them. In the subsequent decade or so the regional war escalated, not least as a result of South Africa's own actions to prolong it, but South Africa also embarked on a major project of social and political engineering within its *de facto* colony, with a view to creating a society and polity which it would find acceptable at independence.[4] Such changes included applying some of the principles of apartheid ideology, in an attempt to establish a political leadership and following which would gain material and ideological support from the 'internal' administration, and which would therefore oppose SWAPO.[5] The election was to reveal a partial success in this regard, especially outside SWAPO's heartland of the north.

During the subsequent decade of delay, which was marked by extensive international negotiations, as well as conflict, changes in the regional politics of the war drew in further the UN Security Council in its own right, as it did the self-styled Western Contact Group (WCG) from 1976, consisting of Britain, France, and the USA (who were also permanent members of the Security Council) along with Germany, and Canada. Jabri usefully casts the WCG members as 'interested third parties' in her evaluation of their effectiveness.[6] The WCG came together to try to persuade South Africa to agree to the implementation of UNSCR 435/78 and took on the role of negotiator, liaising also with the Organisation of African Unity and other Third World countries at the UN.

The agreements struck during this period with South Africa were handled by different members of the WCG playing lesser and greater roles, with few of them also being put to SWAPO, and some of the details not officially being passed to SWAPO, Namibia's internal Administration, or even to the UN Security Council itself.[7] The bundle of agreements then were as much about ending the *regional* conflict, involving the Angolan government, UNITA, Cuba, USSR and, increasingly after the repeal of the Clark amendment in 1986, the USA itself, because of its direct support for UNITA, as well as South Africa and SWAPO. Linking the resolution of these international dimensions of a regional conflict with the transition to Namibia's independence became known as *the linkage issue* and was pushed by the USA to the extent that it led to the break-up of the WCG, whose other members wished to keep the two issues separate. So by the time South Africa was ready to see UNSCR 435/78 implemented, the collection of associated agreements spelled out some of the detail of the transition process, although they had different signatories, had not even been circulated to all interested parties, and different parties had drawn contrasting conclusions from them, as was to become apparent during the transition itself.

The Cease-fire and conditions for the election

South Africa's agreement finally to go ahead with the implementation of UNSCR 435/78 (which was used as a sort of short-hand by all parties to include the associated agreements[8]) coincided with the ending of the Cold War. Considerable detail had yet to be agreed about the role and capacity of UNTAG and the details of the political processes involved in the transition. Debates in the Security Council and the General Assembly focused on the size of the UNTAG force and its timing. The final agreement, which was supported by the USSR, was for a force much reduced in size and scope from that proposed in UNSCR 435/78, in spite of widespread protests from Third World Countries, and for the first time the USSR voted against a Third World bloc in the General Assembly, in support of the proposal. Such moves were widely interpreted as reflecting the withdrawal by the USSR from contesting strategic interests in the Third World with the USA, and the distancing of the Western powers from SWAPO to ease their accommodation with South Africa.[9]

The role of UNTAG thus remained simply to oversee the processes of Cease-fire (and demobilisation of troops), election to a CA (which would write a constitution), and subsequent transition to independence. The processes would actually be carried out by the existing regime, under the leadership of the Administrator General (AG), in the person of Louis Piennar. To match this office the UN agreed to put in place the UNSGSR, in the person of Martti Ahtisari. The finally-agreed composition of the funded UNTAG force, in January 1989, was: 4,650 military personnel and 500 police monitors, compared with that envisaged under UNSCR 435/78: 7,500 military personnel and 1,860 civilian monitors.[10] This decision was taken in the face of evidence presented to the General Assembly about the inevitability of the reduced force being too scattered to be effective.[11] Further delays resulting from disagreements about the funding of the UNTAG force resulted in 75 per cent of UNTAG arriving late in Namibia, with hardly any at all being stationed in the north of the country on the very eve of the official Cease-fire on 1 April 1989. The full (but much reduced) contingent did not arrive until after the debacle of nine days' fighting in northern Namibia beginning on 1 April itself.[12]

The Nine Days' War

Some of the interim agreements made by the WCG, the USA, South Africa, Angola and Cuba, had already established some basic parameters for the transition in addition to the broad picture of UNSCR 435/78, which included the regulations for demobilisation of fighters. However, crucially, the first job of the UNTAG forces in Namibia, ie to oversee the formal Cease-fire on 1 April, was a disastrous failure. The details of where PLAN fighters should go prior to the election had not only been hotly contested by South Africa and SWAPO, but also the proposal from the WCG, which had been accepted by South Africa in 1988[13], had never been formally passed to SWAPO, let alone subject to its agreement, and did not, in any case, specify what should happen to any PLAN troops which were inside Namibia before 1 April, or whether they should be monitored by UNTAG.[14] Such obfuscation has been put forward as the reason why armed PLAN fighters crossed the border, ostensibly searching for UNTAG stations at which to register and hand over their weapons into Namibia, and were evidently not expecting to come under attack from South African forces.[15]

The AG was alerted to the presence of PLAN troops in the North in the early hours of 31 March[16] and immediately remobilised South African troops, including Koevoet, the fearsome military unit which had played a crucial security role in the north of the country in preceding years. The UNSGSR had the right to veto this action, although he had only arrived the day before, but was utterly reliant on South African intelligence and, as there were few UNTAG military personnel in place in the northern region, he felt he had little option but to agree. In the event there were very few witnesses to the fighting, but only one PLAN fighter was taken alive, with perhaps 250-300 combatants being killed, 30-40 of whom were SADF personnel[17], which is probably more than occurred in active military service within Namibian territory during the whole of the liberation war. Accounts have emerged which paint a slightly clearer picture than was available at the time, but there are still uncertainties about what happened.[18]

This conflict triggered a political major crisis, with both sides of the war claiming injustices, and the South Africans once again threatening to derail the transition process. The UNSGSR became embroiled in resolving these tensions, but prioritised keeping to the election timetable. The clash undermined what little trust already existed between the South African administration and SWAPO supporters in the country, making UNTAG's job much harder in the lead up the election. Some observers have argued that this was the intention of the South Africans all along, carried out with the collusion of the AG.[19] In any case the late arrival of UNTAG forces on the ground left the UNSGSR with little room for manoeuvre and a curtailed timetable.

Preparation for the election

The details of the election processes themselves had not been settled in international agreements and were to be drafted by the AG and then approved, or not, by the UNSGSR. As the timetable was not adjusted for lost time, the regulations for the registration of voters, one of the most potentially contentious issues of an election where population data are very poor, and the issue of citizenship is hotly contested, had to be scrutinised in a shortened period of time, and certainly were not subject to as many refinements as later stages of the election. The AG's proposals took an inclusive approach to the definition of eligibility, including not only people who had been born, or whose parents had been born in Namibia (with proof), but also anyone who had been living in the country for the four years before 1989. This latter inclusion allowed many white South Africans to fly in from the south to register (and indeed they were given incentives to do so) and a good number of people regarded as Angolans to come from over the northern border.[20] At the time this approach was defended as a way of avoiding unnecessary conflict and complication, and was not contested by the UNSGSR. After the election a number of analysts emphasised the point that all the 'extras', who might not have been deemed eligible under different rules, were most likely to support SWAPO's main opponents. None were expected to vote SWAPO, and their participation led to a swing of perhaps three seats to SWAPO's main rival, the Democratic Turnhalle Alliance (DTA).[21]

Once the AG had 'caught up' with the timetable, the UNSGSR seemed more willing to subject later proposals to greater scrutiny. There were prolonged discussions in the months between May and November about the actual mechanics of the election; all that had been agreed internationally was a system of proportional representation to a CA. The AG's office reflected the South African preference for a system which allowed the greatest representation of small parties as possible, and initial proposals from his office would also have allowed considerable scope for lessening the secrecy of the ballot and for high levels of tendered ballots.[22] The South Africans' strategy here was clearly (and now admitted to have been) to prevent SWAPO from achieving the two-thirds' majority which would enable it to write the constitution alone[23], so there was quite a lot at stake for the 'side' which was actually administering the election. The UNSGSR successfully negotiated changes in these regulations to minimise the chances of fraud, albeit only four weeks before the commencement of voting, but most of the regulations which facilitated the representation of small parties were allowed.

Ensuring a peaceful political climate

In preparation for the registration period and the lead up to the election, one of the most important responsibilities for UNTAG was to remove, or at least minimise, a climate of intimidation. For the military personnel this was a straightforward responsibility of continuing to oversee demobilisation and ensuring that the former military players in the war remained demobilised or were confined to bases. In the event of any armed incidents occurring they had the usual rights of recourse to the use of arms in self-defence but, in spite of the anxieties caused by the nine-days' war, there were relatively few incidents for them to deal with during the period of campaigning. There was significant loss of life amongst SWAPO supporters nonetheless (in contrast to only one death attributed in any way to SWAPO supporters). The SWAPO leadership was evidently targeted, including the assassinated Anton Lubowski in September 1989[24], and although it has been admitted that forces in South Africa were behind this assassination no one has been brought to trial.[25] Nonetheless the presence of UNTAG military forces no doubt prevented large numbers of deaths.

The situation was much more complex for the civilian police contingent (UNCIVPOL) which had a brief to monitor the actions of the existing police force, the South West African Police (SWAPOL). Briefly, problems in this regard were twofold; first SWAPOL had taken on considerable counter-insurgency roles in much of the country, regularly using terror tactics against the local population and torture techniques in interrogation, and so patently did not have the trust of the local population, especially in the north of the country. As UNTAG, and specifically UNCIVPOL, was supposed to *monitor* the actions of SWAPOL, it could not act directly in response to the complaints which citizens might make to it, but simply urge SWAPOL to be more responsible to its 'clients' and make complaints to the office of the AG[26], who set up a commission to hear such complaints, if it failed to do so satisfactorily. That the UNTAG force was powerless to take action against

SWAPOL in the face of documented brutality is testified to in the records of the commission and the closing statement of the commissioner himself[27] (although apparently there were some isolated successes in UNCIVPOL personnel undertaking on-the-spot retraining of SWAPOL personnel[28]).

The second major challenge for UNCIVPOL was presented by Koevoet, a unit which had been established as part of a number of military units under the South African administration within the 'national' South West African Territorial Force (SWATF). SWATF was made up of Namibian forces (which were conscripted towards the end of the war) and, whilst being ostensibly separate from SADF, in practice was subordinate to it and the links were made clear as some battalions were transferred into SADF and moved to South African territory once the peace process began.[29] Koevoet (*crowbar* in Afrikaans) was made up of local men, with little education, who were trained in basic counter-insurgency, brutal interrogation methods and terror tactics, and played a strong role in the north of the country during the last, highly militarised, years of the war (when they are said to have been responsible for 80 per cent of the deaths in the north of the country[30]). As a military unit it came under the rules for demobilisation and monitoring by the military component of UNTAG (although this had not been literally envisaged by at the time of the original agreements, as they pre-dated the formation of SWATF in 1980), but many of its members were incorporated, in units, into SWAPOL before the transition began, and some of these were re-mobilised and used to attack PLAN fighters in the nine-days' war. A number of observers argued at the time, and have documented since, that Koevoet was not disbanded in the way it was intended, but its ambiguous status also meant that the military component of UNTAG also did not monitor it closely.[31] The Koevoet forces seem to have kept their weapons for longer than they were supposed to and were able to stay in contact with their ex-commanders.[32]

Under cover of complete disbandment, or employment within SWAPOL, Koevoet undertook direct harassment of SWAPO supporters, working closely with their main political rival, DTA. Even when witnessing acts of political and physical intimidation, UNCIVPOL had no powers of coercion, arrest or detention and no recourse to the use of arms other than in self-defence. Very little guidance was given to these personnel[33] in how to deal with ex-Koevoet, or with other situations of intimidation of campaigners, such as those who were prevented from talking to voters on farms or other places of employment, as often happened to SWAPO campaigners.

An issue which was fanned by some of SWAPO's opponents was the fate of members of SWAPO who had been detained as its prisoners, but who had not returned safely to Namibia, or whose death or whereabouts could not be established.[34] This issue continues to be of great significance in Namibian politics today, but its relevance here is limited to an assessment of the effectiveness of UNTAG'S intervention. In response to the protests it received about 'missing' ex-detainees, UNTAG did undertake a mission to Angola and Zambia to investigate the SWAPO camps where detainees had been held. UNTAG was criticised for not allowing any ex-detainees themselves to accompany the mission, which certainly limited the credibility of its conclusion that no one was still being detained and the number of missing people was much smaller than many had alleged.[35] The investigation did not satisfy SWAPO's critics, but it is very difficult to say what effect this action had on the election result and therefore to assess UNTAG's effectiveness in carrying out this part of its mission.

The voting itself

In contrast to the fears cast by the nine-days' war, the assassination of Lubowski, attacks on other individuals, and the relatively frequent incidents of political intimidation in the north of the country, the days of voting passed very peacefully. A large number of experienced international civilian monitors were placed at polling stations and the polling days were extended to compensate for the late announcement of all the detailed regulations which had to be agreed between the AG and the UNSGSR.

There was relatively little of the directly threatening intimidation of voters which many had feared and this was one of the main reasons why the international pronouncement of the election as 'free and fair' was so quickly made. However, observers at the time noted the prevalence of what has been called *structural intimidation*[36] where people might not receive an outright threat but, because of their position in society, are nonetheless constrained in their electoral choice. The classic example of this was that of farm employees who lived in very isolated circumstances and were often totally reliant on their white employer for transport to the distant polling stations (or were not given time off work to make the journey themselves) and even for explanations of what the election was for and how to vote. With such a largely illiterate and scattered population over much of the country, many observers believed that there was an inevitable loss of votes which might have been expected to be cast in SWAPO's favour.

The results and their impact on the final stage

The results of the election were: SWAPO 57.3 per cent (giving it 41 of the 72 seats in the CA, and thus falling short of the two-thirds), and DTA 28.6 per cent (with 21 seats, which was three short of a potential blocking-vote by itself). The rest was divided between 10 parties or fronts, none of which were clear allies of SWAPO.[37] The results were widely celebrated as a SWAPO victory even though it failed to achieve the two thirds' majority which would have allowed it to write the constitution alone. In spite of the large number of contenders for the election, it was really seen as one between the 'nationalist' side (SWAPO, along with the very small fronts UDF, NNF) and the 'collaborators' with the previous regime (primarily DTA, along with all the others[38]). In evaluating the effectiveness of UNTAG in ensuring a free and fair election, one does therefore need to turn to more political analyses of these results. South Africa seems to have achieved its main objective for the election, ie. to prevent SWAPO from obtaining a two-thirds' majority. Analysts have calculated that the potential loss of votes to SWAPO as a result of the regulations put forward by the AG, and structural intimidation, did actually cost SWAPO the two-thirds majority.[39]

Looking at the outcome of the decisions in the CA reveals more of a mixed picture, however. The main issues which the South Africans were thought to be most concerned about were those of the property rights, especially land, of Namibian (white) citizens, and the risks of transition to a one-party state. In the event all of the *constitutional principles*, which had been agreed with the WCG in 1982, were accepted by SWAPO from the word go, and although land rights were discussed heatedly in closed session, a united front was kept in public, with the relevant clauses in the constitution being acceptable to both 'sides'. The main issues which SWAPO did contest were the terms of office of the President, on which it relented, and it agreed to a bicameral system, and SWAPO leadership's desire to keep the preventative detention legislation, which it relinquished.[40]

It was commonly believed that SWAPO members of the CA took such a conciliatory approach because SWAPO's leadership had adjusted its own political stance to suit the political changes of a post-Cold War world, and also because of members' eagerness to take up office. One might therefore argue that the South Africans' relatively successful attempts to influence the outcome of the election were needless. Perhaps this is the case[41] but the lesson here is surely that it was possible for South Africa to do so, although it was not easy to prove at the time, and - more significantly -

was not effectively challenged by UNSGSR or UNTAG.

Conclusion

The starting point of a negotiated peace process leading to an election and some formal political transition is usually presented in the form of a documented agreement. Almost by definition such agreements represent compromises, achieved perhaps solely through vagueness on issues where compromise has been most difficult. Using such agreements as the 'rule book' is very difficult, if not impossible, for a UN peacekeeping force and so there has to be some process where further definition is given to the detailed regulations about the processes associated with such transitions, such as demobilisation, the type of election (whether proportional representation etc, and election to what body), registration, voting and the counting of votes, and the writing of a constitution. In Namibia's case matters were complicated because even the conditions of the basic peace agreement did not exist in a single document, and some of the parties had not seen important components. So even though the relevance of a UN presence during the transition was not disputed by any of the major actors[42], UNTAG was caught on the hop on 1 April because of a lack of clarity about what had been agreed to in the first place, arising directly from the long drawn-out nature of the negotiations.

The peace process suffered a major 'failure' with the bloodbath of the nine-days' war and arguably with the successful assassination of Lubowski, and whilst neither derailed the process, certainly the former could have been avoided had there been adequate resourcing of UNTAG, as well as more clearly spelt-out agreements. The force was too small, not in place in time, did not have adequate logistics or independent sources of intelligence, and perhaps was insufficiently prepared for the particular conditions of Namibia. All of these weaknesses could have been avoided with the resources which were originally envisaged for UNTAG by UNSCR 435/78. The reluctance of the UNSGSR to delay the timetable was a more profound factor limiting UNTAG's scope for intervention which was clearly related to anxiety about the cost - political and financial - in Namibia's particular situation. Such anxieties are, however, also likely to be generic to peacekeeping forces in other places which come under pressure to avoid delays which a) would seem like failure and might risk the impatience and withdrawal of one or more of the parties and b) are inevitably costly.

The preparation for the election, including the repatriation of refugees, the demobilisation of troops from both 'sides' and the maintenance of a political climate which is relatively free from violent intimidation was widely seen as a success, but there were serious limitations here too. The thorny problem of SWAPO's ex-detainees was not handled to everyone's satisfaction, although perhaps it never could be and it is not clear what impact this had on the outcome. The demobilisation of Koevoet was a confused and messy business which had very real consequences for the political climate, and perhaps for the outcome in some places. Fundamentally, however, it was the relatively limited roles of the UNSGSR and UNTAG in the definition of all the detail of the elections subsequent to the major international agreements, as supervisor and monitor, which created very real problems in the degree of slant which one side in the contest was able to give to the process. The AG, with support from South Africa, had a sophisticated grasp of the local situation and successfully manipulated the electoral system itself, as well as tactics of assassination, violence and political intimidation, to prevent a SWAPO two thirds' majority. Some of the mechanisms used by South Africa are also used elsewhere: defining the eligibility of voters is often a crucial issue after a war involving neighbours; rules about the funding and representation of parties can clearly affect who is able to enter the contest; different electoral systems do lead to different kinds of outcomes[43]; and voting regulations can be made more or less suitable for illiterate voters.

The issue of limiting the extent of voter intimidation to a level which allows an election to be pronounced 'free and fair' is one of the major challenges of a force such as UNTAG. Whilst officially, UNTAG was successful in its mission, there were significant examples of intimidation which UNTAG failed to alleviate and which in a different political situation might have had a greater impact on voting patterns. The strength of UNCIVPOL was drastically limited by its role as monitor of SWAPOL, particularly as SWAPOL itself was so closely associated with one side during the war, as is surely common in post-conflict settlements. Moreover, UNCIVPOL's ability to tackle structural intimidation was even more severely curtailed, as was that of other civilian election monitors, restricted as it was to intervening where there was suspicion of foulplay around the act of voting itself. In a situation where high rates of illiteracy and total lack of experience of voting in a secret ballot is the norm for whole communities, there is certainly a need for much more comprehensive voter education to be provided by a neutral party. Thus, although the 'success' of the election was certainly conditional on the presence of the UNTAG force, the problems associated with it were also strongly related to the conditions of its mandate.

In spite of the highly significant interventions of the WCG members, and particularly USA, in the politics of negotiations which progressed and then ended Namibia's war, the transition to a peaceful, democratic, independent state has been accredited to UNTAG itself. Lessons were clearly taken from experience of Namibia's transition, not least by the UN in the elections in Angola and Mozambique, and definitely in the case of South Africa. Exactly what lessons were visible, through the triumphant celebration of the SWAPO victory, to those most concerned to see a free and fair election in those countries, is certainly less clear, as explored elsewhere in this volume.

Notes

1   This chapter relies heavily on the results of a collaborative research project led by Lionel Cliffe (published as Lionel Cliffe with Ray Bush, Jenny Lindsay, Brian Mokopakgosi, Donna Pankhurst and Balefi Tsie (1994), *The Transition to Independence in Namibia*, Lynne Rienner: London.
2   For an introduction to Namibia's history, see: Wood, B. (ed) (1984), *Namibia 1884-1994. Readings on Namibia's History and Society*, Namibia Support Committee: London; Wood, B. (1984) 'The Militarisation of Namibia's Economy', *Review of African Political Economy*, No. 29; Katjavivi, P. (1988), *The History of Resistance in Namibia*, James Currey: London.
3   Cliffe et al, op. cit., p. 69.
4   See Cliffe et al, op. cit., pp. 49-51 for a review of the possible motivations of South Africa for delaying.
5   Cliffe et al, op. cit., p. 33-9; Pankhurst, D. (1996), *A Resolvable Conflict? The Politics of Land in Namibia*, Peace Research Report No. 36, University of Bradford: Bradford, pp. 18-22.
6   Jabri, V. (1990) *Mediating Conflict. Decision-Making and Western Intervention in Namibia*, Manchester University Press: Manchester, p. 40.
7   These agreements are reproduced or listed in Cliffe et al, op. cit., pp. 239-247. They include: *The Western Settlement Plan, 1978; UNSCR 435/78*; The 'Constitutional Principles' document; a further 9 Security Council Resolutions; 6 Statements/Reports from the Secretary-General; the agreements of 1988 between Cuba, Angola and South Africa (known as the *Protocols of Geneva and Brazzaville*, and the *Tripartite Agreement*); *The Annexure on the Joint Commission* (between Angola, Cuba and South Africa); *Mount Etjo Declaration,*

1989 (which re-affirmed the Cease-fire in Namibia).
8   Cliffe et al, op. cit., p. 40.
9   Cliffe et al, op. cit., pp. 70-1.
10 Cliffe et al, op. cit., p. 70.
11 Ibid.
12 Cliffe et al, op. cit., p. 84.
13 In the *Geneva Protocols* (Cliffe et al, op. cit., pp. 86-7).
14 Cliffe et al, op. cit., p. 74; Jabri, V. op. cit., p. 98.
15 Cliffe et al, op. cit., p. 89.
16 Cliffe et al, op. cit., p. 84.
17 Cliffe et al, op. cit., p. 84-6; Waldman, J. A. (1995) *Serving the Peace: NZ Police, Professionalism and UN Peacekeeping*, unpublished MA thesis, University of Auckland, p. 98.
18 Cliffe et al, op. cit., pp. 84-91; Leys, C. (1989) 'The Security Situation and the Transfer of Power in Namibia' in *Review of African Political Economy*, No. 45-6.
19 As reviewed in Cliffe et al, op. cit., especially pp. 90-91.
20 See Cliffe et al, op. cit., pp. 117-120.
21 Cliffe et al, op. cit., p. 120.
22 Cliffe et al, op. cit., pp. 128-33.
23 The South Africa campaign strategy, known as *Operation Agree*, was revealed in subsequent inquiries in South Africa about its own past. See Leys, C. and Saul, J. 'The Legacy: An Afterword', pp. 199-200, in Leys, C. and Saul, J. (1995) *Namibia's Liberation Struggle. The Two-Edged Sword*, James Currey: London, pp. 199-200; Cliffe et al, op. cit., pp. 83, 90.
24 Cliffe et al, op. cit., pp. 99-100.
25 Cliffe et al, op. cit., p. 106.
26 Cliffe et al, op. cit., pp. 136-8; Waldman, op. cit., p. 104.
27 Leys, C. (1995) 'State and Civil Society: Policing in Transition', in Leys and Saul, *Namibia's Liberation Struggle ...*, p. 136.
28 Waldman, op. cit., pp. 108-9.
29 Leys and Saul, 'The Legacy ...', p. 199.
30 Cliffe et al, op. cit., p. 24.
31 Cliffe et al, op. cit., pp. 135, 139-141.
32 Cliffe et al, op. cit., p. 140; Leys, C. 'The Security Situation ...'.
33 Waldman, op. cit., p. 128.
34 Cliffe et al, op. cit., pp. 167-175.
35 Cliffe et al, op. cit., p. 171.
36 Cliffe et al, op. cit., pp. 107-110.
37 See Cliffe et al, op. cit., pp. 183-196, for a full analysis of the

results.
38 See Cliffe et al, op. cit., pp. 145-179 for a comprehensive analysis.
39 Cliffe et al, op. cit., pp. 143-44.
40 Cliffe et al, op. cit., pp. 213-4.
41 Cliffe et al, op. cit., p. 200.
42 Cliffe et al, op. cit., p. 65.
43 Cliffe et al, op. cit., pp. 116, 250-2.

11 Liberia: lessons for the future from the experience of ECOMOG

Gerry Cleaver

Introduction

The continuing debate on the future of 'peacekeeping' operations in Africa has focused attention on, amongst other things, the most recent example of what is a purely African peacekeeping operation, namely the continuing mission of the ECOWAS Monitoring Group (ECOMOG) to Liberia. Given that the most likely scenario for future peacekeeping operations on the continent is one of African forces operating under the mandate of either the OAU and/or a sub regional organisation such as ECOWAS, it is natural to examine a current example of the genre to attempt to identify examples to be followed and mistakes to be avoided. Within this context I propose in this chapter to try and identify some of the lessons for future African peacekeeping operations that might be drawn from the ECOMOG involvement in Liberia. It is not possible within the space limitations of a single chapter to cover all the issues raised by the Liberian crisis that might be deemed portentous for future operations and the selection made is subjective and governed, at least to some degree, by the problems that have arisen during the discussion of proposed peacekeeping operations elsewhere in Africa.

Neither is it practicable or relevant to engage in a lengthy narrative of the evolution of the Liberian crisis. Suffice it to say that in December 1989 forces of the National Patriotic Front of Liberia, under the leadership of Charles Taylor, crossed the border from the Ivory Coast and launched an invasion of Liberia designed to overthrow the regime of Samuel Doe, who had himself seized power in a military coup in 1980. The fighting rapidly escalated with Doe's government forces faring badly. As is all too common in African conflicts, civilians became the preferred targets of the armed factions and as Taylor's forces overran most of the country apart from Monrovia, mounting evidence of atrocities against civilians increased pressure for external intervention to put an end to the killing. With the attention of most of the international community diverted by the growing crisis between Iraq and Kuwait, it fell to African states themselves, and particularly those in the immediate vicinity, to formulate some sort of response to the Liberian tragedy.

Legitimacy

One of the most persistent problems that has bedevilled ECOMOG is the legitimacy of the force itself and of its mandate for action. This problem reflects a wider one of the Francophone/Anglophone split within ECOWAS and also a fear of growing Nigerian hegemony in West Africa. It is of course not solely a question of legitimacy in the international context but also a question of the legitimacy of ECOMOG in the eyes of the various parties to the Liberian conflict. The questioning of the right of ECOWAS to intervene reflects the sacrosanct way in which internal sovereignty is regarded in Africa and which is reflected in the charter of the OAU. Indeed ECOWAS's own Protocol on Non-Aggression and Mutual Defence, signed in 1981, is designed to deal with external threats and inter-state conflict rather than the more prevalent intra-state conflicts such as the Liberian crisis.[1]

ECOMOG grew out of a decision by the ECOWAS summit in Banjul in May 1990, to adopt a Nigerian suggestion to establish a Standing Mediation Committee to deliberate on possible solutions to crises such as that in Liberia. This Committee, consisting of representatives of Nigeria, Ghana, The Gambia, Mali and Togo, held discussions with the belligerent parties in Liberia but were unable to secure an agreement. The Committee, at its meeting on 6-7 August 1990 decided on the despatch of a cease-fire monitoring group to Monrovia, with a mandate to establish a cease-fire, secure Doe's resignation, set up an interim government and organise elections to be held within twelve months.[2] Undoubtedly action was needed to prevent further civilian casualties, but the processes behind the establishment of ECOMOG exposed two fundamental problems that can be fatal to the effectiveness of an intervention force. Firstly it led to rift between the members of the sponsoring organisation, ECOWAS. The Francophone/Anglophone antipathy amongst the member states of ECOWAS had been a constant fact of life for the organisation since its inception. However the issue of ECOMOG turned this into a serious rift. A number of Francophone states were suspicious of Nigeria's motives in particular. Nigeria had been the prime mover behind the establishment of ECOMOG and was contributing the largest share both in terms of manpower and finance. President Babangida stated that Nigeria did not lightly breach the convention of non-interference but that in the absence of any legitimate authority in Liberia it was incumbent upon neighbouring states to intervene in order to prevent further loss of life and to prevent the spread of the conflict.[3] Nevertheless the Francophone states believed that Nigeria was using ECOMOG as a vehicle for its own regional hegemonic ambitions and Burkina Faso's Blaise Compraore openly denounced the intervention as illegal and was supported by Ivory Coast and Senegal. The two Francophone members of the Mediation Committee, Mali and Togo, expressed their disapproval by refusing to contribute to ECOMOG.[4] What might have been mere technical disagreements over legality or even a continuation of a long standing political row had serious implications for ECOMOG since both Burkina Faso and Ivory Coast continued to support Taylor's NPFL and provide not only a safe haven for his forces but also a conduit for his supplies, thus reducing the incentive for him to negotiate in good faith and prolonging until very recently a situation whereby he could still entertain ideas of an ultimate military victory after the premature withdrawal of ECOMOG as a result of divisions within ECOWAS. It has also been in Taylor's interests to exacerbate divisions within ECOMOG itself, between the Francophone and Anglophone elements and this may in some way explain the attack by NPFL forces on the newly arrived Senegalese detachment of ECOMOG in March 1992.

The principle lesson to be learnt from this is that unanimity amongst the member states of any organisation sponsoring a peacekeeping operation is essential. Undoubtedly the split within ECOWAS has impacted upon the effectiveness of ECOMOG and contributed to the prolongation of the fighting. The second fundamental problem that faced the ECOMOG forces arriving in August 1990 was that they had failed to obtain the consent of the belligerent parties to their mission. Taylor regarded ECOMOG as a Nigerian force sent to deny him his 'deserved' triumph over Doe.[5] The latter on the other hand must have had mixed feelings about ECOMOG. Its arrival undoubtedly relieved the pressure on his forces, if only because the NPFL now had another target to aim at, but part of ECOMOG's mandate called for his removal from office and this might well have caused him to regard its arrival as a dubious blessing. The only group to welcome openly ECOMOG was the newly formed splinter group of the NPFL, led by Prince Johnson, which was contesting control of Monrovia with Taylor. The failure to obtain the consent of the warring factions, particularly the NPFL, meant that ECOMOG, far from being a peacekeeping force, immediately found itself in a war-fighting situation which has often characterised its operations in the ensuing six years. In addition any claims to impartiality by ECOMOG were fatally flawed from the outset and with the subsequent appearance of even more factions, some of which it openly supported or used as auxiliaries, ECOMOG appeared to be just another party to the continuing struggle for Liberia. This lack of consent from the belligerents and the naked hostility of Taylor and the NPFL forced ECOMOG to adopt a peace enforcement role that has at times evolved into outright war-fighting, roles which the original mandate did not envisage for the force and which it does not cater for.

A clear lesson emerges for future operations and that is, that where possible strenuous efforts must be made to obtain the consent of the belligerent parties to a conflict before an intervention force is despatched. If that consent is not forthcoming and intervention is still considered necessary then those parties withholding their consent must be isolated from their external sources of supply so as to make them more amenable to negotiation and the intervention force must possess overwhelming military superiority so as to overcome any resistance from these parties, preferably by overawing them but if necessary by the application of force.

The size and composition of ECOMOG

An important lesson to emerge from the experience of ECOMOG in Liberia is that the size of any intervention force must be sufficient to match the tasks allotted to it. The nature of these tasks must also be reflected in the equipment inventory of the force and ideally the composition of the force should reflect the political commitment of its supporters. In all these respects ECOMOG's record is, at best, chequered.

At the outset it needs to be pointed out that the short time lag between the decision to despatch a force, taken on 7 August 1990, and its actual deployment on 24 August 1990,[6] demonstrates that African states can deploy their forces rapidly when the need arises and circumstances permit. The speed of deployment was assisted by the fact that it was an operation largely carried out by the armed forces of one country, Nigeria, using maritime transport facilities to reach quickly the central area of conflict, Monrovia. Had Liberia been landlocked and the insertion necessary by either air or land, it is questionable whether the deployment would have been quite so rapid. In addition had the force been unable to call upon the resources of a sizeable military power but instead had to rely upon pooling the assets of smaller militaries, then this too would have affected its speed of deployment.

On the question of the size of ECOMOG, the initial deployment of 3,000 troops was inadequate to the tasks allotted to them. I do not think it unfair to suggest, given the lack of consent from the belligerent parties, that ECOMOG might have anticipated some of the hostility that greeted them, particularly from Taylor's NPFL. The armed resistance of the NPFL made it impossible for ECOMOG to carry out its mandate and unnerved its Ghanaian commander. The abduction and murder of Doe whilst visiting the ECOMOG Headquarters, by Prince Johnson's forces, dealt a fatal blow to ECOMOG's plans for the establishment of a cease-fire.[7]

Subsequently a Nigerian force commander was appointed and ECOMOG's strength was doubled. A more aggressive strategy was adopted and the ensuing three-week offensive cleared Monrovia of the NPFL and established it as a base for ECOMOG's operations and for the delivery of humanitarian aid. In the following six years the size of ECOMOG has fluctuated to reflect both the levels of commitment and frustration of the contributing countries and the emphasis placed on the military element of any solution to the crisis. These fluctuations have meant that ECOMOG has never been able to establish itself throughout the whole of Liberia in order to implement a cease-fire or monitor adherence, or the lack of it, by the various factions to the numerous agreements that they have signed up to since 1990. Until very recently ECOMOG has been unable to effectively supervise the disarming of fighters as required under the latest agreements. The peak strength of ECOMOG was achieved in early 1993 when 16,000 troops were deployed in an aggressive campaign against the NPFL, that included the use of air power and also brought the force perilously close to conflict with the Ivorian military.[8] Since then ECOMOG's strength has been reduced until in April 1996 it had to concentrate nearly all its remaining 8,000 men in Monrovia to deal with renewed factional fighting.

More recently the outgoing Force Commander, Major General John Inienger, has called for ECOMOG's strength to be increased to 18,000. He argued that the force needed 'an overwhelming presence in Liberia' in order to compel adherence by the various factions to the agreements they have signed. To this end he believes that ECOMOG should be properly equipped with armoured vehicles and helicopter gunships so that it can 'assert' itself.[9] This recommendation appears to have been endorsed by ECOWAS, with increased contributions from countries with forces already deployed and, somewhat significantly given their original opposition to ECOMOG, first time troop contributions from Burkina Faso and Ivory

Coast.[10] All this is a long way from the original concept and size of ECOMOG and is a salutary lesson in how nations who commit themselves to such interventions must be prepared for changes of circumstances that will alter the demands placed upon them. All peacekeeping and related intervention operations undergo transformations of one form or another and flexibility, both political and military, on the part of their sponsors is a vital ingredient for their success.

The composition of ECOMOG has always reflected Nigeria's dominance of the force. This too has been the case with the position of Force Commander, who since September 1990, has always been a Nigerian. This has had the advantage of bringing a certain continuity to the command structure as well as an element of homogeneity to the force. However the hostile nature of the relationship between Taylor's NPFL and the Nigerians had meant that ECOMOG had never been able to gain his trust and has often been engaged in open warfare with his forces. This has undoubtedly hindered the peacemaking process in Liberia. To offset this problem of acceptance by one of the leading belligerent factions, ECOMOG has been augmented, at various times, by contingents from Senegal, Tanzania and Uganda. These deployments were designed to counter the accusation that ECOMOG was a puppet of Nigerian policy and to bolster its credibility as an impartial actor in the eyes of Liberia's armed factions. These efforts have been largely unsuccessful but do illustrate how necessary it is for an intervention to be perceived, by all parties to a conflict, as being impartial and trustworthy. This is absolutely essential when an intervention force is asked to supervise the disarmament of warring factions. This is much more easily achieved with the co-operation of the parties concerned and the fate of UNOSOM II illustrates what can occur when disarmament by force is attempted.

In the case of the recent promised addition of Ivorian and Burkinabe contingents to ECOMOG, their significance lies not in their size but in the signal they send, particularly to the NPFL, that the latter can no longer look to these countries for support. Hopefully this will induce Taylor and the other faction leaders to respect the agreements they sign. It can only be speculated what sort of an impact the inclusion of these forces in the original deployment, might have had on the whole Liberian tragedy.

ECOMOG's relations with the international community

The experience of ECOMOG's relationships with states and international organisations with interests in the Liberian conflict highlights a number of problems that can either deliberately or inadvertently impede the progress of an intervention force toward the achievement of its goals. In the case of ECOMOG the actions of both the USA and France have impacted on its operations to a significant degree.

The USA had long standing historical and economic ties with Liberia as well as being responsible for arming Doe's forces. However in 1990 the attention of the US administration was focused on the growing crisis in the Gulf and initially its interest in Liberia was limited to the provision of humanitarian assistance to refugees and to the evacuation of foreign nationals in Operation Sharp Edge, conducted by the Marines just prior to ECOMOG's deployment in August 1990.[11]

The effective disengagement of the USA from the Liberian conflict, at least in political terms, made ECOMOG's task more difficult than it might have been since the presence of overt US support and political leverage might have induced the various faction leaders to negotiate in good faith. This disengagement on the part of the USA may well have been initially determined by a necessity to concentrate on events in the Gulf but subsequently has been driven by the experience of the disastrous intervention in Somalia. Following on from that episode US policy towards peacekeeping changed. The US has effectively ruled itself out of future UN operations, particularly in Africa. The new policy was embodied in Presidential Decision Directive 25, issued in May 1994, which limits US involvement to the provision of logistical support for peacekeeping operations and imposes stringent criteria which need to be met before the US will support future UN operations financially.[12] This policy has been an instrumental factor in curtailing UN peacekeeping activity in Africa, particularly in the case of Rwanda but it has also affected Liberia where the onus of peacekeeping and conflict resolution remains squarely on ECOMOG, with little effective help from the UN.

On the positive side the US has provided substantial assistance towards the costs of ECOMOG, to the tune of some $40 million worth of logistical assistance in the fiscal year 1996 alone.[13] In addition it has provided economic support for the deployment of non-ECOWAS units to ECOMOG. However it is arguable that more active US involvement earlier on might well have helped bring the conflict to an early conclusion.

France's role in Liberia is less clearly defined but there is little doubt that for most of the time since 1990 she has opposed the deployment of ECOMOG and has encouraged her allies within ECOWAS to do the same. As stated earlier the Francophone countries of Ivory Coast and Burkina Faso supported Taylor's NPFL in its attempt to take over Liberia and whilst there is no concrete evidence of French military support for the

NPFL, they must have at least turned a convenient 'blind eye' to the provision of that support by Libya and Burkina Faso. The architects of France's African policy may have come to the conclusion that a Liberia governed by the NPFL would gravitate towards the Francophone members of ECOWAS thus expanding French influence in the region, diminishing American influence and curtailing, at least to a degree, Nigeria's ambitions to become a regional hegemonic power. Needless to say this interference has contributed to the prolonging of the conflict and to the difficulties of obtaining compliance from the Liberian factions to the various peace agreements that have been signed.

The UN's direct involvement on the ground in Liberia has been limited to the dispatch, in December 1993, of unarmed peacekeepers to monitor violations of the cease-fire, theoretically in force at the time, and to observe ECOMOG's disarmament of the factions. This UN presence, known under the acronym of UNOMIL, continues to this day and its mandate was extended in August 1996, until the end of November 1996.[14] This was despite the continuing violence and the limited progress at that time towards disarmament of the factions. ECOMOG is charged with providing security for the members of UNOMIL and thus yet another burden has been added to its load. If UNOMIL was intended to assure those faction leaders opposed to ECOMOG that they had nothing to fear by adhering to the disarmament agreements, then surely the necessity of UNOMIL's close co-operation with and reliance upon ECOMOG, calls into question, at least in the eyes of those particular leaders, any claims it may make toward impartiality.

What has transpired in Liberia with ECOMOG raises a number of issues which are particularly relevant to current discussions over peacekeeping operations in Africa. Firstly, there can be no realistic expectation of direct participation by US forces in operations on the African continent in the near future. The exceptions to this would be contributions limited to the provision of equipment and support but with no actual deployment of ground forces, and the less likely scenario of a purely US military operation in pursuit of specific US goals.

With the direct intervention of the world's largest military power effectively ruled out, it becomes even more important to secure the political and financial support of the US. Active US support for a peacekeeping operation can encourage others, particularly in Europe, to provide assistance and can perhaps discourage some countries from meddling in an unhelpful manner. There are of course negative aspects to any US involvement in an African peacekeeping operation, not least the hostility of certain African countries themselves, and the pros and cons would have to be weighed very carefully in each case. However the fact remains that only the US has the military capacity to move significant numbers of troops rapidly over great distance and to keep them supplied once deployed. Any African force that could obtain access to this resource would surely be operating at a distinct advantage to one that could not.

The ECOMOG experience also highlights the necessity for any organisation committing forces to a peacekeeping operation, to be fully aware of all the international implications of its actions. There needs to be proper assessment of the potential threats to the success of the operation that may emanate not only from inside the particular territory involved but from outside the region and beyond the continent itself. Measures need to be taken to identify malign international influences and to apply pressure politically in order to get them to curtail their activities. Serious political problems arise when certain countries who wield considerable influence in Africa decide to act in the pursuit of their own self interest rather than in the broader interests of peace and stability. The Liberian tragedy shows a urgent need for African countries to develop political relationships that are not predicated on allegiances rooted in the colonial past. Such a development might go some way to diminishing the influence of external powers.

Finally, it has to be admitted, albeit sadly, that no great reliance can be placed on the UN when it comes to peacekeeping in Africa. For a multitude of reasons, not the least of which is the antipathy toward the UN currently in vogue amongst US politicians, the UN is effectively hamstrung when considering peacekeeping operations in Africa. The UN will still remain important as the provider of legitimacy for any operation and as the organiser of humanitarian aid. But when it comes to the deployment of military forces, then for the foreseeable future it would appear that this will become the province of African states themselves, as has been the case in Liberia.

The 'image' of ECOMOG

The image of ECOMOG has been damaged in two crucial areas. Firstly its failure to gain acceptance by the various factions as an impartial force has led it away from a purely peacekeeping role to one of peace enforcement. Secondly the discipline of the force has been called into question on numerous occasions and looting by members of ECOMOG has severely undermined its reputation in the eyes of many ordinary Liberians. As a consequence of the first two shortcomings, ECOMOG's claim to be an effective intervention force has been undermined by numerous failures to enforce agreements and disarm the factions.

ECOMOG's neutrality was put in question by its initial failure to obtain the consent of warring parties to its initial intervention. The violently hostile reaction it received from the NPFL forced it to adopt a more aggressive stance than was originally anticipated and has coloured its relations with the various factions that have emerged in the subsequent years. Generally speaking the only constant in what was otherwise a fluid environment of shifting alliances had been the antipathy between ECOMOG and the NPFL. This has at times led to open warfare with ECOMOG fighting alongside other factions, such as ULIMO and the AFL, against the NPFL. On other occasions ECOMOG has found itself in conflict with its earlier allies, notably with ULIMO-J and the AFL in separate incidents in September 1994.[15] Ironically the disturbances this April in Monrovia saw ECOMOG pitched alongside the NPFL in combat with Roosevelt Johnson's ULIMO-J. At times it has seemed that ECOMOG has operated more like another faction in the Liberian civil war rather than a peacekeeping or even a peacemaking force. Parallels can be drawn with the US experience in Somalia and these serve as examples of the pitfalls of inserting forces, ostensibly deployed for peacekeeping or humanitarian purposes, into complex multi-factional civil wars.

On the question of discipline, ECOMOG has been badly let down by certain elements within the force itself. Pilfering and looting has gone on to such an extent that among many Liberians ECOMOG is said to stand for Every Car Or Movable Object Gone![16] The Nigerian contingent are usually singled out as the prime orchestrators of this looting which has gone well beyond the theft of the more obviously mobile type of plunder. There are reports of whole buildings being sold for scrap and of an entire iron ore refinery being stripped bare.[17] This scale of activity is indicative of a high level of organisation and the use of significant military resources with the active participation of senior officers. Although some of the smaller scale looting may be attributable to the sometimes lamentable pay arrangements of ECOMOG contingents, it is clear from the evidence of large scale and systematic criminal activity, that some Nigerian officers in particular regard service with ECOMOG as a lucrative opportunity to enhance their personal wealth and are not all that concerned with ECOMOG's peacekeeping activities.

The overall effect of all of this has been to undermine ECOMOG's credibility, not just in Liberia but also internationally, as well as diverting precious resources away from ECOMOG's designated tasks into criminal activity. The impact on Liberia's economy and infrastructure has been pernicious, exacerbating an already difficult situation and boding ill for any attempts at post war reconstruction. The lessons for future operations are the need for proper pay arrangements for force contingents, well trained and disciplined units and some form of monitoring to nip any criminal activity in the bud. It is perhaps an unfair requirement, but in order to maintain any sort of authority, peacekeeping forces need to be seen to be operating to a higher standard of behaviour than the belligerent forces in any conflict. This is the foundation of the respect that they need in order to be effective and once that respect is lost then it is extremely difficult to regain.

In order to address some of these concerns over its image ECOMOG has sought to dilute the impression of Nigerian dominance by the introduction of contingents from those countries with no obvious connection with Nigeria and her alleged hegemonic ambitions. At various times contingents have been brought in from Senegal, Tanzania and Uganda, to name but three.[18] This policy has by and large failed to alter the impression that ECOMOG is not a neutral force. These contingents have come under attack from the various factions and have suffered financial problems. This was particularly the case with the Tanzanians whose funding was supposed to be provided by the UN.[19] The recent promised expansion of ECOMOG to include Burkinabe and Ivorian contingents will hopefully, given the past policies of their governments, meet with more success in persuading the Liberian faction leaders to disarm their forces and seek a political solution to their country's problems.

Conclusions

The Liberian imbroglio continued throughout 1996 without any concrete signs of the establishment of a permanent peace. Inter-factional fighting persisted and remained a severe hindrance to the delivery of humanitarian relief supplies particularly in the rural areas. This enduring rivalry took a most dramatic form in the assassination attempt against Charles Taylor, who remained the pivotal character in the conflict.[20]

There were however hopeful signs not the least of which was the election of Ruth Sando Perry as President of the Liberian Council of State.[21] In addition the frustration of ECOWAS members with faction leaders who refused to abide by agreements had at last manifested itself not just in threats to withdraw from ECOMOG but in the more effective form of promised sanctions against individual faction leaders.[22] As mentioned above the promise of Burkinabe and Ivorian units for ECOMOG hopefully presaged a more unified approach from ECOWAS members than has been the case in the past. Together with the expansion of ECOMOG these factors lead to real progress towards the goal of disarming the various armed factions.

There are numerous lessons for would-be peacekeepers to learn from the experience of ECOMOG in Liberia. Among the most important is the desirability, where possible, of obtaining the consent of the parties involved in a conflict, to the deployment of a peacekeeping force. Where this is not possible then any intervention force ought to be of sufficient strength to overcome any anticipated opposition and the countries taking part must be prepared for the consequences of engaging in what becomes a de facto invasion.

In either case a clear mandate for the force is essential and this should reflect a unanimity of purpose by the nations or organisation sponsoring the mission. In addition the aims and mandate of the force should be clearly understood by the parties to the conflict in order to minimise the possibility of the force's role being misinterpreted.

As stated above not only should the size of any force be commensurate with its goals but its equipment must reflect the nature of the tasks that it is asked to undertake. Lightly armed units are unlikely to be able to enforce a peace should that become necessary and on the other hand a heavily armed force may be counterproductive to the aim of building confidence in a peace agreement. A careful balance needs to be struck between the security of the peacekeepers and the avoidance of them becoming perceived as just another party to the conflict. To this end it is also vital for any intervention force to maintain its impartiality. If it does not then it runs the risk of becoming sucked into the conflict that it was intended to help conclude.

The composition of any force should also be such as not to lead to the conclusion that the force is merely an instrument of a particular nation's foreign policy. The inclusion of units from a number of states not only avoids this possibility but helps spread the burden of intervention and also makes the belligerent parties to the conflict aware of the extent of support for and depth of commitment to, the intervention force by the wider international community.

In the global context the Liberian experience shows that African peacekeeping forces and their sponsors need to seek the widest possible support from outside the continent as well as from Africa itself. This is particularly the case when it comes to financing an operation where the costs are usually quite beyond the capacity of African states, either individually or collectively, to meet. The financial assistance of the USA and European states is increasingly important given the parlous state of the UN's finances. Whereas there are significant question marks over the likelihood or even desirability of intervention on the ground by forces from these countries, logistical and technical assistance from them will remain a vital ingredient for African peacekeeping operations for the foreseeable future.

In addition any intervention force needs to be composed of disciplined units properly trained for their mission. In order to avoid the kind of looting seen in Liberia these units need to be paid adequately and regularly and their activities monitored, preferably by an independent agency.

The ECOMOG intervention in Liberia will continue to provide lessons for future African peacekeeping operations for many years to come. Certain facets of the ECOMOG experience of course reflect the idiosyncrasies of the Liberian conflict and may not have a bearing on crises elsewhere. However a great many valuable lessons can be learned from this tragedy and not just by African nations but by the wider international community as a whole in order to make future peacekeeping interventions in Africa more effective.

Postscript

The ECOWAS heads of state and the Liberian faction leaders signed a renewed Abuja Accord on 17 August 1996. This provided for a cease-fire to be implemented by the 31st of that month and disarmament and demobilisation of the factions to be achieved by 31 January 1997. Elections were scheduled initially for 30 May 1997 and were subsequently put back to 19 July 1997.

Between 22 November 1996 and 7 February 1997, ECOMOG, now with a strength in excess of 10,000, disarmed more than 23,000 of the estimated 35,000 fighters in Liberia. On 27 June 1997, the UN extended the mandate of UNOMIL until 30 September 1997.

The elections held on 19 July 1997 were declared free and fair by the international monitors and were won by Charles Taylor's party with some 75 per cent of the vote. He was inaugurated as President on 2 August 1997. ECOMOG is scheduled to stay in Liberia for up to another six months to train the army and police.

The future of Liberia of course remains, to a degree, uncertain. However, despite the problems of the past and the continuing spill-over conflict in Sierra Leone, ECOMOG is for the moment, being hailed as an African peacekeeping success story.

Notes

1. Vogt, M. A. 'Nigerian in Liberia: Historical and Political Analysis of ECOMOG' in Vogt, M. A. and Ekoko, A. E. (1993) *Nigeria in International Peacekeeping 1960-1992*, Malthouse Press.
2. Ibid.
3. Babangida, I. B., Foreword in Agetua, N. (1992) *Agetua Operation Liberty: The Story of Major General Joshua Nimyel Dogonyaro*, Hona Communications Ltd: Lagos.
4. Adebajo A. (1996) 'Journey without Maps' in *West Africa*, 9-15 September, pp. 1432-1433.
5. Clapham, C. (1995) 'Problems of Peace Enforcement: Lessons to be Drawn from Multinational Peacekeeping Operations in On-going Conflicts in Africa', a paper for the Conference *South Africa and Peacekeeping in Africa*, 13-14 July.
6. Op. cit., Vogt, op. cit., Adebajo.
7. Op. cit., Adebajo, Gunston, J. (1990) 'Africa's Prince of Darkness', *Mail on Sunday*, YOU Magazine, 02.12.90.
8. Op. cit., Adebajo.
9. Ejime, P. (1996) 'ECOMOG Needs 10,000 More Troops in Liberia', *Pan-African News Agency*, 29.07.96.
10. Ejime, P. (1996) 'More West African Troops set for Liberia', *Pan-African News Agency*, 28.08.96.
11. Parker, Lt. Col. T. W. (1994) 'Operation Sharp Edge' in Venter, Al. J. *The Chopper Boys: Helicopter Warfare in Africa*, Greenhill Books: London.
12. *The Clinton Administration's Policy on Reforming Multilateral Peace Operations*, May 1994, United States Information Service Reference Centre: London.
13. *U.S. Situation Report on Liberia*, United States Agency for International Development, Washington, 30.09.96.
14. *UN Council agrees to continue Liberia Mission*, United Nations Press Release, 30.08.96.
15. Op. cit., Adebajo. Atkinson, P. (1996) 'Conflict heightened by Western Meddling', *The Independent*, 23.04.96.
16. Atkinson, P. (1996) 'What chance for a country plundered by its peacekeepers?', *The Independent*, 24.04.96.

17 Ellis, S. (1994) 'Liberators or Looters?', *Focus on Africa*, Oct-Dec 1994, BBC Publications.
18 Op. cit., Adebajo.
19 *Africa Research Bulletin*, 1994, p. 11481.
20 'ECOMOG Commander orders review of security for faction leaders' *Pan-African News Agency,* 03.11.96.
21 Sotinel, T. (1996) 'Good News for Liberia at Last', *Mail and Guardian Johannesburg,* 03.09.96.
22 'ECOWAS Summit Examines Sanctions', Pan-African News Agency, 27.07.96.

12 Rwanda and Burundi: peacekeeping amidst massacres

Oliver Furley

In April, May and June 1994 one of the most horrifying conflicts in Africa took place in Rwanda, when somewhere between 500,000 and a million people died either in massacres or as a result of disease, starvation and exhaustion in refugee camps. This war was an internal conflict, but as usual in Africa it had strong overtones of foreign interference and efforts to intervene. Efforts by the UN and the international community to end this conflict and to establish a peacekeeping role have met with severe criticism.

After a series of clashes involving several massacres between rival Tutsi and Hutu groups, and after an invasion of Rwanda by exiled Tutsis from Uganda, who formed the Rwandese Patriotic Front (RPF) in 1990, the UN and OAU had brokered a peace agreement in 1993 at Arusha in Tanzania, in an attempt to introduce democracy and power-sharing. The Arusha accords were never accepted by the Hutu extremist party, who may have been responsible for the mysterious shooting down of President Habyarimana's plane on 6 April 1994, when he and the President of Burundi perished.

The signal for a prepared massacre

Whoever was responsible, it was the signal for a prepared massacre of Tutsis and Hutu moderates by the Hutu extremists. It had been planned since 1990. There was a prepared list of leaders to be killed, who were deliberately sought out and eliminated. Since 1991 young Hutus had flocked to join the *Interahamwe*, 'Those who act together'. They were trained in two camps and given weapons by the Ministry of Defence, and were worked up into a frenzy of hatred for the Tutsis. Radio broadcasts, especially by the private station, Radio Mille Collines, poured forth propaganda saying the RPF were coming to steal Hutu farms: all Tutsis must be exterminated once and for all.[1] This struck a chord in the peasant masses, both men and women, who armed themselves with machetes and clubs, and killed every Tutsi man, woman and child that they could find. Many Hutus suspected of being moderates or members of the better-off classes were killed as well. The details of these massacres over a two-month period are sickeningly familiar to the world through newspapers, television and radio and need no further elaboration here. The concern of this chapter is with the international reaction, to what was by this time both a civil war (Rwandan government versus the RPF) and an ethnic conflict (Hutus versus Tutsis).

The United Nations' reaction

After the Arusha peace accord, the UN had sent 2,500 troops to Rwanda as peace-keepers for the UN Assistance Mission in Rwanda (UNAMIR). Already depleted to 1,705, the Security Council's reaction to the outbreak of massacres was to withdraw nearly all of them, leaving a token force of 270, beleaguered in their headquarters in the capital, Kigali. It considered that these troops had been powerless to stop the massacres, and were in considerable danger themselves. A group of Belgian UN soldiers sent to investigate the crash scene of the President's plane were all murdered. Belgian soldiers were particular targets of hostility, and they were all ordered to withdraw. Some of them cut up the UN insignia on their blue berets in disgust at this order and in frustration at their powerlessness. The peace-keeping force did not have orders to use force to safeguard lives and could only fire in self-defence: it was said that many Rwandans were killed in full view of UN soldiers. The massacres were carried out on a country-wide scale very quickly. The result was a massive exodus of refugees to the neighbouring countries of Tanzania, Zaire (now the Democratic Republic of Congo), Burundi and Uganda, in one of the largest and quickest refugee movements ever seen, involving up to two million people.

There was immediate criticism of the UN withdrawal. Dr Salim Salim, Secretary-General of the OAU, said, 'It is absolutely incomprehensible for Africa that the UN should withdraw the majority of its troops from Rwanda and refuse to change its decision at the very time when its presence is required to end the massacre of innocent people. The Security

Council must recognise it is the responsibility of the international community to end the large-scale killings and genocide being perpetrated in Rwanda.' The OAU itself however had no plans for intervention, and looked to those countries that might have the logistical capabilities to do so. Meanwhile the Security Council was 'groping for a response to genocide' in Rwanda.[2]

The UN Secretary-General, Dr Boutros Boutros Ghali, was well aware that UN credibility was at stake. Only ten days after the Security Council had unanimously voted to withdraw all but a handful of the UN force, Boutros Boutros Ghali made an urgent appeal to the Council for a new force of 5,500 troops to be sent. At first his appeal fell on deaf ears. The big powers with immediate military capability - USA, Britain and France - said they favoured 'an African solution' to this problem, but it was expected that USA in particular would help finance African countries to send troops. The response took some time, but it did materialise. Nigeria and Ghana said their resources were already stretched with the intervention in Liberia. Zimbabwe and Botswana said they might assist but only if a western power led the peace-keeping force. Kenya and Tanzania were loath to interfere, and Uganda was in any case a supporter of the Tutsi RPF guerrilla force, which of course was now renewing the fighting and invading the north of Rwanda. The Tanzanian government tried to mediate in the renewed war by holding separate peace talks with both sides. The Africa countries were waiting to see which big power would pay for the costs and logistics involved. By the middle of May, the UN had obtained troop commitments from Ghana, Nigeria and Tanzania; others such as Senegal and Ethiopia were to follow. Such a force was to begin by creating 'safe areas' for refugees, while both the RPF and the Hutu Rwandan government said they would accept a UN peace mission provided it did not repeat the Somalia operation, that had developed into an attempt to disarm both sides.

Following pledges of troops from various African countries, the Security Council moved towards a new resolution to send 5,500 troops to Rwanda. But then came the revelation that USA was balking at support for this move. The talks broke down after the US insisted on conditions for the deployment of the troops. The majority of the Council wanted these troops to be in Rwanda, but the US wanted them only on the borders. US diplomats said the plan should wait until UN had 'a clearer concept of operations'. Instead, Washington proposed sending just 150 military observers plus 500 Ghanaian peace-keepers who had been withdrawn the previous month as described above. US diplomats asked what will 5,500 troops do? Who will pay? How long will they stay? How will they get there?

They wanted Boutros Boutros Ghali to make a report on how many troops he had been able to muster for an all-Africa force, and what were the views of the two warring parties about such a force. A second vote of approval should be called for only after this report was presented, which would take a further two weeks. The world press viewed this prevarication with dismay. By 17 May, the US had backed down and agreed to the force of 5,500 but still sought three criteria: the consent of the warring parties, the speedy securing of Kigali airport, and availability of troops and funds. It thus took the UN nearly six weeks to resolve to do something about Rwanda, and undoubtedly the US had delayed the final decisions. Its insistence on definite objectives has of course to be seen in the light of harsh lessons learnt in Somalia, where the US military effort in sending thousands of its troops there had been regarded as largely a fiasco, and its objectives had been diverted by a process of 'mission creep' into a hunt for General Aidid. President Clinton's hesitations over what to do in Haiti were another example of US post-Somalia psychosis at this time. Certainly the prospects for effective intervention in Rwanda were not good, and the point about the attitudes of the two warring parties was valid: it was clear that while the Rwandan government might welcome UN troops as a way to stop the RPF advance, the RPF declared it would not tolerate any UN interference in their advance and would attack any UN force that barred their way.

Further, it appeared that the UN would have difficulty in raising 5,500 African troops. Ghana, Senegal, Ethiopia and Zimbabwe each offered a battalion of 800, while Nigeria, Congo and Mali would make up a fifth battalion. They would go to Kigali and fan out across the country to set up 'humanitarian zones' where refugees would be safe. The US was to supply fifty armoured personnel carriers but these were to be leased, on terms which the US government continued to quibble about - such delays were 'a tragedy' and the troops would not arrive for another three weeks - *three months* after the massacres began, as Richard Dowden angrily pointed out.[3] In fact, it was reckoned that another three months would pass before sufficient forces arrived. The whole process has illustrated the inability of the UN to act quickly even in cases of the most dire emergency.

The French intervention

The ponderous process of UN decision-making was soon to be hijacked by the French. Since decolonisation France had held on to an interventionist role in its former African possessions, keeping their economies closely linked through the 'franc zone', maintaining military bases in these countries, and frequently intervening militarily in internal conflicts. They now maintained 11,000 troops in Africa, and both President Mitterrand and the Prime Minister, M. Balladur, spoke of France's 'calling', and the duty to act. The Times commented 'Forty years after its colonial defeats, France is emerging as the western state most eager to don the Képi of gendarme to the world'. Le Figaro said 'Nearly 200 million Africans live in France's orbit. It is up to the French to remain worthy of their trust'. Talk of trusteeship was old doctrine indeed, and it should be noted that strictly speaking Rwanda was not within the French 'orbit' - it had been ruled by the Belgians. But more to the point is that it was part of francophone Africa, and France had supplied arms to the Rwanda government - and even continued to do so after the killing had started - and French 'advisers' were rumoured to have helped Rwanda forces fight the RPF invasion of 1990. 'The French have one obsession with regard to Africa - the spread of the English Language. Admiral Jaques Lanxade, Chief of General Staff, calls it 'the Anglo-Saxon Conspiracy' wrote Sam Kiley.[4] And the RPF, as everyone knew, was anglophone, did not speak French, and came from bases in anglophone Uganda. Furthermore, President Mitterrand's son, Jean-Christophe, had been closely associated with French support for Habyarimana's government. Cynicism regarding French motives in sending a force, and disbelief in its neutrality, was widespread.

Yet the offer to send French troops to Rwanda was very tempting for the UN, in view of the appalling humanitarian situation. France sought UN approval to send 2,000 French troops, mostly marines, paratroops and Foreign Legion units, all of them with African experience, and many of them readily accessible in bases in Zaire, Gabon or Djibouti. They said they would use force to stop the killings, but that they would remain neutral between the two warring parties. They would not penetrate far into Rwanda, and their operations would be humanitarian only. This offer presented a dilemma for UN member states. Everyone knew that France was serving her own interests and was not wholly altruistic in her motives: most members were in fact highly sceptical. Could such a move be seen as a genuine UN humanitarian operation? Could it contribute to a peace settlement and a peacekeeping operation?

The Rwandan government of course saw it as their salvation and the way to halt the advance of the RPF; the RPF immediately accused France of a partisan plan seeking to support one side only. They declared they would treat the French as an enemy and confront them by force if they obstructed their campaign.

The temptation to use an immediately available force won the day, and the Security Council voted to give France a mandate to send its troops in. China, Brazil, Nigeria, Pakistan and New Zealand opposed it. The French 'operation turquoise', as it was called, was intended to last only a few weeks, and was to end as soon as other UN troops were available to take over. There were many cavils about the decision. France applied to the West European Union (the nine-nation defence group) for outright endorsement of the operation, but they offered only 'co-ordination' and some logistical support but only if the African states would participate. At the Union's second meeting only Italy offered to send troops, conditional on UN approval, and the other members said logistical and financial support would depend on backing by the Security Council. While francophone African countries backed the operation, the OAU spoke of possible complications and said intervention should only be with international support.

By 20 June, an advance party of 20 French troops were already in Goma on the border. More soon arrived, and their first aim was to assist a refugee camp nine miles inside the border from Zaire, to protect fleeing refugees. Their reception was very mixed. The RPF repeatedly declared the French were interfering for cynical purposes in the French interest only, and expelled all French journalists from the large area under their control. The French relief agencies had to evacuate staff from border areas, and 42 UN military observers in Kigali were forced to leave because their home countries - Senegal, Congo and Togo - had backed France. The World Council of Churches criticised the French intervention, as did most other humanitarian agencies, except the Belgian-based Médicins Sans Frontières. Nevertheless the French saved 1,000 Tutsis from seemingly certain death near Kibuye, and rescued many from Butare - in spite of being fired on by the RPF as they evacuated refugees. Their orders were to fire back if fired on, and they did so. They announced clearly that attempts by the RPF to stop their rescue operations would be met by force, and there was a tense period when it looked as if the French were going to confront the RPF advance and take part in the war. Very soon however they saw the folly of this and switched their policy, to stay clear of the fighting, and concentrate on creating 'safe zones' in the south-west for refugees whether Hutu or Tutsi. This proved to be a very important switch, and led to positive results, lending what seemed to be a degree of respectability to the whole French operation. They more or less took over the south-west as a safe haven for refugees, and this action saved lives. The 'interahamwe' militia could not carry out further massacres there.

The French faced a new dilemma, however, because of the very success of this move. Thousands upon thousands of the population gathered there, where there was safety and food, and these included leaders and members of the nearly-defeated Rwandan government, and Rwandan soldiers and militia who had previously been labelled as pariahs by the international community. Were the French to harbour murderers? Even a French soldier was quoted as saying 'This seems crazy, we are protecting the killers'. The RPF said they were doing just that, and trying to save a tyrannical government from total defeat. In early July the situation remained very tense as the French, now with their full complement of 2,500 troops with helicopters, anti-tank missiles and other heavy weapons, had orders to block the rebels' advance. There was tough talk about 'drawing a line in the sand'. The switch of policy ended this situation however, and the RPF in fact kept clear of the French area and made an agreement with the French that they could police a refugee zone. The RPF by early July had declared themselves to be the legitimate government of Rwanda, and France recognised it, abandoning any attempt to back the Hutu government. They said they would try to disarm the Hutu soldiers in their area, and to arrest the Interahamwe. They expected to occupy this zone until the troops arrived.

Suddenly the French intervention was seen to be better than no intervention. A senior French officer declared 'This is an excellent outcome to what looked like a nasty situation earlier in the week', and the Times did not disagree.[5] The French problem was now how to extricate themselves. M. Balladur said he wanted the French out by 31 July if possible but some would have to stay until August. France stepped up its request to the UN for replacement troops, for 'an honourable exit from Rwanda'.[6] In fact, in the continued absence of UN troops, the French stayed until their final deadline of 22 August. During that time they were charged with shielding some of the most notorious ringleaders of the massacres, and the RPF demanded that they hand over war criminals in their safe haven. For the same reason the non-government relief organisations (NGOs) still refused to co-operate with the French for fear of being labelled partisan and pro-Hutu. Yet by now there was intense pressure for the refugees to return into Rwanda from the overcrowded camps in Zaire, Burundi and Tanzania. Malnutrition and disease were taking a terrible toll; the NGOs had an almost impossible task to sustain these huge camps, and meanwhile the crops in Rwanda were ready for harvesting if only the population would return. Refugees were very reluctant to go, in spite of the awful conditions in the camps, because they feared reprisals on them by the RPF. Some of them of course had reason to fear. Furthermore, the soldiers of the defeated Hutu army, in camps nearby, used terror tactics to force them to stay, as they could use the refugees as pawns in a power struggle whereby they hoped to win back at least a share of power in Rwanda. In August the UN troops, chiefly Ghanaians and Ethiopians, began arriving and taking over from the French. But they were uncertain of their role, and mistrusted by the civilian population, who had got used to French protection in the south of the country. It was feared that when the French left, there would be a massive exodus of new refugees into Zaire, and indeed this was attempted. After a short time it was stopped by Zairean troops, as Zaire had no wish to provide for and feed more refugees. This was a period when the conflict was shown to throw up huge problems of 'refugee management', both for governments and NGOs and the UNHCR. These problems had not been nearly well enough thought out. It was for instance a long time before a UN 'Blue Beret' radio station was set up, urging the refugees to return home, to counter Radio Mille Collines which had poured out hate propaganda and excited alarmist fears among Hutus wishing to return. Eventually stacks of food were made available at strategic points along the roads back into Rwanda, to persuade the refugees to return - a strategy that gradually succeeded, although some have met with hostility and attacks in Rwanda.

By late July both USA and Britain had taken the decision to intervene actively. The US ambassador to Rwanda returned to Kigali - the first western head of mission to do so - where the RPF was firmly installed. USA committed 4,000 troops to Rwanda for purely humanitarian work, it was stressed - not for peace-keeping operations which should be in the hands of UN African troops. Britain also sent troops with a similar declared purpose - they were not peacekeepers, but they were engineers, technicians and medical staff who could help to repair and restore electricity, water supplies, health provision etc.

The transport of UN African troops as peacekeepers, for which USA was now willing to pay, proceeded more rapidly, though by 10 August troops from Chad, Congo, Guinea-Bissau, Niger and Senegal were all in the French zone (all from francophone countries). One difficulty however was to get the nervous population to trust them. The UN pleaded with the French to stay, to prevent further exodus to Zaire. This must have been a sweet moment for the French after all the international scepticism they had faced. Alain Juppé, the French Foreign Minister, rebuffed the plea, and the French troops were duly pulled out by their deadline date. So ended this remarkable unilateral intervention, which will be the subject of debate for years to come. What began as intervention seen to be serving chiefly the interests of France, came to be something that the UN could not do without.

The former French zone remained insecure. In spite of UN troops, both the RPF soldiers and various Hutu groups carried out murders and vendettas which still convinced many refugees to stay in the camps. The UN sent a very inadequate squad of human rights monitors with the huge task of keeping this situation in check. There was a chorus of protests from the NGOs. Save the Children said that the UN had recommended 150 monitors be sent, but only four had arrived and the 26 more promised were not nearly enough. Amnesty International declared,

> It is scandalous that because of bureaucratic and political delay by governments, the unarmed and observer component of the UN peacekeeping operation still is not fully deployed. Monitors alone cannot make the country safe, but their very presence can help build confidence and dissuade further human rights abuses by government forces. They need to be a visible presence in every one of the 70 districts in Rwanda.[7]

By mid-September Karen Kenny, head of the UN human rights investigating team in Rwanda, had resigned in protest at the lack of staff, vehicles and communications equipment, as Action Aid angrily protested. Oxfam added its complaint in mid-October, that only 40 monitors had been deployed in Rwanda so far.[8] Such monitors clearly have a very important role in the aftermath of the conflict, safeguarding the lives and well-being of the returning refugees and indeed the whole population. If they had been in place in every district *before* the conflict, this might have prevented it or diminished its scale. There was still a danger that the conflict might break out again: the defeated Hutu army was still present in large numbers in Zaire, possibly 20,000 strong, very evident in the camp areas on the border, and apparently still well armed, in smart uniforms, and with plenty of money. They were constantly threatening to re-invade Rwanda. This did not happen, but the danger remained, and the sporadic raids from Zaire which occurred could have escalated into a more serious invasion.

The UN as a preventive agency

The UN's record in Rwanda has been heavily criticised, as acting too little too late. An early criticism, and a very strong one, was in the failure of the UN to condemn the genocide taking place in Rwanda, and to urge the international community to do the same. In the middle of this the foreign minister of the Hutu interim government was permitted to make a racist anti-Tutsi speech in the Security Council, and only New Zealand protested. The Rwandese government continued to take its seat on the Security Council: there was no move to expel it. It was almost as if the world shrugged its shoulders when genocide took place in a country so deep in the middle of Africa. As we have seen, the decision to send 5,500 troops came two months after the decision to cut its small force already there as monitors of the Arusha peace accord. Even then, because of US hesitations there were further long delays before they arrived. As the Guardian wrote, 'The general impression of hesitation did not encourage troop-contributing countries to commit themselves speedily'. The USA did not have a force available for Rwanda, and it and the other western powers who might be expected to support action in the Security Council did not effectively do so. The truth was that Rwanda counted for very little in western interests. Andrew Sullivan commented: 'The massacres were so great, the situation so complex and *western interests so minimal* that intervention is clearly unrealistic and unwise'.[9]

The second phase in Rwanda: peacemaking and peacekeeping

With the installation of the new RPF government in Kigali, and the UN forces under a new mandate in UNAMIR II, the hope was that the country would gradually settle into a peaceful state: massacres and killings would end; Hutu rebel groups would lose their hold on the masses; external and internal refugees would return home; rehabilitation and economic reconstruction would take place. Expectations were too high however. The RPF made attempts at power-sharing in the government, and a Hutu prime minister was appointed, but its general efforts to achieve reconciliation among the shattered communities, the restoration of home owners to their properties, the safeguarding of returning refugees, the bringing to justice of the main perpetrators of the massacres etc, were slow and inadequate. The RPF clearly remained a partisan regime. UNAMIR II could not itself build a new peace: militarily and politically its mandate from the UN was inadequate even in the task of providing protection. The Security Council has been criticised for seldom obtaining expert military advice, and as a consequence it made impractical decisions, for example, regarding the role of the military in Bosnia.[10] The same appeared to be true in Rwanda: it was awash with arms and control over security was desperately inadequate. The new government was extremely short of funds, having taken over an empty Treasury, while possible donor countries held back aid because the peace process seemed so uncertain. Political solutions were required, sponsored by whoever could help, but neither the UN, the OAU or neighbouring countries showed the required initiatives. The International Red Cross commented,

> Rwanda needs massive aid, but like many of today's disasters, no amount of aid will 'solve' this crisis of peace and security, justice and resources. A political solution is required to address the humanitarian needs, security, justice and far more... the need now is for unflinching support for reconstruction and reconciliation.[11]

Meanwhile, huge populations of refugees built up in camps in Zaire, Tanzania and also within Rwanda itself. The UNHCR and relief organisations strove to cope with this humanitarian disaster, made worse by a cholera outbreak which caused thousands of deaths. NGOs quite often had to enlist the help of the former Hutu army and Hutu ex-government officials to distribute aid, which enabled rebel groups to establish control over the refugees. They were forcibly restrained from returning home, and were kept as virtual hostages. The peacekeeping operation became to a significant extent one of 'refugee management' and NGOs in particular found themselves having to make political decisions on how to dispense aid without helping Hutu rebel fighters to gather strength for re-invasion of Rwanda. The Rwandan conflict was being transferred to the camps in Zaire and Tanzania. The international community appeared 'paralysed and ineffective' according to Human Rights Watch Africa, and Major-General Guy Tousignant, commander of UNAMIR II, warned that 30,000 of the former Hutu army were in Zaire camps and 10,000 militia trained with them. They used the camps as bases for raids to destabilise Rwanda. In Rwanda itself, there were 370,000 refugees in camps, who were not only forcibly restrained from leaving by Hutu militia but then faced expulsion by RPA (the army of the RPF government) soldiers who could be just as violent, for the government was trying to clear the camps. The UN mandate of 17 May directed UNAMIR forces to protect displaced persons and refugees in Rwanda, but they frequently failed in this task and did not intervene when RPA soldiers used force to clear the camps.[12]

The Security Council extended UNAMIR's mandate for six months on 30 November and added the duty to protect human rights monitors and staff of the International Tribunal attempting to trace the perpetrators of the massacres, but tensions were so high that the RPA would go on the rampage at the slightest explosion or outbreak by rebel militias, and the civilian population suffered. The Hutus were politicising the repatriation process from the camps, hoping to come back in the context of power-sharing. The Tutsis, on the other hand, had been out of power for thirty years and were very nervous, reacting to the slightest threat.[13]

The tragedy of Kibeho camp

Kibeho, in south-west Rwanda, was one of the largest refugee camps and was a focus of the RPF's campaign to close the camps because they were bases for Hutu militia activities. UNAMIR was aware of this pressure and in December 1994 sent twenty trucks to try to begin a process of evacuation. They collected only twenty-one refugees. UNHCR radio programmes had some effect and before the government announced a deadline for the camp to be closed, the UN had assisted 60,000 to leave. Before the final crisis, UN troops entered the camp with megaphones urging refugees to leave under their protection.[14] By mid-April 1995 it was too late: the RPA soldiers were ordered to clear the camp. They moved in with rockets, machine-guns, rocket-propelled grenades and small arms, and lost all discipline in what developed into a massacre as refugees tried to flee. The UN appeared to be powerless, and UN Zambian troops in the camp were beleaguered, sheltering those they could. Some 80,000 refugees fled towards Butare, but many were attacked and beaten by the local population. The Times wrote:

> The tragedy of Kibeho reflects the continued failure of the UN and the international community to confront the reality that, after last year's genocide, Rwanda's Hutus and Tutsis may never be able to live alongside each other without protection from an independent force.[15]

The crisis could have been foreseen, as there was a build-up of RPA troops round these camps, but UNAMIR had not increased its own military presence, with just 200 troops in Kibeho, who had to face the RPA attack on the camp by 2,000 well armed soldiers. UNAMIR tried to find RPA officers to negotiate with, or to locate General Kagame, vice-president and chief of staff, but failed. UNAMIR's mandate gave them the right to fire, not just in self-defence but to protect refugees and humanitarian agencies, but clearly on this occasion they did not have the necessary force to leave their bunkers. One comment was that the UN troops 'were just stretcher-bearers'.[16] Appeals to the UN for a 7,000 strong policing force, to break the hold of Hutu extremists in the camps, had failed, as the international will was not there. A European diplomat in Kigali said the RPF 'have been begging for the international community to help them break up the Hutu militias inside Rwanda and in the refugee camps in Zaire and Tanzania, and we have done absolutely nothing except make sure that those responsible for genocide are fed, watered and sheltered. There is no great surprise that the RPA has finally cracked; the pressure cooker has blown.'[17] The bitterness of these comments reflects the feeling of helplessness that so little protection could be given and that reconciliation and resettlement could receive such a set-back. Tom Walker, a former aid worker in Rwanda, blamed the fact that there were three divisions within the UN in Rwanda, which created a recipe for ineffectiveness and uncoordinated action. There was the UN's Rwanda Emergency Office (UNREO), its military wing (UNAMIR) and its refugee agency (UNHCR).[18]

Whatever the fault with questions of organisation, the UN agencies compounded the now worsening relations with the RPF government by first announcing an estimate that 8,000 had been killed at Kibeho. This was quickly amended to 2,000 at which the UN was accused of a cover-up by aid workers and diplomats. Australian troops said they counted 4,500 dead before abandoning the operation. Oxfam and Médecins Sans Frontières said the UN was suppressing the scale of the killings: the RPF government on its part claimed that only 300 had died. After the EU threatened to cut aid of eight million pounds, the RPF government announced that there would be an enquiry, and asked the UN, the OAU and donor countries to send experienced investigators. Aid was in fact suspended, but the international investigation concluded that although excessive force was used by the RPA, a massacre was unintentional. This is a rather surprising conclusion when one considers the heavy weapons used in the attack. Afterwards it appears that the troops were not publicly disciplined in any way. 'This will make national reconciliation even harder - which means very hard indeed, if not impossible - in any foreseeable future', declared the Economist.[19] After Kibeho, refugee mistrust of the RPF government was heightened, and the return of refugees both from camps in Rwanda and from Tanzania and Zaire slowed to a trickle. The RPF in turn thought that hesitation by the refugees was a sign of their guilt. In June Joel Boutrone, UNHCR head in Goma, said 'ninety per cent of the solution lies with the Rwandan government, but the RPF just does not want these people back'.[20] A researcher in the camps has recently published his findings which reveal a contrary twist to this situation: the refugees believed that UNHCR and other UN agencies were allied to the RPF government, pressurising the refugees to return when it was far from safe to do so. They knew it was easy for them to be accused of murder and put in gaol; furthermore the return of Tutsi 'old-case' refugees (that is, from earlier conflicts) meant that they and their cattle had take up available land, so that new refugees thought they would not be able to claim their property back. Thus the nearly two million refugees were unlikely to return in the near future.[21]

Failures in peacekeeping in one country can quickly lead to the extension of the peacekeeping task to other countries, and this was the case with Rwanda. Indeed, the massacres in Rwanda had international implications immediately, in that the neighbouring states of Zaire, Tanzania, Burundi and Uganda were drawn into the crisis. After Kibeho, it was Zaire that finally lost patience with the seemingly insoluble problem of huge refugee camps on its territory. Most of the NGOs had pulled out of the camps already, saying that 'bandits' had taken over and threatened aid workers: 'We are not soldiers or policemen', said the ICRC, implying that only such personnel were the ones now to be of use.[22] What sparked Zaire's reaction was the news that the Security Council had suspended the arms embargo on the RPF government for one year as they needed weapons to deal with the external menace from Hutu extremists. For Zaire this was seen as a hostile act, laying the country open to raids from Rwanda in retaliation for Hutu incursions. Zaire said this would endanger the Zairean population and therefore the prime minister said he was justified in delivering an ultimatum that the camps must close.[23] In response, the UNHCR was desperate to find solutions. Already in May the High Commissioner, Mrs Ogata, had met President Mobutu in Geneva and former US President Jimmy Carter put forward the idea of a neutral zone between Zaire and Rwanda where the refugees could go and it would be jointly patrolled by Zaire and UN observers.[24] But after the lifting of the arms embargo, Zairean troops attacked the camps and cleared four of them, using much violence and looting the refugees' possessions. Some 100,000 of them fled but they were determined not to go to Rwanda, especially after Kibeho. International pressure forced Zaire to suspend the expulsions, but Zaire insisted the UN must make it possible for the voluntary repatriation of the refugees.[25] But only small numbers volunteered, in spite of the new pressure. By March 1996, Mr Lafiq Saidi of UNHCR in Geneva said UNHCR 'had tried everything' but there was little sign yet of the refugees returning and their refusal could be justified: property restitution was hardly working, and those who return or might accept office could be accused of genocide by just two people. UNHCR had built 30,000 houses for 'old-case' refugees returning, so that newer refugees could take over their former houses, but this could only touch the problem. Meanwhile, neighbouring nations were suffering from 'asylum fatigue', and were no longer willing to host the camps. Quite apart from the political and security problems, camps caused degradation of the environment and also serious medical problems.[26]

Tanzania, which originally took a more positive and pro-active role in the Rwanda crisis, also hardened its policy towards refugees. President Ali Mwinyi was the facilitator and host for the Arusha peace accord, and provided premises later for the International Tribunal in Arusha to bring just punishment to the perpetrators of genocide. After the massacres Tanzania was flooded with Rwandan refugees and Benaco camp in Ngara District, with 5-700,000 refugees, became the second largest 'city' in Tanzania. With UNHCR's help Tanzania, an extremely poor country, did the best it could for the refugees. But in March 1995 a sudden incursion of 40,000 refugees from Burundi caused a dramatic switch of policy: the borders with both Rwanda and Burundi were closed and troops posted there, as the government decided it had had enough, with a total refugee population of 1,438,000. The financial burden was too great, and political opposition was stirred by the social, security and ecological problems as well.[27] Peacekeeping in so many areas involves huge operations in refugee management, and Rwanda proves that international policies and norms fall far short of needs in this area. If Burundi really erupted in a major civil war, as it threatens to do, then the pressure on Tanzania to receive yet more refugees would be enormous, and better international funding and planning for them would be needed.

For the UN, the major commitment to Rwanda was to be scaled down, with a partial withdrawal of UNAMIR troops. In June 1995, vice-president Paul Kagame called for this, as he said UN soldiers were 'lolling about in a now-peaceful Rwanda.' In the next three months, numbers were to be reduced by half, from 5,500 to 2,330, and then to 1,800 the following month.[28] Their role was regarded as nearly completed, and the focus had already shifted to Burundi. The UN peacekeeping task was over, but 'peace-building' was at a strange juncture indeed when a considerable proportion of the population was still in exile as refugees. The outbreak of civil war in Zaire in October 1996 has compounded the situation. When the Zairean-born Tutsis in the south east of Zaire, the Banyamulenge, rose up in rebellion, apparently with help and support from the RPF, their advance northwards swept through the area where some of the remaining Hutu refugee camps were. Thousands fled at last back to Rwanda, but unknown thousands fled westwards into the forests, to be 'lost' to the UNHCR and other agencies until they assembled in new camps in Zaire, up to 200,000 of them, to be 'discovered' early in 1997. Their presence is merely one factor in the further destabilisation of the Central Lakes region as a whole. They scattered into various parts of Zaire (now the Democratic Republic of Congo) and the fate of very many of them is unknown.

Burundi: on a knife edge

Burundi, Rwanda's neighbour to the south, has like Rwanda suffered a recent history of extreme violence between Tutsi and Hutu rival groups, generated by rivalry among complex hierarchies struggling for political and economic power.[29] After independence, attempted coups by Hutus were followed by rounds of killings, until 1972 when a major Hutu rebellion took place, put down by the Tutsi army, when some 250,000 were killed and 150,000 driven out as refugees. The pattern was set for Burundi's appalling record of coups and counter-coups followed by murderous retaliations in which soldiers and others could kill with impunity while the international community took little interest - indeed the massacres hardly made headlines in the press. By June 1993 things had improved a little; the country was actually able to carry out elections and a Hutu majority government took power. This lasted only four months before the Hutu President and three ministers were assassinated in a Tutsi attempted coup (in which the present leader General Pierre Buyoya was said to be involved). This was the signal for yet another civil war in which estimates of killings vary from 100,000 to 200,000 with 600,000 or up to one and a half million people displaced from their homes. This was out of a population of only 5.6 million,[30] and the figures for the internally displaced persons (IDP's) illustrate the state of anarchy the country was sliding into. The violence naturally affected neighbouring countries: Hutu refugees spread from Burundi to Rwanda, Zaire, southern Uganda and north-west Tanzania; no country in the region was isolated from this and they were at risk of a spreading conflict. Burundi itself 'in many areas resembled a leopard's skin, with patches of concentrated Tutsi, "surrounded" by dispersed Hutu'. The Tutsis sought to safeguard their communities by clearing towns of Hutus, and 'ethnic cleansing' began in Bujumbura, the capital city, early in 1994.[31]

After the attempted coup of 1993, the UN and the OAU, realising these dangers, sent special representatives to try to mediate. The UN's Ould Abdallah in particular made great efforts, taking over the radio and TV, calling for calm, and calling on military leaders to co-operate; in the better sense of the term he behaved 'like a colonial governor', which was perhaps what was needed among some thirteen political parties, most with their own violent militias.[32] Burundi could explode at any moment, warned Richard Dowden, but there appeared no UN contingency planning for this: 'There is no chance that a peacekeeping force will be available or able to stop a disaster'.[33] Burundi would clearly not allow a peacekeeping force to enter the country in any case, though it allowed a small OAU International Observer Mission (MIOB) of 47 officers and ten civilians, and various agencies went in to try to reduce the violence, notably Human Rights Watch Africa, which established a Human Rights Centre in Bujumbura, and started a campaign in the media to uphold human rights and especially to try to educate the young.[34] The OAU Secretary-General went on a fact-finding mission to Burundi, and the OAU's new body, the Mechanism for Conflict Prevention, Management and Resolution, strengthened the mission to Burundi and called on it to try to defuse tension, promote dialogue, regain peace, confidence and security within a framework of national reconciliation. This followed the UN's request for the OAU to set up an International Force for Stabilisation and Confidence-Building.[35] Amid a host of 'early warnings' of further conflict, both the UN and the OAU were making positive moves. Could diplomacy, observers' teams and education campaigns be enough? Could a sprinkling of human rights monitors constitute a peacekeeping operation?

A further test came when the newly elected President Cyprian Ntaryamira, was killed in the plane crash which also killed the Rwandan President and sparked off the Rwandan massacres, in April 1994. Fortunately this time UN mediation helped an interim President to be appointed and all parties agreed on a new government, in what was described as a 'fragile alliance'. International concern was strong, and the UN, OAU and EU all sent missions to enquire ways of reconciliation. The Security Council called on all parties to end extremism and reach a settlement on the presidential succession and democratic principles. The Tutsis refused to agree to army reform while the Hutus pressed for a truly national army. The UN mission advocated assistance to rebuild the collapsed judicial system to end the 'murder with impunity' phenomenon, and to bring the actors in the coup to justice.[36] Yet international commitment remained minimal: the OAU had 46 human rights monitors in Burundi; the UN had about 100 personnel there by December 1994. There was no lowering of tension; the killings went on and Amnesty International believed Burundi was 'poised on the edge of a horrific slaughter'.[37]

The calls for an international intervention force

By June 1995, the warnings appeared to be coming true. Tutsi army groups fought with Hutu militia; tit for tat killings were an everyday occurrence: fighting on the Mutanga university campus caused the deaths of Hutu and Tutsi students in a week-long siege in a neighbourhood of Bujumbura; the army used tanks and armoured cars. Thirty people were killed and 40,000 fled from the area. By the beginning of 1996, it was reckoned that 200,000 had been killed in the last three years, 1,500 of them in the last two months.[38]

Boutros Boutros Ghali had been pressing for two plans of action to try to save Burundi from a worsening conflagration. First, he urged the neighbouring countries to meet together and produce regional solutions through negotiation. Second, he said the international community must launch a major initiative, if necessary, with an international intervention force. In particular, the UN should help the OAU in the provision of a peacekeeping force. Western diplomats in Bujumbura agreed but said 'because their governments were preoccupied by the NATO deployment in Bosnia, they had no interest in saving Burundi from itself'. Indeed, the Security Council also rejected the proposal to send a force but would consider sending 'guards' to protect aid workers in Burundi (some of whom had been attacked and one UNHCR worker killed).[39] The Burundi government was reluctant to allow in human rights monitors and also strongly protested against Boutros Boutros Ghali's recommendation for a standing force. Zaire had been proposed as a possible base for the force but Zaire was not keen on the idea.[40] These comments illustrate how far Burundi was, for the West, an obscure part of an already marginalised continent, and for the region, how far the idea of direct intervention was disliked. Meanwhile the situation got steadily worse, with both the Tutsi army and the Hutu rebels carrying out raids and killings - avoiding fighting each other but instead attacking the civilian population. It was no longer safe for aid workers: by June the ICRC withdrew the last of its aid workers and suspended operations after the murder of three of its Swiss staff, and France suspended its military co-operation which it had hung onto so far with dubious justification.

At a regional summit meeting the neighbouring states began to galvanise themselves into action, and Uganda and Tanzania agreed to send troops while Kenya would send police. They actually persuaded the Tutsi prime minister, Antoine Nduwayo, to request this assistance for security and to agree to talks with Hutu rebels. This could have been an historic moment when the East African states might have galvanised themselves into an act of regional co-operation, sending a force with a conflict prevention and peacekeeping mission. But Nduways's own party, UPRONA, called it a betrayal and high treason: an invading force would be deemed aggression and would be opposed.[41] The proposal hung fire, and helped to precipitate the military coup by Major Buyoya at the end of that month, 25 July 1996. The prime minister had to take refuge in the American ambassador's residence, and yet again Burundi was saddled with another military government, in which the predominantly Tutsi army was in control. World reaction, verbally at least, was speedy. The UN revived its calls for the immediate deployment of a multi-national peacekeeping force, and the OAU said it would not allow the coup to succeed. The UN effort was headed by Kofi Annan, the Ghanaian UN Under Secretary-General for Peacekeeping (later to succeed Boutros Boutros Ghali), who envisaged a force of 20,000 to provide safe areas in Burundi. But neither USA, Britain nor France were keen to become embroiled (though USA and Belgium offered to contribute to costs and help with logistics). Indeed many of the comments were that in the circumstances the coup was the best thing to happen for Burundi as it might produce stable government. Only six African countries - Chad, Ethiopia, Malawi, Tanzania, Uganda and Zambia - responded to Kofi Annan's appeal for promises of troops,[42] and the Security Council remained unmoved.

Buyoya, however, knew he was under strong pressure - more than almost any African leader had been - to put an end to the habit of conflict in the country. He promised a new government of national unity; he would open talks with the Hutu rebel leader Leonard Nyangoma; he would halt the forced expulsion of Rwandan Hutu refugees to Rwanda; he would discipline the unruly Tutsi army, and he promised to end the 'immunity' for anyone who had been involved in massacres.[43] He paid a quick visit to President Museveni of Uganda, known to be friendly towards the new Tutsi government in Rwanda, who might be persuaded to moderate the stand of the regional summit leaders when they met again on 31 July. Museveni did not do so and apparently took a strong line. However, the summit balked at sending an intervention force and instead resolved on sanctions against Burundi, imposing a total economic blockade, to be ratified by the OAU and the UN. This was not to be lifted until 'constitutional legality' was restored - which was defined as restoring the deposed President and the Parliament, unbanning the political parties, and abiding by the terms of the Arusha peace initiative and Julius Nyerere's peace process.[44] This device represented an expression of international disapproval rather than a positive attempt at peacekeeping. To date, the boycott has not been very firmly adhered to but it has caused much economic hardship in Burundi. Buyoya claims he is trying to meet the conditions but the regional powers are far from satisfied.

Conclusion

Rwanda and Burundi can only provide a mixed verdict on international peacekeeping efforts, and the task is by no means completed. In Rwanda's case, it was an especially difficult task, as peacekeepers had to face several different aspects of this situation. First, it was a civil war between an invading force and an entrenched government. The Arusha Accords appeared to work temporarily but soon proved to be flawed. The war ended with the complete conquest and victory of the RPF. The threat of a counter-invasion by the defeated Hutu forces was very real for a time but appears to have receded. The international community has simply gone with the flow and recognised the new government.

Secondly, it was an ethnic conflict between two communities whose hatred for each other was so deep that no peacekeeping force could really hope to transform the situation. Against a long history of 'killing with impunity', the peacekeepers had only limited success and the process of the defence of human rights, and bringing to justice the perpetrators of genocide, has only just begun. This is linked with the third aspect, the return of the hundreds of thousands of refugees and international efforts to help their rehabilitation and the process of reconciliation. Here the UN and its agencies and NGOs have made enormous efforts and saved thousands of lives, but their successes may be diminished if reconciliation is not achieved, and that could take decades or even generations.

In Burundi, it may be questioned whether peacekeeping has taken place at all. International efforts to broker peace and secure governments of national unity have failed in the face of numerous coups, while the same ethnic hatred as Rwanda has continued to dominate Burundi, with continued examples of 'ethnic cleansing' taking place in different areas, accompanied by murders and massacres. International 'observers' can do nothing. The attempt to scrape together an international intervention force, even at the regional level in East Africa, failed, and all we have is a trade boycott. At least it is an indication that regional action by African states is a possibility in East Africa, and there is hope that this could develop for peacekeeping operations in the future, provided that some assistance with funding and logistics could be assured by the UN and the big powers.

Notes

1. A good general account is by Alex de Waal, in the Church Times, 1-7 August 1994, and The Times, 18.6.94. See his *Rwanda: Who is Killing, Who is Dying, What is to be Done?*, African Rights, London, 1994. See also R. Lemarchand, 'Genocide in the Great Lakes: Whose Genocide?', paper presented at the conference on *Peace and Human Rights in the Great Lakes of Africa*, Makerere University, December 1997, who asserts that the Tutsi RPF was also guilty of genocide during its invasion of Rwanda.
2. The Times, 2.5.94; 'This was UNAMIR's darkest period', wrote Major-General G.C. Tousignant, Force Commander, UNAMIR II, 'Peacekeeping in Africa: The Rwanda Experience', South African Institute of International Affairs and Institute of Defence Policy, July 1995, p. 15.
3. In the Independent, 10.6.94 and see The Guardian, 10.6.94. See letter of Boutros Boutros Ghali to President of Security Council, S/1994/923, 3.8.94.
4. The Times 22.8.94. Allegations were made in November 1996 that British companies also supplied arms to the Hutus in violation of the UN Arms Embargo imposed on Rwanda in June 1994, Le Monde, 21.11.96.
5. The Times, 7.7.94. See also The Independent, 13.7.94, and the Daily Telegraph, 14.7.94. Major General Tousignant wrote, 'I must state that the French action did have some positive effects', op. cit., p. 18.
6. Financial Times, 11.7.94.
7. Quoted in The Independent, 20.8.94.
8. The Times, 13 and 15.9.94, and 14.10.94.
9. Sunday Times, 24.4.94.

10 General Rickhye, at the Conference on the Role of the Military in Humanitarian Emergencies, Refugee Studies Programme, Queen Elizabeth House, Oxford, October 1995.
11 ICRC, *World Disasters Report*, 1995, p. 65.
12 Human Rights Watch Africa, 'Rwanda: A New Catastrophe?', December 1994, Vol. 6, No. 12. For the camps in Zaire, see Johan Pottier's article 'Relief and Repatriation: Views by Rwandan Refugees' in *African Affairs*, Vol. 95, No. 380, 1996, which is highly critical of UNHCR's over-optimism regarding repatriation.
13 Interview with Mr Mahiga, UNHCR Co-ordinator for the Special Unit for Rwanda and Burundi Operations, Geneva, 26.3.96.
14 Daily Telegraph, 25.4.95.
15 The Times, 24.4.95.
16 Human Rights Watch Africa, 'Release' of 24.4.95, and ITV News, 24.4.95.
17 The Times, 24.4.95.
18 Daily Telegraph, 24.4.95.
19 The Economist, 29.4.95, and Amnesty International Annual Report, July 1995.
20 The Economist, 3.6.95.
21 Johan Pottier, 'Relief and Repatriation', pp. 420-421, 425, note 49.
22 ICRC, *World Disasters Report*, 1995, p. 63.
23 Interview, Mr Mahiga, UNHCR, Geneva, 26.3.96, and The Times, 23.8.95.
24 UNHCR, 'Rwanda-Burundi Operation', internal update, No. 81.
25 The Times, 23 and 26.8.95.
26 Interview, Mr Lafiq Saidi, UNHCR, Geneva, 25.3.96, and *Africa Report*, May-June 1995, p. 32, and The Times, 13 and 14.2.96, and 17.5.96.
27 Bonaventure Rutinwa, 'The Tanzanian Government's Response to the Rwanda Emergency', Paper for the Refugee Studies Programme, Queen Elizabeth House, Oxford, 1995.
28 *Africa Research Bulletin*, 1-30 June 1995, p. 11893.
29 See R. Lemarchand (1994), *Burundi*, Cambridge University Press, for a general picture, and J. Abrams 'Burundi: Anatomy of an Ethnic Conflict', *Survival*, 37, No. 1, Spring 1995.
30 *Africa Report*, March-April 1995, pp. 26-27, and J. Abrams, op. cit.
31 Reyntjens (1995) 'Burundi: Breaking the Cycle of Violence', Minority Rights Group, Manchester, pp. 6, 15.
32 Ibid, and Michael Ignatieff, BBC2, 1995.
33 Richard Dowden in The Independent, 11.5.94.

34 Human Rights Watch Africa, Release of 11.7.94.
35 OAU Press Release NY/OAU/BUR 43/93, and OAU CM Res/1524(LX), Resolution of Council of Ministers, 6-11 June 1994.
36 UN S26631 and S/1994/1039.
37 J. Abrams, op. cit., p. 157, n. 57, Daily Telegraph, 3.4.95.
38 *Africa Research Bulletin*, June 1-30, 1995, p. 11889-90, The Independent, 7.6.95, The Times, 19.1.96 and J. D. Kayigamba, (1995) 'Burundi, a Call for Sanity', Human Rights Bulletin, InterPress Service Agency, October-December. Amnesty International made similar reports.
39 The Times, 19.1.96.
40 Interview with Mr Mahiga, UNHCR, Geneva, 26.3.96.
41 The Guardian, 28.6.96. Lt. Col. Longin Minani, a Tutsi Army spokesman, declared 'Burundi is not going to be colonised again. This is an independent country and we are not going to be governed by foreigners', The Guardian, 26.7.96.
42 The Times, 26 and 27.7.96, and The Daily Nation, Kenya, 14.8.96. A leader in The Independent was entitled 'Should the West Remake Broken African Nations?', 26.7.96.
43 The Times, 29 and 30.7.96.
44 The East African, 5-11 August 1996 and 12.8.96.

Part Three: WIDER ISSUES

13 NGOs and conflict resolution in Africa: facilitators or aggravators of peacekeeping ?

Timothy Murithi

In the area of peacekeeping, NGO activities have to a large extent paralleled the changes which have taken place with the United Nations itself...the vast enterprise of building peace presupposes that non-governmental organisations will be involved at every stage.
Boutros Boutros-Ghali, UN Secretary-General, 1994

Introduction

In the various complex emergencies that have proliferated the African continent, domestic and international non-governmental organisations (NGOs) are increasingly establishing themselves as the primary providers of basic needs, essential for the survival of human polities in these fragmented societies. In cases where the state has 'collapsed' NGOs and other transnational and regional organisations, like the UN and the OAU, in many respects take over the security-providing functions of the state. This often includes food, medical and social security provision. For the most part, the institutional mandate and ethos of these NGOs is to provide humanitarian relief to communities that find themselves subsumed into conflict situations which are typically defined by: the loss of life, the displacement of large numbers of people as well as the destruction of a population's ability to procure sustenance vital for physical survival. In most cases the NGOs are working in areas where war between insurgents is still a going concern. Thus, on the face of it their task is one that involves a high degree of risk. The provision of security to these aid workers is often rudimentary at best, if not virtually absent. In war zones where disputants are committed to achieving their political objectives through military means order is a rare commodity. This chapter will attempt to examine the impact that NGO activity has on peacekeeping efforts on the African continent, as well as explore the type of role that humanitarian relief workers can play in peacemaking efforts at the dawn of the new millennium.

The recent experience of international peacekeeping operations in Africa has placed into sharp focus the precarious nature of trying to 'keep' the peace in places where belligerents are still committed to war. In 1992 the US-led United Nations Operation in Somalia (UNOSOM), which was mandated to intervene in the inter-clan war with the objective of alleviating starvation and restoring peace and stability, concluded with the death of 25 Pakistani peacekeepers on 6 June 1993 and subsequently casualties were also incurred by the US troops when 18 Americans were killed in October 1993.[1] As a consequence of this the US President Bill Clinton announced the withdrawal of US forces from Somalia. By March 1995 the complete withdrawal of UN peacekeeping troops was effected. As Woodhouse observes 'over 130 peacekeepers had died in Somalia during the three-year intervention between 1992 and 1995, the highest fatality rate recorded in the history of UN peacekeeping'.[2] The net effect of this outcome was a change in US, and more generically, Western attitudes towards providing their troops for peacekeeping operations on the African continent. This event had a significant impact on subsequent UN peacekeeping efforts in the Rwandan conflict. The UN Assistance Mission to Rwanda (UNAMIR), established on 5 October 1993, found itself embroiled in a conflict situation. When 10 Belgian soldiers serving with UNAMIR were killed, in April 1994, the force was reduced to a minimal contingent of 270 soldiers; paradoxically this occurred at the height of the genocide against the Tutsi and moderate Hutu. Stern criticisms of this action came from most quarters particularly when the carnage forced huge numbers of Rwandan refugees to flood to neighbouring countries. In effect, after the take-over of the state by the Tutsi-led Rwanda Patriotic Front (RPF) UNAMIR was still in Rwanda and was subsequently mandated to assist the Rwandan government and the UN High Commission for Refugees (UNHCR) with the safe and voluntary return of approximately two million refugees in neighbouring countries. In March 1996 UNAMIR II was withdrawn but the refugee conundrum in the Great Lakes region was still potentially explosive. Peacekeeping in Africa had become an anathema to Western governments. A culture of Western disengagement most aptly describes the peacekeeping efforts in Africa today. As an uninterested international community seeks to disengage from a continent deemed to have no intrinsic 'strategic' value to the powerful nations, the mantra of 'African solutions to African problems' is audible in the corridors of Western governments. Yet Gerry Cleaver and Roy May maintain that as far as an 'African peacekeeping structure' is concerned 'the political and military structures are not yet in place, nor is there any likelihood that there is any organisation to fill the post-Cold War security vacuum'.[3]

The task of security and relief provision is thus, as a consequence, increasingly being left to actors not necessarily familiar with such roles. The London-based NGO African Rights asserts that 'the increase in donor-funded NGO relief operations and Western disengagement from poor countries are two sides of the same coin'.[4] When these 'poor countries' disintegrate as a consequence of war NGOs are for the most part the primary actors still remaining in war zones when all other forms of international presence have left. This has led John Prendergast to remark that 'as NGO responsibilities have grown, so too have their self-defined mandates, as their remits have been pushed beyond the provision of humanitarian relief to conflict resolution and human rights issues'.[5] In an attempt to explore the nature of this extension this chapter will analyse the role of NGOs as 'peacekeepers' in the wider sense of the term. The fine line that divides humanitarian relief and politico-military humanitarianism[6] is becoming distinctively blurred. Increasingly as peacekeepers find themselves having to take on humanitarian roles so are relief workers being drawn into activities which involve finding ways of engendering peacemaking and ways of 'keeping the peace' between disputing groups. From recent literature on the subject the view has emerged that a certain degree of 'complementarity' necessarily exists between relief work and peacekeeping.[7] In this respect the role of NGOs in conflict resolution and peacekeeping is at a crucial crossroads.[8] This chapter will proceed by addressing NGO activity in the wider context of international relations with a brief discussion of their growing presence in Africa. Subsequently a brief analysis of the various debates surrounding peacekeeping in the post-Cold war world will then be carried out. This will lay the foundations for an assessment of the positive and negative impact of NGO activity in complex emergencies with a specific reference to peacekeeping. The final part will consolidate the themes that emerge from this discussion with a view to putting forward the proposition that the way in which these relief associations begin to adapt themselves to the conditions they confront in war zones, will be integral to the evolution of an African peacekeeping structure. Indeed, the moment has arrived in which NGOs have to begin to acknowledge that 'politics' is inherent in anything which can be 'politicised'; and with the politicisation of humanitarian relief NGOs are already implicated in what is essentially a political activity.

Conceptualising non-governmental organisations

Non-governmental organisations (NGOs) are an integral part of international life. Interaction between human beings is gradually taking on a transnational character. The net effect of this is manifest in a world where social mobility has become heightened. The movement of trade, people, capital, ideas and values is more fluid today than at any other point in human history. NGOs, both domestic and international, are steadily increasing in number on every continent. As the former UN Secretary-General Boutros Boutros-Ghali observed, 'non-governmental organisations are a basic form of popular representation in the present-day world'.[9] But what are they and more importantly what are their goals? In his historical analysis of NGOs Bill Seary suggests that NGOs, as we know them today, first appeared in the international scene in the nineteenth century, with numbers growing from an estimated four NGOs in the 1850s to approximately sixty at the turn of the century.[10] The most prominent of these was an organisation founded in 1859 by Henri Dunant, a Swiss national, as a reaction to the effects that taking care of the war-wounded at the battle of Solferino had upon him. He spear-headed the formation of a small committee in Geneva, Switzerland, which would focus on continuing to help the victims of war. The committee blossomed into what is today known as the International Committee of the Red Cross. In 1919 the needs of societies that found themselves in war zones encouraged an American, Henry Davidson, to take on from where Dunant had left off and inspire the creation of what has come to be referred to as the International Federation of Red Cross and Red Crescent Societies. This narrative of the formation of this Federation, which today has an annual operating budget world-wide of six hundred million US dollars, typifies the process which underpins the majority of NGOs that we are familiar with today. It is primarily down to the drive and motivation of one person or a small group of people, who identify a need in international or domestic activism, which leads to the establishment of an organisation to respond to that need.[11] With the formation of the United Nations in 1945 a provision was included in the UN Charter which granted NGOs a consultative status. This was enshrined in Article 71 and stated that 'the Economic and Social Council may make suitable arrangements for consultation with non-governmental organisations which are concerned with matters within its competence'. Today the hundreds of thousands of domestic and international NGOs are central to drawing our attention to situations of injustice or expanding our awareness of the need for proactive measures to secure the sustainability of our social and physical environment. NGOs vary greatly in size from small groups of a few individuals, usually based in local communities, to larger transnational NGOs which maintain national offices in different countries as well as having international headquarters. Thus, the type of work that these organisations perform also varies greatly. The larger NGOs that routinely partake in relief efforts in complex emergencies in Africa are, for example, the Red Cross and Red Crescent Societies, Médicin sans Frontières (MSF), CARE, Oxfam, International Rescue Committee (IRC), and Save the Children Fund (SCF). It was estimated that at the height of Operation Restore Hope in Somalia, in 1993, there were upwards of 40 NGOs stationed in the country.

NGOs rely on both public and private sources of financial support. The meteoric growth of NGOs has coincided with the shift in the policy of the main donor nations and institutions. Based on the argument that the states in many parts of the developing world are riddled with 'economic mismanagement', their ability to transfer the funds donated for the benefit of their populations has been severely compromised. NGOs have stepped into the equation which has led to a shift in donor funding away from states to NGOs, who are viewed as being more financially accountable for their expenditure and its effects on the recipient communities. In the post-Cold War period it is possible to discern a significant expansion of NGO involvement in development projects and relief work. With reference to Africa Mark Duffield notes that 'by the end of the 1980s the reputation of NGOs as emergency program implementors was well established. From the Horn, safety net systems spread to other parts of Africa. This enhanced relief role was also synonymous with the increasing development of donor/NGO sub-contracting relations.'[12] In cases where NGOs from the developed north establish themselves as actors in countries in the south there are mixed reactions to their presence. Andrew Natsios makes the observation that 'NGOs do their relief and development work at the grassroots level, which is labour-intensive from a staff perspective, both expatriate and indigenous. Thus, they tend to have large field staffs that can carry out complex operations in remote areas.'[13] Governments, particularly in the south, tend to be sensitive to the possibility of their authority being eroded by these NGOs. According to Gordenker and Weiss governments are 'often hostile about the formation of grassroots and intermediary NGOs...some governments harbour suspicions of expatriates whom NGOs usually employ to supervise or inspect activities. This suspicion easily develops into accusations of espionage against NGOs.'[14] Some commentators are even more sceptical, for example with reference to Africa Chango w'Obanda contends that 'today the so-called non-governmental organisations (NGOs) have taken over the role that was played by the missionaries during former colonial rule'.[15] He goes on to suggest that the NGO presence in Africa represents an informal institutionalisation of the structures for 'recolonization'; whereby Western presence disguised as humanitarian and developmental assistance is one more step in the projection of Western values on the African continent. What is not made clear are his views on domestic NGOs. In any case, w'Obanda's conclusion rests on the assumption that Western-based NGOs and Western governments have a unified consensus on what sort of activity is necessary for the African continent. Whereas, the evidence points to the contrary in that some Western-based northern NGOs tend to be as vocal as their southern counterparts in their criticisms of the injustice that pervades the international system, promulgated by Western economic, political and cultural hegemony and compounded by tyrannical rule in the south. It comes as no surprise, therefore, that this view is contested by other commentators who believe that NGOs are performing tasks vital to the physical survival of societies particularly in complex emergencies, where the state for all intents and purposes may have ceased to exist. Among the proponents of NGO activity in these situations is Samia El Hadi El Nagar, a social researcher in Khartoum, Sudan, who suggests that:

> the governments in the Horn countries are attempting to reduce the stressful situations of war, but such efforts have been greatly constrained by the continuity of the wars and political aims. Government assistance to victims of war is largely dependent on NGO support. Many NGOs are distributing food and clothes, and providing health services in displaced camps and refugee settlements. Some NGOs provide educational services and many projects have been established, particularly in the Sudan and Ethiopia, with the aim of achieving self-reliance among refugees.[16]

These disparate view points suggest that there is a need for examining the gap between the intentions and the consequences of NGO activity in war zones. In particular, this study is concerned with determining how NGOs impact upon peacekeeping in these areas. However, before proceeding to such a discussion it may be illuminating to engage in a brief examination of the multifarious dimensions of peacekeeping in the post-Cold War world.

Complex emergencies and humanitarian intervention: the peacekeeping paradigm reconsidered

At the close of the millennium 'peacekeeping' remains one of those enigmatic activities performed by the international community. Michael Walzer states that 'humanitarian interventions and peacekeeping operations are first of all military acts directed against peoples who are already using force, breaking the peace'.[17] Indeed, in what can only be described as a decade of complex emergencies this observation holds true for most of the peacekeeping operations currently active. This has fuelled quite an intense debate in the corridors of policy-making at the UN, within the military establishments of various countries and in the research forums of relief organisations and academic institutions. Peacekeeping in the absence of a peace to keep has meant that peacekeeping troops invariably find themselves endeavouring to secure avenues for transportation and communication using coercive action which facilitates the dissemination of humanitarian assistance. Traditionally peacekeeping had entailed 'a UN presence in the field, with the consent of the parties, to implement or monitor the implementation of arrangements relating to the control of conflicts and their resolution, and/or to protect the delivery of humanitarian relief'.[18] This definition established in 1994 is distinguished from earlier definitions by the addition of the last phrase. The 'delivery of humanitarian relief' has become part and parcel of peacekeeping operations in war-torn areas. As we discerned at the outset of this chapter this changing remit has led to peacekeeping efforts being drawn into a more proactive form of military activity. With regards to Africa this has proved to be a damaging experience for both recipients of humanitarian intervention and the peace-keepers alike. UN peacekeeping efforts in Somalia and Rwanda throw into sharp relief some of the issues that have led to calls for the reconceptualisation of what peacekeeping is intended to do and what it cannot be asked to do. In the events in Somalia and Rwanda there were no peace agreements between warring parties to monitor or implement and in both cases the peacekeeping process was not functioning on the basis of the consensual agreement of the disputants as to the presence and role of the peacekeeping force. This was most vividly illustrated in the situation in Somalia whereby UN/US peacekeeping troops failed to act with impartiality but rather were drawn into 'war-fighting' with the faction led by Mohammed Farah Aideed. UN peacekeeping was drawn into the territory of so-called peace-enforcement when UNOSOM II detained members of militias at the end of 1993.[19] As UN troops became engaged in hostilities their position as 'peacekeepers' was severely compromised, reminiscent of the ONUC United Nations intervention in the Congo (now the Democratic Republic of Congo) between 1960 and 1964. By 1994 the UN had defined peace-enforcement as 'action under Chapter 7 of the Charter; including the use of armed force, to maintain or restore international peace and security in situation where the Security Council has determined the existence of a threat to peace, breach of the peace or act of aggression'.[20]

Views are mixed as to the course that future developments should take. Alan James for instance maintains the position that there is no middle ground between peacekeeping and peace-enforcement.[21] This view is echoed by Charles Dobbie and Mats Berdal who question the possibility of such a link existing.[22] They argue that both operations should be distinct from each other which implies that UN troops mandated for one activity cannot then, midway through the operation, be used to fulfil a different mandate as was the case in the US/UN effort on Somalia. David Rieff argues that 'the increasing sense that peacekeeping is so ineffective a tool for resolving crises like Somalia' is an indication 'that it might well be better to scrap it altogether and leave the policing of the world's trouble-spots to great powers or regional hegemons'.[23] To some extent this view has found its way to the policy position of several Western governments who advocate the need for peacekeeping efforts to be carried out by countries who are in the proximity of the conflict. By extrapolation, this means that future complex emergencies in, say, Africa need to be dealt with by African contingents. Clearly, there is no conclusive end in sight; as far as this debate is concerned it is likely to remain a defining feature of the transition from a world of politico-military certainties to a world of contingency. The Special Assistant to the UN Under Secretary-General for Peacekeeping operations sums up the overall situation when he intimates that:

> traditional peacekeeping is all very well if the only crises confronting the United Nations are those which are ripe for the peacekeeping treatment. But classical, consensual peacekeeping does not respond fully to the nature of the world we live in and the challenges the new world disorder poses to the international community. If UN peacekeeping has acquired a certain elasticity in recent years, it is precisely because circumstances have led the world to make demands on the military capacity of the United Nations which vastly exceeds anything it was called upon to do.[24]

This elasticity is evident at the other end of the peacekeeping spectrum, namely; the humanitarian relief dimension. It is self-evident that humanitarian operations can only function effectively within a secure environment. As a consequence linkage becomes forged between military and humanitarian operations. In complex emergencies the presence of peacekeepers improves the security which in turn enables humanitarian work to proceed. More recently, UN peacekeeping contingents have been mandated to provide relief and social welfare provisions.[25] Fetherstone argues for the need to go even further and suggests that peacekeeping should be conceptualised as a part of an integrated framework of conflict resolution, in which peacekeepers are trained in communication skills, negotiation, facilitation and mediation. Thus, beyond their traditional remit of keeping the peace these contingents would be proactive in encouraging a de-escalation in the conflict stance of warring groups; as well as engaging in active peace-building at the grassroots level.[26]

Aiding the peace: NGOs as peacekeepers

This nexus between peacekeeping and humanitarianism is also evident, to some extent, in the changing role of NGO relief workers in conflict situations. Most NGOs refuse military protection due to the legitimate concern that their credibility as humanitarian workers, who are by definition supposed to be impartial, is compromised when they are closely associated with a peacekeeping force.[27] It is however becoming clear that the relief work done by NGOs can also be systematically undermined by the absence of security provisions. This suggests that NGOs have to begin to contribute towards activities that promote and keep peace in line with the integrated framework of conflict resolution and peacekeeping, to which peacekeepers themselves are currently having to adapt. In failed states, or even failing states, a condition which is afflicting parts of Africa, the presence of only a token peacekeeping force means that to effect relief distribution NGOs will invariably, in one form or another, be drawn into self-initiated efforts to encourage a truce or even promote cease-fire agreement between belligerents.

The traditional role of NGOs in Africa included addressing the symptoms of internecine conflict which involved providing food and medical support for war-affected populations or refugees displaced beyond the recognised borders of their country of origin. During the Cold War NGOs largely restricted their activities to areas which respected the sovereign will of the state concerned. Thus, NGOs worked closely with African governments. Permission from the recipient state was an essential precondition for providing relief on its territory. Christopher Clapham notes that 'even when access to parts of a country was prevented by insurgent warfare, government forces almost invariably controlled the ports, roads and other infrastructural facilities through which famine relief food and other resources had to be distributed'.[28] The provision of humanitarian assistance clearly favoured the government. As Duffield observes:

> Up to the end of the 1980's, warring parties usually attempted to deny humanitarian assistance to areas controlled by opponents. They were able to pursue a strategy of humanitarian denial largely as a result of the importance previously attached to traditional notions of non-interference in internal matters. As a result, during the Cold War non-government areas in internal wars were out of bounds for most aid agencies. NGOs tended to operate on the side of the recognised government.[29]

Changes in the structure and ethos of international politics after the end of the Cold War contributed towards an increase in both the scope and the legitimacy of NGO humanitarian assistance to grassroots communities. Intervention became more common, as Clapham remarks: 'the decline in respect for national sovereignty, coupled with the removal of the constraints imposed by superpower competition, helped to redefine such operations as a universal humanitarian obligation, rather than as an intervention in the domestic affairs of sovereign states'.[30] The unofficial operational remit for NGOs altered. Today the relationship between NGOs and warring parties tends to be defined by an agreement, usually brokered through the UN, which stresses that all humanitarian relief activity should be deemed as being neutral and designed only to assist civilians in a non-strategic way. This form of 'negotiated access' has become the approach preferred by NGOs in making sure that assistance gets to all the war-affected. According to Duffield's definition 'in its most basic form, negotiated access involves gaining the consent of warring parties for the movement and delivery of humanitarian aid to civilian populations'.[31] Thus NGOs are, in one sense, already drawn into the process of 'mediation' by their attempts to secure a country-wide access to conflict areas. By establishing internationally mandated relief operations which cover all sides of the dispute NGOs legitimise 'cross-border or cross-line type programmes that were previously out of bounds to most aid agencies'. It is this factor which places NGOs in an advantageous position from which they can undertake efforts to promote peace and engender cross-border links upon which humanitarian assistance can develop into assistance which contributes towards keeping the peace. Whereas such activities may not constitute peacekeeping, they are nevertheless the basis upon which the expansion towards an integrated peacekeeping and conflict resolution structure can be developed in present and future emergencies. Consent after all is central to even the traditional notion of peacekeeping, as evident in Duffield's reasoning when he states that 'wider peacekeeping, and helping to secure and maintain humanitarian access, hinges upon the management of consent'.[32] NGOs in this context can partake in the activities, loosely defined as wider peacekeeping, as far as playing a role in forging consent among warring factions is concerned. Historically, as Clapham explains, 'NGOs engaged in attempts at conflict resolution in Africa were characteristically reluctant to envisage force as a means to arrive at a solution, and sought instead to settle conflicts through reconciliatory mechanisms managed by external mediators'.[33] In 1992, the conflict settlement in Mozambique was brought about with the contributory efforts of a Catholic lay community based in Rome, called San Egidio.[34] In the case of Somalia, the Head of UNOSOM, Mohamed Sahnoun, points out that he had very few resources with which he was expected to help supply food, restore the infrastructure and mediate in the myriad of disputes that defined social relations in the country at the time.[35] As far as he was concerned 'it was largely thanks to the NGOs that the population began to gradually return to Mogadishu'. Sahnoun further makes the point the 'the provision of humanitarian assistance and the maintenance of the cease-fire are closely linked'. In the absence of food and medical provisions the situation can lead to the rapid escalation of hostilities. In this sense, humanitarian intervention 'contributes to an atmosphere propitious to dialogue and compromise'.[36]

More recently NGOs specialising in conflict management are beginning to play active roles in war-prone areas. For example, the UK-based NGO, International Alert, attempted to promote activities in Burundi between 1994 and 1995 upon which the building blocks of reconciliation could be developed between Tutsi and Hutu youth. Typically, their programmes consist of training the youths in ways of strengthening civil society such as backing an independent and reliable media as well as holding meetings, away from the volatile atmosphere in Burundi, in which they are encouraged to explore ways for developing reconciliatory relationships. International Alert resumed their efforts in 1997 in partnership with a Washington-based NGO, Search for a Common Ground, which had been working in Bujumbura. Since 1995 Search for a Common Ground has been working with a team of Hutu and Tutsi journalists to produce broadcasts that counter 'hate radio' and advocate tolerance. It has also been running a Hutu-Tutsi women's centre for co-operation.[37]

In the area of human rights monitoring NGO participation also contributes to peacekeeping efforts. With reference to the human rights NGO Amnesty International, Helena Cook explains that:

> UN peacekeeping is not a field in which Amnesty previously sought to have an input. Since 1988, however, the United Nations has launched more operations than in the previous forty years and the nature and scope of these operations have changed radically. They have developed well beyond the traditional mandate and tasks of the old-style peacekeeping forces, and human rights issues have been more prominent.[38]

Thus, the maintenance of peace and security is gradually being linked to the promotion of the respect for human rights. The 1993 report, by the then Secretary-General of the UN, Boutros-Ghali, to the Security Council concerning peacekeeping and conflict in Angola proposed that the 'respect for human rights constitutes a vital, indeed a critical, component among measures to resolve, on a long-term basis, conflicts of this nature, including efforts to promote enduring conditions of peace, national reconciliation and democracy'.[39] Besides Angola, Amnesty has monitored, and continues to monitor, the human rights situation in Burundi, Liberia, Mozambique, Rwanda, Somalia, South Africa and Western Sahara all of which have been beset by political violence, with some situations escalating to complex emergencies. Amnesty uses its channels directly to approach and influence UN policy makers and governments; and to raise public awareness through publishing reports and recommendations. Reiterating this view Felice Gaer observes that 'Amnesty International has set forth human rights principles to be followed in designing all peacekeeping operations, calling for UN peacekeepers to be more than silent or indifferent witnesses, demanding that troops be impartial, properly trained and ready to uphold international law and to adhere to it in their own conduct as well'.[40] A similar view has been echoed by Rakiya Omaar and Alex de Waal, co-directors of the London-based NGO Africa Rights, who have highlighted the conceptual and operational contradictions which plague humanitarian NGOs, UN agencies and peacekeepers. They suggest that human rights 'objectivity' means that an emphasis has to be placed on solidarity with the victims of injustice and genocide. When such 'objectivity' is upheld it will inevitably from time to time be at variance with 'operational neutrality' on the field.[41] On the advocacy side of things effective campaigning by the NGO Human Rights

Watch, with the participation of Amnesty, directed at the Security Council of the UN, culminated in the establishment of a human rights monitoring mission in Rwanda, as a response to the 1994 genocide, by the UN High Commissioner for Human Rights.[42] In this way it is becoming evident that NGOs are increasingly playing a constructive role in peacekeeping, through their activities in the spheres of humanitarian assistance, conflict resolution and human rights monitoring. But there is an important sense in which their activities have resulted in dire consequences for the populations that they seek to serve.

NGOs as 'war-keepers': a case of provision exacerbating division

NGOs have traditionally endeavoured not to get entangled in the 'political' issues of a conflict situation, a move which they felt would compromise their standing in the eyes of the parties concerned and make it difficult for them to carry out fully their primary function of providing relief to grassroots communities. Since the objective of NGOs in complex emergencies, as they see it, is to respond to the massive human suffering being perpetuated among the war-affected, their main priority has tended to be to find ways of establishing immediate and direct access to innocent civilian victims. The political dimension of the conflicts and their settlement tended to be left to the international governmental organisations to manage. In post-Cold War Africa, defined by the retreat of the superpowers, political movements no longer coalesce around bi-polarised ideological positions, but rather they tend to take on a more ethnic, cultural, or religious character. The net effect of this is that the representational divisions of the military conquest on the ground tend to be more fragmented and less coherent. Given this situation, Duffield makes the point that 'as a consequence providing humanitarian aid is more dangerous and often represents the acceptance of situations of high and continuous risk'.[43] In this altered geopolitical terrain NGO humanitarian workers have to confront the logic of internal conflict. The pitfalls of their activities become magnified in such circumstances. The logic of communal conflict means that, to some extent, NGOs invariably become aligned. In the absence of such alignment their efforts would become unmanageable.[44] Through negotiating access NGOs provide the warring groups with contacts to governments that they may be pitted against and by extension they are also able to channel their grievances out to the international community. Due to the reluctance of NGOs to concede that they are invariably engaged in 'politics' - with many of them operating under provisos which prohibit political activity- both the political causes of the crisis and the political impact of the humanitarian relief operation is easily overlooked or even suppressed.[45] Amir Pasic and Thomas Weiss argue that 'even without military forces, humanitarian efforts are profoundly political; and unless they are carefully designed, they can actually exacerbate conflicts'.[46] According to Clapham past experiences illustrate that as far as NGOs carrying out relief work in war zones is concerned 'the resources which they distributed, necessarily conferred power on some groups and in the process at least relatively disadvantaged others'.[47] Rather than empowering the grassroots polities through providing them with resources for rehabilitation and social reconstruction these resources can, and have been, just as easily diverted into the war effort to further entrench destruction. In such situations NGOs effectively become inadvertent 'war-keepers'. The experiences in Somalia are quite telling in this regard. The armed factions competing for control of Mogadishu would often fight over the aid. These resources would then be used to enhance their military organisations making a volatile situation more explosive. In Rwanda the displaced refugees settled in a camp in neighbouring Goma (in the Democratic Republic of Congo) but so did the soldiers of the fallen Habyarimana regime who organised the genocide of the Tutsi. A report by the Economist, at the time, remarked that these camps 'which are reckoned to house 30,000 soldiers and 10,000 militiamen, provide recruits, a base for weapons training and, say aid workers, the chance of almost daily armed incursions into Rwanda'.[48] Following events like these the refugee camps effectively become militarised and the situation is such that combatants:

> threaten force against NGOs to extract payment, either in cash or in kind, for access to civilian populations, resulting in nominally neutral NGOs providing logistical support for active combatants. Humanitarian supplies are regularly confiscated from relief workers by combatants...the diversion of humanitarian supplies heightens the dilemma by tainting short-term emergency civilian assistance with forced augmentation of the long-term capacity of combatants to continue fighting.[49]

Aid is actively being used as an instrument of war by the unrepentant authors of genocide. Gerard Prunier, in his illuminating study of Rwanda, has castigated such NGOs for effectively helping these militia and soldiers, albeit, under the guise of providing 'aid to the refugees'.[50] The former President of the medical aid NGO, Médecins sans Frontières (MSF), Rory

Brauman, also maintained with regard to this case that 'humanitarian intervention, far from representing a bulwark against evil, is in fact one of its appendages'.[51] Whether or not one concurs with this assessment the point that emerges is that there is clearly a greater need for an integrated peacekeeping and conflict resolution structure in Africa; particularly given the token UN presence in Goma which has enabled chaos to flourish. However, it is also important for NGOs to recognise that the delivery of relief aid is a political action with inescapable political consequences. Humanitarian relief can prolong wars by sustaining the territories which militia depend upon to maintain their fighting capability. Michael Ignatieff further suggests that the delivery of humanitarian assistance, necessary as it is, probably reduces the incentives of both sides to negotiate a settlement.[52] It remains a paradox that the primary element which would make NGOs effective in contributing to an integrated peacekeeping and conflict resolution structure - namely their emphasis on establishing consensual arrangements with the warring parties - is also the primary factor which makes their activities more likely to exacerbate conflicts if, or when, these self-same warring groups decide to bend the activities and resources of the NGOs to their will. Thus, there are limitations to providing aid to war zones. The politicisation of humanitarian relief makes NGOs quasi-political actors. A realisation of this necessarily points towards the need for a reconceptualisation of humanitarian relief.

Towards integrated peacekeeping: NGOs - practitioners in the politics of rescue

Cleaver and May have illustrated how the African continent is at the moment not sufficiently endowed with the resources and logistics which are essential for effecting and implementing peacekeeping operations. The absence of an African peacekeeping structure thus remains an issue of vital concern as far as the mitigation and management of Africa's conflicts are concerned. While it is reasonable to see why NGOs are reluctant to become closely associated with the military humanitarianism of a UN peacekeeping force, there has been more linkage with military operations than is generally acknowledged. Pugh notes that 'in Somalia, agencies such as Oxfam and CARE supported the UNITAF mission, while Save the Children and Médecins sans Frontières (MSF) were either ambivalent or opposed'.[53] MSF has maintained its consistency in being critical of UN military humanitarian missions. In Rwanda it actively campaigned for military intervention. Antonio Donini observes that 'most humanitarian actors would probably agree that direct military intervention in humanitarian programmes, whether UN or NGO, should be a last resort. This is not to deny the useful support role that the military can provide, particularly in the breaking phase of a complex emergency.'[54]

Humanitarian intervention is by definition deemed to be well-meaning. But when a disparity emerges between the intentions and the consequences of a particular effort, as has been the case in Africa, then 'reflective practitioners' and observers, alike, need to re-evaluate their fundamental assumptions.[55] In the case of peacekeeping and relief work it is necessary to ask the question - what is the impetus behind humanitarian intervention? Following a taxonomy developed by Pasic and Weiss, we can distinguish between three types of humanitarian intervention: *custodial intervention* which is primarily geared towards the relief of suffering; whereas *restorative intervention* seeks to restore at the very least a semblance of political order; and finally *revolutionary intervention* which endeavours to go a step further and secure justice for the victims.[56] While there is going to be a great deal of overlap between these constructions the possibility of trade-offs also exists. Pasic and Weiss note that there can be a trade-off between the relief of suffering and the restoration of political order. In a similar fashion, the goal of stability can also be at variance with the quest for justice. According to Pasic and Weiss seeking 'to institute political order is to attempt to create and sustain viable social institutions which will prevent the need for subsequent rescue efforts'. Thus, on one level a certain amount of synthesis can prevail between custodial and restorative intervention; particularly if the task of providing relief and building a sustainable order is carried out by different actors in parallel - for example NGOs and peacekeepers respectively. However, Pasic and Weiss also point out that political strategies which seek to create 'an enduring sociopolitical order will sometimes require reining in the impulse to save lives'.[57] Rescue in this sense is compromised for the establishment of justice in the long-run. However, as we encountered earlier, there is an important sense in which efforts only to relieve suffering can be systematically undermined by the absence of order. Alain Destexhe, the former Secretary-General of Médecins sans Frontières, notes that 'humanitarian action is noble when coupled with political action and justice. Without them, it is doomed to failure.'[58] Elsewhere Stanley Hoffman makes a similar point when he suggests that 'as long as the causes of humanitarian disasters have not been addressed, very little will be accomplished'[59] by humanitarian relief intervention.

It is this coupling of relief, the restoration of order and the search for a just and enduring socio-political order that would underpin an integrated peacekeeping and conflict resolution structure. It is also within such an integrated structure that NGOs can provide the service that they are best at, that is to say, rescue. Clearly this would also demand a parallel commitment to co-operation with UN or OAU efforts to co-ordinate the creation of a stable political order. In this respect, NGOs would necessarily become practitioners in the politics of rescue. NGOs will increasingly complement peacekeeping operations not only by the provision of relief aid but also by the provision of active mediators involved in encouraging the warring parties to forge institutions for political coexistence. Subsequently they will help the parties to establish an equitable arrangement in the medium to long-term.

Given the emerging fact that the traditional roles of the peacekeeper and the relief worker are no longer strictly applicable, NGO activity will be effective if it endeavours to complement peacekeeping efforts. Likewise peacekeepers would be more effective in their tasks if they complement rather than substitute, and hence replicate, NGO humanitarian relief work.[60] Role demarcation would obviously need to be established, together with greater coordination between NGOs who tend to overlap each other in their projects - driven in part by the highly competitive nature of obtaining grants based on their ability to justify their efforts in complex emergencies. The peacekeepers are in a better position to deal with the logistics of humanitarian intervention such as providing transportation and the building of infrastructure as well as securing relief areas, while NGOs carry out the provision and dissemination of food and medical aid. Pugh proposes that 'humanitarian skills can be incorporated into peacekeeping training, with recognition of the limitations of military humanitarianism and the requirement to co-operate with, or defer to, civilian humanitarian expertise on matters such as developmental priorities and humanitarian law'.[61] In recognition of the changing landscape of humanitarianism on the African continent NGOs also need to ensure that their staff grasp the fundamental political and economic dimensions of internal conflict, so that their interventionary activities can focus on de-escalating the pressures of war. As Mark Bradbury suggests, this would necessarily entail training NGO staff in conflict resolution and mediation skills.[62]

Conclusion

In the absence of an institutionalised African peacekeeping structure, NGO relief organisations working in war zones, with only a token military presence, find themselves often co-opted into undertaking various peacemaking and peacekeeping activities as the situations demand. Through their ability to obtain a cross-line 'negotiated access' between warring groups NGOs are in an advantageous position to promote efforts to de-escalate an internal conflict. Paradoxically, having obtained this access NGOs are often vulnerable to coercion, obstruction and interference by the same combatants. Given that humanitarian assistance is invariably a form of political action, with inescapable political consequences, NGO activity can also exacerbate conflict, as experiences in Goma in the Democratic Republic of Congo, and Mogadishu in Somalia, illustrate.

The complex nature of the conflicts currently afflicting the African continent, with the high levels of suffering experienced by the war-affected at the grassroots level, evokes the need for a greater degree of complementarity between humanitarian NGO relief work and peacekeeping operations. Thus, NGO and peacekeeping activity are effectively coextensive within the general peace-building process. Military and non-military input is equally vital in brokering peace and setting in motion efforts in rehabilitation and social reconstruction. NGOs are also in an advantageous position to maintain the continuity necessary to support the transition of the war-affected populations towards development and the establishment of consensual institutions for local governance, built from the grassroots up.

The events that are defining Africa in the post-Cold War world suggest that peacekeepers and NGO relief workers will need to become 'reflective practitioners' and design their activities in ways which reduce the pressure of war situations. In the decade coming to a close the efforts to address complex emergencies in Africa have been woefully lacking in coherency or consistency. As a consequence humanitarianism has gone through a steep learning-curve, typified by lessons learnt through trial and error. The experiences of NGOs as makers and keepers of peace are no exception. Suffice to say, as Boutros-Ghali contends, that by constructively drawing upon past experiences NGOs can only become better facilitators at 'building peace'. Any future attempts to establish and institutionalise an integrated structure for peacekeeping and conflict resolution in Africa would be incomplete without the incorporation of NGOs.

Notes

1   Woodhouse, T. (1996) 'Commentary: Negotiating a New Millennium? Prospects for African Conflict Resolution', *Review of*

African Political Economy, No. 68, pp. 129-137.
2 Woodhouse, T. (1996) 'Negotiating a New Millennium', p. 129.
3 Cleaver, G. and May, R. (1995) 'Peacekeeping: The African Dimension', *Review of African Political Economy*, No. 66, p. 484.
4 Africa Rights, 'Grass and the Roots of Peace', Discussion Paper No. 3, p. 19.
5 Prendergast, J. (1997) *Crisis Response: Humanitarian Band-Aids in Sudan and Somalia*, Pluto: London, p. 12.
6 Weiss, T. and Campbell, K. 'Military Humanitarianism', *Survival*, Vol. 33, No. 5, pp. 451-465.
7 Liu, F. T. (1990) 'The Significance of Past Peacekeeping Operations in Africa to Humanitarian relief', in Gordenker, L. and Weiss, T. (eds) *Humanitarian Emergencies and Military Help in Africa*, Macmillan: Basingstoke, pp. 24-27; Jackson, R. (1993) 'Armed Humanitarianism', *International Journal*, Vol. 68, No. 4, pp. 579-606; Lewer, N. and Ramsbotham, O. (1993) 'Something Must be Done: Towards an Ethical Framework for Humanitarian Intervention in International Social Conflict', *Peace Reports*, No. 33, Department of Peace Studies: Bradford; Evriviades, M. and Bourantonis, D. (1994) 'Peacekeeping and Peacemaking: Some Lessons from Cyprus', *International Peacekeeping*, Vol. 1, No. 4, pp. 403-404; James, A. (1996) 'Humanitarian Aid Operations and Peacekeeping', in Belgrad, E. and Nadmias, N. (eds) *The Politics of International Humanitarian Operations*, CT, Greenwood: Westport.
8 Dellaire, R. (1996), 'The Changing Role of UN Peacekeeping Forces: The Relationship Between UN Peacekeepers and NGOs in Rwanda', in Whitman, J. and Pocock, D. (eds), *After Rwanda: The Co-ordination of United Nations Humanitarian Assistance*, Macmillan: Basingstoke.
9 Boutros Boutros-Ghali (1994), Statement at the UN Department of Public Information's Forty-Seventh Annual Conference of Non-governmental Organisations - 'We the Peoples: Building Peace', United Nations: New York.
10 Seary, B. (1996), 'The Early History: From the Congress of Vienna to the San Francisco Conference', in Willets, P. (ed), *The Conscience of the World: The Influence of Non-Governmental Organisations in the UN System*, Hurst: London.
11 Ibid., p. 16.
12 Duffield, M. (1994), *Complex Political Emergencies: With Reference to Angola and Bosnia*, United Nations Children Fund (UNICEF), p. 110.

13 Natsios, A. (1996), 'NGOs and the UN System in Complex Humanitarian Emergencies: Conflict or Co-operation?' in Weiss, T. and Gordenker, L. (eds) *NGOs, the United Nations, and Global Governance*, Lynne Rienner: London, pp. 67-83.
14 Gordenker, L. and Weiss, T. (1996), 'Devolving Responsibilities: A Framework for Analysing NGOs and Services', *Third World Quarterly*, Vol. 18, No. 3, pp. 443-455.
15 Chango Machyo w'Obanda (1995), 'Conditions of Africans at Home', in Abdul-Raheem, T. (ed) *Pan-Africanism: Politics, Economy and Social Change in the Twenty-First Century*, Pluto: London, pp. 33-66.
16 Samia El Hadi El Nagar, 'Children and War in the Horn of Africa', in Doornbos, S., Cliffe, L., Ahmed, A. G. and Markakis, J. (eds) *Beyond Conflict in the Horn: The Prospects for Peace, Recovery and Development in Ethiopia, Somalia, Eritrea and Sudan*, James Currey: London, pp. 19-20.
17 Walzer, M. (1995), 'The Politics of Rescue', *Social Research*, Vol. 62, No. 1, p. 58.
18 United Nations (1994), *Improving the Capacity of the United Nations for Peacekeeping*, Report of the Secretary-General, A/48/403, para.4(c), United Nations: New York.
19 Amnesty International (1994), *Peacekeeping and Human Rights*, Amnesty International: London, p. 20.
20 United Nations (1994), *Improving the Capacity of the United Nations for Peacekeeping*, para. 4(d).
21 James, A. (1990), *Peacekeeping and International Politics*, Macmillan: Basingstoke, p. 368.
22 Dobbie, C. (1994), 'A Concept for Post-Cold War Peacekeeping', *Survival*, Vol. 36, No. 3; Berdal, M. (1993), 'Whither UN Peacekeeping?', *Adelphi Paper*, International Institute for Strategic Studies, No. 281, October.
23 Rieff, D. (1994), 'The Illusion of Peacekeeping', *World Policy Journal*, Vol. 11, No. 3, p. 3.
24 Tharoor, S. (1995), 'Should UN Peacekeeping Go "Back to Basics"?', *Survival*, Vol. 37, No. 4, p. 53.
25 Dellaire, R. (1996) 'The Changing Role of UN Peacekeeping'.
26 Fetherstone, A. B. (1994), *Towards a Theory of United Nations Peacekeeping*, Macmillan: Basingstoke.
27 Weiss, T. (1995), 'Military-Civilian Humanitarianism: The "Age of Innocence" is Over', *International Peacekeeping*, Vol. 2, No. 2.
28 Clapham, C. (1996), *Africa and the International System*, Cambridge University Press: Cambridge, p. 227.

29 Duffield, M. (1997) 'NGO Relief in War Zones: Towards an Analysis of the New Aid Paradigm', *Third World Quarterly*, Vol. 18, No. 3, pp. 533-534; see also Keen, D. and Wilson, K. (1994), 'Engaging with Violence: A Reassessment of the Role of Relief in Wartime', in Macrae, J. and Zwi, A. (eds) *War and Hunger: Rethinking International Responses to Complex Emergencies*, Zed Books: London, pp. 209-222.
30 Clapham, C. (1996) *Africa and the International System*, p. 259.
31 Duffield, M. (1997) 'NGOs and the New Aid Paradigm', p. 534.
32 Ibid., p. 537.
33 Clapham, C. (1996) *Africa and the International System*, p. 260.
34 For a more detailed discussion see Schneidman, W. (1993), 'Conflict Resolution in Mozambique', in Smock, D. (ed) *Making War and Waging Peace: Foreign Intervention in Africa*, US Institute of Peace: Washington.
35 Sahnoun, M. (1994), *Somalia: The Missed Opportunities*, United States Institute of Peace: Washington, p. 16.
36 Ibid., p. 17.
37 Evans, G. (1997), 'Responding to Crises in the African Great Lakes', International Institute of Strategic Studies, *Adelphi Paper*, No. 31, August, pp. 39-40.
38 Cook, H., 'Amnesty International at the United Nations', in Willets, *The Conscience of the World*, p. 207.
39 Boutros Boutros-Ghali (1993), Report to the Security Council on Angola, UN doc. S/25840, United Nations: New York.
40 Gaer, F. 'Reality Check: Human Rights NGOs Confront Governments at the UN', in Weiss and Gordenker, *NGOs, the United Nations and Global Governance*, p. 62; see also Amnesty's' first major paper on UN peacekeeping and human rights, Amnesty International (1994), *Peacekeeping and Human Rights*, IOR 40/01/94, Amnesty International.
41 Omaar, R. and de Waal, A. (1994), *Humanitarianism Unbound: Current Dilemmas Facing Multi-Mandate Relief in Political Emergencies*, Working Paper No. 5, Africa Rights: London, November, pp. 18-33.
42 Gaer, F., 'Reality Check', pp. 2-63.
43 Duffield, M. (1997) 'NGOs and the New Aid Paradigm', p. 536.
44 Clapham, C. (1996) *Africa and the International System*, p. 260.
45 Ibid., p. 260.
46 Pasic, A. and Weiss, T. (1997), 'The Politics of Rescue: Yugoslavia's Wars and the Humanitarian Impulse', *Ethics and International Affairs*,

Vol. 11, p. 133.
47 Clapham, C. (1996) *Africa and the International System*, p. 260.
48 'Rwandan Refugees: Crime and Nourishment', *Economist*, 1 April 1995, pp. 68-69.
49 Smith, E. and Weiss, T. (1997), 'UN Task-sharing: Towards or Away from Global Governance?', *Third World Quarterly*, Vol. 18, No. 3, p. 605 .
50 Prunier, G. (1995), *The Rwanda Crisis: History of a Genocide*, Hurst: London, p. 83.
51 MSF ultimately left the Goma camp towards the end of November, but several other NGOs remained. Cited in Prunier, G. (1995) *The Rwanda Crisis*, p. 279.
52 Ignatieff, M. (1995), 'The Seductiveness of Moral Disgust', *Social Research*, Vol. 62, No. 1, Spring, p. 91.
53 Pugh, M. (1996), 'Humanitarianism and Peacekeeping', *Global Society: Journal of Interdisciplinary International Relations*, Vol. 10, No. 3, September, pp. 205-224.
54 Donini, A. (1996), 'The Bureaucracy and the Free Spirits: Stagnation and Innovation in the Relationship Between the UN and NGOs', in Weiss and Gordenker, *NGOs, the United Nations, and Global Governance*, p. 96.
55 Schon, D. (1983), *The Reflective Practitioner*, Basic Books: New York.
56 Pasic and Weiss, 'The Politics of Rescue'; for a fuller discussion and a critique see Natsios, A. (1997), 'NGOs and the Humanitarian Impulse: Some Have it Right', *Ethics and International Affairs*, Vol. 11, pp. 133-136.
57 Pasic and Weiss, 'The Politics of Rescue', p. 110.
58 Destexhe, A. (1995), 'Foreword', in Francois, J. (ed) *Populations in Danger 1995*, MSF: London.
59 Hoffman, S. (1995), 'The Politics and Ethics of Military Intervention', *Survival*, Vol. 37, No. 4, Winter, p. 41.
60 Pugh, M. (1996) 'Humanitarianism and Peacekeeping', p. 20.
61 Ibid., p. 220.
62 Bradbury, M. (1993), *The Somali Conflict: Prospects for Peace*, Oxfam, Research Paper, No. 9, October, p. 3.

14 The military, peacekeeping and Africa

Richard Connaughton

Introduction

'We shall be in Africa for 40 years'
- Major General Romeo A. Dallaire, former UNAMIR Commander

The challenge of writing on the subject of the military, peacekeeping and Africa in one 6,000 word chapter has been fortuitously simplified by what has appeared in earlier chapters. By now we have examined the international framework within which Africa sits and also eight separate case studies. This presents us with an ideal opportunity to focus upon the military and its relationship with peace-associated operations, with special reference to Africa. It is important to mention at the outset, however, that when we discuss the roles and capabilities of the military there is a universality of political and military principles under which they operate, which are not just Africa specific.

Peacekeeping

If ten different people were to be asked what they understand by the word *peacekeeping* they are likely to give ten different interpretations, none of which might be correct. For the soldier, the definition is of vital importance, for it is a precise selection and use of such words which provides the basis upon which to formulate the mission and to match forces to courses.

At the top of the spectrum of military commitment is General Global War, or High Intensity Conflict (HIC) which, for the foreseeable future has a zero probability. Next, there is Limited War (Vietnam and the

Falklands) and those fought under UN mandates, such as Korea and the Gulf Conflict. This is Mid Intensity Conflict (MIC), synonymous with traditional Chapter VII Peace Enforcement. Existing treaty obligations (United States treaties with South Korea and Taiwan) mean that MIC cannot be ruled out in the foreseeable future, but the incidence of inter-state conflict is becoming less frequent. The next level of conflict is within a wide band which fits between Chapter VII and Chapter VI, Low Intensity Conflict (LIC). There are approximately 30 major conflicts fought throughout the world each year. They are not peacekeeping *per se* because there is an absence of peace to be kept. Of late, all these conflicts have been intra-state affairs.

Traditional Chapter VI Peacekeeping was a product of the Cold War arising from the United Nations Security Council's Permanent Members' inability in 1948 to install a permanent collective security regime. Certain understandings evolved vis-à-vis the employment of blue beret peace-keepers. They were not normally drawn from the states of the Permanent Members and they used force only for the purpose of self defence. There were two implicit understandings. Firstly, peacekeepers were to be impartial at all times and secondly, their presence required the consent of the host states. The temperament of the troops was more important than their military skills, and their patience and non-threatening presence enabled them to hold a line until a political solution to the local problem could be found. It was not until the 1961-63 Katanga episode that the notion of Chapter VI peacekeeping first became compromised. From that point on, the obligatory abstention from the use of weapons other than in self defence, in an increasing number of environments where the settlement of disputes by armed force had become the norm, became increasingly difficult to sustain.

At the time of its inception in 1945, the United Nations was implicitly an organisation concerned with affairs between (inter) states. Katanga was an intra-state phenomenon within the wider Congo imbroglio and represented a portent of what was to come. Change was not instantaneous, for UN Article 2(7) still provided states with a well nigh watertight guarantee of domestic sanctity within borders. The world body had no difficulty in setting aside its coyness in overlooking the sovereignty of Southern Rhodesia and South Africa, but it was not until 1991, when western troops occupied Northern Iraq without Saddam Hussein's permission, that a coach and horses were driven through the concept of non-intervention in intra-state affairs. The environment was changing, yet past concepts of peacekeeping were not universally deconstructed, so that prevailing interests picked up the established notion of peacekeeping and took it into conflict environments where it was never intended to go, and where it was soon to be found wanting. Confusion as to the direction in which peacekeeping had now gone can be illustrated by the Belgian paratroop battalion's experience with United Nations operations in Somalia (UNOSOM II) and United Nations Assistance Mission (UNAMIR) in Rwanda. In Somalia, where the Belgians were not at great risk, they had Chapter VII authority on operations to use 'all necessary means'. However, when they then moved to Rwanda, they were tied to an inappropriate Chapter VI, traditional peacekeeping mandate, and suffered cruelly as a consequence.[1]

The future for peacekeeping remains uncertain. Largely as a result of its Somalia experiences the US Congress has refused to support what they understand as peacekeeping, and this political dissociation can be seen in the field. In 1994 in Rwanda, the American forces insisted that they were 'on a humanitarian assistance mission (and) could not appear to be taking sides, or co-operating with UNAMIR, a UN military command with a peacekeeping mission'.[2] Dr Boutros Boutros-Ghali subsequently let it be known that he favoured a return to what the UN did best, traditional Chapter VI peacekeeping. These UN-*sponsored* operations are likely to continue wherever possible. In those environments where the UN does not have the ability to command and control or does not command the confidence of contributing states, we are likely to see an increase in UN-*sanctioned* operations. This is where the UN authorises a state or security organisation to command and control a military operation on behalf of the international body. Examples are Korea, the Gulf Crisis, the United Task Force (UNITAF) in Somalia, the French Operation Turquoise in Rwanda, and the Implementation Force (IFOR) in Bosnia. However, the grey area lying between traditional enforcement and traditional peacekeeping requires urgent definition and expectations expressed, otherwise, like the Belgian paratroopers, the military will continue to find themselves at Chapters VIs and VIIs.

The military

If the civilian practitioner in the peace associated field is to remember one thing, it is this: the 'military' is no monolith. National armed forces are as varied in their characteristics, customs and levels of training and expertise as is possible to imagine. Taking a balance of quality and quantity, there are four world class armies: the USA, the UK, France and India. There are professional armies and conscript armies. The small, professional British army has become increasingly hollow as it strives to remain a capability-centred force structure supported by its domestic (thus more expensive than need be) industries. Perhaps the British army will not be able to remain in the front rank of excellence as it threatens to implode due to political negligence. The French army is a conscript army but recently M. Chirac announced the intention to convert French forces to a professional status, reducing their size from 500,000 to 350,000 over the next decade. The French President's unusual, publicly expressed justification was to enable the French armed forces 'to become as good as the British'. The problem associated with small and relatively small, quality armies is that if they are employed to the level seen in Bosnia in 1996, there are insufficient troops to deploy in any strength to Africa.

Africa's armed forces have undergone a qualitative decline. In some cases, there is a sound political rationale for not improving military professionalism. However, in colonial days there were some first class African armies - the King's African Rifles (KAR) comes to mind. The downward trend was arrested during the Cold War as the East-West camps assisted their client states - principally with training and equipment. With the ending of the Cold War, the overall, general decline in the standards of Africa's military continued.

In the recent past, military support for peace associated operations has been patchy to indifferent. Rarely has supply matched demand and rarely has the representative total force been other than a mishmash, ranging from the truly good to the truly awful. States support peace associated operations for a number of reasons at different levels. At the higher plain, states will become involved either because they have an *interest* or because they feel a moral obligation. If a state has a national interest in assisting another state, contingency plans will invariably be in existence. In the case of a nation's *conscience* being sufficiently aroused by media images for the public to tell their political representatives to do something, there may well not be pre-existing plans due to the absence of a perceived national interest. Operations which are launched at the public's insistence, at short notice, will often be found to be wanting in organisation and function. At a lower plain, and this applies more often to the armed forces from developing states, their participation might be to take advantage either of the force-building opportunity or perhaps of the hard currency $ payments the UN makes for the provision of each military representative, or both.

The nature of the crisis dictates the type of troops required. Infantry are best suited to peacekeeping and there is a wide choice of states who have infantry capable of filling the role. It is not a role that requires the crème de la crème, but the culture of some forces does not lend itself to patient, often protracted, traditional peacekeeping. The United States is a case in point. There is also a difference in the composition of troops which present themselves on operations. There are formed or composite units. Formed units are one entity which has pre-existed as one unit with the same men and officers, and who have lived and trained together. A composite unit will invariably have been assembled for the specific operation and therefore its cohesion and efficiency may be found to be not of the best. Composite units are normally found by states who are either short on assets or who want to spread loads and widen the operational experience within their armed forces. It would be wrong to believe that composite units will always be inferior to formed units.

Most external support for crises in Africa will be related to humanitarian support. There will be infantry in the military package; the numbers will be directly proportional to the perceived risk. In a virtually risk-free environment, however, it would be the norm to expect a predominance of logistic troops - engineers, communications, transport, supply and medical. Generally their effectiveness will relate to the equipment they either bring with them or procure locally. The sheer size of Africa presents particular problems in the availability of equipment either in situ or moving it from the donor state to the host state. France has seven equipment depots within Africa, while the United States is unique in having embarked depots on pre-positioning ships. Costs and budgets will have an increasing influence upon peace associated operations, thus cost-effective options will be sought out. Contractors have a role, as have had the Russians in supplying Antonov heavy-lift aircraft at a rate which cannot be matched by others.

A major challenge facing the military in deploying to Africa is to have the capability to do so rapidly. 'Rapid' has become a relative term which the military tend to play long and beyond civilian expectations. Again the French have garrisons[3] in Africa to support the former African colonies with whom they have treaties. However, the impact of conversion from a conscript to professional army will mean that France will no longer be able to afford to keep 8,000 troops in Africa. A rapid reaction capability is expected to be built-in to their new forces, and a willingness to assist with the training of pan-African forces has been expressed. The United Kingdom has recently created a brigade-sized Joint Rapid Deployment Force (JRDF), and the United States European Command (USEUCOM) has contingency plans for rapid deployment within its sphere of responsibility. The UN has examined and supported studies into the creation of its own, standing, rapid response formation, but politics and cost considerations have meant that it has become little more than an academic study. One solution adopted by the UN was the UN Standby Arrangement System (UNSAS), introduced in 1993 with a view to increasing the speed with which troops could be deployed on UN peace associated operations.

UNSAS is a database containing the details of member states available in principle to the UN at short notice. In April 1994, details of the armed forces of 19 states were on the database. When called to assist, not one agreed for service in Rwanda. What the database had succeeded in doing was to accelerate a universal, negative response. Potential troop donor states require quality intelligence as they engage in the decision-making process, weighing the pros and cons of commitment. Since the UN, or rather a significant part of its membership, has been persistently diffident with regard to the matter of intelligence, it has been unable to help states with this key ingredient in the decision-making process.

Of late, the call to deploy military forces has been the option of first resort. There is a dichotomy. The UN Charter requires graduated coercion prior to the ultimate use of military force. However, in some cases, a graduated response to a crisis may mean that once the delayed decision to send in the military is taken, the situation may have deteriorated beyond their control. It is a difficult decision, but one that has to be made case by case. However, in a conflict situation it is entirely wrong to believe that the military represents an ultimate option. Many military interventions have failed because they had no chance of succeeding. Indeed, our recent history is replete with examples where ill-considered intervention has polarised and intensified opposition within the target state. The question intervening states should have been asking is not only, can the intervention be justified but also, can it succeed?

The Red Cross has said of the military: 'There are not better logisticians than military ones and their resources are enviable. They are disciplined, organised and fast. But it is an uneasy marriage since humanitarians and the military have different agendas, different objectives.'[4] Such a view is only partially valid, for the humanitarian and the soldier will have the shared agenda and objective of achieving stability. The humanitarian's agenda and objectives run-on beyond those of the military, into long-term development. It is this reality which is the rationale for a civilian lead, because it is the civilians who provide continuity. Humanitarian operations of the type which recur in Africa can be divided into three stages: *intensive, consolidatory* and *transitional*. As a general rule, the intensive phase requires highly trained military with sophisticated equipment, material and resources at their disposal. The military and their tools are engaged to gain control of the situation. The NGOs and Agencies may well be in country but, at this stage, often of high risk and danger, their capabilities are limited. In the consolidatory phase, soldier and civilian will be working together to achieve stability in the region. Once the situation has been consolidated, the military will hand over to the civilians (if not already done) who then manage the transition towards development.

The role the military adopt in a target state will be a reflection of the prevailing levels of risk and instability. In high risk situations the military are likely to exert draconian control within their tactical areas of responsibility. In the intensive phase, the majority of agencies and NGOs will automatically accept the reality of a pre-eminent military position, if only because they require the shelter of the proffered protective umbrella in order to conduct their work. There will be parties who find themselves doctrinally opposed to having their own agenda influenced by military decisions. It is an occasion for patience. In a low risk situation, however, there is no need for a military lead, nor should they seek it.

One point to emerge from the Rwanda experience, and one confirmed by IFOR in Bosnia, is that the assembled coalition requires to be rather more than simply a *military* coalition. It has become evident that the military require an in tandem civilian police contingent to control areas pacified, liberated or relieved and may also require legal experts to deploy with them in order that no delay occurs in dealing with the investigation of alleged human rights abuses. In an operation, the sooner a working relationship is struck with GOs, Agencies, NGOs and the media, the better.

The military has to be acquainted with, and understand, that the environment into which it has deployed has, by tradition, been sub-divided by the NGOs into areas of specialism and interest. There is obvious scope here for friction, which can largely be militated against through education and understanding. One particular area where expertise differs is in the very important field of medicine. Military doctors support the young, fit, almost exclusively male force, not mother and child feeding. The strategies differ - the military curative, the humanitarian preventive. The military must become accustomed to developing a plan and programme for handover on departure, the time of which should be declared well in advance. They should introduce local people into their work at the outset so that the vacuum created by their departure can be filled without adverse effect on the ground. Experience gained thus far in Africa underlines just how essential it is to formulate a complete and collaborated strategy between the military and humanitarians. This ideal state of affairs depends upon a willingness on the part of both parties to achieve dialogue at the outset.

Part of the difficulty in achieving rapport between soldier and civilian lies in their totally different functions and structures. The military has a vertical, hierarchical structure. Its culture is based upon obedience to authority, hence orders are well nigh universally accepted and obeyed rather than being the first stage in what could be a long debate. The slight limitations that might have been noticed in the previous sentence reflect the fact that in certain high risk situations, obedience within a military coalition may not be immediately forthcoming. In all operations where national forces are subordinated to a foreign body or international organisation, the national commander will have his own whistle to blow if he believes what he is being asked to do is either unwise or contrary to what he or his government would wish to do. In Mogadishu on 3 October 1993, a number of American Ranger troops had been pinned down by General Aideed's forces. The rescue plan was delayed while a number of national representatives consulted with their governments. There can also be sensitivity, leading to a delayed response. That was evident in Kigali when the Bangladeshi battalion commander first reported to the Belgian office commanding the sector. 'I will not', he told the Belgian, 'carry out your orders unless they are in writing'. These examples are exceptions to the rule and reflect the existence of risks - political and military.

Civilian humanitarian organisations operate in unstructured operational planes, similar to labelled steps of co-ordination, co-operation, consensus building and assessment. There is of course no compulsion, and response can be pedestrian. A neutral body has to be created, to act as an intermediary from the earliest stages. It could be a senior military figure but the rule of civilian primacy, either at the outset or ultimately, is predominant.

The military are answerable to their political masters. One senior humanitarian representative observed that the 'military' were not entirely dedicated to humanitarian assistance, responding instead to the dictates of governments. That fact of life is as inescapable now as it has been from Clausewitz, to Mao, to Clinton. The military is a manifestation of politics in action. The ending of the Cold War heralded a new situation whereby security and foreign policy converged, enabling the principal states, if they wished, to use their armed forces in pursuit of foreign policy goals. Thus, the ending of the Cold War did not mean that the military had lost their purpose but, rather, it heralded the introduction of a new range of possibilities which, earlier, had not been available. The military will only perform to the level of ability that their government will allow. The fear of 'mission creep' can be so obsessional that military professionalism is unable to compensate for the absence of political will.

The politico-military interface

The timing of the main intervention into Rwanda was significant for it took place after approximately one million Tutsis and moderate Hutus had been slaughtered at the behest of extremist Hutus. What prompted the international intervention was the emergence of the refugee crisis of 1.5 million Hutus moving out of Rwanda, principally to the area of Goma in eastern Zaire (now the Democratic Republic of Congo). The importance of Goma, and what was in effect the creation of refugee warrior communities, was that it marked a turning point from the earlier position where there was no national interest among the majority of the interventionist states to one where the CNN factor had forced upon those states, through public attitude, a stimulation of consciences. In such cases, where there is a dramatic shift from a condition where there is no apparent national interest and no intention to be involved, to an effective, rapid reversal of that policy, the whole decision-making process is turned on its head.

Under normal circumstances, the UN Secretary-General or other interested states begin the process of forming an interventionist coalition. The recipient governments of such a request go through a process of analysis to reach a decision. Often that decision-making process will be abbreviated as states intuitively decline to become involved in another state's internecine warfare. More often than not, the final decision will be based upon a finely balanced assessment of the factors. There will be domestic and international factors to consider and they will rarely move in harmony.

Understandably, the decision-making process will begin with an assessment as to whether national interests are at stake and, if they are, whether they are vital interests upon which the government has a duty to act. If vital, national interests are not at stake, the government has to reflect upon its international responsibilities and also consider the disadvantages of not intervening. There can be disadvantages. For example, if State A declined to be associated with an intervention into Africa in which State B had a national interest, it might present problems in the future if State A wished to solicit the support of State B for an intervention which was in State A's interest. Legality is becoming an important consideration vis-à-vis intervention. The would-be interventionist government will invariably require assurance that there are unequivocal moral and legal grounds for the putative operation. The national aim has to be decided upon and, from this, there may be a compromise as the coalition's political aim and military mission are agreed. This is a vital step. Coalitions can only be held together where there is unity of purpose, an unequivocal aim and an agreed mission statement. The maintenance of the aim is crucial, but there is no reason why, with an evolving situation and with the agreement of the parties concerned, the aim may not be redefined or changed.

Inevitably, the coalition has to come to a collective decision as to how success should be measured and defined. The constituent coalition governments will examine the political and military consequences of success and failure. They will be aware of the failure of earlier interventions and the danger of descending the slippery slope of expanding commitment. Governments will be much more positive in deciding upon intervening in situations which require a naval or airforce response, or both. The political risks and stakes rise exponentially once soldiers are put out on the ground. All politicians are concerned that there will be military casualties. That concern is stronger in the USA than in the UK or France.[5] Visitors to US bases in Rwanda have written of having seen 'posted' the Army's first priority in the country, to suffer no casualties. The implications of such a policy do not look good out on the ground:

> ...when women were driving throughout the countryside, alone, as were the rest of the NGO personnel, one begins to wonder whether or not this particular appreciation of 'security' is appropriate. Many recall the curious juxtaposition between unarmed NGOs going anywhere they wanted and the armed-to-the-teeth military having to be in before dark while not being allowed in the refugee camps at all.[6]

Rwanda was of course an intervention which did not have the benefit of contingency planning and, in these circumstances, political paranoia associated with the 'body bag' syndrome was at its most intense. However, there is some evidence that the issue of US military deaths impinges more intensely upon the political leadership than upon its public. In a 1995 poll, when respondents were asked what their reaction to seeing 'the bodies of Americans on television' would be, only sixteen per cent said they would want to withdraw all American troops.[7] The assertion that the public will not stand for casualties has not been verified by opinion polls or through negative public support of peace-associated operations. It is a myth inspired by governments. What it means, however, is that in those circumstances where there is the perceived risk of high casualties, potential contributors will either decline to participate or to so tie the hands of the military commanders as to severely constrain the military's potential. On most other issues, policy-makers will be asking themselves whether public opinion can be sustained and what effect national involvement will have upon the standing of the government. American attitudes and the political processes there are important given the strong possibility of a US lead in some form or other.

The modern military have become budget conscious and budget driven. In the past, operations were conducted in a laissez faire, financial fog with little accountability. A recent Red Cross report commented: 'today's immensely costly use of soldiers to carry out and support humanitarian operations is a transformation which neither government nor troops have fully understood or mastered'.[8] If Treasuries indulge in full-cost accounting, that is, including items such as the military's wages which would be paid whether the troops were in Africa, Arizona, Andover or Avignon, then, naturally, costs will be high. By the same token, the cost of using military resources can be so set as to be prohibitively expensive. The cost of flying a kilo of freight from Europe to Kigali by Sabena was £1.70; the Royal Air Force quoted £7.00.[9] As if creative accounting by itself was not an unwelcome deterrent, add the fact that the UN is verging on bankruptcy and the USA is reducing her contributions to peace-associated operations to emphasise just how critical a consideration financing has become for future military operations in Africa.

The three fundamental test statements for military intervention are likely to be: low risk, low cost and short duration. Political leaders will consider a permutation of six questions:

- Is there a national interest or moral obligation to intervene?

- Is there a real threat to international peace and security?

- Does the mission have a clear aim?

- Can the proposed mission succeed? How is success to be defined?

- Can the conclusion be envisaged, or, is there an exit strategy? How, therefore, may failure be defined?

- Is there enough money?

What, therefore, are the key military doing during this period of political analysis and prevarication when decisions to deploy forces are left unresolved for the longest possible period? The United States has a number of Unified Commands which have responsibility for the execution of military operations within prescribed zones. They will be maintaining watching briefs and changing states of readiness commensurate with the rise in tension within their own area. The British and French early warning systems are of recent origin and are broadly similar in design. There is a designated permanent joint headquarters with a rapid deployment force at its disposal. Potential crises are monitored according to the level of impendence: quiescent, stirring, quickening and surfaced. There are three stages in the process towards the deployment of forces. The first is *normal*, a low level of activity during which a watching brief is maintained on areas of potential or actual operational interest. When a possible need to deploy national forces becomes evident, step two is initiated, whereby a contingency planning team is formed for the dedicated monitoring of a specific potential operation. That contingency planning team may be stood down once the crisis evaporates or the political decision is taken to proceed no further. If, however, the crisis escalates, step three involves the formation of an operations team and the subsuming of the contingency planning team. In that manner a joint team is established for the planning and execution of a precise military operation.

The next logical step is to examine the construction of future military coalitions for operations in Africa. The most militarily capable world alliance is NATO. Despite assertions to the contrary, NATO has not come to terms with post-Cold War realities. She is now seeking to extend membership to the states of Central and Eastern Europe who, in the absence of a threat, have a more pressing need for political and economic support. That is to say, their needs are best satisfied in the EU rather than NATO. NATO ground forces did make belated moves into Bosnia, but it was an unopposed operation. The domination of IFOR's agenda by Washington has caused dissent both within the military organisation and among the humanitarian agencies with whom they have had to work. The universal criticism of NATO is that it could have achieved more than it did. The reason for its timidity has been the fear of taking casualties as much as fear of polarising the situation out on the ground. If, therefore, NATO is circumscribed in an environment on the fringe of Europe, where western interests are paramount, NATO is less likely to be effective in Africa.

The Western European Union (WEU) is the senior European security organisation and has its origins in the 1948 Brussels Treaty, thereby predating NATO. However, since France is considering rejoining all the NATO military structures from which it withdrew in 1966, the continuing relevance and need for the WEU has to be subjected to the closest examination. The WEU has the authority to use NATO command structures and assets in European-led operations in regional crises when the USA is not involved. The circumstances when such a contingency is likely to arise is difficult to imagine. The British Foreign Secretary, Malcolm Rifkind, declared the WEU mission to be 'restricted to humanitarian assistance, helping refugees and coming to the aid of civil powers'.[10] Since combat missions are by definition excluded, the value and relevance of the WEU in assisting Africa is likely to be minimal.

The principal problem of the WEU lies in its association in the minds of European Foreign Ministries with the Maastricht Declaration. The Franco-German Axis in Europe is still inclined to bring the WEU under the charge of the EU. The implication of maintaining the status quo is that the examination of other options for the building of new coalitions for operations in Africa and elsewhere are not being seriously addressed. There have been recent, ad hoc; bilateral defence agreements between France and the UK which are important in this context because of the inclination of both the UK and France to be interventionist states. However, the charge of neo-colonialism can still be laid against an Anglo-French initiative into Africa.

There is a risk in the near future of America becoming isolationist, in which case, now is the time for new ideas. (Even if American isolationism is not total, the military operations in continents such as Africa will be limited. The analogy can be drawn of the wholesaler and the retailer, the USA providing services up to rear bases from where regional forces will continue the action.) To return to the British and the French and their residual expertise in Africa, there are two seeds to develop. The Commonwealth is an under-utilised organisation. Its members are in the vanguard of UN-sponsored or sanctioned military operations. Its military enjoy high standards of professionalism, a common language, common operating procedures and a common ethos. It also bridges the First/Third World divide. The same is true of La Francophonie. Both groups could be cultivated to do more for Africa.

But what can Africa's military do for itself? A serious problem which arose during the UN's Congo operation was the divide which occurred among the UN's African troops due to a 'definite degree of partisanship among African contingents in the Congo, which was not surprising in view of the vested interests involved'.[11] Vested interests will be present in any regional or sub-regional organisation, but the problem seems to be more acute in Africa. For that reason, regional and sub-regional organisations are frequently too close to the problem to be effective.

The ECOWAS (Economic Community of West African States) peacekeeping operation (in Liberia) has been questioned as it found difficulties in maintaining the traditional principles of peacekeeping established by the United Nations. That is, that forces should operate without offensive arms (except in self-defence), under the strictest rules of engagement, and with impartiality, while attempts at a peaceful settlement are brokered elsewhere.[12]

The author was to write later:

The rivalry within West Africa between anglophone and francophone states has made the achievement of peace in Liberia more difficult and that is why the growing involvement of states from outside the region is a positive development.[13]

The Pan-African Organisation of African Union's (OAU) first real challenge came in attempting to resolve the 1981 Chad crisis. Its failure affected the Union's confidence as much as what has been a continuing lack of political will and resources. In 1995 in Burundi, an under-resourced OAU was struggling gamely on in its urgent endeavours to defuse a potentially critical situation. It is not a question of western forces coming to Africa to absolve African armies of participation in the resolution of Africa's problems but rather in providing some of the essential support with command, control, intelligence and equipment. In Rwanda, an Oxfam spokeswoman said: 'The African battalions adjust to doing nothing very easily but when employed and properly led, one felt proud of them - the Ethiopians were particularly brave and knew how to deal with the rebels'. In essence, it is a matter of whether the level of security provided by African military is sufficient to reassure the fellow Africans they are assigned to protect. In Rwanda, a refugee remarked: 'If American or English troops were deployed, many people would stay. African soldiers do not reassure people. We judge the strength of an army by its equipment; that is why the French have been so effective.'[14]

The bottom line is that we should not become totally mesmerised with regional and sub-regional defence and security organisations. In reality, consensus may be difficult to achieve within bodies which are frequently divided internally on many issues, including that which is their raison d'être. It is much more likely that future African crises will form their own coalitions involving one or more of, the USA, the UK and France as principal contributors in UN-*sanctioned* coalitions.

Notes

1 On 6 April 1994, 10 disarmed Belgian paratroops were massacred by elements of the Hutu RGF Reconnaissance Regiment.
2 Lieutenant General Daniel R. Schroeder, 'Operation Support Hope 1994'. *After Action Review*, 4.
3 Djibouti 3400, Central African Republic 1300, Senegal 1200, Ivory Coast 1200, Chad 800, Gabon 400.
4 *World Disasters Report*, 'Special Focus on the Rwandan Refugee Crisis', (1994), p. 31.
5 The British and French were visibly more relaxed in theatre than the Americans. One of the French contingent's so-called 'behaviour guidelines' forbade them to wear helmets or flak jackets except when engaged or in immediate danger.
6 Chris Seiple, *The US Military/NGO Relationship in Humanitarian Interventions*, Peacekeeping Institute, Center for Strategic Leadership, US Army War College, 1996, p. 163.
7 *Americans on UN Peacekeeping. A Study of US Public Attitudes.* Program on International Policy Attitudes, Maryland, 27 April 1995.
8 *World Disasters Report*, 'Special Focus on the Rwandan Refugee Crisis', 1994, p. 31.
9 Save the Children Fund Representative, Rwanda, April 1995.
10 *The Times*, 4 June 1996.
11 Michael Harbottle, *The Blue Berets*, London, 1975, p. 44.
12 Comfort Ero. *Subregional Peacekeeping and Conflict Management: The Liberian Civil War.* UN Conflict Programme, UNA-UK, London, April 1915, p. 5.
13 Ibid, p. 28.
14 *The Times*, 16 August 1994.

15 Being peacekept

Christopher Clapham

Introduction

As the previous studies in this volume have demonstrated, the recent experience of international peacekeeping in Africa has been extensive, and has at the same time had decidedly mixed results. This chapter seeks to review this record, and to assess some of the underlying reasons for relative success or failure, looking in particular at the characteristic problems of African peacekeeping operations, and the reasons why they have so often failed to measure up to the optimistic aspirations with which they were launched. It will attempt to approach these problems, not from the relatively familiar perspective of the peacekeepers, but from the generally understudied viewpoint of the 'peacekept': the parties to the conflicts which peacekeepers seek to resolve, and the populations whose aspirations the conflicting parties claim (often meretriciously) to represent.

The reasons for the customary emphasis on the peacekeepers are evident. Engagement in peacekeeping operations requires a policy initiative on the part of those governments which send their forces into potentially hazardous situations in often distant parts of the world. Such actions require justification, especially when the governments concerned are publicly accountable to their own electorates. When operations fail, as they often do, observers correspondingly tend to look for explanations to the inadequacies of the peacekeepers: to the inadequate size or tardy despatch of the peacekeeping force; to problems of defining the 'mission' of the force, and the resulting 'mission creep' that occurs as the force has to adapt to changing and often unexpected situations on the ground; or to largely technical problems of training, equipment, deployment or leadership. Such post-mortems are in any case generally concerned to alert the governments and international institutions responsible for peacekeeping to the problems that previous missions have encountered, in the hope that these can be taken into account in planning and implementing future operations - and as such they have a great deal to contribute.[1] Others seek to apportion the blame for failure, in terms which necessarily assume the possibility of success, and concentrate on the relationships between different individuals and organisations engaged in running the peacekeeping operation.[2] Yet this is only a very partial viewpoint, and it is the lesson of many of the case studies assessed in this volume that the conditions making for their success or failure lie every bit as much in the situations and reactions of the conflicting parties, as in those of the peacekeeping forces. In some cases, indeed, peacekeepers have even exacerbated the very conflicts that they were meant to resolve.

Peacekeepers and peacekept

It may therefore be useful to switch the angle of vision, and to ask how conflicting parties view the role of peacekeepers, and how this viewpoint differs from that of the peacekeepers themselves. With this in mind, we can then look at the interface between peacekeepers and peacekept, and relate this to the conditions under which peacekeeping operations are most likely to succeed, and to the problems which they must avert if they are not to fail.

The first and obvious point is that the conflicting parties are likely, at least in their own estimation, to be fighting for good reason: conflicts which from the outside appear to be 'irrational' and meaninglessly destructive will almost invariably seem to those engaged in them to be very important indeed, endowed with a 'rationale' for which they are prepared to risk their lives. Outsiders characteristically have difficulty even in distinguishing Tutsi from Hutu, Mano from Krahn, or Abgal from Habr Gidir, and find it difficult to understand why these divisions should fuel and channel (even if they do not directly 'cause') the conflicts which they have come to settle. For insiders, they matter. In any case serious enough to call for external peacekeeping, moreover, the conflict will already, almost invariably, have been taking place for a considerable period, and in the process have destroyed lives, property, and domestic political institutions, exacerbated distrust, and intensified the divisions along which they have been socially structured.

Some conflicts are characteristically more accessible to outsiders than others, depending on whether or not they can be fitted into social categories which are familiar and legitimate to the peacekeepers. In Africa, conflicts have been structured in racial terms as between peoples of African and European origin, and which can thus be understood within the parameters of the idea of decolonisation, like those in Zimbabwe and Namibia (if *only*, in each case, those between 'whites' and 'Africans'), present few problems to external peacekeepers, and equally lend themselves to appropriate solutions derived from post-colonial conceptions of majority (and thus African) rule. Conflicts structured in terms of ethnic divisions within the indigenous population, on the other hand, are often deeply puzzling, because they do not fit into legitimate categories, and do not present the same ready-made formula for their resolution. Kriger's analysis in this volume shows very clearly how the Zimbabwe settlement, which appeared to be 'successful' when interpreted in post-colonial terms, took on an altogether more ambivalent aspect with respect to other internal conflicts, which were ignored or overridden because they did not fit into these terms.

Second, domestic combatants can rarely be expected to share the broad value orientations of the intervening forces. As earlier chapters in this volume have indicated, peacekeeping forces tend to be drawn disproportionately from the armies of Western liberal states (the United States, France, the United Kingdom, Canada, the Scandinavian states, and other small European states), which share a relatively long tradition of stable democratic government, and a deep aversion to violence as a means of resolving conflicts. Only the ECOMOG force in Liberia, among those examined here, was drawn from and commanded by nationals of neighbouring states, even though subordinate contingents of African and other 'third world' forces were included in many of the operations. Within the domestic politics of the major peacekeeping states,[3] a broad value consensus can generally be assumed, and the resolution of conflict can correspondingly be reduced to essentially procedural issues: the commitment to 'peace' itself is inherently procedural, since it presupposes that conflicts can be resolved by means from which violence is excluded; from it follows a belief in negotiation and compromise, validated by reference to the democratic rights of the majority, and the universal human rights of minorities, as the means through which disputes should be resolved.

For combatants, on the other hand, substantive questions take precedence over procedural ones: they are basically concerned about who wins, not about the means by which victory is secured. A lack of any deep commitment to peaceful conflict resolution, among at least a substantial element of the conflicting forces, is presupposed by the fact that conflict is taking place at all. Nor can it be assumed that combatants will share the values which, to many of the peacekeepers, form part of an elementary conception of 'humanity'. The Rwandan genocide provides the most traumatic example of deliberate behaviour on the part of combatants which most of the would-be peacekeepers felt way beyond any conceivable idea of human action; but the actions of Somali warlords, or the casual butchery of civilian populations in Liberia, provide further examples of the gulf in expected standards of action between peacekeepers and peacekept. In some cases, this gulf creates deep antipathies for the peacekept among the peacekeepers, and helps to account for (though not, of course, to justify) human rights abuses by the peacekeepers which would otherwise be difficult to understand.[4]

This lack of commitment to 'humanitarian' values, and concern for substantive rather than procedural issues, is often especially marked among the leaders of conflicting parties, who are at the same time the people with whom the peacekeepers have to deal. Leaders such as Mohamed Farah Aidid in Somalia, Charles Taylor in Liberia, and Jonas Savimbi in Angola have readily been condemned for their lack of humanity, and for their selfishness and unscrupulousness in undermining peacekeeping proposals, and reneging on commitments that they had promised to honour. But condemnation, however justified, is no substitute for explanation: and as political entrepreneurs who are fighting for very high stakes, and who have placed their own lives (along with those of many other people) in the balance, such leaders can only be expected to fight by every means at their disposal.

Third, the peacekeeping operation itself is necessarily viewed in a very different light from the two sides. Peacekeepers necessarily view themselves as bringing *solutions* to the conflicts which they are concerned to resolve: that is why they are there. These solutions, of course, vary widely according to the nature of the conflict itself, and the level of agreement that has been reached by the internal parties; in some cases, as in Zimbabwe, Namibia and Mozambique, the peacekeepers see themselves as simply helping to assure the proper implementation of a settlement which has already been broadly agreed; in others, as in Liberia and Somalia, they intervene in an attempt to impose a solution on parties who have not been able to achieve it themselves. Regardless of these variations, they differ from participants, for whom peacekeepers are perceived as contributing *resources*, which may be captured and used by one or more of the internal parties to the conflict, in order to improve their own position within the conflict itself.

Earlier chapters in this volume have shown how true this is, even in cases where the role of the peacekeepers appears to be most technical and restricted. In Namibia, for example, Pankhurst argues that the peacekeepers were in some degree 'captured' by the South African administration of the territory, and used to ensure that at least some of its residual objectives (notably, preventing SWAPO from gaining a critical two-thirds majority in the elections) were achieved. The more distant the prospects of a settlement, and the more fluid the internal military situation, the greater are the opportunities offered to conflicting parties to manipulate the peacekeepers in such a way as to strengthen their own position vis-à-vis their internal rivals. The troubles of UNOSOM in Somalia and ECOMOG in Liberia, as well as the strained relations between UNAMIR II and the newly installed RPF regime in Rwanda, all described in earlier chapters, arose from the way in which peacekeeping forces were absorbed into the very conflicts that they had expected to resolve.

Nor are the resources that peacekeepers have to offer only political ones. In some cases, and here Somalia provides the extreme example, peacekeepers bring with them financial resources which can be captured or expropriated in one way or another by the parties to the conflict, and used in order to sustain the conflict itself.[5] Given that Somalia is an extremely poor country, offering a very limited economic base from which to maintain a long-lasting and highly destructive form of warfare, it can plausibly be argued that the peacekeepers, with the massive amounts of money and aid that they brought with them, helped to keep the conflict going at a level which would scarcely have been possible had the competing factions had to rely on the resources available on the spot. The provision of relief aid to Rwandan refugee camps in Zaire (now the Democratic Republic of Congo) after July 1994, controlled as these were by the elements in the former Rwandan government who had been responsible for the genocide, is a further example of how external resources can be diverted in such a way as to foment conflict rather than resolve it.

Finally, peacekeepers tend to think in the short term, whereas combatants necessarily have to think in the long term. Peacekeeping is an 'operation' that is bounded in time. There is no permanent role for peacekeeping forces in the domestic politics of the states in which they intervene: their mission is to come in, sort things out, and then leave. Almost invariably, they badly underestimate the length of time for which they will have to stay: the UNITAF forces despatched by President Bush, who stormed ashore at Mogadishu in December 1992, initially expected to leave in time for the inauguration of President Clinton in the following month. But regardless of how long they have to stay, the end-point for peacekeepers is the moment when they can pull out, preferably leaving behind them some form of internal settlement which enables them to present the operation as a success. But the end-point for the peacekeepers is often no more the starting point for the peacekept. They are - unless exterminated or driven out - permanent actors on the local political stage. Their prime concern is to position themselves as advantageously as possible for the moment when they are left to resume their domestic rivalries without external interference. What matters then is whether the peacekeepers have left behind them a domestic government capable of seeing off any challenges to its position, or whether their departure is no more than the signal for internal combatants to resume their rivalries unencumbered by external forces.

The outcome of all of these considerations is to give the peacekept enormous leverage over the peacekeepers, in the constant struggles for bargaining advantage that characterise the peculiar politics of peacekeeping operations. Peacekeepers readily assume an assumption of their 'superiority' in approaching the situations that confront them. Characteristically drawn from the sophisticated armies of industrial states, with their high levels of discipline, training, equipment and technological expertise, they view themselves as coming in from the outside, in order to help sort out the problems of underdeveloped states whose people have been unable to resolve those problems without external aid. In practice, the boot is almost invariably on the other foot. Domestic combatants have a clearer and longer-term view of what they are trying to achieve; they are uncluttered (or uninhibited) by the value systems within which the peacekeepers are operating; they are often very well aware of the domestic and international constraints on the behaviour of the peacekeepers, while suffering from few such constraints themselves; and they have a far better grasp of the local political scene. Peacekeeping operations are therefore often most appropriately analysed, not from the perspective of the peacekeepers, but from the perspective of local combatants using peacekeepers within the framework of their own internal conflicts.

Structures of interaction

The preceding case studies in this volume provide a highly varied range of situations within which to explore the relationships between internal political factions and those who come to keep the peace between them, and correspondingly make it possible to sketch out broad typologies of the way in which these relationships may work. These cases fall into three main categories. First, exemplified by Zimbabwe and Namibia, are those that may be characterised as 'pacted transitions': that is to say, there is an internal political (and not merely constitutional) settlement which is broadly accepted by the major actors, and which the external peacekeeping forces are brought in to guarantee. Second, there are 'provisional settlements', which have been negotiated, usually under strong external pressure, by the internal combatants, but which do not incorporate any broadly accepted political formula; in these cases, which include Angola, Mozambique and Rwanda, the role of the external peacekeeping forces which are brought in to help manage the settlement is very much more uncertain. In the third category, that of 'direct interventions', the peacekeeping forces intervene in ongoing conflicts, in which no settlement has been agreed, and their relationship with the combatants carried a very high potential for conflict; Liberia and Somalia are the clearest examples of this type. The remainder of this section will examine each in turn.

Pacted transitions

In Zimbabwe and Namibia, as later in South Africa, the outlines of a settlement were clear from the moment that the white minority regime recognised that it could not continue to govern without the domestic and external legitimacy provided by internationally accepted majority rule. On the one hand, open and internationally supervised elections would take place on a universal franchise, the winners of which - necessarily the African national movement which won most votes - would take over the government. On the other hand, the minority could use the constitutional negotiations in order to entrench residual rights which would likewise need to be internationally guaranteed. This settlement, moreover, could be expected to hold politically. The white minority would accept the advent of majority rule, because they recognised their inability to resist it, and because acceptance was preferable to continuing war as a means of maintaining their own continuing interests in the management of the state and the economy. The incoming majority could likewise be expected to accept the pact, because they relied on the minority to supply essential services in the management of the state and the economy, which they needed but could not provide themselves. In short, they wanted to inherit an effective state and a working economy, and needed the whites to run it.

In these circumstances, the role of the peacekeepers was relatively straightforward, because they could - short of thorough mismanagement on their own part - rely on the acquiescence and even the support of the most powerful groups among the peacekept. They were always liable to be manipulated, more or less knowingly or willingly, by one or both of the major internal parties to the settlement, in the way that Pankhurst describes in Namibia. But the underlying pact on which the settlement was based was robust enough for inevitable (and sometimes justified) charges of favouritism not to upset it. The anti-ZANU bias shown by the British force in Zimbabwe, and the anti-SWAPO bias shown by the UN force in Namibia, did not prevent either of these parties from taking power. The problems in these cases arose from the predicament of those who were abandoned in the process of reaching an agreement acceptable to the holders of state and economic power on the one hand, and majority votes on the other: the Muzorewa faction and DTA on one side, and ZAPU on the other - there was no major nationalist rival to SWAPO in Namibia, despite the existence of the SWAPO detainees, whose position was in some ways analogous. These however were not problems for the peacekeepers, but could be left for resolution (however brutal) once they had been withdrawn.

Provisional settlements

The position was very different in the case of provisional settlements. In these cases, even though the internal combatants had been placed under sufficient external pressure to induce them to accept a negotiated solution, this solution did not have built into it any broadly accepted underlying pact. The key prize, control over the state, remained unallocated, and was due to be determined by a subsequent election in the case of Angola and Mozambique, and by an extraordinarily complex and unworkable power-sharing agreement (to be followed at some future date by a new constitution and elections to be held under it) in the case of Rwanda. In Rwanda in particular the two major actors - the MRNDD government and the RPF insurgent movement - were deeply irreconcilable, while it could not be assumed in either Angola or Mozambique that the incumbent MPLA and FRELIMO governments, or the UNITA and RENAMO insurgencies, would willingly accept electoral victories by their opponents. Even though the Mozambican settlement proved to be remarkably successful, 'many more people died in Angola and Rwanda *after* peace agreements failed than during the years of war that preceded them',[6] a horrifying fact which indicates that misconceived peace settlements can result in damage far greater than would have occurred had no attempt at conflict resolution been made at all.

In such cases, peacekeepers are placed in a critical and invidious intermediary position. Rather than simply monitoring the implementation of a settlement that has in its essentials been agreed between the major internal parties, they are required to enforce a settlement which - signatures on a piece of paper notwithstanding - has never really been agreed at all. Combatants frequently agree in principle to peace proposals which they have no intention of implementing, or to settlements which they will accept only if they emerge as the winners. Though they sometimes simply miscalculate their prospects of success, apparent acquiescence is often a useful bargaining strategy, designed to improve their access to external diplomatic, military and financial resources, and to place the onus for continuing conflict on their opponents. The relationship between peacekept and peacekeepers under these circumstances depends in part on the leverage which the peacekeepers are able to exert on the internal factions, and in part on the resources available to the factions themselves, and their capacity to manipulate the peacekeepers to their own advantage. The first of these has understandably gained the greater attention, especially from those concerned to account for the failure of peacekeeping operations from the viewpoint of the peacekeepers. Both in Angola and in Rwanda, this failure led to appalling suffering and loss of life, and the need for peacekeepers to learn the appropriate lessons was therefore acute and deeply felt. In each case, the small size and tardy deployment of the peacekeeping force could be blamed, along with the precipitate withdrawal of the UNAMIR force, against the urgent pleas of its commander, at precisely the moment when it could have saved the lives at least of a great many of those who were being slaughtered in such numbers.

At the same time, the differences between Angola and Rwanda on the one hand, and the successful implementation of the peace process in Mozambique on the other, lay far more in the peacekept than in the peacekeepers. The factions responsible for breakdown - the MRNDD government and its supporters in Rwanda, and the UNITA insurgent movement in Angola - in each case disposed of substantial political and military resources, and had little if anything to gain from the implementation of a settlement from which they could only be the losers. In Angola, it had been an article of faith with Savimbi, ever since the precipitate Portuguese withdrawal in 1975, that had there been an election at the time of independence, he and his FNLA allies would have won it. It was on the assumption that this still held good that he agreed to take part in the 1992 elections. With the failure of that assumption, readily rationalised as due to electoral fraud, he could immediately fall back on the army that he had not demobilised (and which it is extremely unlikely that he would ever voluntarily have demobilised), and on the financial resources provided especially by his control over many of the country's diamond fields. Had the vote gone the other way, the acquiescence of the MPLA government would have been every bit as problematic.

In Rwanda, it was the incumbent government - and notably the die-hard Hutu supremacists within it - which stood to lose from the settlement, and who had the capacity to nullify it. The peculiar circumstances under which the Arusha accords had been negotiated had given an exceptional degree of leverage both to the RPF, and to the minority parties within the governing coalition in Kigali which the MRNDD had been obliged to accept under international pressure.[7] The Habyarimana regime and its allies, which had entrenched themselves deeply in power over a period of twenty years, were reduced under the transitional arrangement agreed at Arusha to a mere five members of a twenty-one member council of ministers, within which a two-thirds majority was necessary for any measure to be passed. Given that their would-be partners under the Arusha settlement were people to whom they were virulently (and, as it transpired, genocidally) hostile, that they controlled the national army, the regional administration, and the *interahamwe* death squads which they were then training, and that they had (so they felt, at least) an unconditional assurance of French support, their incentive to abide by the Arusha settlement was non-existent. In Rwanda, certainly, an actively deployed peacekeeping force could have saved a great many people from the appalling fate which befell them; but there as in Angola, the formally agreed settlement could only plausibly have been implemented had this force been large, well-armed, and prepared to take a combatant role which lay well beyond the normal bounds of 'peacekeeping' by multinational forces.

The Mozambican story was different, not because of any major differences in the peacekeeping operation, but because of the very different situation of the peacekept, both the FRELIMO government and the RENAMO opposition. Mozambique had no equivalent to the oil and diamonds which, as Munslow shows, gave the Angola factions their autonomy. Both government and insurgents were deeply dependent on Western aid, which could be used to lever each of them to the negotiating table, and to ensure that they would broadly abide by the outcome. RENAMO, in particular, had lost the autonomy that it had gained from its relationship with the *apartheid* regime in South Africa, and it lacked independent resources. Consistent external pressure, coupled with 'side payments' in terms of development aid and a role in local government to which Barnes refers, were enough to keep it in line.

Direct interventions

The most critical problems, however, have arisen in those cases - illustrated in this volume by Liberia and Somalia, and in some degree by the Inter-African Force (IAF) in Chad and *Operation Turquoise* in Rwanda - in which peacekeepers directly intervened in on-going conflicts, without even the very limited security afforded by a provisional settlement. In Liberia and Somalia especially, the assumption that since the peacekeepers were more powerful than any of the local factions, in terms of their numbers, weaponry and organisation, this would be enough to enable them to impose a solution to the conflict, turned out to be completely misconceived.

For a start, any claim by the peacekeepers to be neutral as between the different contending parties to a conflict in which they intervened rapidly became unsustainable. This claim, for a start, was not always made in good faith. In three of the four cases discussed in this volume, it is plausible to suppose that the intervening forces always favoured one domestic faction over the others. In Chad, the states constituting the IAF may well have preferred Habre to Waddeye, because of Waddeye's close links with the Libyans - and at all events, the IAF intervention helped Habre to succeed. In Liberia, the ECOMOG states sided first with Doe and then with Sawyer's IGNU, against Taylor's NPFL. In Rwanda, relations between France and the Habyrimana regime and its successor had been so close that no pretence of neutrality could plausibly be sustained. In Somalia, however, the United States had no evident reason to support any of the numerous warlords against any of the others, and its claim to neutrality *in intention* may be accepted. In practice, however, it made no difference. Intervening forces become involved in the conflicts in which they have intervened, and in the process come to favour some parties more than others, entirely regardless of what their initial intentions may have been. Neutrality proved as impossible to maintain in Somalia, where the US forces were barely aware of the identify of the different factions before they moved in, as in Chad or Liberia.

The central problem is that the arrival of the intervening force in itself affects the balance of power between the different internal factions. By interposing itself between the combatants, or by taking control of places or resources which these had hoped to gain for themselves, it necessarily disadvantages some of them and in the process advantages others. Those that gain from its presence will therefore welcome it, whereas those that lose will treat it with suspicion. Normally, the intervention freezes the military situation, and thus prevents whichever faction is currently on the offensive from pressing home its military advantage. It thus helps the faction which is in the weakest military position, which therefore looks to the intervening force to protect it against its rival. In Liberia, the strongest faction at the time of ECOMOG's arrival in August 1990 was Taylor's NPFL, which then controlled most of the country and was about to launch an attack on Monrovia; from its viewpoint, ECOMOG cheated it of victory. In Somalia, Aidid's was the stronger of the two main factions fighting for control of Mogadishu, and viewed UNITAF in much the same way as Taylor did ECOMOG, whereas his weaker rival, Ali Mahdi Mohamed, had every reason to see UNITAF in the light of the relieving cavalry. The situation was rather different in Chad, where Habre could view the IAF's arrival with relief, both because it replaced the Libyan force which was directly opposed to him, and because the leaders of at least two of the intervening states could be expected to support him against Waddeye; although it ostensibly placed a barrier between the contending factions, and thus appeared to maintain the Waddeye government in Ndjamena, it did not actually do so. In Rwanda, the French presence soon became unsustainable, and they were obliged to help their allies by covert action in Zaire, rather than by direct intervention in Rwanda.

It is in any event very hard for an intervening force, suddenly thrust into an unfamiliar and dangerous environment, to avoid regarding those who help and support it as its friends, and those who oppose it (and very possibly shoot at it) as its enemies. Even if it does not choose sides itself, sides will effectively be chosen for it by the combatants. Once the force is on the ground, incidents will almost inevitably occur which serve to confirm the preconceptions of the local contestants. In Somalia, in February 1993, for example, an anti-Aidid faction managed to seize part of the town of Kismayo by a *coup de main,* catching the UNITAF peacekeepers by surprise; when Aidid's ally Omar Jess tried a similar trick a few days later, the peacekeepers were on their guard, and managed to foil it. From Aidid's point of view, it was hard to avoid the conclusion that UNITAF had sided with his opponents - but if this particular event had not occurred to create that impression, almost certainly some other incident would have had the same effect.

But the intervening force is not merely forced to take sides: almost inevitably, it finds itself lining up against the strongest of the domestic factions. This in turn not only exacerbates its military position, but impedes any attempt to negotiate a political settlement and achieve its own withdrawal. Its presence becomes essential to the weaker groups which have become its clients, and an affront to the stronger groups whose support is needed in order to achieve any lasting settlement. An understandable reluctance to abandon its allies to retaliation by its opponents only drags it deeper into the mire.

In both Liberia and Somalia, and to some degree also in Chad, the manipulation of the peacekeepers by the peacekept is likewise illustrated by the numerous and invariably unsuccessful attempts to negotiate a settlement. A mere roll call of failed mediations, named after the places where they took place, conveys a sense of their futility: the Kano I, Kano II, Lagos I and Lagos II agreements on Chad; the Freetown, Banjul I, Bamako, Banjul II, Virginia, Yamoussoukro I, Yamoussoukro II, Yamoussoukro II, Yamoussoukro IV, Geneva, Cotonou, Akosombo and Accra agreements on Liberia; the Djibouti I, Djibouti II, Addis Ababa I, Addis Ababa II, Addis Ababa III and Nairobi agreements on Somalia. There is no point in going into the details. The attempt to establish a political structure which all of the indigenous parties can be induced to accept is virtually built into the peacekeeping enterprise. The peacekeepers cannot simply impose a settlement themselves, after the manner of a conquering army of occupation; nor can they blatantly side with one of the combatants, and help it impose a settlement on the others. It is therefore a necessary part of the operation that all - or virtually all - of the contending parties should agree. This in turn gives any major party a veto power over the settlement.

At the same time, however, the fact that the peacekeepers have arrived in order to impose a settlement, at a time when the contestants were not yet ready to agree on a settlement among themselves, means that the local factions are unlikely to have any real commitment to any agreement that is reached. For the peacekeepers, the settlement has a strategic goal: it is intended to put in place a new political order, which will ensure stability and enable them to withdraw. For the peacekept, on the other hand, it is no more than a tactical device, intended to buy time while they regroup for further conflict. Even though combatants may be induced to accept a settlement when this is negotiated in some outside location, simply because they do not want to lose external support by appearing to reject it, this does not carry any assurance that they will actually abide by it once they return to their forces on the ground.

The process of negotiation in itself tends to strengthen the position of the leaders of the various armed groups or warlords, since these are the people who have to take part in it. The patient creation of a civilian political structure is much too costly, in terms both of the time required and of the need to disarm the military factions, to be a practicable option for the peacekeeping force. During the first months of the UNOSOM I operation in 1992, before the UNITAF intervention, UN special envoy Mohamed Sahnoun tried to follow a strategy of building up links with clan elders in order to slowly undermine the position of warlords like Aidid or his rival in Mogadishu, Ali Mahdi Mohamed; he was later to describe this as trying to pluck a bird's feathers one by one, until it could no longer fly. Whether or not this strategy could have demanded faster results, and eventually pushed him into resignation. Subsequent UN representatives took the *realpolitik* approach that it was necessary to do a deal with the people who had the power, and these were the leaders of the military factions. In the process, they helped to give these leaders a level of external legitimacy that they might not otherwise have possessed, and enable them equally to reinforce their domestic control.

In Liberia, it worked rather differently, but the eventual result was much the same. After Doe's death in September 1990, ECOMOG sought to establish a regime in Monrovia with which it could do business, and held a meeting of Liberian notables in The Gambia in order to select an interim president. Their choice of Amos Sawyer, a man universally respected for his courage and integrity under both the Doe and the preceding Tolbert administrations, could scarcely have been faulted. Established under ECOMOG protection in Monrovia, deprived of the opportunity to build up a political following in the rest of the country which was controlled by Taylor, and obliged to work with the military factions which had sided with ECOMOG (and which notably included the unsavoury remnants of Doe's brutal army), Sawyer nonetheless become little more than the prisoner of ECOMOG. He was eventually happy to give up the presidency and retire to private life.

Another way in which the external attempt to negotiate a political settlement easily becomes self-defeating is through the proliferation of factions. On the one hand, the peacekeeping force protects factions against being suppressed and absorbed by more powerful groups. On the other, by holding negotiations in which faction leaders bargain under the aegis of ECOMOG or UNOSOM for positions in a newly established government of national unity, the peacekeepers encourage each and every would-be leader to establish his own faction, in order to protect his negotiating position. Sometimes this proliferation of factions is encouraged by the intervention force, in order to divide and weaken existing groups; ECOMOG has plausibly been accused of establishing and arming factions in Liberia, so as to undermine the NPFL. Sometimes factions divide because subordinates within them try to displace the leader, or secede within their supporters to set up new factions on their own; the NPFL split when the representatives whom Taylor had appointed to the newly established transitional government in 1994 rejected his leadership. In Liberia, factions which had not been represented at the meeting which established the transitional government, such as the Lofa Defence Force, demanded a place in it; factions which had been involved in the negotiations (such as the Armed Forces of Liberia) reinvented themselves under a different name (as the Liberia Peace Council), in order to avoid adherence to the cease-fire conditions which they had agreed to.

Neither in Liberia nor in Somalia did any of the participating factions feel any obligation to abide by the conditions that they had accepted under pressure from external peacemakers. They were not 'real' negotiations or 'real' conditions, since the discussions in Addis Ababa or Akosombo bore no discernible relationship to developments in Mogadishu or Monrovia. The saddest commentary on the process was provided by the UN special envoy for Liberia, a decent but entirely ineffectual Jamaican diplomat named Trevor Gordon-Somers, who complained after one of the Liberian faction leaders had instantly reneged on a commitment to disarmament that he had assumed that the negotiations had been conducted in good faith. He should have known better. It was only once Charles Taylor and the Abacha government in Nigeria came to appreciate the futility of fighting against one another - at enormous cost to Liberians - that it became possible to broker a settlement in which the dominant regional state allied with the dominant internal faction to produce at least the possibility of restoring peace, a deal which was then validated by the July 1997 elections. In Somalia, any viable settlement had to await the complete withdrawal of the peacekeepers.

Conclusion

The massive expansion in peacekeeping operations after 1990, in Africa as elsewhere, resulted from changes in the global system, rather than from any significant changes either in the nature of peacekeeping itself, or in the nature of the conflicts which these operations were designed to help resolve. Even though the end of the Cold War helped to remove an important factor which had often helped to exacerbate conflicts in Africa and elsewhere, these conflicts were seldom if ever *caused* by the Cold War, and could not be expected simply to disappear when it ended. The resources available to local combatants to prosecute their conflicts differed widely, but in many cases were still considerable.

The application to these conflicts of relatively uniform principles of international peacekeeping has therefore had very different outcomes, and these have depended much more on the impact of peacekeeping on the local combatants - the peacekept, as they have been called in this chapter - than on the peacekeepers. Only where a peace settlement or 'pact' had already been broadly agreed between the major combatants could the peacekeepers play the role, in helping to ensure that the terms of the pact were honoured on both sides, that conventional peacekeeping assumed. On occasion, and notably in Mozambique, the bargaining position of the internal parties was sufficiently weak, and the leverage exercised by the peacekeepers was sufficiently great, for peacekeepers to be able to play a critical role in helping to resolve a very damaging conflict. In cases where the internal combatants continued to maintain considerable war-making capabilities, and these included the majority of the conflicts with which this volume is concerned, peacekeeping would only have had any plausible prospect of success had the peacekeepers both disposed of substantial military force, and been able to use it with a skill and determination (including a disregard for inevitable casualties), that would have carried them well beyond any conventional conception of peacekeeping. In practice, even when (as in Liberia and Somalia) the military force has been available, the skill and determination have been lacking. In all too many cases, including Angola and Rwanda as well as Liberia and Somalia, an approach to peacekeeping which took insufficient account of the resources, interests and manipulative skills of the peacekept has resulted in the exacerbation rather than the resolution of the conflicts which it had been meant to solve.

Notes

1 For a classic example of such a study, see Walter Clarke and Jeffrey Herbst (eds) (1997) *Learning from Somalia: The Lessons of Armed Humanitarian Intervention*, Westview: Boulder; a generally excellent appraisal of Operation Restore Hope from the peacekeepers' point of view, it scarcely considers what it was like for Somalis to find a massive US-led intervention force suddenly arriving in their midst.
2 See Margaret Anstee (1993) 'Angola: The Forgotten Tragedy: A Test Case for UN Peacekeeping', *International Relations*, Vol. 11, No. 6, pp. 495-511.

3   Not always: the British in Northern Ireland face a conflict every bit as intractable as those that they confront in peacekeeping operations abroad, and have every bit as much trouble in understanding it.
4   Human rights abuses by Belgian, Canadian and Italian forces in Somalia have attracted particular notice.
5   See Andrew S. Natsios 'Humanitarian relief intervention in Somalia: the economics of chaos', Clarke and Herbst, *Learning from Somalia*.
6   Stephen J Stedman and Donald Rothchild (1996) 'Peace operations: from short-term to long-term commitment', *International Peacekeeping*, Vol. 3, No. 2, pp. 17-35.
7   I have examined the problems of the Rwanda settlement in Clapham, C. 'Rwanda: the Perils of Peacemaking', *Journal of Peace Research*, forthcoming. For an excellent account, see Gerald Prunier (1995), *The Rwanda Crisis 1959-1994: History of a Genocide*, Hurst: London, especially chapters 4 and 5.